EXPATRIATES AND PATRIOTS

🌾🌾🌾🌾🌾🌾🌾🌾🌾🌾🌾🌾🌾🌾🌾🌾🌾🌾🌾🌾🌾🌾🌾🌾🌾🌾🌾🌾🌾🌾

EXPATRIATES AND PATRIOTS

American artists, scholars, and writers in Europe

Ernest Earnest

DUKE UNIVERSITY PRESS   Durham, North Carolina   1968

ACKNOWLEDGMENT

I wish to express my thanks to Temple University and to the Committee on Research and Publication for a grant-in-aid which covered the secretarial and travel expenses involved in the preparation of this work.

Also I wish to thank Professor Jay B. Hubbell for his many helpful suggestions.

My thanks are also due to Mrs. Ellen C. Masters for permission to quote "Archibald Higbie" from *The Spoon River Anthology* (Macmillan, 1914, 1915, 1942).

CONTENTS

INTRODUCTION

For a hundred and fifty years after the founding of the United States, a considerable number of Americans lived at least part of their lives in Europe. One theory about this, stemming largely from Henry James, is that our culture during much of our national life was too thin to nourish writers and artists. Another theory, one especially popular among critics between 1910 and 1930, was that because of puritanism and commercialism the United States has been actively hostile to the artist and the intellectual. The expatriation, brief or extended, of many of our artists and writers has been used as an indictment of American civilization.

As recently as 1957 the novelist Wright Morris cited Henry James as "the archetype of the [American] problem . . . a now-immortal reminder of our fear and distrust of real intelligence. In leaving the country he almost spared us the trouble of exiling him." Others have cited the careers of Ezra Pound, Gertrude Stein, and T. S. Eliot as evidence of our alleged hostility to the intellectual.

Over sixty years ago William Dean Howells felt it necessary to answer a charge by a visiting English lecturer to the effect that "the Americans who are most prominent in cultivated European opinion in art or literature live habitually out of America and draw their inspiration from England, France and Italy." As Howells pointed out, expatriation is by no means an exclusively American phenomenon. He cited Byron, Shelley, Hunt, the Brownings, and Landor, all of whom preferred to live in Italy; Kipling, who lived for a time in Vermont, Björnson and Ibsen, who spent many years in France and Italy; Heine, who preferred Paris to Dusseldorf; and Voltaire who went to Prussia for a number of years. He might have cited Henry James's friend Turgenev, who lived in Paris.

However, several questions remain: To what extent has the United States "exiled" its writers, artists, and intellectuals? What has the expatriate experience of a number of sensitive and thoughtful people revealed about the nature of American culture, and for that matter of European culture? To what extent has this experience abroad been an important factor in the artistic or literary work of the expatriate? It is to these questions that the present study addresses itself.

For the purposes of this book the term *expatriate* will be used very loosely. Length of stay abroad is not a reliable criterion. Longfellow, who spent relatively few years in Europe, was more of an intellectual expatriate than Lowell, who lived there many years. Irving, who by choice lived much of his life in England, France, and Spain, came to regard his cottage at Tarrytown as his real home. It is ironic that Cooper, an Anglophobe, was more characteristically English than Henry James, who became a British subject. As a working definition the term *expatriate* will be used to describe anyone who has lived abroad for a considerable length of time.

Expatriates have of course lived in all parts of the globe, but those who lived in Europe have been by far the most important in our cultural history. Artists, scholars, and writers have been chosen for several reasons: they have been, as a rule, the most articulate commentators on their experiences and impressions; they are the people who most often examined the conflicting values of the civilizations on both sides of the Atlantic; and they have had great influence upon American manners, taste, ideas, and values.

The selection of persons to be discussed is based on two criteria: their importance in our cultural history, and the extent and perceptiveness of their observations. For instance, James Fenimore Cooper is a far more penetrating and voluminous writer on European and American society than is Longfellow or even Lowell. Henry James is of course central to a study such as this one. And the noisy expatriates of the 1920's had a lot to say about the conflicting values on both sides of the Atlantic.

Obviously many persons touched on lightly or not at all could have been included, but faces can become lost in a crowd; impressions of a variety of people become homogenized. Therefore I have chosen to examine in some detail the expatriate experience of a relatively small number of people in the hope that this method will more adequately give the texture of that experience, and in the belief that the extended comments of a perceptive and thoughtful observer like Hawthorne are more valuable than an anthology of brief comments by a variety of people.

There were, of course, expatriates before 1783. As will appear, the American was very early recognized as a new type. Like the Australian today he did not regard himself, nor was he looked upon, as merely a transplanted Englishman. However, after 1783 he was further set apart by a political system which was suspect in the eyes of most Europeans. The traveling American felt and was made to feel that he belonged to a different civilization. He might be boastful or apologetic about his own land, but very often he learned to see it with fresh eyes.

Just as 1783 is a convenient date for beginning the account of American expatriates, 1929 serves as a good terminal point. The stock-market crash and the long depression brought home numerous writers and artists who could no longer afford to live abroad. The explosive expansion of American libraries, universities, and schools or art and music which followed World War I made it no longer necessary for scholars, musicians and artists to study in Europe. An editor of a great American publishing house says that about 1929 the tide shifted from European to American authors. Before that date the house published more books by foreigners than by native writers; since then American titles have predominated. As a nation, therefore, our period of cultural dependency on Europe came chiefly between 1783 and 1929.

To sum up: the purpose of this study is to examine the experiences and reactions of a selected number of important American scholars, artists, and writers who lived abroad for extended periods between these dates. It is hoped that this examination will shed light on the nature of American society and will trace one of the important cultural influences upon it.

EXPATRIATES AND PATRIOTS

PROLOGUE

One of the enduring themes in the literature of the United States is the conflict between American and European values. On the one hand there has been the obvious cultural heritage from the Old World; on the other, the break with many of the old traditions. As might be expected, the break with the past was more self-conscious than the preservation of much of it. Literary historians in particular have emphasized the new, the characteristically American elements in our culture. Like the writers of advertising copy for a new model car, they give their chief attention to the innovations, even minor ones. Cotton Mather began his *Magnalia* with the words, "I write the wonders of the Christian religion flying from the depravations of Europe to the American strand. . . ." Yet as Perry Miller points out, probably 90 per cent of the folk ways of the New England Puritans were those of the same social class in England.

Cotton Mather exemplifies the nature of the seventeenth-century break with established European religious tradition. Roger Williams and William Penn, with their insistence on the right of private judgment, represent another direction taken by the revolt against the church-state pattern of the old world.

In the eighteenth century the revolt was economic and political. "The new world has been the asylum for the persecuted lovers of civil and religious liberty from every part of Europe. Hither they have fled, not from the tender embraces of the mother, but from the cruelty of the monster," wrote Paine. Crèvecoeur went a step further: "The American is a new man, who acts upon new principles; he must therefore entertain new ideas and form new opinions."

Crèvecoeur was talking chiefly about new political and economic ideas, but in the nineteenth century writers carried this theme into other cultural areas. Horatio Greenough preached a new, functional architecture; Emerson said, "We have listened too long to the courtly muses of Europe," and Whitman sounded his "barbaric yawp over the roofs of the world." Less self-consciously perhaps, painters like Charles Willson Peale, Copley, Sully, and Morse developed an American style of portraiture. Irving, Cooper, Hawthorne, and Lowell, among others, sought for American themes in literature.

But there were counterforces. Many Americans tried to bring religion, political institutions, art, architecture, and literature back into European patterns. For one thing many of the artists, scholars, and writers went abroad to study. Until after the Civil War there were in the United States no great libraries, no genuine universities, no first-rate instruction in music and art. Political and social conservatives were often appalled at the rapidity of social change in America. Some of them, like the Loyalists during the Revolution and numerous Southern aristocrats following the Civil War, expatriated themselves from their homeland. James Fenimore Cooper stated that the upper-class American was "accustomed to sneer at democracy, to cavil at its fruits, and to colour and exaggerate its faults." From Thomas Hutchinson to Edith Wharton many of this class expatriated themselves, and a much larger number traveled extensively abroad.

The American in Europe is one of the earliest aspects of the cultural history of the new world. As early as the 1760's he was recognized by Europeans as a distinctly new breed, typified in both England and France by Benjamin Franklin. The sayings of Poor Richard, which had preceded him, were regarded as an American document. Nothing could be less European than this scientist and diplomat who called attention to his plebeian origins by presenting to his aristocratic friends cakes of crown soap made, as he proudly pointed out, by his sister according to a formula handed down in the family.

Yet like many Americans who have lived for some time abroad, Franklin seemed to his compatriots to be dangerously Europeanized. Abigail Adams, seeing Mme Helvetius playfully sit on his lap, wrote in shocked indignation about the corruption of French manners. Irving, Cooper, Bancroft, Motley, Henry James, and many others who lived abroad were to experience similar criticism of alleged un-American tendencies despite the fact that they were not observed with ladies on their laps.

On the other hand Europeans were always aware of the American qualities of visitors from the New World. At times, for reasons which will be discussed, they were hostile to the travelers and expatriates, but the usual attitude was one of curiosity about the strange breed. "Is he white or black?" asked the blind Cardinal Albani on being introduced to young Benjamin West in 1760. To the Cardinal the word *American* connoted Indians. The next morning the young man was taken to the Vatican museum so that the experts could observe the effect of the great art of

Europe on this visitor from the wilderness. A large group of connoisseurs in their carriages followed the aged Cardinal and his blond guest. As a dramatic climax the old man ordered doors thrown open to reveal the Apollo Belvedere. It was the first nude statue West had ever seen.

His response was hardly Quakerlike: "My God, how like a Mohawk warrior!"

For a moment there was indignation; then West explained to an interpreter what noble savages they were. He had seen one, just after discharging an arrow, in the same attitude as that of the statue. The virtuosi around him, remembering their Rousseau, declared that a better criticism of a statue had never been heard.

When John Singleton Copley sent over his painting of a boy with a tame flying squirrel, it was recognized as something strange, a work unlike that of any European painter. Benjamin West wrote to Copley, advising him how to make his work conform to the current style. After 1774 when Copley, a Loyalist, settled in England, he learned how to soften and prettify his sitters. Most critics will agree with the painter's comment on his own work when toward the end of his life he said that the American canvases, which had once been scorned as crude, were better than any of the highly polished works of his transatlantic career. Thus, long before Henry James took up the theme, we have the conflict between a naïve, vigorous America and a polished, enervating Europe.

The early American painters especially felt this conflict. Before 1806 there was no art school in the United States. According to Rembrandt Peale the first collection of paintings was sent over about 1786 to John Swanwick, a Philadelphia merchant. In 1780 John Adams, after a visit to Versailles, wrote to his wife, "It is not indeed the fine arts which our country requires; the useful, the mechanic arts are those which we have occasion for in a young country." He himself needed to study politics and war so that his sons could study mathematics and philosophy, and their children might study painting, poetry, and music. However, American artists were not content to accept Adams' delayed timetable.

The careers of such men as Benjamin West, John Singleton Copley, Washington Allston, Charles Willson Peale, and Samuel F. B. Morse represent various steps in the process of bringing the fine arts to America. West was a Pennsylvania Quaker who went to England to study, and who remained there the rest of his life. He became a favorite of George III; following the death of Reynolds in 1792 he was elected president of the Royal

Academy by an almost unanimous vote. After the King went mad, West lost favor and resigned, but was re-elected in 1806. When he died he was given an immense funeral costing £1000 and was buried in St. Paul's. Yet despite his apparent anglicization West could not forget he was an American. He refused a knighthood and hankered to return to his native land. Nostalgically Mrs. West tried to grow Indian corn in an English hothouse. Certainly his influence on American painters was immense. He was always ready to loan money to an art student from America or to invite him to stay at his home. Among those he taught were Copley, Gilbert Stuart, Charles W. Peale, Rembrandt Peale, Matthew Pratt, John Trumbull, Allston, Morse, Charles Leslie, Earle, William Dunlap, and Thomas Sully.

Some of these men were to help realize West's hope, expressed to Trumbull, that the fine arts should take root in America, for in Europe he believed they had passed their zenith. Charles Willson Peale founded the first art school in America, and Morse became the first professor of fine arts at New York University. It is symbolic that Morse complained that in his studio at N. Y. U. the roof leaked. Copley remained in England, but even this former Loyalist rejoiced that America would become a great empire, and he expressed the modest thought that "it is a pleasing reflection that I shall stand amongst the first of the Artists that shall have led that Country to the Knowledge and cultivation of the fine Arts, happy in the pleasing reflection that they will one Day shine with a luster not inferior to what they have done in Greece or Rome in my Native Country."

Charles W. Peale was a more characteristically American type. He too went abroad before the Declaration of Independence but he subscribed to its principles. During his two-year stay in England during the agitation over the Stamp Act be became more than ever an American patriot. He swore to bend all his energies to making America independent, and upon leaving for home would not take English clothes back with him.

Peale was American in a number of other ways: he could turn his hand to anything. Although trained as a saddler he made for himself a watch and a violin. In England he studied oil and miniature painting, modeling in plaster, and mezzotint scraping while supporting himself by painting miniatures. On one occasion he called upon Franklin, whom he found with a pretty lady on his knee. Peale tiptoed out, made a sketch, and then tactfully stamped as he re-entered the room.

Back in Philadelphia he founded the first art school in America, the

Pennsylvania Academy of the Fine Arts, in 1806. Unable to get anyone to pose in the nude for his classes, he did so himself. One of his most famous paintings is of George Washington in uniform, done in a straightforward realistic manner quite unlike the idealized, prettified English style of the time. Like Copley's early work and Morse's portraits, this is definitely an example of native American style—what John A. Kouwenhoven calls the vernacular tradition.

Peale also established the first public art gallery as part of his museum in Independence Hall. The museum included animals stuffed by himself and the skeleton of a mammoth he had discovered in the New Jersey marshes. To get it out Peale had invented a machine with buckets on a revolving chain, and then painted a picture of the whole operation. Some of the reasons for adding a museum to his art gallery are revealed in the comment of his son Rembrandt Peale: "There the Italian pictures were deposited and displayed to a public but little prepared to appreciate them; for they were less disposed to admire some really excellent memoranda of the fine art than to censure their deep shadowings."

However it was probably this collection which fired young Rembrandt Peale with a desire to visit Italy. The lives of father and son illustrate the two forces in American culture. Charles Willson Peale exemplifies the native, vernacular tradition, slightly modified by English influences; Rembrandt Peale, although an ardent patriot, shows more dependence on European culture. The work of the younger Peale also suggests a flagging of creative vigor in the new nation during the early years of the republic.

American letters show the same hiatus. It is as if, following the Constitutional Convention in 1787, the creative and intellectual vigor of the United States of America paused for breath. The new document crystallized in institutionalized form the revolutionary thinking from Roger Williams to Jefferson and Madison. The ideas embodied in the Declaration and the Constitution were to disturb Europe for at least half a century. It remained, of course, for Washington to prove that the revolutionary theories would work; for Jefferson and Jackson to extend their application, and for Lincoln to preserve them through our greatest national crisis. But between 1787 and about 1827 the United States developed its muscles faster than its mind. Philip Freneau in 1788 expressed the problem of the American writer:

On these bleak climes by Fortune thrown,
Where rigid reason rules alone,

Where lovely Fancy has no sway,
Nor magic forms about us play,
Nor nature takes her summer here;
Tell me, what has the muse to do?

An age employed in edging steel
Can no poetic raptures feel;
No solitude's attracting power,
No leisure of the noonday hours,
No shaded stream, no quiet grove
Can this fantastic century move.

Emerson said that "from 1790 to 1820 there was not a book, a speech, or a conversation, or a thought" in Massachusetts.

This does not mean that no writing was being done in the United States during the early years of the Republic. A few writers stand out: Philip Freneau, William Bartram, Charles Brockden Brown, Joel Barlow, William Cullen Bryant—and of course Washington Irving and James Fenimore Cooper. It is significant that the last two were expatriates for long periods—Irving for a total of twenty-four years, Cooper for nearly eight years. But not until Poe's *Tamerlane* (1827) and Emerson's *Nature* (1836) did a really major writer emerge. The influence of European experience on Irving and Cooper will be treated in later chapters.

An important influence on the writers of the early Republic was European opinion. As the representatives of a new nation and a distrusted political system, Americans felt themselves to be on trial. In fact, they were on trial before the bar of European, especially British, opinion. Sydney Smith's remark of 1820 is famous even today: "In the four quarters of the globe, who reads an American book or goes to an American play, or looks at an American picture or statue?" It is significant that this sort of criticism came after the United States became independent. For many years to come no one demanded a Canadian or an Australian literature or art or music. The new American was made to feel defensive in a way in which his Colonial predecessors had not been. This defensiveness sometimes led to violent counterattack in American periodicals and such books as Cooper's *Notions of the Americans* and *Gleanings in Europe*. On the other hand it led Americans to adopt the protective coloring of imitation as in Irving's *Bracebridge Hall*, Bryant's *Thanatop-*

sis, or Poe's use of foreign settings, Renaissance palaces, English castles and manor houses. When *Thanatopsis* appeared, the editor of *The North American Review* stated that no one of this side of the Atlantic could have written it.

American sensitivity to criticism was further heightened by a series of books by English travelers who discovered pay dirt. It was not mere provincial sensitivity which caused Americans to resent the remarks of foreign travelers: there was a genuine failure of communication. To an American, a frontier city like Cincinnati was a blueprint or the foundation of a structure to come; to Frances Trollope it was democracy incarnate—tobacco chewing and shoddy. The fact that she had failed in business there heightened her perceptions. She bemoaned the fact that for the people on a frontier farm, "No village bell ever summoned them to prayer. . . . When they die, no spot sacred by ancient reverence will receive their bones." Secure in a belief in beef and boiled cabbage, she deplored the "strangest incongruity imaginable" of mixing such foods as eggs and oysters or ham and apple sauce.

In like manner Fanny Kemble, accustomed to the waddle of the over-fed English women described by Hawthorne, said that American ladies walked with "a French shuffle." An American autumn with its gorgeous—and therefore un-English—colors was for her "a whole forest dying of consumption." Even going to church was an ordeal: "I must say it requires a deal of fortitude to go into an American church. There are no pew openers. . . ."

All this may seem remote from political institutions, but English travelers insisted on a connection. The preface of Frances Trollope's *Domestic Manners of the Americans* announced that "by describing, faithfully, the daily aspect of ordinary life, she has endeavoured to show how greatly the advantage is on the side of those who are governed by the few, instead of the many." Fanny Kemble would have agreed. Captain Basil Hall, a much more judicious observer than either of the ladies, on seeing some decaying country estates, reported that the ancient aristocracy was withering away "before the blighting tempest of democracy."

It is not strange, then, to find a certain defensiveness on the part of Americans in the early days of the republic. As Henry Adams sums up the reports of Europeans from 1790 to 1840:

> No foreigner of that day—neither poet, painter, nor philosopher—
> could detect in American life anything higher than vulgarity; for it

was something beyond the range of their experience, which education and culture had not framed a formula to express.

The expatriated Washington Irving included in *The Sketch Book* an essay of uncharacteristic sharpness, "English Writers on America." In it he suggested that the type of English traveler in America was likely to be "the broken-down tradesman, the scheming adventurer, the wandering mechanic." Irving warned that time was on the side of America and that it was dangerous for England to alienate a nation which she might sometime need as an ally. The more usual response to criticism and calumny was a series of spread-eagle screams in American newspapers and magazines. Apropos of the reception of Hall's book Mrs. Trollope says:

> I am induced, ere I conclude, again to mention what I consider as the most remarkable traits of the national character of the Americans; namely, their exquisite sensitiveness and soreness respecting everything said or written concerning them.

Other nations might be thin-skinned but "the citizens of the Union have, apparently no skins at all."

When Americans went abroad they encountered the same supercilious attitude. Fifty-five years after Cardinal Albani asked concerning Benjamin West, "Is he white?", young George Ticknor wrote from Germany that Americans were a curiosity: "It is supposed we can hardly be civilized." Cooper was irritated by a British hostess who asked where he had learned to speak such good English. In 1864 James Russell Lowell wrote bitterly to his friend Leslie Stephen:

> England *can't* like America, do what she or we will. . . . But I think the usages of society should hold between nations, and see no particular use in her taking every opportunity to tell us how disagreeable and vulgar we are. What *riled* me was the quiet assumption that we hadn't, couldn't, and had no right to have a country over here.

To Thomas Hughes, Lowell told of an experience Longfellow had in Rome. On the way to the races Longfellow's carriage drew abreast of one containing two English ladies who were discussing American girls: "Well, you know, what can be expected of people who are all descended

from laboring men or convicts?" In the 1920's an Englishman said to
Conrad Aiken, "But you're an American. And you speak English!" To
which he replied, "Oh yes, at will."

On the whole, it would seem that Americans abroad have been more
understanding about Europe than Europeans have about the United
States. The exceptions stand out: de Toqueville, James Bryce, and more
recently Alistair Cook and Denis Brogan. On the other hand, it would be
hard to match in American writers on Europe such jaundiced views as
those of Frances Trollope, Fanny Kemble, Rudyard Kipling, D. H. Lawrence, and Simone de Beauvoir on the United States. Two of the sharpest
critics of Europe, Fenimore Cooper and Mark Twain, are equally severe
on their own countrymen. In contrasting the values of the two civilizations probably no writer can match the American Henry James.

By contrast the Englishman abroad, whether traveler or expatriate, has
been notorious for his inability to admire anything foreign. Even an
anglophile like Washington Irving could write in Amsterdam: "The most
prominent character here was an Englishman with a sour discontented
face, apparently travelling to find whatever is bad out of England."
Cooper commented that English travelers were proverbially grumblers,
especially about anything different from what they knew at home. Lawrence Sterne's character Smellfungus and Meredith's Egoist are British
portraits of the traveling Englishman.

The different attitude of the American abroad was due in part to the
fact that he had been brought up on English literature and history. With
his mind filled with Shakespeare, Milton, Scott, and Byron—and later
Dickens—he regarded London, Oxford, Kenilworth, and Newstead
Abbey as holy places. The tombs in Westminster Abbey were those of his
spiritual ancestors. For instance just before leaving England, Irving took
Martin Van Buren and his son on a tour which included all these places.
One night Irving slept in Byron's bed. Hawthorne complained that Americans visited the Coliseum by moonlight to feel raptures that were not
their own but Byron's. Certainly they saw the Forum as the scene of
Shakespeare's *Julius Caesar*. Europe was a vital part of the American's
cultural heritage; in fact Hawthorne wrote of England as "Our Old
Home."

There was however, another element in the American's feeling about
Europe—a distrust of its morals. This inheritance from the Puritans
appears in some degree in Irving and Cooper—neither one of whom

came from New England. When in 1818 President Kirkland of Harvard proposed that George Bancroft study in Europe, Andrews Norton took the young man to consult the aged John Adams. Adams advised against it: from what he had seen of European society it was no fit environment for a young theologian. Samuel F. B. Morse ran into similar objections from his mother. All Americans in Europe, she believed, were "dissipated infidels" with the exception of West and Allston. Hawthorne, after looking at Titian's "Magdalen," decided that "Titian must have been a very good-for-nothing old man." Even Hiram Powers, whose nude Greek Slave so titillated visitors to London's Crystal Palace and Philadelphia's Centennial Exhibition, tried to discourage young girls from entering "so perilous a profession" as modeling for sculptors.

Above all, perhaps, the American in the early days of the Republic, felt himself a representative of his country. He had a dual responsibility to demonstrate to Europeans that an American could be a gentleman, a writer, or an artist, and to report back to his friends and relatives about his experiences and impressions. Two of those who felt these responsibilities keenly were Irving and Cooper. In very different ways each tried to represent his country abroad, and both men left extensive records of their European experience.

AT EASE IN ZION

WASHINGTON IRVING

To a considerable degree Washington Irving foreshadowed a half century of American expatriate writing and experience. Like most expatriates of the nineteenth century he came from the old Federalist aristocracy. It was this class which most often found itself uncomfortable in a raw, expanding nation.

Irving himself was not especially uncomfortable in the United States; he had a rare gift of being at home wherever he was. Like his literary model, Walter Scott, he was a delightful companion. Among his friends were many people of importance on both sides of the Atlantic; a list including Lafayette, Louis Philippe, Andrew Jackson, Franklin Pierce, Martin Van Buren, Prince Albert, and many others. When Napoleon III was crowned emperor, Irving remarked that he had entertained him in his cottage near Tarrytown and had dandled on his knee a child, Eugénie Mantijo, who was now empress of France. His intimate friends were most often painters and writers: Washington Allston, Charles R. Leslie, Walter Scott, Thomas Moore, John Howard Payne, Sydney Smith, Samuel Rogers, and Thomas Campbell. This roster is the result rather than the cause of Irving's long residence abroad. As a young gallant in New York he showed no indication of discontent with the gay companions who went in for stag dinners with much madeira and champagne. One of this New York group, Henry Brevoort, was a lifelong friend and correspondent.

There is no indication that Irving ever intended to become an expatriate. The process was gradual—more drift than direction. Because he had no desire to enter the family business, he took up in a rather desultory fashion the study of law. The death of Matilda Hoffman, with whom he was in love, was perhaps the cause of his own ill health. The usual prescription for ailments which nineteenth-century doctors could not diagnose was a trip abroad. His brothers put up the money, and Washington sailed for Bordeaux in May of 1804.

Then he remained for six weeks to improve his French. Characteristically he wrote about the display of feminine charms. Ladies in New York once displayed only the foot, later the "ancle," but those of Bordeaux showed the garter. However at Marseilles he was shocked by the ballet: "These lascivious exhibitions are strong evidences of the depraved morals and licentiousness of the public." As will appear, this kind of puritanism was almost universal in Americans abroad throughout the nineteenth century. Unlike most of his countrymen, Irving soon took a more tolerant view. By the time he reached Italy he commented that "to a single man the Italian women are a mighty agreeable accommodating set of beings." However he "would as soon put his neck into a hempen noose as into a hymneal one with any of them." In Sicily, he engaged enthusiastically in masquerades, wine drinking, and flirtation.

His biographer, Stanley Williams, comments that although Irving was no libertine: "Compared with other American men of letters with whom he shared fame in the nineteenth century, it must be said . . . that in these matters he was less aloof." His notebook of 1805 is filled with racy anecdotes. In the garden of the Palais Royal he took walks with "a frail nymph." He often expressed a wish that more Americans could be exposed to European civilization.

Irving's traveling companion, encountered in the diligence to Paris, was a Dr. Henry of Lancaster, Pennsylvania. The doctor, who spoke fluent French, knew many people of importance and carried a snuffbox presented by Lavater. With an American love of practical jokes, he introduced Irving variously as an English prisoner in the custody of a French officer, and as a Mameluke of distinction. Irving, anxious not to be taken "for one of the Smellfungi of this world," was usually an appreciative traveler. He climbed Vesuvius, where he nearly suffocated, but on the whole he enjoyed himself:

> There is no country . . . where the prospects so much interest my mind and awaken such a variety of ideas as in Italy. Every mountain, every valley, every plain, tells some striking story. . . . I am lost in astonishment at the magnificence of their works, at their sublime ideas of architecture, and at their enormous public undertakings!

At Rome:

> To describe the emotions of the mind and the crowd of ideas that arise on entering this "mistress of the world," is impossible.

Like most Americans of the time, Irving approached European scenes with a mind filled with classical history and English literature—especially

Byron. The impact of Byron upon American travelers can scarcely be overestimated.

In Rome he met Washington Allston, the twenty-six-year-old painter from South Carolina, who knew both Byron and Coleridge. Through Allston he met Coleridge, who was a frequent visitor at the studio, and whose fascinating conversation led the painter to feel that he had listened to Plato in the groves of the Academy. Allston, a modest man of considerable learning, loved to spend his evenings discussing art. This was a far different world from that of the balls and oyster suppers—the drunken stag parties of New York.

Allston's studio was also far different from the dull law office to which Irving expected to return:

> He [Allston] was to reside among these delightful scenes, surrounded by masterpieces of art, by classic and historic monuments, by men of congenial minds and tastes, engaged like him in the constant study of the sublime and beautiful. I was to return home to the dry study of the law, for which I had no relish, and, as I feared, little talent.

The painter, discovering a certain amount of talent in the unwilling law student, offered to take him as a pupil and share an apartment with him. Irving was greatly tempted, yet doubted his ability to become a painter. The fact is that at twenty-three he was not ready to settle down to any occupation.

Instead of studying painting he went on to Paris for a stay of four months. Almost every night he went to the theatre: vaudeville, tragedy, opera—his tastes were catholic. He attended a ball.

> Of all the places I have seen in Europe Paris is the most fascinating. . . . The favorableness of the climate, the brilliancy of the theatres, operas etc., the beauty of the public walks, the gaiety, good humor, and universal politeness of the people, the perfect liberty of private conduct, are calculated to enchant a stranger, and to render him contented and happy with everything about him.

However, perhaps remembering his brother's urgings to return home, he added:

> You will smile to see that Paris has obtained complete possession of my head, but I assure you that America has still the stronghold of my heart.

He went on to England, where between November 9 and January 17 he saw twenty-nine plays. One evening an actor came forward to announce Nelson's victory at Trafalgar. Altogether he had experienced a new and exciting world.

However, he was not unhappy on his return home. On Broadway he observed the "pretty *Democrat* à la mode Francoise" and the "sweet little *Federalist* à la mode Angloise." No city in Europe from Cantania to London satisfied him so well as New York of 1806. He told Kemble that he had "resigned the feverish enjoyments of Madeira and Champagne," and was "hasting with rapid strides towards perfection." He even worked for the Federalists in an election campaign in 1807. "I shook hands with the mob—whom my heart abhoreth." Three years later he was in Albany "to witness the interesting scenes of intrigue and iniquity." Such comments reveal his distaste for the American political scene and suggest that his Federalism was less a reasoned conviction than a distaste for the mob. The untypical savagery of his satire on Jefferson as "William the Testy" in *The Knickerbocker History* shows more prejudice than perception.

On the other hand, at no point in his life did Irving prefer the political and economic systems of Europe to those of his homeland. At Syracuse in Sicily he had noted the gloomy, ill-lit streets, the filth and misery on every side. Traveling to Palermo he spoke of the wretchedness of the peasants. Years later as minister to Spain he wrote to Mrs. Storrow: "I am wearied and heartsick at the wretched politics of this country, where there is so much intrigue, falsehood, profligacy, and crime, and so little of high honor and pure patriotism in political affairs."

Nor was Irving without some intellectual companionship in New York. In 1807–1808, along with his brother Peter and James Kirke Paulding he produced *Salmagundi, or the Whim-Whams and Opinions of Lancelot Langstaff and Others.* As the title suggests, this shows the influence of Addison and Sterne. Diedrich Knickerbocker's *A History of New York* followed in 1809. In this too Peter had a hand.

Peter was much like his brother but without his talent. After trying his hand at medicine, he entered the family business and was sent to Liverpool. With a view to counteracting the un-American tendency toward literature of the youngest brother, the four older ones took Washington into the business as inactive partner and agent at large. This provided Irving with the necessary excuse for another trip abroad. Peter was already installed in Liverpool as purchasing agent for the firm.

For Washington Irving the first two years of his stay abroad proved something less than a pleasure jaunt. He found Peter down with erysipelas and rheumatism. And, expecting a demand for English goods following the War of 1812, he had overbought. Irving gave up his playboy way of life and tried to untangle Peter's affairs; he even studied bookkeeping. Occasionally he managed to get to the theater, and he stole off for visits to his sister Sarah, married to Henry Van Wart, a Birmingham businessman. Sarah was his favorite sister and he enjoyed playing the bachelor uncle to her growing family. With Peter he rambled in Wales and Derbyshire. With the American expatriate painters Leslie and Allston he planned a new edition of *Knickerbocker*. But for the most part, these were years of anxious days and sleepless nights.

Despite his dislike of commercial life, the failure of the firm in 1818 was "frightful and humiliating." His heart went out in anxiety for his relatives involved in the crash.

Irving's two years in business in England and his later service as a diplomat in England and Spain must not be considered as an exception to the pattern of the American expatriate. A large proportion of Americans abroad have had business there. As will appear, the sculptors especially found it more profitable to work in Italy. Irving, Hawthorne, Lowell, Motley, and Bancroft all held diplomatic posts abroad. For most of these men their expatriation was partly a matter of business, partly of choice and temperament. Irving certainly found much to his taste in European life. But until after the Civil War the expatriate as dilettante and *flaneur* was the exception rather than the rule. Irving had some of these qualities, but it is possible that his biographers and the literary historians have exaggerated them. Economics—the business of making a living—played an important part in expatriation during the first hundred years of our national life. The Henry James, Edith Wharton, Gertrude Stein, and T. S. Eliot types come later. One must not read the motives of later expatriates into the lives of Irving and his contemporaries.

Following the collapse of the firm of E. and P. Irving, Washington sought an antidote for his very real mental distress by studying German day and night. Apparently he never became very good at it: years later during a residence in Dresden he confessed to his difficulties with the language. But his attempt to learn it was tied up with his rather amateurish interest in folklore. This was the period when Scott had captured the imagination of England and America with his tales of a romantic past.

The influence of German romanticism was beginning to be felt. Among Irving's associates following his release from business were Allston, Kemble, Charles Leslie, Campbell, and Coleridge. Campbell had recently published *Gertrude of Wyoming,* a verse tale based upon American history. Coleridge, as is well known, was an avid reader in folklore and legend. Irving's own travels in England and Wales were always undertaken with an eye for picturesque and historic scenes. With a letter from Campbell, he called on Scott at his imitation castle at Abbotsford: "The glorious old minstrel himself came limping to the gate, took me by the hand in a way that made me feel as if we were old friends. . . ."

The two-day visit was filled with story, incident, and song. Scott urged him to stay longer and Irving promised himself to pay another visit. Legend has it that he told of Rebecca Gratz in whose arms his beloved Matilda Hoffman had died, and that Scott used the American Jewish girl as the model for Rebecca of *Ivanhoe.* Be that as it may, Scott wrote a friend asking him to thank Campbell for introducing Irving, "who is one of the best and pleasantest acquaintances I have made this many a day."

Francis Jeffrey was also cordial and made his house a home for Irving. The romantic mood which appears so often in Irving's accounts of travel shows in his letters:

> Arthur's seat is perfect witchcraft. I don't wonder that any one residing in Edinburgh should write poetically; I rambled about the bridges and on Calton Height yesterday, in a perfect intoxication of mind. I did not visit a single public building, but merely gazed and revelled in the romantic scenery around me.

This mood and theme: the pilgrimage to the romantic past, appears over and over in the letters, journals, and published works of Americans from Irving to Henry James. It is the prevailing note of *The Sketch Book* written almost entirely in England. In it, Irving developed himself as the romantic wanderer. In the *Knickerbocker History* he had already used the American past. Now he domesticated two German tales by placing them in the Hudson River Valley. So completely has he visualized the romantic scenery of the Catskills and Sleepy Hollow that the stories have become a part of the mythical past of America.

The modern reader brought up on Hemingway and Faulkner usually has a vague recollection of *The Sketch Book* as a collection of American essays and stories. Yet only six of the thirty-four pieces in it have any connection with Irving's homeland. Most of the essays are a traveler's impressions of England, the England of country houses and historic shrines.

In the opening section he tells of his "rambling propensity" and his early passion for books of travel. Then:

> I visited various parts of my own country; and had I been merely a lover of fine scenery, I should have felt little desire to seek elsewhere for its gratification. . . . Her mighty lakes, like oceans of liquid silver; her mountains, with their bright aerial tints; her valleys teaming with wild fertility; her tremendous cataracts. . . . no, never need an American look beyond his own country for the sublime and beautiful of natural scenery.
>
> But Europe held forth the charms of storied and poetical association. There were to be seen the masterpieces of art, the refinements of highly-cultivated society, the quaint peculiarities of ancient and local custom. My native country was full of youthful promise: Europe was rich in the accumulated treasures of age. Her very ruins told the history of times gone by, and every mouldering stone was a chronicle. I longed to wander over the scenes of renowned achievement—to tread, as it were, in the footsteps of antiquity—to loiter about the ruined castle—to meditate on the falling tower—*to escape in short, from the commonplace realities of the present, and lose myself among the shadowy grandeurs of the past.* [Italics mine.]

For many years to come Americans saw Stratford and Westminster Abbey through Irving's eyes. Because such things caught the imagination of a country which felt a lack of a romantic past, and because of Irving's own charming eighteenth-century style, *The Sketch Book* became at once an American classic. It displaced the *Spectator* as a model of prose, and for over a century was used as a school textbook. In Maine young Longfellow read the *Sketch Book* with delight and promised himself to write like Irving. His *Outre Mer* proved that it was not easy to do. To what extent *The Sketch Book* and the later books like *Bracebridge Hall* and *The Alhambra* created an American attitude toward Europe it is difficult to say. Certainly they fell in with a trend already created by Scott and other Romantic writers. Almost inevitably Americans abroad would have looked for the things so lacking at home: ruins, cathedrals, literary and historic shrines, even if Irving had never written a line. All that can be asserted with confidence is that Irving reinforced a point of view that was to influence American education and literature for over half a century.

Nor is *The Sketch Book* a peculiarly American phenomenon; rather it reflected the sensibility of its time on both sides of the Atlantic; in a minor key it strikes notes found in Lamb's essays, the Waverley novels, and *Childe Harold*. Coleridge, Scott, and Byron read *The Sketch Book* with enthusiasm. It was a flower of the Romantic movement.

Upon its publication Irving was taken into the Holland House circle, a group which included Sydney Smith, who only a year before had asked, "In the four quarters of the globe, who reads an American book?" Holland House was a lavish London mansion surrounded by its own park, and in Irving's day owned by Henry Richard, the second Lord Holland. His wife was the former Lady Webster, with whom he had eloped. With the nonchalance characteristic of the Whig aristocracy of the Regency, the Hollands had not married until after the birth of their first child. Because of Lady Holland's preference for continental ways of life they had lived abroad until 1805. On their return to England, Holland House became the gathering place for Whig politicians and writers. Visiting Americans, looked upon with suspicion by the Tories, were frequently entertained at Lord Holland's famous breakfasts, which lasted through much of the morning. Lord Holland was himself something of a writer. He collected manuscripts and books which he later used in his lives of Lope de Vega and Guillen de Castro. However, his literary reputation rests chiefly upon his *Foreign Reminiscences, Memoirs of the Whig Party*, and *Further Memoirs*. The chronicler of Holland House, Lloyd Sanders, speaks of "a curious leaning toward Republican principles which, we may be sure, would never have been translated into practice."

It was a skeptical, tolerant circle in which Irving found himself. Byron had met Lady Caroline Lamb there, and was still welcome after the famous scandal even though the lady had satirized Holland House in *Glenarvon* as Barbary House. "Holland's society is very good," said Byron in 1813; "you always see some one or other in it worth knowing." Tom Moore considered Lord Holland equal to any talker of the time—no small compliment in a circle which included Samuel Rogers, Sydney Smith, Lord Brougham, Thomas Campbell, Sir James Mackintosh, and of course Byron himself. Scott, however, refused to dine there because he did not wish to be suspected of changing his Tory principles. When Mme de Staël visited England, she was taken into the group. While he was a refugee in England, Louis Philippe was entertained there. Rogers, who made much of Americans, seems to be the one who introduced visiting statesmen and diplomats like Monroe, Van Buren, and Daniel Webster. The Harvard scholar George Ticknor was an intimate, as was the American painter Charles Leslie. Fenimore Cooper was later taken into the group, though not without some misgivings.

Here in this acre between Regent's Park, Pall Mall, and St. James Park, which Sydney Smith described as the center of intellectual life in London, Irving found himself at home. All accounts indicate that he was liked and respected. His letters to America contain no hint of invidious comparisons, but there is reason to believe that his association with interesting people abroad had much to do with his continued stay.

Irving had planned to return home in 1817, but the death of his mother led him to change his plans. Shortly after his meeting with Scott, Commodore Decatur obtained for him the offer of a post as first clerk of the Navy Department at $2400 a year. This salary, said Decatur, would enable one to live like a prince in Washington. Irving declined the offer. About the same time, and possibly influencing his refusal, his brother Peter decided to remain abroad. Washington wrote home saying that his own talents were "merely literary" and adding that he had no talents to be an active politician. Apparently he felt that a political appointment would involve an active participation in party strife. The apologetic phrase "merely literary" is significant: in the New York world of his brothers, a legal or business career was more respectable than writing.

As a further excuse for staying abroad Irving spoke of the advantages of foreign copyrights and added:

> To carry this into better effect it is important for me to remain a little longer in Europe, where there is so much food for observation, and objects of taste on which to meditate and improve. . . .

> Do not, I beseech you, impute my lingering in Europe to any indifference to my own country or my friends. My greatest desire is to make myself worthy of the good-will of my country, and my greatest anticipation of happiness is to return to my friends.

The somewhat defensive note reoccurs in Irving's correspondence with his brothers and with Henry Brevoort. Certainly his alleged longing to return home must be weighed against the fact that he stayed in Europe for thirteen years more. That Irving had moments of homesickness seems clear, but he continued to find much to hold him in Europe. In fact his occasional protestations of a longing to return most often follow a letter from home accusing him of abandoning his country.

The copyright problem was real enough. In the absence of an international copyright publishers on both sides of the Atlantic pirated books of other countries. Because there were many more important writers in England than in America, this most often worked to the disadvantage of the English, and to a considerable degree accounts for the hostility to America on the part of writers like Dickens. American publishers, profiting by this situation, brought pressures on Congress to prevent a copyright agreement. It was a situation which gave support to the European view that Americans were unscrupulous when it came to money.

To meet this situation authors endeavored to get their work copyrighted almost simultaneously on both sides of the Atlantic. The proof sheets of a book to be published in England would be sent to America by clipper ship so that a publisher willing to pay royalties for exclusive rights could get an American copyright before some other publisher got hold of a copy of the book. For as soon as an uncopyrighted book got into a publisher's hands he would set up type and print copies within two or three days. He could then obtain a copyright with no payment to the author. Because of a British requirement that anyone applying for copyright must be a resident, it was to the advantage of American authors to be in England at the time of application. Also because of the likelihood of greater sales in England, a copyright there was often more valuable than one at home. "If the American public wish to have a literature of their own," wrote Irving, "they must consent to pay for the support of their authors."

Americans sometimes acted as agents in their own country for British authors. Emerson, a shrewd man in dealing with publishers, acted for Carlyle in America; Irving obtained an American copyright for his friend Campbell. When *The Sketch Book* was ready, Irving wrote to Henry Brevoort asking him to obtain an American copyright. However, even with the most careful planning, a simultaneous copyright could fail because of the uncertainties of navigation. The ship carrying proof sheets might arrive after one which sailed two weeks later with a copy of the book. Considering the popularity of Irving's books in America and the fact that his brother Peter lived abroad and could act for him, it is quite possible that the copyright problem need not have detained him.

To find Irving's real reasons for remaining abroad one must read between the lines. At home he had been looked upon as a dilettante, a man unable to make his way in law or politics. In England he was regarded as a person of importance. Scott made him an offer of £500 a year to edit an anti-Jacobin periodical which was being planned in Edinburgh. Irving declined on the grounds that he disliked politics and that his habits of work were so desultory that they unfitted him for any periodically recurring task. After all, he had left New York to avoid both of these things. His pride in his European standing appears in a letter written a year or two later to Brevoort: "The success of my writings has given me ready access to all kinds of society, and I have been the rounds of routs, dinners, operas, balls, and blue-stocking coteries."

A few weeks later he added that he had "got on sociable terms with most of the men of letters and the leading artists of the day that are in London." And on another occasion he proudly told Brevoort that he had achieved a position "entirely independent and self-created."

At home Irving had been a younger brother, often disapproved of and urged to show more energy, to make a place for himself in the business or political world of America. Just as the younger-brother status seems to have been a factor in the expatriation of Henry James, it may have influenced, if only subconsciously, Irving. Although he was too kindly a soul to mention it, Washington was the one who was able to send £100 to his brother Peter in France. In New York the Irving firm was not doing well, and William, worried over financial reverses, died at the age of fifty-five. On the other hand, Murray, who had rejected *The Sketch Book*, paid 1000 guineas for *Bracebridge Hall*, and because of its popularity offered 1500 guineas for Irving's next book, sight unseen. It was a mark of distinction to be accepted by Murray, the publisher of Scott and Byron.

In addition to his income in England Irving was getting good prices at home. Brevoort had arranged for the American publication of *The Sketch Book*. When *Bracebridge Hall* was ready, Irving asked his brother to arrange for it to come out before the English edition arrived, "throwing me at the mercy of American publishers."

But there were more subtle forces than money and social distinction to keep Irving abroad. He was in his late thirties and had not been home for five years. He wrote Brevoort of his longing for past times and past scenes in New York and added: "But I shall return home, and find all changed, and shall be made more sensible how much I have changed myself." Even on his last visit home he had, according to himself, held aloof from the Madeira parties and champagne suppers. Now his old friends were married or dead; they were involved in political and business affairs in which he had no interest. Their lives and interests must have seemed dull and narrow to a man accustomed to the Holland house circle. But much of this Irving was too polite to say.

His nearest approach to bitterness was in response to a letter of Brevoort's accusing him of renouncing his country. On March 10, 1821, Irving wrote: "I am endeavoring to serve my country. Whatever I have written has been written with the feelings and published as the writing of an American. . . . How else am I to serve my country? by coming home and begging an office of it . . . ?"

The fact is that he seems to have liked the footloose life. In the same letter to Brevoort he mentioned that he was seeing Moore almost daily. This was in Paris, where he had gone for a six-month stay. Moore, who was there with his family, frequently had Irving in to dine. Charming and improvident, Moore was congenial company. He let Irving read Byron's *Memoirs,* presumably that fabulous manuscript which was later destroyed as too scandalous for publication. Another associate in Paris was John Howard Payne, the American actor and playright now remembered for one song, "Home, Sweet Home." The association was pleasant but certainly not profitable. Payne, always out of funds, borrowed money. Together they wrote several plays which had no success.

Irving also had a brother and a sister living abroad. Peter, the semi-invalid who had failed in Liverpool, had a scheme for making money out of steamboats on the Seine. Washington invested and loaned money in this venture, and tried to get his American brothers to release some of the family funds for this purpose. The New York brothers, seeing no reason why both Peter and Washington should not come home, refused to do so.

Irving's favorite sister, Sarah Van Wart, lived in England. To his American sister, Catherine Paris, Washington sometimes revealed his own doubts and worries. As James and Hemingway were to report later, Irving spoke of the difficulties of a writer trying to work in "a world of people living at their ease, with nothing to consult but amusement and society, the least notoriety takes away from a man all command of his time and person, unless he becomes absolutely rude and churlish." There was also a self-doubting note: "My life has been for the greater part a desultory and unprofitable one, owing perhaps to the greater ascendency of my imagination over the more valuable faculties of the mind. I have often felt distressed by the idea that I must be an object of censure among friends. . . ."

He added the hope that he could enjoy the affection of his relatives "and leave a name that may be cherished by the family when my poor wandering life is at an end." Obviously there were times when Irving was influenced by the American idea that the "valuable faculties of the mind" were those which led to success in business and politics. Yet, as has been shown, he recognized that his only chance of serving his country and making a name for himself was through his writing. This ambivalence about himself is a reflection of the nineteenth-century American's ambivalence toward Europe. Europe stood for leisure and the arts—and these were to be valued—but were they the true values? Were not hard work and business acumen more important? Irving's experience taught him that his talents, his social graces fitted him best for the European pattern, but his upbringing and the letters from home left him with a sense of guilt.

This conflict within himself may well account for several periods of apparently psychosomatic illness, extended bouts with allergic skin ailments which were relieved only by courses of baths at some spa. Also it is not surprising to find that periods of comparative idleness alternated with others of furious work. Moore reported that in Paris Irving wrote 130 pages of *Bracebridge Hall* in ten days!

Just after the publication of *Bracebridge Hall* he wrote to Brevoort saying that the thought of a return to America "is daily becoming clearer and dearer to my imagination, as the lapse of time gives it all the charms of distance." Instead of going home, however, he made a tour of the Rhine and the Black Forest, where the romantic scenery enchanted him. "I have a taste for the antique, particularly for the antique of the middle (Gothic) period," he wrote his sister Mrs. Van Wart. At Munich he enjoyed the opera and the music of Mozart. In Salzburg he found a French translation of *The Sketch Book*. At Vienna, with *Ivanhoe* in his mind, he visited the prison where Richard Coeur de Lion had been confined. Thinking he would find a more intellectual society at Dresden, he settled there for six months. Here he became intimate with the court of

Frederick Augustus and Queen Marie. His reputation had preceded him: on sale in the city were a German edition of *Bracebridge Hall* and a French one of *The Sketch Book*.

He went boar hunting with the King and took part in amateur theatricals. On one occasion he was fined for firing a pistol from a window during the course of a performance. At a court ball the Queen sent the master of ceremonies to bring Irving to her. She had not seen him for a century, she said, and she wanted to compliment him on his works which she had just received from Paris. It was all very flattering.

Also he was seeing much of the Fosters. Mrs. Foster, the daughter of Lord Carhampton, was in Dresden for the education of her lovely daughters Fanny and Emily. With Mrs. Foster he reviewed his Italian and with Miss Foster his French. Irving fell more or less in love with Emily, who described him as

> Sweet tempered, gentle, fastidious, sensitive and gifted with the warmest affections, the most delightful and invariably interesting companion, gay and full of humor, even in spite of occasional fits of melancholy . . . a gift of conversation that flowed like a full river of sunshine. . . . He was thoroughly a gentleman, not merely in external manners and look, but to the innermost fibres and core of his heart.

To her he confided that he felt at times "the least fitted being for this wandering life, into which chance and circumstance have thrown me. I have strong domestic feelings."

However, the habit of drifting was too strong. He returned to Paris, but for a time was unable to write. He got up in the morning with a kind of horror that almost incapacitated him. He realized that that was "an affair of nerves."

To his nephew, Pierre Irving, who was starting in business in New York, he wrote saying that young people in America went into fashionable society too early, at a time when Europeans were still at school. "How many an hour of hard labor and hard study I have had to subject myself to, to atone in a slight degree for the hours which I suffered society to cheat me of." He might have added that he continued to let social life cheat him of working hours. In a letter from Dresden he said that he went out so much in society that he had little time to write. Back in Paris he entertained his nephews, the Van Wart boys, who were there at school; and he looked after his ailing brother Peter. He heard anecdotes of Byron from Captain Medwin, Samuel Rogers, and Benjamin West.

He did some work with Payne, and managed to finish *Tales of a Traveller,* an inferior book based on his German experience. Here again he retold folk tales which he had picked up on the way. Strangely enough this thin concoction was attacked in both England and America for "droll indecencies and equivocating ribaldry . . . offensive to the chastity of the Georgian home." To Irving, familiar with the marital history of Lord and Lady Holland and aware of the many illegitimate children fathered by Lord Egremont, a member of the Holland circle, this offense against the chastity of the Georgian home must have seemed strange indeed. What may have hurt him more was the increasing American clamor about his celebration of the aristocratic virtues.

Irving's three years of rather desultory writing were followed by his journey to Spain in 1826. Here a new and romantic world opened for him, and with it came an access of literary energy. The journey may have had its origins in conversations in Paris with Alexander Everett, who was on his way to Spain as head of the American legation.

At first Irving lived in the house of the American consul, Obadiah Rich, who had an excellent collection of rare books on Spanish history. Here and in the Escorial and in private archives he worked for two years on his *Life and Voyages of Columbus* (1828). Longfellow, calling with a letter of introduction from Ticknor, found Irving difficult of access: "He seemed to be always at work." He was honored by election to the Real Academia de la Historici, to which Ticknor had been elected in 1818.

Even while working on Columbus he wrote to Brevoort saying that the longer he remained in Europe the more charm home held for him: "I look forward to my return as to the only event of any very desirable kind that may yet be in store for me." He was mistaken. At the age of forty-six he set out with an attachè of the Polish legation, Prince Dolgorouki, for the Alhambra. According to his biographer, Stanley Williams, Irving's stay there was his last romantic play-day in Europe.

"I tread haunted ground," he wrote. "From earliest boyhood . . . often have I trod in fancy the romantic halls of the Alhambra." To his sister Mrs. Paris he said that he felt as if he were living in the Arabian Nights. He took an apartment in the old palace from which he could look out upon beautiful rolling scenery. To Brevoort he wrote: "Here, then, I am nestled in one of the most remarkable, romantic, and delicious spots in the world. . . . It absolutely appears to me like a dream; or as if I am spell-bound in some fairy palace."

Here he collected oral legends of the place. He sat by the fountains and told stories to the children, among them Marie Eugénie Montijo, future empress of France. He even engaged in a flirtation with the daughter of a Polish officer. Later he was to put his feeling for the romantic palace into *The Alhambra.*

To literary historians this work is far less important than the *Knickerbocker History* and *The Sketch Book,* but its romantic, out-of-this-world character gave it an immense popularity in their time. Irving's biographer argues that along with the sentimental travel books of Longfellow and Bayard Taylor those of Irving gave Americans an escape from shirt-sleeve democracy.

That is only part of the story. It is quite true that literate Americans were fascinated by the past of Europe. That fascination is one of the themes of the present study. But it must be remembered that the Romantic movement in both England and Germany was filled with this love of the past and of exotic scenery. Scott and Byron were perhaps the most popular writers on both sides of the Atlantic. And it was not Byron the satirist, but Byron the painter of exotic landscape and teller of tales of adventure who was chiefly admired. Longfellow's love of the romantic past was contemporaneous with *The Idylls of the King* and *The Ring and the Book.*

The Alhambra and *Tales of a Wayside Inn* are on a similar pattern to *The Earthly Paradise* of William Morris. Ruskin was to write of Gothic architecture with the same enthusiasm Irving showed for that of the Moors. In fact, the revolt against this sort of antiquarianism appeared in the United States before it did in England. In 1837 Emerson wrote: "Give me insight into to-day, and you may have the antique and future worlds. . . . We have listened too long to the courtly muses of Europe." And four years before Irving's death Walt Whitman threw the courtly muse into the street and sounded his barbaric yawp over the roofs of the world. Nine years later Tennyson published *Idylls of the King.* In sentimentalizing the past Irving was closer to the British than to the American tradition.

At the end of his Spanish idyll he packed up his books and other

belongings for a return to New York. Regretfully he said farewell to the Alhambra: "Never shall I meet on earth with an abode so much to my taste. . . ."

Before he sailed, however, he was informed that he had been appointed secretary of the legation at London. Under pressure from his relatives in New York he accepted the post.

If the story in the Alhambra was the high point of Irving's life as a romantic wanderer, his experience in the legation may well mark the end of his spiritual expatriation. Very early he was jolted out of his sense of English-American brotherhood when he discovered the extent of the enmity toward America. Like many of his countrymen since, he complained of the English passion for field sports which made it extremely difficult to find anyone in his office.

He and his superior, Louis McLane, proposed to Congress a reciprocal trade agreement permitting American vessels to trade in the West Indies. Van Buren helped to get it through Congress. Because of McLane's illness, much of the work of the legation fell upon Irving. Then McLane was recalled and Van Buren appointed in his stead. During the interim, Irving was in charge. Altogether he was virtual head of the Legation for about eleven months. As he could upon occasion, he worked hard. Curious about the attitude of France toward English reform, he made a trip to Paris where he saw the coronation of Louis Philippe.

In England Moore dragged him to evening entertainments at Lady Holland's, Lady Donegal's, and Murray's. Despite their long friendship Irving must have found Moore's anti-American sentiments irritating. Nevertheless he arranged for the publication of Moore's *Life of Byron* in America. For one thing Irving regarded Byron as the greatest English poet of the nineteenth century.

In 1830 the Royal Society of Literature gave its medals to Irving and Henry Hallam. Three years before Scott had been thus honored. Also in 1830 Oxford conferred on Irving the degree of LL.D.

In fact the anti-American British were often kinder than his own countrymen. In the process of getting Bryant's poetry published in England Irving changed a line of "Marion's Men" to overcome the understandable objections of the publisher. The offending line originally read:

And the British soldier trembles
When Marion's name is heard.

This was changed to "The foeman trembles in his camp." Although Irving's change prevented the rejection of the poems, Bryant was annoyed. The Cleveland *Plaindealer* charged Irving with pusillanimity and a lack of manliness.

In the United States newspapers hostile to his diplomatic appointment denounced him "as a toadeater, an alien to his country." Even Van Buren, before he reached England, had his doubts. However, when he found the kind of a job Irving was doing, he wrote enthusiastically about him to President Jackson. Van Buren wanted Irving to stay on the job, but at long last the expatriate was ready to go home. Before he left, he took Van Buren and his son on a tour to Oxford, Stratford and Kenilworth. Almost certainly at Irving's suggestion they made a long side trip to Newstead Abbey where Irving slept in Byron's room.

The seventeen-year expatriation was over. On April 11, 1832, he sailed for New York. Today's sentimental pilgrims can find in the Red Horse in Stratford memorials of Irving's stay there on his own last sentimental pilgrimage.

II

The nation which had often attacked Irving as a renegade now took him to its bosom. After all, not many American writers in 1832 were world famous. Here was someone Americans could boast about without drawing condescending smiles from British travelers and periodicals. Then too, Wouter Van Twiller, Rip Van Winkle, and Ichabod Crane were already a part of American folklore. In an all-is-forgiven mood New York gave a public banquet in Irving's honor.

Much as he loathed such occasions, Irving responded handsomely to the toasts. Apparently some speaker had asked if he could be content in America.

> Can I be content to live in this country? . . . What sacrifice of enjoyments have I to reconcile myself to? I come from gloomier climes to one of brilliant sunshine and inspiring purity. I come from countries lowering with doubt and danger, where the rich man trembles, and the poor man frowns—where all repine at the present and dread the future. I come from these to a country where all is life and animation; where I hear on every side the sound of exultation. . . .

It had not taken him long to catch the oratorical style of Clay and Webster. On a quieter note he wrote to his brother Peter, saying he wished they could be together and telling of life in New York, now a booming city of 200,000: The mode of living, the sources of quiet and social enjoyment, and the sphere of friendly and domestic pleasures, are improved and multiplied to a degree that has delightfully surprised me."

However there were shadows in the picture. To Fanny Kemble he deplored this "commonplace civilization" and the vulgarity of American life. It must be remembered, of course, that these were Fanny Kemble's own sentiments, and that the gallant Irving always knew how to say the right thing to an attractive woman. Nor is there any reason to doubt his disgust at the corruption of American politics. He had renewed his acquaintance with Clay and had dined with Jackson in the White House. "Certainly official life in Washington must be harassing and dismal in the extreme," he told Peter.

Once he got out of cities, however, America was delightful. The steamboats were "floating hotels"; the inns were the best he had found outside of England; even in places remote from cities the food was excellent. On a nostalgic visit to the Catskills, "The wild scenery of these mountains outdoes all my conception of it." From Trenton Falls he wrote to Peter, ". . . indeed the natural beauties of the United States strike me infinitely more than they did before my residence in Europe."

It was as if Irving were determined to take the country at one gulp. For one thing, he wanted to answer his critics by writing an American book. After his trip to the Catskills and a visit to New Hampshire he set out on a tour of the West with Henry Leavitt Ellsworth, Commissioner of Indian Affairs; Charles Joseph Latrobe, and young Count Pourtales. His letters are filled with enthusiastic remarks upon the scenery. He was sorry to realize that the lovely forests of Ohio would be rapidly cleared. In a theater in Cincinnati the manager announced that Irving was in the house; everywhere he was embarrassed by the attention he attracted.

But even in his enthusiasm for the American landscape he could no longer describe it quite as directly as he had in *Rip Van Winkle*; the European scene intervened. ". . . the prairies of the Missouri are extremely beautiful, resembling cultivated countries, embellished with parks and groves rather than the savage rudeness of the wilderness." Or again: "Yesterday I was out on a deer hunt . . . which led me through some scenery that only wanted a castle, or a gentleman's seat here and there interspersed, to have equalled some of the most celebrated park scenery of England." After camping out and living on game he had never been in finer health or enjoyed himself more.

As Edward Everett, a former expatriate, said in his review of the book which resulted, *A Tour on the Prairies*: "It is a sort of sentimental journey, a romantic excursion. . . . We thank him for turning these poor barbarous *steppes* into classical land, and joining his inspiration to that of Cooper in breathing life and fire into a circle of imagery, which was not known before to exist, for the purposes of the imagination." This must have irritated Cooper, who regarded Irving as too Anglophile.

Irving was greatly moved by the cordiality and affection with which he was received everywhere, but when the Jacksonians tried to get him to run for Congress he rebelled. To his brother Peter he wrote: "The more I see of political life here, the more I am disgusted with it. . . . There is such coarseness and vulgarity and dirty trick mingled with the rough-and-tumble contest. I want no part or parcel of such warfare." Unfortunately Irving became involved in another characteristically American activity—speculation in western land. Hoping to make a quick profit of at least 100 per cent he instead lost about $9000. He and his brother Ebenezer also invested about $20,000 in lots on Lake Erie near Toledo. These too did not yield the "advantages" he expected. By 1836 he was deploring the American mania for becoming suddenly rich.

A much more happy investment was his building of a little turreted house near Tarrytown. At this cottage, which he alternated in calling "Sunnyside" and "The Roost," he planted ivy from Abbotsford. His household consisted of his brother Peter, his niece Sarah Paris, two servants, Imp (a cat), and Fanny, "a pig of peerless beauty." He raised vegetables and fruits at what he said was not more than twice the market price.

Here he continued to write and to entertain friends. When Fanny Kemble paid a visit she threw her arms around him, "he looked so like a bit of home, England." But to Irving, happy in his first real home, "neither Spanish nor Italian skies, so bright and cloudless, can compare with ours, forever shifting in their tints, and at times so gorgeous with their floating regions of 'cloudland.' " The description is reminiscent of the opening paragraphs of *Rip Van Winkle* written twenty years before.

Williams argues that the lack of critical standards in America led to a weakening of Irving's writing during these years. If so, it was an enervating effect which missed Poe, Emerson, and Thoreau in these same years. More likely reasons are to be found in the fact that Irving was over fifty and enjoying the easy-going life at Sunnyside. As for critical standards, the English critics hailed his hack work *Astoria,* done during these years. *The Spectator* called it a *chef d'oeuvre* and the acid Sydney Smith called it entertaining and well written.

Although he avoided active politics he was known as an anti-nullification man and was an advisor to Van Buren. Occasionally he tried to get political jobs for his relatives. When Van Buren became President, he offered to appoint Irving Secretary of the Navy, a post he declined because he could not face the "bitter personal hostility, and the slanders and misrepresentations of the press, which beset high station in this country."

It is not strange that Irving's letters show both favorable and unfavorable comment on the United States—after all, what writer other than a blind partisan does not show the shadows as well as the sunlight of a scene? On the whole Irving seems to have enjoyed his ten years of repatriation and to have left for Europe with regret.

His reason for going abroad once more was his appointment to a post he could not easily decline, that of Minister Plenipotentiary to the Court of Spain in 1842. To his brother Ebenezer he expressed his astonishment at the appointment and said, "It will be a severe trial to absent myself for a time from dear little Sunnyside." Cooper, on hearing of the appointment, groaned with disgust.

For Irving, despite his lack of enthusiasm for further expatriation, there were compensations. In London he stayed with Mr. James Bandinel who had quarters in Little Cloisters, Westminster Abbey. To Mrs. Paris he wrote in his old romantic vein:

> How strange it seems to me that I should thus be nestled quietly in the very heart of this old pile, that used to be so much the scene of my half-romantic, half-meditative haunts, during my scribbling days. It is like my sojourn in halls of the Alhambra. Am I always to have my dreams turned into realities?

He looked up Leslie, now gray haired. Rogers took him in his arms and Moore rushed to him as "the man of all others I wanted to shake hands with once more." He dined at Lady Holland's, talked with Wordsworth and suffered through public dinners, one of them with Prince Albert present. In Paris he called upon King Louis Philippe, who chatted about Irving's essays and about international affairs.

But the charm of Europe had largely gone for him. His letters are filled with nostalgic references to home. To his niece Sarah he wrote:

> My visit to Europe has by no means the charm of former visits. Scenes and objects have no longer the effect of novelty with me. I am no longer curious to see the great sights or the great people, and have been so long accustomed to a life of quiet, that I find the turmoil of the world becomes irksome to me. Then I have a house of my own, a little domestic world, created in a manner by my own hand, which I have left behind, and which is continually haunting my thoughts, and coming in contrast with the noisy, tumultous, heartless world in which I am called to mingle.

Irving was fifty-nine. After a round of dinners and social functions in Paris "My heart yearns for little Sunnyside."

In the European perspective even American politics seemed less violent than those abroad. When he presented his credentials at the palace in Spain, he noticed the marble doorways shattered by gun fire during the recent attempt of the Queen Mother's party to get possession of the little Queen and her sister. After only two years in Spain he wrote to Mrs. Storrow that he was heartily sick at the wretched politics of that country; there was so much intrigue, falsehood, profligacy, and crime and so little honor and patriotism.

In his observation of Spanish life Irving showed more puritanism than was characteristic of him in earlier years. At the theater he saw a lady who had appeared years before in a tableau as Murillo's Virgin of the Assumption. Now she was matronly and accompanied by her *cavalier servente*.

> The charm was broken, the picture fell from the wall. She may have the customs of a depraved country and licentious state of society to excuse her; but I can never think of her again in the halo of feminine purity and loveliness that surrounded the Virgin of Murillo.

As he told Dolgorouki, Europe was "full of half melancholy recollections and associations. The scenes of past pleasures and friendships were now vacant and desolate."

In 1845 he went to Paris for a vacation. Louis McLane in London asked him to come there to help with the Oregon question. He felt that Irving's intimacy with persons connected with the government would be useful. Irving studied the question and wrote an article on it. He was pleased with his part in facilitating the discussions between McLane and Lord Aberdeen which did much to bring about a settlement of the dispute.

Then after another year in Spain he insisted on going home. He was tired of being an expatriate. After only four years of absence he found New York more crowded and noisy. It reminded him of a great European city during an annual fair.

Irving had thirteen years more to live. Most of that time he spent in the happy domestic circle at Sunnyside. Distinguished visitors came from time to time. Occasionally he went down to Philadelphia or Washington. On one such trip he found Thackeray on the ferry boat. It was a happy reunion. Thackeray, who was on a lecture tour, was enjoying the United States.

Then, after some years of comparative idleness, Irving embarked upon a project which he felt would demonstrate once and for all that he was an American. As a baby he had been patted on the head by the first President whose name he bore. It seemed fitting that Washington Irving should crown his life's work with a biography of George Washington. Irving had been born the year that ended the American Revolution. In his youth the United States had no past in the usual sense of the word. Now, in the words of Longfellow, "hardly a man was now alive" who remembered the beginnings. Irving, who had tried to give the Hudson River region a legendary past, undertook the task of preserving the historic past of his country.

He was not a trained scholar but in his work on *Columbus* and *The Conquest of Granada* he had learned to use historical materials. The task he embarked upon was enormous, one which a more scholarly writer would have found impossible—that of writing one volume a year for four consecutive years. This is not the place to analyze the work or assess its value. There is general agreement that it is uninspired, but it remained for years a popular work.

There is some tendency today to attribute the weakness of Irving's works to the cultural limitations of the America of his time. His biographer, S. T. Williams, tends to take this view. A more tenable position is to hold that Irving's limitations are those of the man himself. Nowhere does he show any great originality of thought. His books, like his letters, are those of an urbane, easygoing, kindly, and very charming man. The literary feuds of his time left him largely unmoved. Even Cooper's long hostility was not reciprocated: Irving rather admired his rival's work, and later became chairman of a committee to raise funds for a Cooper memorial.

There is some possibility that because of changes in literary fashion—such as the obsolescence of the familiar essay and the vogue of the hard boiled style—Irving is undervalued. Compared to Cooper he is lacking in vigor and originality, but he is immeasurably superior to Cooper in style. It might even be argued that Irving's style is more easy and graceful than that of his model Addison. As early as the *Knicker-bocker History* there is a hint of the colloquial—the rhythms of actual speech—which was to become one of the trademarks of American writing. He talks of "long sided, hard fisted Yankees" and compares the appearance of Wouter Van Twiller to "a beer barrel on skids."

However, an assessment of the value of Irving's work is not the object of the present discussion. Rather, Irving has been presented as a talented American who faced the problem of becoming a literary man in the first half of the nineteenth century, and also as a sensitive observer of both European and American life. For him a literary career involved expatriation, but it is not certain that it was chiefly the cause of his expatriation or that his long residence abroad was essential to his career. And with the possible exception of his first Spanish residence, his happiest life seems to have been at Sunnyside.

There is considerable evidence that as he got older, the glamor of Europe somewhat faded. Much as he had enjoyed his friends of the Holland House set, he, like other Americans, was often irritated by the British assumption that anyone from the States was an illiterate semi-savage. When the American minister, Richard Rush, told Irving that Lady Littleton had written to ask about the rumor that Scott wrote *The Sketchbook*, Irving answered: ". . . the doubts which her ladyship has heard on the subject seem to have arisen from the old notion that it is impossible for an *American to write decent English*." As a patriot he hoped that he had helped "to stagger this prejudice."

On another occasion he complained that he was isolated in English literature, without a coterie to cry him up or reviewers partial to his work.

In fact, "the very review of my publisher is hostile to everything American." Late in life he was in London when he heard of the war with Mexico: "I feared some humiliating blow, and saw that the English press was preparing to trumpet it forth to Europe with the customary insults and exaggerations." In another letter he stated: "A rancorous prejudice against us has been diligently inculcated of late years by the British press, and it's daily producing its fruits of bitterness."

As has been noted (p. 34) Irving was even more disgusted with the corruption of Spain and he deplored the fact that in France "every political change is a military convulsion." This last was apropos of the coup of Napoleon III. A year later he wrote to Mrs. Storrow about the inauguration of Franklin Pierce:

> I was present at the going out of one Administration and the coming in of another . . . It was admirable to see the quiet and courtesy with which this great transition of power and rule from one party to another took place. I was at festive meetings where members of the opposite parties mingled socially together, and have seen the two Presidents arm in arm, as if the sway of an immense empire was not passing from one to the other.

It is clear that as he got older the former expatriate became more than ever the patriot. But as this account of Irving shows, he always considered himself first of all an American. To young Charles King, later president of Columbia, he described his ideal of what an American traveling abroad should be: "frank, manly, and unaffected in his habits and manners; liberal and independent in his opinions, generous and unprejudiced in his sentiments towards other nations, but most, loyally attached to his own."

THE SCHOLARS
TICKNOR, BANCROFT, COGSWELL

In 1821 young George Bancroft returned to Cambridge, Massachusetts, after studying abroad for three years. Sporting a beard and velveteen trousers he greeted his old friend and mentor, Andrews Norton, in European style with an embrace and a kiss on each cheek. Norton turned away in disgust and a few weeks later wrote a note suggesting that the young man no longer call at Shady Hill. For six years the two men did not speak.

Three years earlier Norton, as one of the Harvard Overseers, had taken Bancroft to consult John Adams about study abroad. Adams opposed the idea, but the Overseers voted $700 a year for the purpose. Bancroft's father and brother added another $500 a year. Like George Ticknor and Edward Everett he went to Göttingen.

On his first Fourth of July away from home Bancroft and another student, James Patton of Vermont, held a "banquet" at which Bancroft gave an oration on Washington, Jefferson, etc. "We are Americans," he declaimed. "The arts and sciences of Europe cannot make us forget it. Thank God we are Americans." Yet three years later all of Cambridge except Edward Everett tended to agree with Andrews Norton about the young man's foreignness. In a letter to Samuel Eliot, Bancroft said: "I have grown quite estranged from my own country and countrymen. Now that I am at home my best labour must be to make myself acquainted with the state of feeling about me."

Despite his efforts he never entirely succeeded in repatriating himself. To a considerable degree his experiences at home and abroad were typical of those of a group of Brahmins who studied in Europe between 1815 and 1860. As a group these Europeanized Americans were extremely important in the history of American scholarship, education, and literature. The roster includes George Ticknor, Edward Everett, Joseph Cogswell, George Bancroft, John Lothrop Motley, Henry Wadsworth Longfellow, and Charles Eliot Norton—the son of Andrews Norton.

One remarkable element in the experience of these men is that many of them became intimates of the great personalities of Europe—Lafayette, Goethe, Byron, Scott, Mme de Staël, Ruskin and Bismarck. Another common element in their European experience was that despite their enthusiasm for English literature, they studied and traveled chiefly on the Continent—especially in Germany.

There were several reasons for this. Following the Revolution there was some feeling that the new nation should declare its cultural as well as its political independence from Great Britain. Oxford and Cambridge had not emerged from their intellectual doldrums of the late eighteenth century. At Harvard Mme de Stael's *De l'Allemagne* in translation began to circulate and to arouse an enthusiasm for German culture. Edward Everett, at that time a tutor in Greek, read it, as did his pupil George Bancroft. The enthusiasm of these men infected President Kirkland. When Samuel Eliot endowed a professorship of Greek with $20,000, Kirkland offered the post to Everett, with the suggestion that he study abroad at full salary to prepare himself. So it was that in April 1815 the twenty-one year old Everett sailed for a four-year stay in Europe.

On the same ship was George Ticknor, who to a much greater extent than Everett was to be influenced by his European experience. Both men were bound for the university at Göttingen, where two years later they were joined by George Bancroft and Joseph Green Cogswell. Conscious of his responsibility to Harvard, Everett managed to earn his Ph.D. in two years. It was the first such degree awarded to an American.

Despite Everett's European education, and later diplomatic service, his career was to follow a typically American pattern. After teaching a few years at Harvard, where he had Emerson as a student, he went into politics. He served variously as Governor of Massachusetts, Congressman, President of Harvard, Minister to England, and briefly as Secretary of State. Two years before his death he delivered a two-hour address at the dedication of the National Cemetery at Gettysburg where he shared the platform with the self-taught Abraham Lincoln, who spoke more briefly.

Everett's traveling companion and fellow student, George Ticknor, became a more typical example of the Europeanized American. Despite his lifelong loyalty to his own country he showed some of the spiritual expatriation of Irving and Longfellow. Like so many other expatriates of his time Ticknor belonged to the old Federalist gentry. His father, Elisha, graduated from Dartmouth, taught school for some years, and then went into business. In good Boston fashion the elder Ticknor helped to found an insurance company and a system of primary schools. When his son took up the study of law, Elisha provided him with a library of three or four thousand volumes.

However, the America into which George Ticknor was born was one of promise rather than performance. To understand some of the pressures for expatriation the modern reader must disabuse himself of the present connotations of names like Boston, Dartmouth, and Harvard. At the time of George Ticknor's birth in 1791, Boston was a provincial city of 18,000. During Everett's years at college Harvard graduated an average of thirty-nine students a year, as contrasted with an average of forty-three between 1766 and 1776. When George Ticknor entered Dartmouth at the not unusual age of fourteen, American colleges were little more than secondary schools. After graduation, when he became interested in the study of German, he found that, even in Boston, books were hard to come by. He borrowed a grammar from Everett, sent to New Hampshire for a German dictionary, and through the connivance of William Shaw, got hold of Goethe's *Werther* from among the books deposited in the Athenaeum by J. L. Adams when he went to Europe.

Like Everett, young Ticknor had got his first information about Germany from Mme de Staël's *De l'Allemagne*. Then in a pamphlet published by Villers he found a sketch of the university at Göttingen with a description of the courses of study. His astonishment was increased by a second-hand account of its library as reported by an Englishman to the Reverend Samuel G. Thacher. With his imagination thus fired, he sought in vain for someone in Boston to teach him German. At last in Jamaica Plain he found a native of Strasbourg, who taught mathematics, but who was willing to do what he could in language instruction.

Ostensibly Ticknor was studying law, and at the age of twenty he was admitted to the bar. However, during the years following his graduation from college he had continued his study of Greek and Latin—to which, as has been noted, he added German. His father, with remarkable understanding, realized that George was more interested in languages than in law, and consulted learned friends about European study. Elisha Ticknor was a puritanical New Englander of the self-denying type, but he also had the kind of respect for learning that has always made Bostonians suspect in the eyes of other Americans. He was rewarded by the respect and love of his son, who until Elisha's death, wrote long and affectionate letters home. When learned friends agreed that young George should go abroad, Elisha decided to finance two or three years of study.

George Ticknor made his decision with some reluctance. The family circle was close-knit and affectionate, and the prospect of several years abroad was a bit frightening. To his friend Charles Daveis he reported his feelings:

> The truth is, Dear Charles, that I have always considered going to Europe a mere means of preparing myself for greater usefulness and happiness after I return—as a great sacrifice of the present to the future; and the nearer I come to the time I am to make this sacrifice, the more heavy and extravagant it appears.

Before he sailed, however, he made a tour of the Eastern seaboard as far as Richmond—his "first real sight and knowledge of the world." At Quincy, Massachusetts, he stopped to pick up letters of introduction from John Adams, whom he found much worried over the War of 1812. He found Hartford full of prominent New Englanders there for a secret convention to discuss opposition to "Mr. Madison's War." At New Haven he heard Professor Silliman lecture on chemistry, and then drove a few miles out of town to see Eli Whitney's ingenious machinery for the mass production of muskets. New York was the first large city he had ever seen, but it was in Philadelphia that he got a taste of the world of fashion and sophistication. Here was a city of 120,000, one which often reminded foreign visitors of London. At what he called a brilliant dinner party, Ticknor first encountered servants in livery and a full service of silver plate. In his old age, and after having attended many dinners in the great and fashionable world of Europe, he still remembered his Philadelphia experience and the prominent men he met there.

From Philadelphia he went on to Charlottesville, where he spent several days at Monticello. Jefferson reminisced about his own experiences in Europe and offered letters of recommendation to prominent people. Ticknor enjoyed the library and the Southern hospitality, but he was too much the Federalist to quite approve of Jefferson, whose philosophy, dress, house, and conversation he described as "notional."

In April 1815 he sailed with Everett for Liverpool. In addition to the customary letters of introduction Ticknor had a high degree of personal charm. During his brief stay in England he became well acquainted with Byron and Sir Humphrey Davy. At the time Byron was flirting with the idea of visiting the United States. He asked about Joel Barlow and about the number of universities in America. He took the young man to the theater, where their box adjoined that of Matthew Gregory Lewis, the author of Gothic novels. Ticknor, who was well acquainted with English literature, commented on *The Monk* and *The Castle Spectre*. On another occasion Byron recounted the anecdote about West's conversation with Admiral Nelson. Nelson admired the painting of "The Death of Wolfe" and asked why there were not more like it. West answered that he feared the daring Lord Nelson would furnish him with another subject.

Altogether Ticknor enjoyed his London experience. He wrote home: "I think I have received more kindness from Lord Byron than from any person in England on whom I had not the regular claim of a letter of introduction."

From England he went to Göttingen for a stay of nearly two years. Except for a daily walk with Everett he studied constantly. The experience was almost overwhelming: here for the first time he realized how elementary were American colleges. He learned the difference between reciting to a man and being taught by him. Even while he was struggling with the language he wrote to his father about his conviction of the superiority of German modes of instruction. ". . . what a mortifying distance there is between a European scholar! We do not yet know what a Greek scholar is; we do not even know the process by which a man is made one. . . ."

He was taken into a literary club, whose chief occupation was, he said, that of all literary clubs which survived the frosts of the first winter—"to eat suppers." However, he remarked that at Göttingen Americans were a curiosity; "it is supposed we can hardly be civilized."

As was then the custom, he wrote long letters to his family and friends describing university life and student duels; he discussed German history and philosophy. One gets the picture of a rather serious-minded young man, intent upon taking in as much as he could. As Murray's famous guidebooks had not been published, he prepared himself for further travel by collecting facts about the history and geography of the countries he planned to visit.

During the six-week vacation beginning in September of 1816 he and Everett toured northern Germany, visiting all the principal cities, the schools and universities. At Halle, Ticknor presented Professor Karl Sprengel with a letter and botanical specimens from Dr. Muhlenberg of New York. The high point of the journey was a call upon Goethe, who received them informally. The aged writer discussed Byron's poetry and—like everyone else—Byron's domestic difficulties.

Back at Göttingen Ticknor found Joseph Cogswell newly arrived from the United States, bringing with him an offer of a professorship at Harvard. Ticknor discussed the matter in a letter to his father. The salary of $1000 plus $300 to $500 in fees would be adequate for a single man, but George hoped to marry, although he had no one especially in mind. Furthermore he felt that the low estate of literary study in America did not augur well for an increase of students, with the consequent increase in the professor's fees. Was Elisha satisfied with an occupation for his son which might involve further support from home? Then, too, George had hoped to visit Greece and to study in Spain. However, after a year of correspondence with Harvard, involving long intervals between questions and answers, Ticknor accepted the position with the understanding that he could continue his studies abroad before taking up his duties. At a time when other college presidents in America were chiefly concerned with the religious orthodoxy of their faculties, Kirkland of Harvard was looking for trained scholars, and was willing to hold open a position for a good man.

Thus, while his contemporaries at home were demonstrating their academic qualifications by engaging in sectarian controversy, George Ticknor set out for Paris. Here the intellectual life was far different from that of Calvinistic America. On the presentation of his letters of introduction Ticknor was taken up by such people as Benjamin Constant, Schlegel, Baron Humboldt, Chateaubriand, and Mme de Staël. Schlegel's habits of living astonished the American: he woke at four in the morning, read five or six hours, worked until six, and then became a man of the world in society. Promptly at ten he went back to his study. Humboldt was even stranger: he slept, ate, or studied whenever he felt like it. An invitation to a six o'clock dinner did not prevent him from going to a restaurant at five. A man who had survived the tropical heat of Orinoco, he was equally at home in the drawing room. Mme de Staël, although very ill, received the young man and discussed Europe, of which she despaired, and America—"l'avant garde du genre humaine." This lady, who so much shocked and fascinated Americans, had Ticknor in to dine on several occasions. On another occasion the Duchess de Broglie, learning that he was anxious to meet Chateaubriand and Mme Récamier, placed him between them at dinner. He noted that although at forty-odd Mme Récamier had faded, she still had a fine figure and beautiful arms.

Sunday evenings he usually went to the salon of Helen Maria Williams, a minor poetess and translator of *Paul and Virginia*. Here he met

Southey, who talked about Roger Williams, William Penn, Cotton Mather, and Joel Barlow. One evening Mrs. William Godwin was there—a person the conservative Boston *Federalist* described as "wife of the notorious William Godwin, and successor to the no less notorious Mary Wollstonecraft." Although he did not say so in so many words, Ticknor obviously enjoyed the salons and dinners of the continent better than the British gatherings he had attended. His accounts of Humboldt, Schlegel, Mme de Staël, Benjamin Constant are filled with enthusiastic phrases. It would also appear that he was able to converse in French.

On one occasion he became involved in a discussion of French versus English poetry. The ladies hunted up a variety of quotations from the French authors. Ticknor was to match them by quoting Shakespeare and Milton. However, he said he was able to win the contest using only Milton.

Before leaving France he visited Lafayette, then went on to Italy. Here he met John Cam Hobhouse. Byron dropped in and told about hearing Matthew Gregory Lewis read *Faust*. In good Byronic fashion Ticknor visited the Coliseum by moonlight, and was properly overwhelmed. He engaged an archeologist to show him around. He filled nearly a volume of his journals with the results of his walks and studies. Like so many of his countrymen he fell in love with Italy: "With Rome, I find every day more reason to be contented; and if I were condemned to live in Europe, I am sure this is the place I should choose for my exile beyond any other I have yet seen."

He was presented to the Pope, who praised the religious tolerance of America, and talked about the superiority of American ships. One gets the impression that the young man from Boston was at ease in London, Paris, Rome, and Florence; that he got on with princes, scholars, and fashionable ladies.

He went on to Spain, where he felt as if he had stepped backward a couple of centuries. He admired the originality of the folk poetry, but was disgusted by the corruption of the government. On a billboard he saw a decree of the Inquisition calling upon servants to denounce their masters, children their parents, and wives their husbands. For *The North American Review* he wrote an account of bullfighting. He saw a man fall dead after being stabbed by his brother over an argument about this sport. Although he was presented at court and went frequently to the salon of the Duchess of Ossina, he found the country primitive and uncivilized compared to his homeland. But like Irving a few years later, he was entranced by the Alhambra. Americans tended to admire the monuments of continental Europe more than the social order. Ticknor was glad to leave Spain, "a country dead in everything a nation ought to be," and to return to England, "where the smallest village and the humblest peasant bear some decisive mark of activity and improvement and vital strength and power." Like Cooper he admired the fine turnpikes, canals, and coaches on the roads.

But at Cambridge University he found the conversation stiff. He went on to the Lake District to look up Wordsworth, who had been told by Southey of his coming. With the poet he scrambled up mountains to enjoy the scenery. In the evening Wordsworth showed him the manuscript of *The Prelude,* not to be published for another thirty-one years, and read him *Peter Bell.* With admirable restraint, Ticknor called the latter a poem with many beauties, but much greater defects. *The Waggoner* he found "very curious." Wordsworth praised Scott but expressed a dislike for Byron.

Back in London Ticknor met Hazlitt, Hunt, and Lamb. He dined with Godwin, whom he described as having "a great head full of cold brains." Although the American might have been something of a celebrity hunter, he, like Emerson a few years later, retained his critical faculties. Ticknor's journal suggests a man of the world rather than a naïve provincial.

In 1819, after nearly four years abroad, he took one of the regular packets for New York. He was twenty-eight and ready to take up his duties at Harvard. Jefferson tried to get him to come to the University of Virginia, then being planned, but Ticknor was too much a Bostonian and a Federalist to accept. Almost at once he found that things at home looked different; the Harvard Library, which had once appeared impressive, now seemed like a closetful of books. With his experience at Göttingen fresh in his mind he undertook the task of making Harvard something more than a glorified prep school. In this effort he was supported by Everett, and a year later by Joseph Green Cogswell. In 1823 George Bancroft returned from Göttingen to join in this unrewarding task.

Their efforts came at a bad time. Between the Revolution and the Civil War the traditional college in America was far more successful in resisting change than in educating the youth of an expanding nation. As has been mentioned (p. 40) the average number of Harvard graduates per year was smaller during Ticknor's youth than in the ten years before the

Revolution. Until at least 1870 the proportion of the population going to college declined steadily throughout the nation, and even more significantly in New England itself. In new institutions such as Virginia, Oberlin, and Transylvania there were important, even brilliant innovations, but the older colleges clung to a moribund curriculum and methods of instruction. Most of the students' classroom time was taken up in reciting on an assigned number of lines in Greek and Latin. College libraries were customarily opened for an hour or two a week for the issuance and return of books. Collateral reading was discouraged. Kirkland's Harvard was less hidebound than most institutions of the time, but Ticknor, Everett, Cogswell, and Bancroft all found it a frustrating place for men with scholarly interests.

It was not a raw democracy which resisted the development of better college education; it was the classical scholars and the conservatives on governing bodies. Jefferson's University of Virginia, the Jacksonian Transylvania, and pioneering Oberlin—later on the democratic University of Michigan—were often far in advance of the old-line colleges controlled by the moneyed aristocracy and the teachers of the classics.

Ticknor, Everett, Cogswell, and Bancroft were very much a part of this basically Federalist class which controlled most of the early colleges. They undertook their European studies with the encouragement and support of a Harvard hierarchy of businessmen, statesmen, and scholars. (This was in an earlier day before the hierarchy read backwards.) Their attempt to reform college education was therefore not motivated by the pressures of an expanding democracy. Perhaps that is one of the reasons it was largely abortive.

Because Ticknor's experience as a repatriated American at Harvard is so closely linked with that of Cogswell and of Bancroft, it is necessary to say something about these two. (Everett left the scene early; his gift for oratory translated him into political life.)

Joseph Green Cogswell was nine years older than George Ticknor but he was later in finding his scholarly calling. After graduating from Harvard he studied law under Fisher Ames and Judge Prescott, the father of the historian. In 1809 he went to the Mediterranean on a merchant voyage. After various adventures, including capture by brigands, he returned home to marry Mary Gillman, a daughter of the governor of New Hampshire. He tried the practice of law in Belfast, Maine, where the ethical standards of a New England small town disgusted him. Lawyers and judges told him that no man could succeed by uprightness and honorable dealing. The first principles of religion seemed to be unknown to most people, and the laws of morality were "wholly disregarded." About fifty miles away lived young Longfellow, who apparently never having been in Belfast, Maine, visited Paris thirteen years later and found *it* the "modern Babylon."

Following the death of his wife a year after their marriage, Cogswell gave up the law for the post of Latin tutor at Harvard. Unhappy and in ill health he decided with great reluctance to go abroad. So great was the reputation of European travel as a cure-all that his friends insisted that he must go.

At first he seems not to have intended to engage in formal study. Possibly it was the example of Ticknor which decided him. In any event, six months after Ticknor's arrival at Göttingen Cogswell wrote him from Marseilles:

> It is time for Cambridge to take a rank above a mere preparatory school, and to do this she must call to her aid all the talents she can command; she has nothing to fear from the cry of heresy, if she cannot attain a decided elevation above all the other literary institutions of the country. All our early colleges were founded for the express purpose of forming ministers, not scholars, and it is unaccountable that the system of education has been preserved until this time, which never required, even of the instructors, any critical knowledge of the language they professed to teach.

As Cogswell had not yet attended any European university, his remarks suggest that they grew out of earlier discussions with Ticknor. And his remark about the immunity from charges of heresy was premature. The growing theological liberalism of Harvard soon had the soul savers in full cry. And the theory that teachers of the classics should be genuine scholars was to prove repulsive to many of the faculty. Cogswell, however, intended to practice what he preached. He told Ticknor that after a business trip to America he intended to come to Göttingen.

Thus, in November 1816 he joined Ticknor and Everett at the university. At the age of thirty-four he found it hard to become a student once more. His selection of studies was slightly bizarre for a Harvard man in the pre-Eliot era: Modern Arts, European Statistics (given in French),

Mineralogy, Italian, and library organization. This last, under the super-vision of Professor Benecke, was to prove especially valuable.

Cogswell's letters suggest that he had an orderly rather than an imagi-native mind. For instance, as a program for exercise he set himself a walk of 10,000 steps daily—a distance he estimated as at least four miles. Mineralogy, in which he became expert, was then largely a science of description and classification. In his later work as a librarian he seems to have been much less concerned with what books should be selected than with how they should be classified.

On a tour of Italy in 1817 he found Venice a gloomy prison and Italy as a whole uninteresting because of its mineralogical uniformity. But in Switzerland he became more cheerful: here were a people who reminded him of "our good sober folk in Boston" with the same love of talk and tea drinking, of political and religious conversation, "in a word the same general habits and customs except the villainous one of universal card playing." But at Pestalozzi's academy he found a lack of obedience among the pupils.

In view of all this it seems hardly necessary that Cogswell felt com-pelled to insist upon his Americanism. Nevertheless, he wrote to Mrs. Prescott defending himself against the charge of "having made 'new friends' whom I preferred to my early and long proved ones, and with having acquired such a taste for foreign customs and manners as to view 'my own with a jaundiced eye.'" The phrases he put in quotes suggest the kind of home-grown criticism to which Americans abroad were sub-jected. More prominent persons like Irving and Cooper found such com-ments in American newspapers. To Cogswell such allegations seemed especially cruel. He had walked from four in the morning to four-thirty in the afternoon to pick up letters from home:

> You do me cruel wrong. . . . The separation from everything I love in the world preys upon my health, and devours my substance more than all the physical maladies which have attacked me. . . . In truth all I have seen abroad serves only to attach me still more strongly to the substantial parts of my own country, and though I might wish to change some of its institutions and customs, I never was so firmly convinced in my life as I now am, that it is the best and happiest in the world (reserves being made for England which I have not yet seen).

Like other Americans of his time Cogswell found that his letters of introduction opened hospitable doors. He had expected to find Goethe conceited; instead he reported:

> a grand and graceful form, worthy of a knight of the days of chivalry, with a dignity of manners that marked the court rather than the closet. . . . Soon after being introduced to him, with the politeness of a real gentleman, he turned the conversation to America, and spoke of its hopes and promises, in a manner that showed it had been a subject of his inquiries, and made juster and more rational observations upon its literary pretensions and character, than I had ever heard from any man in Europe.

Thus, despite the fact that Cogswell was able to carry on the conversation in French, he demonstrated that cloudy syntax in English and the dangling modifier are not recent inventions of the American college student.

He went on to Paris, where he had a fit of the blues, and to London, which he enjoyed. His first view of the English countryside made him "carol like a bird at the opening of the buds of spring." During a tour of the Lake District he met Southey, whom he regarded as too much of a party politician to be a great poet. He found Southey minutely learned in the history of America but totally ignorant of the character and spirit of the people. After all Southey was connected with the rabidly anti-American *Quarterly Review,* and was shortly to publish his *Vision of Judgment* in which George Washington is shown welcoming George III into heaven.

In Scotland he was entertained lavishly at a laird's home where there was too much wine and whiskey drinking for a man of sober habits like himself. With Ticknor he visited Scott, whom he described as delightful. Back in Germany he again called on Goethe, who "was not merely gracious, but affectionate and playful even. . . ." At Carlsbad, while taking a hike, he encountered a group, some of whom he knew, the members of the Bonaparte family: Jerome, Comte de Monfort, and his wife; Louis, Comte de St. Leu; Princess Elise Baiciochi and her husband; and Count and Countess Posse [sic.]. The ladies shared his picnic breakfast and put themselves under his command for an afternoon ramble. It is understandable that Cogswell should do a certain amount of name dropping in his letters home. What is more important is that in a smaller world than ours, Americans abroad associated on intimate terms with Europeans of distinction. And even allowing for a desire to impress the home folks, there is considerable evidence that the Americans had a certain amount of aplomb. An astonishing number of them became intimate friends of some of the greatest personages in Europe.

Cogswell returned to Göttingen for the awarding of his Ph.D. degree. He felt that American scholars, because they had lost twenty years of their lives through inferior education, deserved more credit for getting an advanced degree than did the Germans. Increasingly his mind turned to the idea of educational reform. To Ticknor he wrote that his earlier description of the low estate of education in America was commendation compared to what he should now say of it. Only at Harvard could he see any hope of a new order of things.

However he had not become Europeanized. Until two months before he left for home he felt that he had made a poor bargain in giving up his happiest life in exchange for a little knowledge. Just before he sailed he visited the highlands of Scotland, where he saw people living in mud hovels far worse than the log cabins of the frontier. The peasants had never seen beds; they slept on peat ashes or heaps of manure.

From Harvard came the offer of three posts: librarian at $660; the professorship of mineralogy at $500 plus additional student fees; and the chair of chemistry at about $800. After some debate with himself he accepted all three. Thus in 1820 he went home to join Ticknor in the attempt to mold Harvard closer to the model of a German university. In 1823 Bancroft was to join in the effort.

Bancroft had reached Göttingen in 1818 while Cogswell was still a student. His intention was to study theology, despite the opinion of John Adams (noted p. 38) that European manners and morals would be dangerous to a young theologian. The Harvard Overseers had voted to give him the income from a bequest, perhaps $700 a year, and his father and brother agreed to add another $500. As his biographer, Russel Nye, wrote: "George Bancroft, literally and figuratively, set sail from New England, and in spirit he never returned to it."

At first, however, he was very much the New England puritan. On reading Goethe he was repelled by the "immorality and indecency." At social gatherings the ladies shocked him with their profanity. At Göttingen he found the students coarse and dirty; they laughed at the word "chastity." A woman of eminence told him that a few years before, twenty of the professors had kept mistresses—a statement which suggests that academic freedom was somewhat broader in Europe than in nine-teenth-century America. Although Bancroft was unaware of it, one of his anecdotes has analogues in every college town. He reported that an old woman with six daughters had set up a brothel, but had gone out of business because of the amateur competition. At a dinner given to the faculty by the Protector of the University the wine flowed so freely that the guests made their way home with "the skins of the professors pretty full."

He was equally startled by the amount of work expected of a student. For two months he worked with Professor Benecke,* who was in charge of English-speaking students. Because German scholars had great curiosity about America, the young man was often invited to their homes. Professor Eikhorn told him that twelve hours of daily study was quite safe— even fifteen or sixteen. "It is a fixed principle," Eikhorn said, "that no man naturally possessed of a good constitution ever died of study." In American colleges of the time, about four hours of study a day seems to have been normal for the more industrious undergraduates.

It was not long before Bancroft's puritanism began to thaw: he learned to waltz and he developed theological doubts. On a walking tour with three friends he visited Goethe, whose writings he had described as immoral and his characters as vulgar. Now he found a very kindly man "with a fine clear eye, large and very expressive features, well built, and giving at once a favorable impression." Goethe defended Byron against the charge of indecency.

Back at the university he became bored: the German professor as a type was a bookworm of lower class origin with no manners, no niceties of sentiment. Even the scholars regarded their profession as a trade. In this mood he joined with another student, James Patton of Vermont, to celebrate the Fourth of July. Patton read a poem and Bancroft gave an oration in which he called the roll of great Americans: Washington, Jefferson, Adams, etc. and then held forth on the national blessings: "the great forests of the west, the hum of business, the vessels of commerce." They toasted the President, the flag, the American eagle—"a terror to the vulture, may she never wound the lamb"—the memory of Washington, the literary prospects of America, the abolition of slavery, the "sweet

* George Frederick Benecke (1762–1844), Professor of English and Old German

nymph Liberty," the heroes of the Revolution, the Fourth of July, the Constitution, the American government, "watered by the dews of Heaven and quickened by the genial warmth of freedom—the nurseries of enlightened patriots." On this occasion it was the Americans who got a skinful.

In September 1820 Bancroft took the oral examination, conducted in Latin, and defended his nine theses. The examination covered Latin, Arabic, Hebrew, ancient history, Greek, and classical literature. He came through the ordeal with credit and was awarded the Ph.D degree.

Nevertheless, he did not consider his education finished. Two days after receiving his degree he set off on foot with two Greek boys for the University of Berlin. Here he found the atmosphere much more congenial: the Göttingen men had been conservative; those at Berlin welcomed new ideas. Instead of emphasizing mere knowledge the Berlin men tried to make their students think.

Here Bancroft began to develop the idea of transplanting some of the new educational ideas to America. A year before, ten young Germans had set up a Pestalozzian school in the city, and Bancroft went to visit it. He discussed with his friend Wilhelm von Humboldt a plan for founding an American school on Prussian principles. Von Humboldt was skeptical, but Bancroft clung to the idea.

Then came the news that the Harvard Overseers had voted to add a thousand dollars to his scholarship so that he might spend a year in France and Italy. Cogswell's idea that Harvard held the chief promise for higher education in America was not without foundation. Rock-ribbed Andrews Norton had not approved of everything in Bancroft's letters, but as the young man's mentor he must have been the member of the Board chiefly responsible for the new grant.

Bancroft left Berlin with reluctance: after five months there he felt more affection for the university than he had for Göttingen, where he had spent two years. On his leisurely journey to Paris he visited schools, both traditional and experimental. Once more he visited Goethe, who once more discussed Byron. The old man, still interested in America, asked about Cogswell and the other *neuen Amerikaner* he had met.

In Paris he met Schlegel and later that same day dined with Washington Irving. Von Humboldt took him to lectures at the Institut de France. Benjamin Constant invited him to dinner, and as he entered the room Lafayette greeted him warmly. Later he called on the old General, who chatted for an hour. The avuncular Irving called to propose a visit to Albert Gallatin's villa. Irving, always a delightful companion, picked up the young man in his carriage, but occasionally they got out to walk or lie on the grass. "Learn all you can in your youth," Irving advised; "buy books, read, listen . . . follow learning, scramble to it, get it wherever and whenever you can." Through Irving he met Tom Moore, Lord and Lady Holland, Sir John Russell. He celebrated July 4 with Lafayette. For a young man of twenty-one it was all very flattering and exciting.

And more exciting events were to come. When he set off for Italy, Lafayette gave him copies of political speeches to be distributed secretly. In Venice he mused: "When I think of the time I ran about Worcester as a boy, that knew nothing of Europe but what little might be learned from books. . . . I cannot but wonder at my own happy destiny." At Montevero, near Leghorn, the frigate *Constitution* lay at anchor. Bancroft as the guest of Captain Chauncey visited the ship in company with some other Americans. Lord Byron also came aboard. The next day Bancroft wrote a note to the poet requesting an interview, which was granted. Byron chatted about Irving's stories and talked of visiting America. Bancroft pleased Byron by telling of Goethe's praise of his work. The young man was invited to stay to lunch, where he met the Countess Guiccioli, whom he thought lovely.

After such pleasures Boston was an anticlimax. Andrews Norton's disapproval of the returned traveler has already been noted. Despite his own sense of estrangement from America, Bancroft took up his duties at Harvard in 1823. Ticknor had been on the faculty for four years and Cogswell for two. In separate ways all three men attempted to use their European experience to improve the work of the college. All of them were to discover the truth of a comment made over a century later that changing the curriculum entails all the physical and psychological difficulties of moving a cemetery.

Ticknor had first run into this problem when he tried to develop his two chairs—the Smith Professorship of French and Spanish and the College Professorship of Belles-Lettres—into what today might be called the field of comparative literature. This he proposed to do in a series of not less than sixty lectures. At once he ran afoul of vested interests: the Greek classics were the property of the Greek Professor; linguistics belonged to the Professor of Rhetoric as was the study of the most celebrated Greek, Roman, and English historians, orators, poets, and divines. As Ticknor said, "This, of course, very much narrows the ground of the professorship of belles-lettres. . . ."

To add to his difficulties he found much idleness and dissipation among the students. American teaching was of poor quality. He asserted that it cost more money in America to be educated badly than it did to enjoy the great advantages of a European university.

> . . . who in this country, by means here offered him, has been enabled to make himself a good Greek scholar? Who has been taught thoroughly to read, write, and speak Latin? Nay who has been taught anything, at our colleges, with the thoroughness that will enable him to go safely and directly onward to distinction in the department he has thus entered. . . .

There followed the process so familiar to every faculty member since—the unsatisfactory conferences with the president, the enlistment of support (Prescott was especially helpful), the questionnaires, the committee reports, the interminable faculty meetings—one of them from 9 A.M. to 6 P.M. The controversy went on for at least six years.

Some of what Ticknor proposed in his plan had been tried out by Bancroft when he joined the faculty. This was to divide his classes in beginning Greek into three sections based on ability. This seemed un-American to the abler students, who were required to do more work than their classmates. Furthermore Bancroft demanded amounts of work unheard of at Cambridge. He proposed the substitution of the lecture system for the time-honored recitation method where students were given daily grades on their mastery of what they had studied the night before. He found the library inadequate. Ticknor had used the lecture system, but this was for the literary histories of France and Spain, subjects regarded as less important than Greek and Latin. It would seem also that Ticknor was the more popular teacher of the two. He opened his own library to students and was generous of his time for consultation. On the other hand Bancroft's students in Greek gathered under his window at night, giving catcalls and mimicking his dandified walk; they composed a song with the refrain from his classroom lectures, "Thus we do in Germany." But they did learn Greek; even the slowest students progressed faster than any previous Harvard class. His best section had to be slowed down to prevent it from covering two years' work in one. After one term he wrote bitterly to Samuel Eliot: "I have the satisfaction of knowing that I have carried my points alone, unassisted by any cooperation whatever from any one individual in Cambridge, and supported by no man in my design except Mr. Ticknor."

Cogswell, meanwhile, had been engaged in developing a systematic catalogue for the library, in which he found gross deficiencies. All three men felt that President Kirkland and the Harvard Corporation were indifferent or hostile to their efforts. In October 1822 Ticknor wrote of Cogswell: "He is weary of the imperfect system of education at the College, and bitterly vexed with the want of liberal views in the Corporation, as to the principles on which the library shall be managed and increased." During that winter Cogswell and Bancroft laid plans for a school which should embody the best of European educational ideas.

They got it into operation at Round Hill, near Northampton, Massachusetts, the following autumn. The newspapers commented favorably and the aged Jefferson wrote that it should prove a great blessing; he only regretted that it was on so small a scale.

At Harvard Ticknor persevered through the interminable conferences, questionnaires, and committee meetings. The chief features of his plan were the division of the whole institution into departments, the right of limited choice of studies, and the division of classes into sections on the basis of ability. He insisted that the young men should be taught as well as examined—in other words lectured to as well as quizzed. Somewhat reluctantly the Corporation and the Overseers sanctioned these changes in 1825; a year later a committee of the Overseers reported that the experiment was not working satisfactorily in any department except Ticknor's. Obviously the rest of the faculty were dragging their feet.

The times were not propitious for academic change. In 1827, the year in which reforms were virtually abandoned at Harvard, a faculty committee at Yale prepared a report damning even mild reforms in the existing system. This report, published the next year, became the bible of educational conservatives for half a century. At the new University of Virginia a fresh air was blowing, but throughout most American colleges in the 1820's the gerund grinders entrenched themselves for another fifty years.

Yet it cannot be said that these German-trained scholars: Everett, Ticknor, Cogswell, and Bancroft failed entirely in their efforts. Under President Quincy, Ticknor found it easier to carry out his ideas. Everett's student, Ralph Waldo Emerson, became one of the most powerful voices for educational reform—not the same reforms proposed by Ticknor, but none the less, a break with the old tradition. And the Round Hill School under Bancroft and Cogswell was perhaps the first in America to give boys a preparation for genuine college work.

In their methods the two men attempted to combine the systems of Fallenberg, Pestalozzi, and the Prussian *gymnasiums*. The boys were kept busy from six in the morning until bed time at eight-fifteen in the evening. The routine included regular morning calisthenics, followed by a mile run. Bancroft, who always ran with them, could do the mile in six minutes, and Cogswell could make it in six and a half. There were three other exercise periods during the day during which the boys engaged in archery, tumbling, sports, and games. This was in a period when college students, having no organized athletic activity, let off steam in riots and free-for-alls. Even more unusual, the social life at Round Hill included frequent balls where both faculty and students danced with young ladies from the village.

On Saturday afternoons Cogswell took the boys for a hike which might cover twelve to sixteen miles. They were permitted to skate and ride horseback. From the Swiss Cogswell borrowed the idea of an annual tour to points of scenic and historic interest. Twenty-five of the smaller boys rode in a wagon; the rest traveled on foot. On one occasion Cogswell rented a fishing smack for the annual excursion.

Despite its unorthodox methods the school grew rapidly. Starting in 1823 with twenty-four pupils, it had seventy two years later, and by 1828 it was turning away applicants despite the increase of schools in America. A large proportion of them came, of course, from Massachusetts, but considerable numbers were from Maryland, South Carolina, and Georgia. A few came from places as remote as Mexico, Brazil, and the West Indies.

In their school work the boys were permitted to go forward as fast as they could; there was not the traditional lock step of regular classes. The curriculum included English, the ancient languages, four modern languages, history, geography, and mathematics. By 1826 native teachers of German, French, and Spanish were connected with the school.

From the first the founders were plagued with the perennial difficulty faced by teachers in America—the inability of their students to read and write. Cogswell found that he had to begin *de novo* with his nine- to fourteen-year-olds, and consider that they were opening a book for the first time. Of the first twenty-five there was scarcely one who could read English decently.

For the masters it was grueling work. Cogswell spent his day from 6:00 A.M. to 9:00 P.M. with the boys. Bancroft, a less popular teacher, became increasingly restive in the job. More interested in scholarly study than in teaching, he usually forgot to bring his spectacles to class; he fell asleep in his chair; his pupils read novels behind their textbooks, or sneaked out of class. Finally in 1830 he sold out his interest in the school to Cogswell. They had accumulated a property worth perhaps $50,000, but the running expenses kept it in continual difficulty. Unable to sell the necessary amount of stock in the corporation, Cogswell finally gave up in 1834 to take a killing job as a schoolmaster in Raleigh, North Carolina.

The trouble was that Round Hill was too good to fit into the American educational pattern. Its graduates had completed work equivalent to the first two years of college; in fact they had gone beyond a Harvard sophomore in mathematics. But the laws of Harvard still required that anyone entering with advanced standing had to pay tuition for the first years anyway. The American colleges, timid on some issues, have been doughty defenders of the lock step and the four-year term of incarceration.

During its brief ten years of existence the Round Hill school turned out a high proportion of young men who had distinguished careers, among them, Samuel Ward, Ellery Channing, John Lothrop Motley, Henry Griswold, and Robert Livingston. Motley, like Bancroft, was to go abroad to study, was to become a distinguished historian, and a foreign minister.

It was Sam Ward, the brother of Julia Ward Howe, who helped to rescue Cogswell from his unhappy situation. In his school at Raleigh Cogswell had found uncouth boys "with the manners of country plantations": he had to make them take off their hats indoors. From the University of South Carolina came an offer of a professorship, but thirty years before Sherman's army got there, he found the college buildings nearly in ruins; roofs falling in and no sash in some of the windows. Another offer came from Jefferson College in Louisiana, but Ward persuaded him to decline it to take over the education of the Ward daughters in New York.

In 1836 Cogswell went to Europe for his health, and four years later made the first of a series of trips abroad to buy books for the library founded by John Jacob Astor. In 1842 Irving tried to get him to go to Spain as his Secretary of Legation. After consulting Ticknor, Cogswell was ready to accept, but was dissuaded by Astor, who put him on salary.

The truth is that Cogswell, unlike Bancroft, was not temperamentally an expatriate. He admired German education and German library methods, but despite his eight visits to Europe he remained very much the homebody. Even after his unhappy experience in the South he found Europe less impressive than formerly. It had gone through gradations of wealth, vice, and corruption, and must reach barbarism unless "the regenerating influence of Freedom should intervene." "I shall love my country a great deal more since I have learned to respect her so much more highly, and shall no longer fear to lay claim to patriotism."

The year after Cogswell gave up the Round Hill School, Ticknor resigned his professorship at Harvard. However, he agreed to remain for a year until Longfellow, then studying in Germany, could return to take his place. To C. S. Daveis, Ticknor wrote that for thirteen of his fifteen years as professor he had contended against constant opposition to make the college more effectual for the education of the community. Despite his satisfaction with what had been accomplished in his own department, he had given up hope of a general reform. If the department of modern languages was right, the rest of the college was wrong. "We differ . . . very largely, both as to what the College can be, and what it ought to be."

As it turned out, he did not remain even a year. For several months he and his wife had been discussing a trip to Europe for her health; now they decided to go in June of 1835 for a stay of three or four years. In addition to the reason of Mrs. Ticknor's ill health, there was the education of the children to be considered. They were now old enough to profit by a European tour.

Although Ticknor proposed to live in various places "in the quietest and most domestic way," his two-and-a-half-year stay was more like a triumphal progress. He was immediately invited to dine at Holland House, where Lord Melbourne took him into the library for a long talk about American politics. Samuel Rogers invited the whole Ticknor family to breakfast. And so it went: Lady Byron asked them to visit a school she was interested in; Sydney Smith put them in his own pew when he preached; a committee of the House of Commons questioned Ticknor on the use of the ballot in America.

Ticknor bought a large carriage which required four post horses. In July the family set off in this for two and a half years of travel. They were invited to visit the Edgeworths, thus beginning a friendship of many years. At Rydal Wordsworth asked them to breakfast and "as usual, talked the whole time."

They went on to Brussels, Bonn, and Weimar. With a letter from Baron Humboldt, Ticknor called on Prince Metternich, with whom he had several conversations on government. He visited Thorwaldsen's atelier, but felt that Greenough was the better sculptor. As for painting there was no one in Europe as good as Allston. In Florence he spent an evening with the Bonapartes: Louis, the Countess Survillier (the wife of Joseph), Jerome. With Mrs. Ticknor he paid his respects to Prince Maximilian and the Princess Amelia. The list of noblemen he met is bewildering, for in his letters and journals Ticknor was something of a name-dropper. Certainly the forty-five-year-old Bostonian had reason to preen himself a bit on the reception he received from European notables.

At Lake Como he bumped into Wordsworth and Crabb Robinson. They all agreed to meet again in Venice, where they made up an evening gondola party. Even Wordsworth enjoyed the singing of the gondoliers.

In Paris he was invited several times by the Duke and Duchess of Broglie; he visited Guizot, Sainte Beuve, and Lamartine. Along with eight or ten other Americans he was presented at court where King Louis Philippe asked about his earlier visit to Paris, enquired after Mr. Gallatin, and praised the hospitality of Boston during his own visit there.

The Ticknors went on to London. Again the names become bewildering: Henry Hallam, Sydney Smith, John Murray, Robert Southey, John Lockhart, Lord Jeffrey—who at a dinner talked all the time, and well—H. N. Coleridge, Lord Holland, Lord Melbourne, etc., etc. There were visits, dinners, breakfasts. At one of the latter Smith and Hallam amazed Ticknor by talking about the noxious influence of aristocracy. On a tour of the Lake District the Ticknors visited the Wordsworths. The poet "explained the scenery" and recited passages from his verse. Mrs. Wordsworth took Ticknor aside to ask him to talk to her husband about finishing *The Excursion* or *The Recluse*; she could not bear to have him constantly writing sonnets. There was another visit to the Edgeworths, and then London and more dinners.

The remarkable thing is that during this second residence in Europe, much of which he obviously enjoyed, George Ticknor became more and more the American patriot. He developed none of Henry James's illusioned view of Europe. And however much Ticknor enjoyed dinners and drawing-room conversations, he did not, like James, confuse them with life. As Ticknor's comments show, he recognized that life went forward in the political arena, the peasant's hut, in the world of sociological and economic developments.

Where, asked the Grand Duke of Tuscany, did Ticknor think it the greatest good fortune to be born? In America, he replied, because the mass of the community was concerned with the affairs of state "instead of being confined as they are elsewhere, to the mere drudgery of earning their subsistence, are more truly men, and that it is more agreeable and elevating to live among them." The Duke blushed a little but made no answer.

To Richard Henry Dana, Sr., Ticknor wrote that in England and Europe he saw "a principle of decay at work, ill counteracted by an apparatus of government." As a good Bostonian he deplored the low moral tone abroad. In the United States there were defects of an opposite kind but he greatly preferred them: there was purity in domestic life and "we have so much more intellect, will, and knowledge, that compared with similar classes here, those I am among seem of an inferior order of creation." This last seems to refer to the common people of Europe. Ticknor was unlike the British travelers in America who compared tobacco-chewing frontiersmen with educated Europeans to demonstrate the evil effects of democracy. Seeing some poverty-stricken English peasants living near the Tweed, he remarked that he doubted whether there was anything so bad elsewhere in Europe outside of Russia.

In France it seemed to him that in the twenty years since his first visit the theater had become more immoral, a view which may have been conditioned by the fact that he was twenty years older. He spoke of "the shameless woman who dresses like a man and calls herself George Sand." Much as this smacks of nineteenth-century Boston, it must be remembered that most Englishmen of the time—and some Frenchmen—felt the same way. A more penetrating remark was his observation that the large number of political parties in France was worse for society than a two-party system.

The original plan had been to travel for four years, but after two years and a half he was weary of Europe; his wife had regained her health, he believed that his fifteen-year-old daughter needed to be at home where she was destined to live, and the five-year-old could be nothing but a plaything while living in hotels. The fact was, he wrote to Miss Edgeworth, they were somewhat homesick.

In June 1838 Ticknor and his family sailed for home. Unlike Cooper, who had repatriated himself five years before, Ticknor was very happy on his return. To Maria Edgeworth he wrote of his large circle of friends

> The town, too, is a good town to live in. It is a part of my enjoy-
> ments—and one that I feel deeply—that is a town of 80,000 inhabit-
> ants,—or, with the suburban towns, 120,000,—where there is a
> great deal of intellectual activity and cultivation, there is no visible
> poverty, little gross ignorance, and little crime.

He was particularly happy that there was universal education in tax-supported schools. All classes benefited: those who got a free education, and the property-owners who paid for the schools. The system produced a stable society and out of it came men like Channing, Norton, Prescott, and Webster—who in Ticknor's italics *could have been produced in no other than this state of things.* It is significant that he omitted Emerson from his list. In fact there is no reference to Emerson in the two volumes of Ticknor's *Life, Letters and Journals.* Possibly this reflects the conserva-tive Boston view that Emerson was dangerously radical and heterodox, a man who associated with Jacksonians like George Bancroft. Certainly, Emerson's demand for an American education and literature divorced from the courtly muses of Europe is at the opposite pole from the attempt of Ticknor, Cogswell, and Bancroft to build on the German model.

Stimulated by the invigorating intellectual climate of Boston, Ticknor began work on a project very much concerned with the courtly muses of Europe: a *History of Spanish Literature.* At first Pascual de Gayangos, a young Spanish scholar, helped him procure books, but when this gentle-man left for Tunis as consul, Ticknor appealed to Irving, then about to go to Madrid. Cogswell's last-minute decision not to go as Secretary of Legation was a great disappointment. Gayangos generously lent books from his own library, and Irving's friend, Mr. Obadiah Rich, purchased numerous others on Ticknor's behalf.

Finally in 1849, eleven years after Ticknor's return to America, the three-volume *History* was published by Harper in New York and by Murray in London. A Spanish translation was begun from the proof sheets. Later it was also translated into German and French. Shirley Brooks, writing in the London *Morning Chronicle*, said that he doubted if there were six men in Europe capable of reviewing it. In America Prescott, who had already published *Ferdinand and Isabella*, ably discussed it in the *North American Review*.

To Sir Charles Lyell, Ticknor wrote that because of the large reading public in the United States he had prepared his book as much for the general reader as for scholars. Furthermore he had dealt with literature as the reflection of a peculiar culture and civilization. His optimistic view of the literacy of his own country was not misplaced. By 1863 when he got out a revised edition, Ticknor said that 3,500 copies had been sold in America, and by 1876, another 1,300 had been sold. It is doubtful that a three-volume history of any foreign literature published one hundred years later would have found so many buyers in the United States unless it was a required textbook.

At the age of sixty-five Ticknor made one more trip to Europe, this time reluctantly. He was persuaded to go to buy books for the Boston Public Library with money from a recent bequest to that institution. With him were his wife, his eldest daughter, and his niece. Once again he was entertained by celebrities and noblemen. On seven different occasions he was invited to meet Macaulay, the current lion in England. He saw much of Thackeray, who had stayed at his house in Boston. But London life seemed more oppressive than ever. Breakfasts which were once modest reunions of half a dozen had grown into dinners in disguise with fourteen or sixteen guests, three or four courses of hot meats and sometimes wine. The advance of luxury, he thought, boded ill for any people.

In Berlin he again visited Humboldt, now a feeble man of eighty-seven. At Potsdam he was invited to dine with the King and the whole court. "Had a jolly good time at table with forty people." The King took him aside for a half-hour chat. Ticknor urged Everett to make another visit to Europe: traveling was now so easy. Even the traveling servants proved to be better than those of twenty years before: now they were even honest. And in Venice there was a full moon and barcarole choruses until after midnight.

Rome reminded him of Mme de Staël's remark, "C'est le salon de l'Europe," and he added, "the phrase has its force." Writing again to Prescott from Rome he said that he had a pleasanter winter than any he had passed before in Europe. He thought the Italians were improving.

The party watched the carnival from a balcony and grew "as crazy as the crowd below us."

Back in London he visited Holland House, now owned by the son of the Lord Holland he had known. In the library he remembered the position of books he had not seen for twenty years. Lord Acton called on him twice. To Palmerston he spoke of a chat with deLesseps, who was full of his canal, but whose canal, he thought, would never be full of water.

It is obvious that the reluctant traveler greatly enjoyed his last European trip. America was now regarded in Europe as an important power. If only the States could avoid disunion they would grow greater and richer. But like most Americans abroad he was embarrassed about slavery. *Uncle Tom's Cabin* was still played in many of the popular theaters in Europe.

He returned home to the panic of 1857. The country, he thought, had brought it on by gambling: bank directors, railroad directors, merchants, and manufacturers were all guilty.

Nevertheless, he remained the patriot rather than the expatriate. In fact as his letters and journals reveal, he became more American in his views as he grew older. Of course he kept up his correspondence with foreign friends, and entertained them when they visited Boston. But during the Civil War he plunged actively into work for the Union cause. Always he had considered slavery a great evil, but almost until Fort Sumter he had believed that its uneconomic nature would bring about its end. In the intervals between work for the Union he worked at the biography of his friend Prescott. Even at the age of seventy-eight he worked with his old friend Cogswell to obtain for the Boston Library a Shakespeare collection which he thought would make Boston the best place on this side of the Atlantic for the study of Elizabethan drama.

Ticknor is now largely a forgotten figure, but as this account indicates, he had considerable influence upon American education and letters during his lifetime. He was trained in European scholarship and spent at least seven years of his life abroad, but like Everett Cogswell, he remained very much an American patriot. All three of these men demonstrated that a European education did not unfit a man for his own country. Ticknor's experience is especially significant. As has been shown, he was at ease in the best intellectual and social life of Europe; yet he had no sense of alienation upon his return home.

His experience and that of Washington Irving suggest the need for a

re-examination of the view later promulgated by Henry James and Edith
Wharton that there was no place in America for the intellectual or the
gentleman. In the best sense of those terms, George Ticknor was a
gentleman and a scholar. Between 1815 and 1856 he experienced the best
Europe had to offer and he greatly enjoyed the experience. But on the
whole he preferred the intellectual life of Boston, and he very much
preferred the political and social organization of America. This preference was not a kind of absentee sentimentality; he was deeply concerned
with the evil of slavery, and aware of the get-rich-quick mania of America. But on the whole he found in his own country a sounder and more
stable society than that of Europe. Even more remarkable, in the era from
Jackson to Buchanan he, like Irving, found a congenial social and intellectual environment.

George Bancroft is a more puzzling figure. After he gave up the Round
Hill School, he began work on the history which was to make him
famous, and he got into politics. His marriage to Sarah Dwight, which
brought him into a family with extensive business enterprises, gave him
the means for the leisure and the expensive research necessary to *The
History of the United States from the Discovery of the Continent.* Oddly
enough, despite his wealthy connections, he became a Jacksonian
Democrat—what in later days was called being a traitor to one's class.
His father had been a Federalist of the old school, and George Ticknor
wrote to warn his friend against associating with "Jacksonians and
Workies."

Bancroft's public avowal of his principles came in a speech at Northampton on that famous July 4 of 1826, when Adams lay dying at Nahant
and Jefferson at Monticello. Bancroft had long ago sought advice from
John Adams, but it was Jefferson he now hailed as one "whose principles
are identified with the character of our government, and whose influence
with the progress of civil liberty throughout the world." He went on to
say, "The popular voice is all powerful with us; this is our oracle; this we
acknowledge, is the voice of God." The speech echoes the patriotic
sentiments of his student days at Göttingen.

Five years later he wrote for the *North American Review* an article
strongly supporting Jackson's stand on the United States Bank. By 1834
he was writing to Everett, "I am radically a republican in feeling and
principle. I am most radical, and to the heart's core." In his notes he
jotted down such ideas as "He who labors should have much and the

reverse. The merchant does not produce; he does but exchange." And "The farmers achieved the Revolution aided by mechanics. The furtherance of our liberty rests on mechanics." "The people is sovereign. The man of letters is his counsellor."

Bancroft's political activities are much too extended and complex to be recounted in detail. They brought him recognition in party counsels, got him the position of Collector of the Port of Boston, made him for a time the Democratic leader of Massachusetts. Under Polk he became Secretary of the Navy and established almost overnight the Naval Academy at Annapolis. After the Civil War he came to the aid of President Andrew Johnson. Bancroft's biographer, Russel Nye, discovered that he was the chief author of the President's important first message to Congress.

During these same years he was working twelve to fourteen hours a day on *The History*. To this task he brought his training in German scholarship, such things as the use of primary sources, which he had learned from H. L. Heeren. His point of view was essentially transcendental; history was to him a working out of a divine plan. On the cover of the first volume was the motto "Westward the star of empire takes its way." Bancroft's rather spread-eagle style led John Quincy Adams to call the first volume a "diffuse and declamatory panegyric," and a later critic remarked that Bancroft wrote the history of America "as if it were the history of the kingdom of heaven."

Other critics over the years have testified to its great value as a pioneering study of American history built upon a solid foundation of original documents. Over the years Bancroft spent more than $100,000 in having documents copied from archives at home and in Europe, and from private papers. He could read German almost as easily as English, and French nearly as well. His fantastic ability to work made it possible, even while active in politics, for him to turn out three volumes between 1834 and 1845. During those same years his first wife died and he married Susan Bliss, the widow of a junior partner in Webster's law firm.

But despite his Jacksonian principles and his super-patriotic view of his country's history, the reward he wanted from Polk was expatriation in the form of a diplomatic post. This he obtained in 1846 when he was sent to replace the ailing Louis McLane as minister to England. He took with him a family of seven: his wife Susan and his two stepsons, his own three boys born of his first marriage, and a daughter by his second wife.

Bancroft was something of an Anglophobe: his history had attacked the British, and his Jacksonian sympathies were opposed to aristocracies. But Mrs. Bancroft's discovery of the first, second, and third class system on British railways made her "feel for the first time the superiority of England over our own country." However, during her three-year residence she was intimidated by the hauteur of her maid, Russell, and was forever asking the wrong servant for coals or wine. But she was dazzled by the social life: "I have the same interest in seeing the really distinguished men of England that I should have in the pictures and statues of Rome, and indeed much greater." She even put aside her New England scruples against a low-cut dress, since it was the fashion among "people of agreeable manners, excellence, and domestic virtues."

The Jacksonian Bancroft bought a court dress complete with wine-colored pantaloons, sword, and plumed hat. When Everett had been minister he used an old yellow coach with one footman; Bancroft bought a handsome maroon affair with silver trim, an American eagle on its panels, and attended by gorgeously attired footmen.

In many ways the resplendent American eagle upon an aristocratic coach is symbolic of Bancroft's whole life. In England and later in Berlin he enjoyed the society of aristocrats, the lavish life of upper-class Europe. Yet, even more than Fenimore Cooper, he considered himself the spokesman for American democracy. However, after two years in England he began to tire of court life. "I begin to sigh a little for republican air, and for the homely sincerity of American life and the rough vigor of our institutions and people," he wrote to Prescott.

Despite an extremely active social life, Bancroft did not forget his history. He put copyists to work in the State Papers Office, the British Museum, and in France, Holland, and Madrid; he persuaded British friends to ransack their attics. Lord Landsdowne himself brought material he considered too valuable to entrust to messengers. George Gray permitted Bancroft to use the Penn Papers, and Lord North's daughter opened the family correspondence to him. After three years in England he shipped home the most important collection of source materials on American history then extant. Before he left for home Oxford gave him an honorary degree.

Back in New York he associated with a literary circle which included Irving, Bryant, Fitz-Greene Halleck, N. P. Willis and Gulian C. Verplanck. A handsome man with flourishing white sideburns and an equally florid oratorical style, he was much in demand as a speaker at banquets. Despite his social life and the death of his daughter Louisa, which caused him to suspend work for a time, he completed Volumes IV and V of the *History* in the two years following his repatriation.

During the Civil War he again dabbled in politics, and was among those who urged upon Lincoln the emancipation of the slaves. Not much impressed by Lincoln on their first meeting, Bancroft came to have a great admiration for him. After Lincoln's assassination Bancroft lent some behind-the-scenes support to President Johnson in the struggle with the Radicals in Congress. He tried unsuccessfully to bring about friendly relations between Johnson and Sumner, and he wrote the President's first message to Congress, a message whose literacy much amazed Johnson's critics. In writing it, Bancroft had woven together ideas which Johnson had expressed in various speeches.

Had the Radical Republicans been aware of this activity, the Congress would not have invited Bancroft to deliver a eulogy on Lincoln in 1866 as he had done for Jackson twenty-one years earlier. In the speech Bancroft revealed both his Jacksonian beliefs and his ability to get into hot water on the subject of foreign affairs. The former expatriate hailed Lincoln as "a child of the West—a child of America . . . Lincoln was through and through an American." No other man was better fitted to preserve a government of and by the people. Yet England had scoffed "at the hopeless vanity" of Lincoln's efforts; had assisted and encouraged the breaking up of the Union. Few home-grown patriots could have twisted the lion's tail more enthusiastically. In London, Lord John Russell called at the American embassy to lodge a formal protest. At this point Bancroft the historian stepped in: he told Congress that when Russell had been British Secretary of State for Foreign Affairs he had on at least four occasions spoken of the United States as "the late Union," and had spread this opinion throughout Europe. Lord Russell quieted down.

President Johnson offered Bancroft his old post as Collector of the Port of Boston, but Bancroft declined on the grounds that he refused to live in Boston. What he really wanted was a diplomatic post. However he declined that of Minister to Austria because he did not want to displace his former pupil, John Lothrop Motley. At last in 1867 he received the coveted offer to be Minister at Berlin. General Grant, the candidate favored by the Republicans, wrote the historian expressing good wishes.

Grant's approval, Bancroft's own fame as a historian, and the Radicals' ignorance of the speech-writing for Johnson led to Bancroft's confirmation by the Senate.

Once more the fiery patriot, the Jacksonian Democrat had chosen expatriation and the allure of court life. His biographer, Russel Nye, says that in his new post Bancroft enjoyed himself as he had not in twenty years. At once he became friendly with Bismarck, who had roomed with Motley at Göttingen. To the Chancellor Bancroft was "the ideal American minister." Soon they were taking daily rides together. The historian, quite possibly with the Chancellor's help, developed a curious blind spot: he came to regard Germany as the leader of a liberal revolution in Europe and Bismarck as another Washington. It would seem that the Chancellor chose his topics of conversation skilfully.

In the growing tension between France and Germany Bancroft sided openly with the latter. He criticized the conduct of France toward America during the Civil War and added a threat that America would express her dissatisfaction concretely when the time came. The French protested to Washington and demanded the minister's immediate recall. General Dix, the American representative in Paris, complained to Seward that Bancroft had embarrassed him. Bancroft wrote to Seward that France, not Germany, was fomenting war. Bismarck, fearing the loss of so useful a friend to Germany, asked Motley to use his influence to keep Bancroft in Berlin.

During the Franco-Prussian War the undiplomatic diplomat stirred up another tempest when in a fiery speech at a banquet he pledged the use of the American navy against France if it became necessary. Then, on the occasion of the renewal of his Doctorate at Göttingen, a ceremony which was customary after fifty years, he answered Bismarck's letter of congratulation with one containing an indiscreet reference to the Chancellor's "work of renovating Europe." Although the letter was private, the wily Chancellor gave it to the German press. Again the French were incensed, but their protest reached Washington after the fall of Paris.

In defense of Bancroft it must be said that Napoleon III was regarded by many other Americans as the chief foe of liberty in Europe. For instance, Margaret Fuller's journals are filled with indignation at the French intervention, during the Second Empire, to put down the liberal revolution in Italy.

Meanwhile, Bancroft's life in Berlin was very pleasant. There was a constant stream of visitors to the embassy, important Europeans and traveling Americans. Motley on his visits to Berlin always dropped in. Bancroft entertained such diverse characters as von Moltke, Richard Wagner, Hermann Helmholtz, Herman Grimm, Henry Adams, and General Sherman.

Partly for the benefit of his wife's health Bancroft took a tour of the Near East in 1872. In Cairo Emerson and his daughter Ellen joined them. Shortly before, Bancroft had contributed $1000 for the rebuilding of Emerson's house after it had burned down. The Americans were entertained at breakfast at the Khedive's palace.

Bancroft spent another year in Berlin; then at the age of seventy-three he decided to come home. His wife was still ailing and he wanted to finish his historical work. He took a house in Washington, decorated with a huge portrait of Kaiser Wilhelm I. Here he entertained visitors from abroad and prominent compatriots with dinners of canvasback, red snappers, and terrapin. In fact an invitation to his house on H Street rivaled one to the White House or an embassy. The list of guests is a roster of the notables of the time: senators, justices of the Supreme Court, writers, scholars. Henry Adams, John Hay, and Dr. S. Weir Mitchell were special friends. Each July he went to Roseclyffe, his Newport summer home, where his collection of roses became famous. Here was another circle: Julia Ward Howe, T. W. Higginson, Helen Hunt, Charlotte Cushman—and the ubiquitous Weir Mitchell.

Despite the social life and the hours spent daily in answering letters, Bancroft finished his history in 1874—forty years after he had begun it. Nye estimates that its ten volumes contained 1,700,000 words. Then Bancroft set about a shortened revision, the first volume of which came out a year later. In rewriting the *History* he pruned away some of the excesses of his earlier style, and reduced the ten volumes to six.

But even in the Gilded Age Americans bought books. In 1876 the revised edition sold 18,000 copies and the old edition 7000. As late as 1880, the two were selling nearly 10,000 a year, and Americans continued to honor the man who had talked with John Adams, Madison, Lafayette, and Jackson. In 1879 the Senate voted him full privileges of the floor. At Bancroft's death in 1891 President Harrison ordered all flags to be flown at half mast. Like Washington Irving the long-time expatriate died a national hero.

Russel Nye argues that Bancroft's democratic liberalism came in part from Europe—the Europe of 1848. But as far back as his student days at Göttingen in 1818, Bancroft had been a fiery patriot. A more tenable thesis is to hold that Bancroft, like many other Americans, read into the Europe of 1848 the history of 1776. Bancroft's own mistake of regarding Bismarck as a second Washington is symptomatic.

Without question Bancroft enjoyed his European experience—the glamour of court life, the association with prominent people. But, like Irving, he seems to have been equally happy at home, to have found equal stimulation in his American friends. His most eloquent tributes were not to the great men he had known abroad; they were to Andrew Jackson and Abraham Lincoln. The project to which he devoted over forty years—the *History of the United States*—is a paean to his native land.

Everett, Ticknor, Cogswell, and Bancroft all experienced the best Europe had to offer between 1815 and 1875—in education and in association with intellectuals and statesmen. All of them, and especially Ticknor and Bancroft, were at ease in Zion. Yet to a man they were primarily Americans concerned with the intellectual and political life of their own country. In the light of their European experience they saw room for improvement at home, especially in education. But no one of them preferred Europe to America—no one was condescending to his homeland. All of them devoted their chief energies to American interests. To a man they found American intellectual life stimulating. Three of them engaged actively in American politics.

If there is any safe generalization to be made on the lives of these scholars it is that between 1815 to 1875 they wanted to bring to America the best to be found in Europe, but they did not become Europeanized. These expatriates went abroad as patriots and they returned as patriots.

THE CHIP ON THE SHOULDER
JAMES FENIMORE COOPER

Both as a patriot and as an expatriate James Fenimore Cooper carried a chip on his shoulder. After Sydney Smith met him in England, he warned Moore that he might as well call Cooper out for a duel as it must come to that before long. Lady Holland, after having Cooper to dinner, wrote to her son, Lord Ilchester:

> *The Red Rover* is very quick, clear and intelligent. I should suspect he was not very good-tempered, not half so amiable as his country-man W. Irvinge [*sic*], and hot upon the subject of American manners & superiority. . . . He is a handsome man.

Fenimore Cooper was indeed different from Irving, who was rarely hot on any subject, especially that of American manners. In fact Irving told one young American tourist that the mark of a gentleman was to avoid nationalism in manners. As might be expected Cooper and Irving were seeking different Europes—the one the romantic world of the past, the other the political and social present. Ironically, Irving had more influence on public affairs than did Cooper. The one helped to settle the Oregon dispute with England; the other fought a rearguard action to preserve the patroon system in New York.

Cooper was born near the frontier in Cooperstown, New York, which his family had founded. After his expulsion from Yale for some prank he went to sea for several years. At twenty-two he married the daughter of the aristocratic De Lanceys and established himself as a country gentleman. After writing one novel, *Precaution,* to prove to his wife that he could do it, he took up novel writing seriously. Then followed *The Spy* (1821), based on American history; *The Pioneers* (1823), beginning the Leatherstocking series, and *The Pilot* (1823) to prove that he could write a more accurate sea story than Scott's *The Pirate.* By the time he sailed for Europe with his family in 1826 he had published six novels, including *The Last of the Mohicans,* and had a considerable reputation in Europe.

His three chief reasons for the six-year stay abroad were his health, the education of his daughters, and the advantage of dealing directly with his European publishers. The extent of Cooper's activities both physical and literary suggests that there was not much wrong with his health.

The education of young ladies was a more serious problem. During the first half of the nineteenth century female seminaries in America were notorious for poor standards and for their emphasis on "accomplishments." At a time when European travel was considered an essential part of upper-class education, it was the fashion to study languages, especially French. Irving had urged language study for his nephew. Students at Harvard and Yale paid for their own instruction in French as an extra-curricular activity. Even before the Cooper family sailed, the children had a French governess. Cooper himself studied with a refugee from St. Domingo, and the three girls were sent to a day school where nothing but French was spoken. William and Susan were also given lessons in Spanish. In addition, Cooper was well aware of American ignorance of and lack of taste in art and music.

The business reasons were also compelling. There was of course the lack of an international copyright. When Cooper tried to explain to Scott the American laws on the subject he ended by saying, "I suppose, after all, a good way of getting an accurate solution of the meaning of the law would be to toss a dollar into the air and cry 'heads' or 'tails.' "

By the time he had been in Europe several years Cooper boasted that a new book of his was published the same day in New York, London, Paris, Vienna, and Rome—in English, French, German, and Italian.

By 1826 sailing packets made regular trips to Europe, making the voyage in about thirty days. An experienced sailor, Cooper was nevertheless uneasy about his family's safety during the first part of the voyage. The family party consisted of Mrs. Cooper, three daughters, a son, and Mrs. Cooper's sister. Near Newfoundland he remained on deck at night to watch for icebergs. He felt that the government should send cruisers to chart rocks and shoals. After landing at Southampton they remained a few weeks, then took a rickety steamboat for Le Havre.

Cooper was enough of an American tourist to be impressed by the ancient monuments of Europe and the prices demanded by French porters. At Rouen they asked ten francs (about two dollars) to transfer some baggage. In America he had paid one dollar for a similar service although the price asked was only thirty-seven and a half cents, so he paid five francs despite the fact that the men hung around for hours demanding more. He attributed the situation to the high taxes on French workingmen. On the other hand, a respectful and well informed guide hesitated to accept a five-franc tip, saying it was too much. "To know when to pay and what to pay is a useful attainment of the experienced traveller," Cooper commented.

But the Rouen Cathedral was "worth crossing the Atlantic, were it only to see this!" For a week "our unpracticed Americans" admired ruins.

> The European who comes to America plunges into the virgin forest with wonder and delight, while the American who goes to Europe finds his greatest pleasure, at first, in hunting up memorials of the past. Each is in quest of novelty, and is burning with desire to gaze at objects of which he has read.

He was impressed by the diligence to Paris—a huge affair which could carry twenty-five or thirty passengers and two or three tons of baggage. But he also admired the landscape partially veiled in clouds: "I love to study a place teeming with historical recollections, under this light."

In fact Cooper, as a traveler, divided his attention between romantic scenery and socioeconomic conditions. The duties on internal trade were, he believed, "the old expedient to tax the poor by laying impositions on food and necessaries." Noting the contrast between the magnificence of Paris and the grubby barges on the Seine, he remarked that trade was a useful thing but one which rarely contributed to the taste, learning, manners, or morals of a nation. Sardonically he observed an English tourist cheering for the French Dauphine "as if he had been cheering a member of Parliament who gave gin in his beer." The French, he thought, treated their servants better than did the English or Americans who allowed coachmen to sit on their carriage boxes "like so many ducks in a drizzling rain." Cooper's comments on the European scene are filled with the kind of down-to-earth observation that one finds only occasionally in Irving and not at all in Henry James.

Like James, however, he was keenly aware of social usages. The protocol governing the diplomatic corps suggested to him the dexterous evolutions of a corps of regular troops, with their wheelings and counter marches. Often he found this sort of thing irksome at formal dinners:

> In America, I have always understood that, on such occasions, silent laws of etiquette exist, in all good company, which are founded on propriety and tact. The young give way to the old, the undistinguished to the distinguished, and he who is at home to the stranger. . . . I confess to some maneuvering in my time, to get near, or away

from a fire, out of a draught, or next to some agreeable woman; but the idea whether I was at the head or foot of the table never crossed my mind.

Almost always Cooper considered any European usage in terms of its possible value to America. Ardent patriot though he was, he was not convinced of the superiority of everything American. French cooking was greatly superior and possibly accounted for the fact that the French were such agreeable companions. The English diet of roast beef, bacon, pudding, beer, and port produced a different and to Cooper a less agreeable breed. Among the improvements he would introduce in America would be "a total reform of the kitchen." In fact the other desirable changes such as less emphasis upon wealth might flow from an improved cuisine. However such niceties as finger bowls were not strange to him; they were used daily in his own home. For along with his admiration for many foreign refinements there is his constant insistence to Europeans on the civilized comforts of his homeland. Most Americans, for instance, except on the frontier, had rugs on their floors.

As it was customary for American travelers to carry letters of recommendation to prominent people, Cooper had come to France equipped with twenty of them. However, because he did not like to push himself, he kept the letters locked up in a secretary. He did call upon Lafayette, whom he had known in America. One morning Lafayette was just driving away from a visit to the Cooper apartment when another caller arrived. This was Walter Scott, who had got hold of Cooper's address from Princess Barbara Vissiliewa Glitzen, whose salon Cooper had visited. Somewhat smugly Cooper wrote to a friend about the visit from the *Great Unknown*—so called at the time because of the mystery over *Waverley*. Such an event, even the visit of a lesser unknown from England, would "throw all the reading clubs at home into a state of moral and poetical excitement."

Cooper and Scott discussed their methods of work. To Cooper's surprise Scott inquired about the proper way to address a princess who had invited both men to breakfast. The American knew the correct form. On another occasion because Scott's French was poor, Cooper took over a conversation when the other began to flounder.

Cooper's curiosity was insatiable. He visited an exhibition of manufactured articles and noted the great difference between the beautiful plows shown and the clumsy affairs in actual use. In France, he thought, articles of common use such as cutlery, hinges, door fastenings, and carpenter's tools were inferior to the same articles in America. It seemed to him that there was such a chasm between the knowledge of the educated classes and the ignorance of the common people that it took a long time for new ideas, new techniques to cross. But as for articles of elegance and luxury in France, no Englishman could see them without astonishment. To him there was something ponderous and purse-proud about the magnificence of England; French taste was much superior.

During his stay in France Cooper wrote *Notions of the Americans* as an answer to the travel books by Englishmen. He used the device of a fictitious traveler who visits the United States in 1824 at the time of Lafayette's triumphant tour. On the whole the book is an interesting and judicious account of American ways of life. Obviously Cooper's European experience had made him more aware of some of the special qualities of his own country.

For instance, he remarked upon the similarity of manners, customs, and opinions as he traveled from state to state. In no other civilized country, with the possible exception of certain English colonies, was a traveler so free from intrusions on his privacy by the police. Although castes existed, "they appear to be separated by less impossible barriers." Americans disliked the obsequiousness characteristic of English servants—as for Cooper himself these servilities "gave me a pain."

He was proud of the state of public education, especially in Massachusetts, and thought American textbooks more up to date than French ones. It seemed to him that the simplicity of American manners among the cultivated classes was founded on good sense; whereas English fashionable society was trammeled by ritual. He even discussed what today would be called "U" speech forms among the British. He attributed these upper-class rituals to a desire to keep the new rich out of society. In America, on the other hand, the dress and deportment of working people did not set them apart. They knew how to dress and behave at public functions.

But there was another side to the American picture. Much as Cooper admired his own country, he recognized its provinciality. New York and possibly New Orleans were the only cities in the Union which had not the air of provincial towns. Europeans sometimes said this about Philadelphia, but Cooper was a New Yorker. Writing amid the libraries, art galleries and universities of Europe, Cooper deplored American smugness:

> I confess, I was a little startled to hear a people who scarcely possess a work of art that attains mediocrity,—among whom most of the sciences are comparatively in their infancy—who rarely push learning beyond its practical and most useful points . . . speak of their pre-eminent civilization with so evident complacency.

Aware that almost every European condemned Negro slavery, Cooper said that most Americans would like to get rid of it but that it could not be abolished by high-sounding declarations. After all, about the same proportion of Europeans suffered hardships equal to those of the slaves. As for the allegation that Americans were money hungry, he answered that money was of more importance in England than in any other country he had visited. Seats in Congress were not put up for sale.

Despite his growing Anglophobia Cooper took his family to England in 1828. Possibly he considered two years in a French school long enough for his daughters. And after all England had a fascination for Americans brought up on her history and literature. Cooper described his own emotions on landing:

> Twenty-two years before, an ardent boy, I had leaped ashore, on the island, with a feeling of deep reverence and admiration, the fruits of the traditions of my people, and with a love almost as devoted as that I bore the land of my birth. I had been born, and I had hitherto lived, among those who looked up to England as the idol of the political, moral, and literary adoration.

At once he was impressed by the fine roads and the orderliness of English inns—no cracked cups, no forks with one tine. Parts of London reminded him of Philadelphia. For a guinea a day he took a furnished house in St. James Place. It had a tiny drawing room, three bedrooms, and the use of offices. The people of the house did the cooking and took care of the rooms although the Coopers had two servants of their own: a maid and a man.

Like a good tourist, Cooper went sightseeing. In St. Paul's he recalled his sensation of dizziness when years before as a raw boy fresh from home he had first seen it. He had returned to astonish his friends by telling them that the steeple of Trinity Church could stand beneath the dome and not reach the top. Now he even took his family to the Tower, saying that perhaps he ought not to confess this weakness. Unfortunately "some musty antiquarians" had recently proved that the armour was not genuine. "I wish with all my heart, the man had not been half so learned, for, like a novel by Scott, or a play by Shakespeare, in this case the fiction was probably more interesting than the reality."

Of Westminster Abbey he wrote in a rare poetic vein:

> the intellectual spirits are crowded together in a sort of vestibule, as if entering, one by one, and finding good companions already assembled, they had stopped in succession to enjoy each other's society. Notwithstanding the gorgeous pomp of the monuments of the noble, one feels that this homely corner contains the best company.

He went driving in a gig with John McAdam over the fine roads which the latter had designed. Cooper greatly admired the roads, and Mrs. Cooper's sister admired McAdam, whom she married.

Cooper's house in St. James Place was just a step away from the home of Samuel Rogers, and not far from Holland House. It was in that magic circle described by Sydney Smith as containing the intellectual life of London. Rogers was hospitable to Americans. At his breakfasts a transatlantic guest might meet Wordsworth, Scott, Lockhart, and Moore. Irving's friend Charles Leslie was a frequent guest. Cooper admitted that in no other country, even his own, had he been so well treated, but like Irving he found an anti-American feeling:

> The English do not like the Americans. There is a strong disposition in them to exaggerate and circulate anything that has a tendency to throw ridicule and contumely on the national character. . . .

The common attitude seems to have been "Some of my best friends are Americans."

Although Cooper presented no letters of introduction, he was enough of a celebrity to be sought out. Godwin called unexpectedly and talked for an hour on America and American poetry. Several times Cooper felt like patting the old man's head and telling him he was a good fellow. At Rogers' house during a discussion of British and American speech a young gentleman said that there was "something peculiar—provincial—he did not know exactly what" in Cooper's speech. "I could have helped him to the word—something not cockney." At one house the hostess asked him where he had learned to speak such good English—a remark encountered in various forms by other Americans, always to their annoyance.

In his *Gleanings in Europe, England,* Cooper spent pages on the subject of English manners. During a two-week period a dozen noblemen laid their hands on his knocker. Because he wrote in the dining room only fifteen feet from the door, he soon learned to recognize a lord by his peremptory knock. Cooper tried out his knowledge. At a lord's house he first knocked quietly, then a little louder. Not a footman stirred. "I then rapped *à la peer of the realm,* and my hand was still on the knocker, as the lazy rogue opened the door."

Only of Lord Grey could he say, ". . . his house was one of the few in England, in which something has not occurred to make me feel that I was . . . not only a foreigner, but an American." For one thing, Lord Grey expressed no surprise that Cooper spoke English. Obviously Cooper was a somewhat thorny guest. Believing that the English particularly despised an American who was in any way "a toad-eater," he took pains never to deserve that epithet.

> I would strenuously urge on every American who really loves the institutions of his country, never to make any concessions to mere politeness, on these topics [politics, etc.], when actually required to say anything in England. Indeed, politeness has few claims when principles are concerned. . . .

Some of the provocation for this attitude appears in the kinds of charges that were brought against America. Someone, probably a reader of Frances Trollope, brought up the subject of drunkenness in Ohio. Cooper answered that his country had as little of this vice as any he had visited. Then there was the old chestnut that the American climate was unhealthful and shortened the life span. No, said Cooper, he could count ten neighbors at home who were over ninety. He stated his belief that a child born in New York State had as good a chance of reaching ninety as one from Kent, Sussex, or Oxford. In his notes, and possibly in his conversation, he expressed his opinion that England ought not to be inhabited between October and January.

Like almost all Americans in England during the nineteenth century he noted the consistent hostility of the press, a hostility especially cultivated by the *Quarterly Review*. It struck him that the higher classes kept themselves free from the national prejudices fostered by the press, which they controlled. He speculated that the aristocracy kept its power by encouraging prejudices in the mass of the people. Anti-Americanism was fostered for the reason that "Power, in America, has nothing to apprehend from English example, while power, in England, has much to apprehend from the example of America."

He denied the charge that Americans were hostile to the English: "*. . . in no other country are the English looked upon with as friendly eyes as in the United States of America*" (the italics are his own). On the other hand, he said that the English were so accustomed to think of us as inferior that they never realized the bad taste of telling a man in society, "Really, now, I do not see but you know how to speak or, to use a fork, or to drink your wine, or to go through the polite manual of polite life, quite as well as one of us." Cooper quoted with approval the saying that a Frenchman goes into society to make himself agreeable, an Englishman to make himself disagreeable.

Like other American visitors, he was struck by the contrast between the extreme luxury of the rich and the misery of the poor. England, he wrote, was the country of the wealthy. Because of the climate the lot of the poor was worse than in countries like France or Italy. One class whose lot he thought worse than that of Asiatic slaves was the female servants in lodging houses and the homes of small tradesmen. They had an air of dogged, sullen misery such as he had never seen equaled. French servants were treated as humble friends, and even American slaves were treated more kindly than English domestics.

But there were compensations. Despite his belief that New York gentlemen set more handsome tables and served better food, he found that almost no one in England left the impression "of vapid ignorance that so often besets us in our own circles." Occasionally there were brilliant moments such as the occasions when Coleridge was present. William Sotheby gave a dinner at which Cooper, Scott, Lockhart, and Coleridge were guests. Someone brought up the subject of a controversial battle between an American and a British ship. Cooper, who considered himself an authority on naval matters, launched into a long defense of the American action. Possibly to change the subject someone mentioned Coleridge's theory that Homer was not one individual. That set off one of the famous monologues. Cooper wrote:

I never witnessed an exhibition as extraordinary as that which
followed. It was not a discourse, but a dissertation. . . . As near as I
could judge, he was rather more than an hour in *possession of the
floor*, almost without interruption. . . . His voice was strong and
clear, but not pitched above the usual level of conversation. . . . I
was less struck by the logic than by the beauty of the language, and
the poetry of the images.

On another occasion Sotheby took Cooper to call on Coleridge at
Highgate. Coleridge showed a painting of a horseman which Washington
Allston had copied from one by Titian in order to study it. However
Coleridge had admired it so much that Allston had presented it to him.
(Although Cooper did not mention it, Coleridge's favorite portrait of
himself had been done by this American painter.) During Cooper's visit
Coleridge held forth on the subject of phrenology, going into detail about
the wonders which a practitioner had found in his skull. "If Coleridge
was scholastic and redundant," wrote Cooper, "it was because he could
not help himself . . . it was a sort of boiling over of the pot on account of
the intense heat beneath."

Altogether Cooper had a stimulating, if exasperating, five months in
England. In June he started with his family for Switzerland and Italy. His
final comment was "England, a country that I could fain like, but whose
prejudices and national antipathies throw a chill over all my affections
. . . a country all respect, but few love." The irony was that Cooper was
much more like an Englishman than he realized, a fact which emerged on
his return to America.

During the four months the family was in Switzerland Cooper, as was
his habit, wrote with the door of his study open despite the commotion
produced by a household of ten. He would stop in the middle of a page to
teach his son how to fly a kite, or to take Mrs. Cooper rowing on the lake,
or to play a game of chess or backgammon with her. Very much a family
man, he disliked going anywhere without his wife, and preferably one or
more of the children. Even when the girls had been in a Paris school,
Cooper took an apartment in the same building.

In Switzerland and Italy he was in a perpetual state of what he called
toosey-moosey over the gorgeous scenery. Traveling in a roomy family
carriage with a coachman's box in front and a rumble seat behind, the
family crossed the Simplon Pass before snow fell. Cooper's daughter

Susan said that he fell in love with Italy at first sight; it was a love which lasted his life-time.

In Florence, where they spent the winter, he found so many "Manhattenese" that he was never without news and gossip from home. Mrs. Cooper wrote home about the cheapness of living in Florence. They went into society very little, she said, and added a touch worthy of her husband: "Mr. Cooper has almost affronted the Lords, the Dukes, and Princes, by declining their invitations."

In Florence Cooper met young Horatio Greenough, who was studying sculpture at the Academy of Fine Arts. It is not strange that Greenough asked Cooper to pose for a portrait bust: this handsome American had already become in Europe a symbol of the land of the woodsman and the Indian. The bust turned out so well that Cooper commissioned the sculptor to do a group in marble, a piece which was first called the "singing cherubs," then the "chanting cherubs." Cooper's motives were at least as much patriotic as artistic. "I believe this is the first piece of regular statuary *in groupe* [sic] that has been executed by an American artist." He believed that Greenough showed promise of making a name for himself and, "In a country like ours, the acquisition of a good sculpture is no trifle." This remark of course led him off into the subject of the purse-proud vulgarity of English taste.

The Coopers spent the summer in Tuscany and on the Bay of Naples, then a winter in Rome. Mrs. Cooper wrote enthusiastically to her sister about spring in Rome and about the historic places she was visiting. For her husband Italy was next to his own country the best place to live. "There is no place where living is such a luxury." This does not mean that he was idle: he wrote two novels in Italy: *The Wept of Wishton-Wish* and *The Water Witch*.

In 1830 the family went back to Paris, where they stayed three years, except for a short summer visit to Switzerland in 1832. Cooper, who had gone ahead to secure lodgings, wrote to his wife naming seven American acquaintances he had met on the streets during his first two hours in Paris. It was the same sort of experience mentioned by travelers and expatriates in London, Dresden, Florence, and Rome. It is a rare American abroad in the twentieth century who meets as many friends from home as did his nineteenth-century predecessor.

Those who stayed at home were inclined to complain about Americans who remained long abroad. We have seen how often Irving felt it necessary to reassure friends and relatives that he had not become an alien. From Paris Cooper wrote to his brother Richard:

> Your aunt Pomeroy is afraid we shall become too Europeanized for home. She knows little of our tastes and wishes. There are people who come here, who see us in the possession of advantages that certainly do not fall to all our countrymen; and as most Americans have an exaggerated idea of Europe and specially of England, they fancy we cannot tear ourselves from a society they imagine so agreeable. Now my longing is for a wilderness—Cooperstown is far too populous and artificial for me, and it is my intention to plunge somewhere into the forest, for six months in the year, at my return.

In answer to this Richard expressed the puritanical views of so many of his countrymen:

> I have heard of the corruptions of Europe, and the total departure from natural sentiment and moral rectitude which characterizes the great body of refined society in that quarter of the world, and I could almost persuade myself that the daily association with human nature in this impure condition had a little obscured the re-membrance of what is your native land.

It was this kind of attitude which so many travelers encountered when they came home. Bancroft's experience with Andrews Norton was a case in point. Thus many an American who did not consider himself an expatriate found that his countrymen thought of him as such. It was one of the pressures which often sent them back for further travel abroad and in some cases led to real expatriation. Cooper, with his ardent patriotism, found this sort of thing especially irksome. As will appear, it helped to make him feel uncomfortable when he did go home.

Like most of his countrymen abroad Cooper had no enthusiasm for European morals. As far back as *Notions of the Americans* he was proud of the fact that with American ladies "the language of gallantry" was not tolerated. He admitted the charge that American ladies were more squeamish in their talk than those of England or France, but on the whole he approved this.

On the other hand, Richard's blanket condemnation of European so-ciety must have seemed pretty silly to a man whose friends included Scott and Lafayette. In Paris he saw Lafayette frequently and advised him on politics. Lafayette entertained the Coopers at his country estate, La Grange. Both men were invited to dinner at the King's palace, an occasion at which the King led Mme Lafayette in to dinner while Lafayette gave his arm to the Queen. In answer to the Queen's question about his favorite European countries, Cooper demonstrated that his years abroad had taught him the language of diplomacy even if he did not always use it. His answer on this occasion was "Italy, in which your Majesty was born, for its nature, and France, in which your Majesty reigns, for its society."

In Paris Cooper was made chairman of a committee of American residents to aid the cause of Polish freedom. At a dinner on the Fourth of July Cooper presided, with Lafayette on his right. An appeal for Poland was prepared to send to the American people. At the suggestion of an Englishwoman, Cooper probably asked Samuel F. B. Morse to contribute paintings for a benefit lottery.

The association with Morse, as well as Cooper's daily life in Paris, is well reflected in a letter to William Dunlap, written in March of 1832:

> I get up at eight, read the papers, breakfast at ten, sit down to the quill at ½ past ten—work till one—throw off my morning gown, draw on my boots and gloves, take a cane that Horace Greenough gave me, and go to the Louvre, where I find Morse stuck up on a high working stand, perch myself astraddle of one of the seats, and bore him just as I used to bore you when you made the memorable likeness of St. Peter. "Lay it on here, Samuel—more yellow—the nose is too short—the eye too small—damn it if I had been a painter what a picture I should have painted."—and all this stuff over again and which Samuel takes just as good naturedly as good old William. . . . Crowds get round the picture, for Samuel has made a hit in the Louvre, and I believe that people think that half the merit is mine. So much for keeping company with one's betters. At six we are at home eating a good dinner, and I manage to get a good deal out of Morse on the way too. We had Greenough up here for three months in the Autumn and then we had a good time of it. I have cut out all Kings and Princes, go to no great officers.

However, Cooper was getting tired of Europe. He told Dunlap that he could not forget that he was born an American gentleman. But almost in the same breath he complained that the American public had repudiated what he had written in the past four years. Somewhat illogically he attributed this repudiation to a group of "quasi litterateurs and soi-disant men who controlled the reviews and had no sympathy with the real taste of the public." In any case he planned to stop writing after finishing the book he had in hand. As events proved, this resolution was somewhat premature: he was to write over twenty more novels.

Some of his dissatisfaction with American reviews of his work grew out of the criticism of *The Bravo* (1831), a story representing a corrupt Venetian Senate under the dominance of the Council of Three. The Three force a man to act as a spy; then have him killed. American reviewers attacked Cooper for an alleged preference for European aristocracy. He regarded it as a picture of the corruption of that class. Morse calling one evening, found Mrs. Cooper and Susan in tears over an article in a New York paper. They felt it unjust that the man who was "scorned" in Europe for his American faith should be traduced and misrepresented at home.

Cooper himself said that no more impudent piece of empiricism had ever been palmed off on the world than the theory that the American public required American themes. In his pugnacious *Letter to His Countrymen* (1834) he came back to the subject, saying that he wrote *The Bravo* and its sequels to demonstrate that power in the hands of an elite class brought intolerable abuses. He said that he was attacked because he wrote about American principles rather than American things.

He suggested that Morse stay over until spring and travel home with the Coopers, but Morse was fed up with Europe. However, once he got back he wrote sourly to Cooper about the plight of the artist in America and about the drive for money—a pursuit which Morse was to engage in for the rest of his life. He warned, "Come prepared to find many, very many things in taste and manners different from your own good taste and manners." It was a prophetic statement.

II. TRAVELER'S RETURN

Cooper's repatriation turned him from a teller of adventure stories into a social satirist, a novelist concerned with manners. In Europe he had traveled with an awareness of the social and political scene; now he looked at America with new eyes.

The Cooper family landed in New York in November 1833 after an absence of more than six years. At first they took a house on Bleecker Street, filled it with French furniture, and employed French servants. At the same time, under the direction of Morse, Ostego Hall near Cooperstown—the wigwam of *Home as Found*—was fitted up for a permanent residence. This became Cooper's permanent home except for part of the winters when he lived on St. Marks Place in New York.

Because Irving had been given a banquet on his return, one was proposed for Cooper. Irving, despite Cooper's well-known animosity to him, set about raising money for it. However Cooper said that he must go to Washington for a talk with President Jackson, and the banquet never took place.

Then Cooper plunged into controversy and literary activity—both stemming from his European experience. The *Letter to His Countrymen*, already mentioned, was an answer to his American critics. This was followed by *The Monikins*, an attempt at satire in the Swiftian manner. The Monikins are a breed of monkeys in which the reasoning qualities of man are developed, and the bestial nature subdued. The seat of reason is in the tail. In Leaphigh (England) the social system is built upon the social-stakes theory that those with property will govern wisely and justly. The American Monikin, Brigadier Downright, speaks for Cooper:

> We have had the property-principle carried out thoroughly in our practice, and the result has shown that its chief operation is to render property as intact as possible, and the loins, and sinews, and marrows of all who possess it, its slaves.

This was a restatement of what Cooper had been saying during his stay in England. But, as Robert Spiller points out, the satire on America is even more bitter. Here was a land where the two-party system took the place of caste and where government was perverted by the money interest. Here Cooper introduces a theme which was to become dominant in his pictures of America—an attack on the leveling tendency of democracy. In Leaplow, the tails of all monikins were cut to a standard length and the residue boiled and served up to the press. Cooper was to nourish a lifelong resentment against allegations in the press that he had imbibed aristocratic prejudices abroad—as perhaps he had. The fact is that he wanted to be an American democrat with all the rights and privileges of an English aristocrat.

Most critics, even those long-suffering scholars who are able to get through Cooper's novels, agree that *The Monikins* is almost unreadable. In contrast, the three volumes of *Gleanings in Europe*, the account of his impressions of and experiences in France, England, and Italy, are delightful. Writing for once in a clear, straightforward style Cooper shows himself the shrewd, informed, and perspicacious observer. In them he makes comparisons—on the whole favorable—to American life and institutions. Because they are based upon notes and diaries kept during his travels, they largely represent his views as an expatriate. Much of the foregoing account has been based upon them.

However, as a repatriated American Cooper was much more critical of his own country in the books which followed. In 1838 there were the two related novels: *Homeward Bound* and *Home as Found*, and a non-fiction work, *The American Democrat*. The novels are primarily social criticism of the United States in the age of Jackson as seen by a repatriated landed country gentleman. Cooper had inherited some money, had married more, and had a good income from his books. He was not wealthy but he was certainly well to do, and he moved in conservative circles. In fact, he found their conservatism appalling. A fictional character, Eve Effingham, on her return from Europe speaks favorably of a republican form of government. Her American friend Grace says that a republic is odious.

> Eve had yet to learn that she had just entered into the most intolerant society, meaning purely as society, and in connection with what are usually called liberal sentiments in Christendom.

(Cooper's syntax in his novels is more cloudy than in his *Gleanings*.) This was the old Federalist society of New York, with its parallels in Philadelphia and Boston. It was the group which called Jefferson a Jacobin and Jackson a barbarian and whose spiritual descendants called Franklin Roosevelt a traitor to his class. Like Cooper himself, its members traveled abroad and had their sons educated in the English manner, their daughters drilled in French. There was even a slang term—a Haggi, which meant "the pilgrimage to Paris instead of Mecca."

Cooper's social satire, however, extends to various classes. In both novels there is an ignorant, pushing young man of the type who represents the rising class of businessmen and politicians. Eighty years before

Sinclair Lewis pictured George F. Babbitt, Cooper put him in *Homeward Bound* as Mr. Dodge; in *Home as Found* he is Aristabulus Bragg—a name looking toward Vergil Gunch and Amandus Pickerbaugh of the later satirist.

Mr. Dodge, editor of *The Active Inquirer,* is a compendium of the prejudices of the American mass. He has "the American mania for hurry." On shipboard he electioneers among the steerage passengers to try to organize one society for total abstinence and another "for the perpetration of the morals and religious principles of our forefathers." As Captain Truck says: "He has no notion of letting a man do as he has a mind to! We are full of such active inquirers in America, and I don't care how many you shoot." A zenophobe, Mr. Dodge believes that the "improper hours" at which meals are served in France have led to immorality and corruption. To him Notter Dam—as he calls it—is an irreligious structure, inferior in true taste to American churches. At the opera—the "Grand Opery"—he had listened to music which was altogether inferior to what he had heard in America. "A judicious remark! exclaimed the Captain. . . . He has acquired a taste for Zip Coon and Long-tail Blue."

Over and over Cooper satirizes the pressures for conformity. He has Mr. Dodge remark: "We eat when the majority eats; drink when the majority drinks; sleep when the majority sleeps; pray when the majority prays."

In the person of John Effingham, Cooper's alter ego, he sums it all up in a remark to a nephew: "You have been dreaming abroad, Ned Effingham, while your country has retrogressed, in all that is respectable and good, a century in a dozen years."

In *Home as Found* the satire gives way to sermonizing. The young lawyer, Aristabulus Bragg, is, if anything, more savagely portrayed than Mr. Dodge:

> An epitome of all that is good and all that is bad in a very large class of his fellow citizens. . . . With him literally, nothing is too high to be aspired to, nothing too low [lowly] to be done . . . a compound of shrewdness, impudence, common-sense, pretension, humility, cleverness, vulgarity, kind-heartedness, duplicity, selfishness, law-honesty, moral fraud, and mother-wit, mixed up with a smattering of learning and much penetration in practical things.

John Effingham, who appears also in this novel, sums Bragg up as a man who "considers life as all means and no end."

The conventional love story is all but lost in homiletics. Cooper discusses everything from table manners (Mr. Bragg's are bad) to church architecture; and from the loud voices of American girls to the variety of religious sects. Few foreign visitors have been less flattering in portraying a rootless society, ignorant of art and literature, and obsessed with making money. To Mr. Bragg the most beautiful tree is one which is cut up into a thousand feet of clear lumber. Towns pass away in a generation. To John Effingham a downtown real estate office seems to be filled with maniacs. A farm which sold for $5000 brought $25,000 the next spring, and a week later $50,000. Then a company paid $112,000 for it and auctioned off lots which brought $300,000. On the wall are maps showing estates whose prices had risen 2000 or 3000 per cent within five years. Even women and clergymen are infected with the mania for speculation; the tulip mania of Holland was trivial by comparison. "All principles are swallowed up in the absorbing desire for gain—national honor, permanent security, the ordinary rules of society, law, the constitution."

Cooper did not despair of his country; rather he saw the present as the second of three stages through which every new country passed: a pioneering period when people are mutually dependent and there are no class distinctions; a period of struggle for place and money; and one in which men and things come within the control of general and regular laws. Because of the migratory habits of Americans the second, and least attractive stage, was unusually prolonged.

It is ironic that Cooper's social ideal was essentially that of the British upper classes: a social caste based on family, land, and manners. While traveling abroad Cooper had always stressed his position as an American gentleman. In *Home as Found,* Eve Effingham believes the position of an American gentleman ought to be "the highest of all human stations, short of that of sovereigns." Her friend Grace, much impressed by titles, is startled when it is pointed out to her that Sir George Templeton's family is less ancient than hers. In a bit of the kind of American bragging he deplored in others Cooper says that the higher classes in America are the equivalent of earls, counts, dukes, nay princes. The novel is pretentiously interlarded with French phrases, not all of them used correctly—for instance *esprit de corps* applied to a servant to mean her code of behavior.

In fact, Cooper's repeated insistence on the superiority of the best American manners and taste betrays the kind of provincial self-consciousness he often satirized. He protests too much about forks and fingerbowls.

His later years were embittered by various controversies growing out of his estrangement from his own country. They present ironic contrasts. The *Letter to His Countrymen* and epistles to various periodicals grew out of insistence on his own patriotism. He resented the attacks upon the alleged aristocratic tendencies in his novels. It is understandable that the loud-mouth and often blatherskite journalism of the time should irritate him; even the mild Irving had suffered from it. More understandably, *Home as Found* stirred things up: James Watson Webb, editor of the *New York Courier and Enquirer* spoke of "Mr. Cooper's wholesale slanders upon our countrymen." Cooper's most effective answers were not his counterblasts; they were the Leatherstocking novels to which he returned. Two of them, *The Pathfinder* and *The Deerslayer*, were written after his repatriation. In addition he wrote *The History of the Navy of the United States of America.*

Another controversy in which he was involved appears in *Home as Found*. In it, John Effingham, like Cooper, owned a point of land which the villagers were long accustomed to use for ballgames and picnics. On his return from Europe Effingham-Cooper asserted his rights as a property owner against the villagers' insistence on the rights granted by custom. In the novel, Aristabulus Bragg gets the ball players off by telling them that they have a right as American citizens to play in the street despite an ordinance to the contrary. The pleasure of flouting an ordinance proves more attractive than that of playing on private property. In actual life Cooper went to law to drive off the villagers. It is not recorded that anyone pointed out a parallel to the enclosure acts in England.

Cooper also took the side of the landlords in the more important controversy over land tenure. In the Hudson River counties there were vast feudal estates going back to colonial times. Many tenants had to render various services in addition to paying rent. If a tenant gave up his lease he had to pay an alienation fine of one-tenth to one-third of the rent. Anti-rent associations were formed to combat this system, which seemed out of place in the United States. They tended to support candidates of the newly formed Whig party, and in 1846 secured enough votes to call a constitutional convention. In the new constitution clauses were included which abolished feudal tenures and limited leases to twelve years. The courts declared the alienation fines illegal. As a result the big landlords rapidly sold off their huge estates.

In a number of novels Cooper dealt with the history and social implications of the old system of landholding. Spiller calls this "the central motivating force for all his writings, the extremes of romance excepted," for the remainder of his life. In *Wyandotte* he dealt with the problem of Dutch and English land grants; in *Afloat and Ashore* he examined the social consequences of this background; and in the Littlepage trilogy (*Satanstoe, The Chainbearer* and *The Redskins*) he dealt with the landed aristocracy from the days of the early Dutch settlers down to the anti-rent war.

In all three of these novels Cooper attacks New Englanders for their manners, their pronunciation, and their egalitarian views. In *The Chainbearer* he is satiric about the New England custom of saying to a subordinate, "Johnny don't you think you'd better do that?" instead of "John, do this," or "John do that." "Mystified nonsense," Cooper calls it. The irony is that in his constant emphasis on "the usages of polite society" Cooper shows himself the true provincial. He finds any custom, e.g., shaking hands upon introduction, barbarous if it does not conform to that of upstate New York. Like many provincials he insists on the aristocracy of his own social group. Even while attacking American provincialism, he emphasizes the antiquity of American family trees and the amount of fine plate and china owned by New York aristocrats.

The *reductio ad absurdum* of these pretensions to gentility comes in *The Chainbearer* (1845). Mordaunt Littlepage, the young son of Corny, has gone to the frontier town of Ravensnest, where he owns thousands of acres. The men of the town are engaged in the dangerous task of lifting the center-beam of the new meetinghouse. If the effort fails, the beam will crush those under it. With their pikepoles the villagers heave the great beam to within a few inches of its proper position, and there it sticks. As Mordaunt tells the story:

> As yet, not a sign, look or word, had intimated either wish or expectation that I was to place myself in the ranks. I will confess to an impulse to that effect; for who can look on and see their fellow creatures straining every muscle, and not submit to human sympathy? But the recollection of military rank, and private position, had not only their claims, but their feelings.

The twenty-year-old young prig waits until the beam is about to crush the men under it, then comes to the rescue. "Hurrah!" shouted the boss, "there comes the young landlord!" One might think that Cooper was parodying a British novel, but by 1845 he was writing thus in all seriousness about the United States.

In the introduction to the third novel of the trilogy, *The Redskins* (1846), he argued not very logically that the destruction of leases in perpetuity would condemn "a numerous class of agriculturalists, either to fall back into the ranks of peasants, or to migrate." This would presumably have included "Uncle Ro" of the novel, who "had passed no less than twenty of his fifty-nine years off the American continent. He was a bachelor with nothing to do but take care of a very ample estate, which was rapidly increasing in value by the extraordinary growth of the town of New York." As with his picture of "the young landlord" Cooper was not attempting satire: Uncle Ro's method of taking care of his American estate by spending twenty years in Europe is not intended to be funny.

Thus the man who had described the inequities produced by the British landlord system could now write: "In point of fact, the relation of landlord and tenant is one entirely natural and salutory in a wealthy community." To Cooper the anti-rent agitation was a part of the leveling process he deplored. It seemed to him that everything was tending toward mediocrity, in manners, opinions, architecture—of taste in general. At various times he argued that a republic did not mean the destruction of social caste: it merely granted equal political rights to every man. In England Cooper had objected to the extreme wealth and privilege of the upper classes as contrasted with the misery and servility of the lower orders. Yet he seems not to have realized that the system of land tenure he sought to preserve tended inevitably to create a social system like that of England.

There is evidence that Cooper had become much more Europeanized than he knew. *Notions of the Americans* (1828) reflects his views on first arriving in Europe; *Home as Found* ten years later gives a very different picture. Cooper believed that his country had changed for the worse, had moved toward mediocrity under the tyranny of public opinion. "No tyranny of one, nor any tyranny of the few, is worse than this."

In *Homeward Bound* and *Home as Found* Mr. Dodge and Aristabulus Bragg are specifically referred to as typical of a large class of Americans.

Their bumptuousness, their prejudices, their lack of manners and taste, their materialism are those of their countrymen.

Yet in *Notions of the Americans* Cooper had made a great point of the good manners and taste of the average man. At a public gathering in honor of Lafayette and at a Presidential reception the fictional traveler is struck by the difficulty of distinguishing the aristocrat from the artisan. A mechanic's daughter can behave like a lady. An innkeeper may be also chief of a militia battalion, a magistrate, or even a legislator. Yet he did not think it beneath him to pick up a guest's luggage. This lack of obsequiousness was all to the good. It was less important for a society to chisel marble or gild salons than to render men more humane.

> In this particular, America is, beyond doubt, the most civilized nation in the world, inasmuch as the aggregate of her humanity, intelligence and comfort, compared with her numbers, has nothing like an equal.

It is possible of course that this idyllic America of 1826 had become during Cooper's absence the multiplied image of Mr. Dodge and Mr. Bragg. But even in the United States social change hardly operates so rapidly. It is significant that the picture of America painted by Cooper on his return was very like that of the British travelers he so much resented: Frances Trollope and Captain Hall. It was to answer them that he had written *Notions of the Americans*. Cooper had become more of an expatriate than he realized. Washington Irving, whom Cooper despised for kowtowing to Europeans, came home to write more sympathetically of his own country than did the once pugnacious patriot.

Thus Cooper could end *The Redskins* with Mr. Hugh Littlepage's remark that should the government in Washington fail to support his stand in favor of rents in perpetuity "he has the refuge of Florence open, where he can reside among other victims of oppression, with the advantage of being admired as a refuge[e] from republican tyranny."

THE ARTISTS

ALLSTON, MORSE, GREENOUGH, POWERS, STORY

I loathed you, Spoon River, I tried to rise above you,
I was ashamed of you. I despised you
As the place of my nativity.
And there in Rome, among the artists,
Speaking Italian, speaking French,
I seemed to myself at times to be free
Of every trace of my origin.
I seemed to be reaching the heights of art
And to breathe the air that the masters breathed,
And to see the world with their eyes.
But still they'd pass my work and say:
"What are you driving at, my friend?
Sometimes the face looks like Apollo's,
At others it has a trace of Lincoln's."
There was no culture, you know, in Spoon River,
And I burned with shame and held my peace.
And what could I do, all covered over
And weighted down with western soil,
Except aspire, and pray for another
Birth in the world, with all of Spoon River
Rooted out of my soul?

> Edgar Lee Masters "Archibald Higbie"
> *The Spoon River Anthology*

Masters' portrait of the American artist torn between the impenetrabilities of Europe and the cultural desert of his homeland became a kind of stereotype which appeared in the literary and art criticism of a whole generation. In letters it seemed to fit Henry James; in painting the model was Washington Allston; in sculpture Horatio Greenough or William Wetmore Story. The stereotype especially appealed to the literary and artistic rebels of the period from about 1908 to 1930—the time when H.

L. Mencken talked of "the Sahara of the Beaux Arts" and said that the Anglo-Saxon was "almost wholly devoid of aesthetic feeling." Van Wyck Brooks blamed the alleged artistic poverty of the nation on Puritanism, a utilitarian view of life, and the lack of an inherited tradition. He argued that in Europe the artist found "the premises of the artistic life taken for granted."

In her *Art in America*, 1929, Suzanne La Follette paints a bleak picture of the artistic scene in the early days of the Republic. Speaking of the artists who returned from European study with high hopes for the future of art in America:

> They were obliged to reconcile this faith as well as they could with a steady decline in quality of the collective life. The forces which dominated the Republic made for cultural aridity rather than florescence. . . . For a time, the spirit of Colonial culture survived with a few statesmen . . . ; and in the work of a few artists whose formative years it had influenced, such as Stuart, Malbone, Allston, Vanderlyn, Morse, and Sully. But the main drift was away from it, toward a debased and vulgar opportunism in politics, toward the dull and the commonplace in art. . . .
>
> America, therefore did not fulfill the hopes of its artists.

In their revolt against the artistic and literary sterility of the late nineteenth century the writer of the twenties read this quality back into the earlier history of the country. The subsequent rediscovery of Poe, Whitman, Emerson, Thoreau, Hawthorne, and Melville has largely contradicted such dim views of our literary past. But our artistic past is perhaps less well understood. The expatriation of so many painters and sculptors is assumed to be the result of the forces Brooks and others described. Nineteenth-century America is supposed to have driven out the artist or starved him physically and spiritually at home.

One fact is of course obvious: the United States had no heritage of great works of art. American painters and sculptors had to go abroad to see the treasures in the Louvre, the Uffizi and Pitti Palaces. Even such an indigenous painter as Charles Willson Peale spent several years in Italy; he named his sons Rembrandt, Titian, Raphael—what English or American artist ancestors could he have found? All this is not a valid objection to American culture; it is merely an accident of history. After all, many of the treasures in the Louvre were stolen from the rest of Europe by

Napoleon. As Horatio Greenough put it, Europe "taunted us, because there were no frescoes in our log cabins; she pronounced us unmusical because we did not sit down in the swamp with an Indian on one side, and a rattlesnake on the other."

It must also be remembered that except perhaps for Blake and Turner, England produced no painters in the nineteenth century more important than Eakins and Winslow Homer. And although such sculptors as Greenough, Powers, and Story are not now highly regarded, there is no British contemporary any better. Early nineteenth-century American sculptors sat at the feet of the Danish Thorwaldsen and imitated the work of the great Italians or of Canova. The painters tended to follow the lead of the American Benjamin West, the long-time president of the Royal Academy.

Because West, Copley, and Peale were men of the colonial period, they fall outside the scope of this study. The problem here is to examine the experiences, both at home and abroad, of the painters and sculptors in our young nation. That it was necessary for them to study in Europe is obvious. But what were their responses to this experience; what did it do to their view of the United States?

For several reasons Washington Allston became a kind of symbol of what America did to the artist. His friend and pupil, Horatio Greenough, after study abroad wished that Allston would return to England: "He always seems like an eagle tied to his roost." William Wetmore Story writing in 1855 was more bitter:

> Allston starved spiritually in Cambridgeport. . . . There was nothing congenial without, and he turned his powers inward and drained his memory dry. . . . I know no more melancholy sight than he was, so rich and beautiful a nature, in whose veins the south ran warm . . . stunted on the scant soil and withered by the cold winds of that fearful Cambridgeport.

As will appear, Story may have been trying to justify his own expatriation. Certainly the case of Allston is worth examination, for he was a central figure among American expatriates, the mentor of Irving, Leslie, Morse, and Greenough.

Washington Allston, the son of a South Carolina planter who had served under Francis Marion, was born November 5, 1779. His father died when the boy was four and his mother remarried. As a youth Washington showed an interest in painting. To prevent such an ungentlemanly career, the step-father sent the boy to Newport to prepare for college. Here Allston took lessons from a Mr. King, a compass and quadrant maker, who also painted portraits. In due course he entered Harvard, where he devoted his leisure hours to drawing and to courting the sister of William Ellery Channing. He got engaged to the young lady and graduated from college with honors.

Allston was an easy-going fellow who liked dancing and the theater. After college he went back to Charleston, where he painted portraits. Finally in 1801 his family gave in and permitted him to go abroad to study art. In London he presented drawings to the Royal Academy in order to gain admission. West, then president, praised the young man's work. Allston, who had been prejudiced against West, came to regard him as the first among London painters; the majority of portrait painters then were "the damndest stupid wretches that ever disgraced a profession."

After a brief stay in London, he went to Paris, where Napoleon had filled the Louvre with the spoils of Europe. "Titian, Tintorett [sic], and Paul Veronese absolutely enchanted me . . . ," wrote Allston. In Paris he became an intimate of the American painter Vanderlyn, a protégé of Aaron Burr's. Allston left Paris to tour Italy, stopping in Siena to learn the language, then spending a year in Florence.

In 1805 he went to Rome, where he said he and Vanderlyn were the only American students. Vanderlyn told how he, Allston, Turner, and Fenimore Cooper frequented the Caffè Greco, where were to be seen Thorwaldsen, Flaxman, Shelley, Byron, and Keats. This was rather re- markable because none of the three poets reached Rome until long after 1805. Cooper did not get there until 1829. However, Allston did meet Coleridge, who became an intimate friend. Allston later wrote:

> To no other man do I owe so much intellectually as to Mr. Coleridge, with whom I became acquainted in Rome, and who has honored me with his friendship for more than five and twenty years. . . . I am almost tempted to dream that I have once listened to Plato in the groves of the Academy.

Allston painted two portraits of Coleridge, one of which now hangs in the National Gallery, and which both Wordsworth and Coleridge thought the best portrait of the poet.

In 1809 Allston returned to Boston and at long last married Ann Channing, who was then thirty-one. The morning after the wedding a friend found Allston at work at his usual time in the Brattle Street studio. Two years later Allston, his wife, and his pupil Samuel F. B. Morse sailed for England. Six months later another American pupil, Charles Leslie, joined them. Of the three only Leslie became an expatriate.

In London Allston associated chiefly with other Americans. Morse said, ". . . he visits me every evening, and our conversation is generally upon the inexhaustible subject of our divine art, and upon home, which is next in our thoughts. . . ." This suggests that Allston, like Morse, was not temperamentally an expatriate. In one of his letters Allston wrote: "Next to my own, I love England, the land of my adoption. I should, indeed, be ungrateful did I not love a country from which I never received other than kindness."

Certainly he enjoyed considerable success as a painter. Sir George Beaumont, Wordsworth's patron and an amateur painter, offered £200 for a painting for the parish church at Ashby-de-la Zouch. "The Dead Man Revived" won the British Institution prize of 200 guineas. After the War of 1812 Thomas Sully and James McMurtrie raised $3500 to purchase the painting for the Academy of the Fine Arts in Philadelphia.

Just after winning the prize Allston was ill with digestive troubles for some weeks. Despite the fact that Coleridge helped to nurse him, Allston sufficiently recovered to go to Clifton, near Bristol, accompanied by his wife, Leslie, and Morse. Here he painted the second and best of his portraits of Coleridge.

On their return to London, Mrs. Allston died suddenly. At her funeral the only people present were the Americans Morse, Leslie, and John Howard Payne. Following his wife's death Allston moved in with Morse and Leslie.

During his last years in London Allston began the mammoth work to which he devoted the rest of his life: "Belshazzar's Feast." By 1818 he was so homesick that he decided to return to Boston. Had he stayed in London he would probably have succeeded West as President of the Royal Academy.

Reaching Boston Harbor on a beautiful evening in October, he jotted down his thoughts:

> Another thought recurs, that I had returned to a mighty empire; that I was in the very waters which the gallant Constitution had first broken; whose building I saw while at college, and whose 'slaugh-

ter-breathing brass,' to use a quotation from Cotton Mather's 'Magnalia,' but now 'grew hot and spoke her name among the nations.'

The following spring he wrote to Leslie expressing the hope that he too
would come home. Allston himself spent the remaining twenty-five years
of his life in America. It is this period of his life that gave rise to the legend of the baleful effect of America on the artist. Allston's biographer,
Jared Flagg, speaking of "Belshazzar's Feast," wrote, ". . . in bringing
it to America, he brought it away from all stimulating and reassuring influences." However, the record does not entirely support this view. In
America Allston had congenial, cultured friends, and the nation of the
1820's and '30's was very ready to welcome and support him. The baleful
psychological forces are more difficult to assess, but there is evidence that
these existed in the man himself.

In America there were usually two avenues open to a painter: murals
for government buildings, and portraits. There were few wealthy patrons
with great mansions as in England. Allston did not regard portrait painting as "high art" and there were few places large enough to display the
huge allegorical canvases in the West style. When West sent his "Christ
Healing the Sick" (1816) as a gift to the Pennsylvania Hospital, a
special building had to be built for it. Sully's "Washington at the Passage
of the Delaware" (1819), painted for the Capitol of North Carolina,
proved too large for the building.

However there was an opportunity to paint murals for the new capitol
at Washington. Trumbull had done four historical panels for the rotunda,
and four remained to be filled. Gulian C. Verplanck, Chairman of the
Committee of the House on Public Buildings, wanted Allston to do the
paintings. Verplanck wanted historical scenes. Allston, saying that he
wasn't good on battle scenes, recommended Morse and Vanderlyn. He
could think of nothing in civil history worthy of "high art." Instead he
suggested scenes from the Scripture. "But I fear this is a forlorn hope.
Yet why should it be? This is a Christian land, and the Scriptures belong
to no country but to man." However, he was still occupied with "Belshazzar's Feast" although it had been nearly done when he brought it home
twelve years earlier. A subscription of $10,000 had been raised to enable
him to finish the picture, but he said it had not been in his power to do so.

Despite the fact that he was in debt, Allston also declined Everett's
suggestion that he do a historical painting for an association in Charles-

ton, S.C., on the theme of the unfurling of the American flag by the U.S. Minister to Mexico when he was about to be attacked by a mob. Again Allston used Belshazzar as an excuse. Again in 1841 he wrote to Mrs. Channing: "With respect to the portrait I had promised . . . it will be wholly out of my power to undertake it with any hope of success until I shall have completed 'Belshazzar.' " In that year Lord Morpeth, on a visit to Boston, spoke of the pleasure his sister, the Duchess of Sutherland, took in Allston's "Uriel in the Sun," which she owned. She wanted another picture, and his lordship suggested "The Court of Titania." Allston made a sketch, but stipulated that he would accept the commission (£500 for a 4 by 6 foot painting) only on condition that he first finish "Belshazzar."

The usual explanation for Allston's inability to finish the painting is that he found the American environment stultifying. But it is also possible to see in his excuses to undertake other work some sort of psychic block, one which may in part have grown out of his sense of guilt at accepting the subscription of $10,000 from ten Bostonian patrons of the arts. In any case Allston made enough out of other paintings to pay back the money. Morse hoped to make enough money out of the telegraph to set Allston free from money worries. The contemporary art historian, William Dunlap, suggested that Allston spent too much of his time in social life, a suggestion which upset the painter. However, there is some evidence for this, especially after his second marriage in 1830. An epicure, he delighted in talking about wonderful dinners in Paris.

In his biography of Allston, Edgar P. Richardson, suggests another reason for the difficulties with "Belshazzar": Allston, after his return to America shifted from the dramatic style to the meditative. This change is linked to that from Neo-Classic to Romantic sensibility. In both theory and practice Allston was much influenced by the theories of his friend Coleridge. Thus of "Belshazzar" Richardson writes, "The aim of his last revision was to create a tone of hushed and tragic solemnity . . . instead of the dramatic conception of the early sketches." As Allston wrote in his *Lectures on Art*, "Human or poetic truth is truth which may be said to exist in and for the mind, as distinguished from the truth of things in the natural or external world." It was essentially this Romantic doctrine that Allston followed in the paintings of his later life.

As to the effect of "fearful Cambridgeport," there is Allston's letter to Cogdell in 1827: "I suppose you have heard of our Exhibition here. . . .

I assure you I have seen worse in London." He was pleased with the "astonishing success it has had with the public." In 1839 there was an exhibition of forty-seven of his works—nineteen of which were done after his return to America. There are at least twenty-two other pictures of this period. The English art historian, Mrs. Anna Jameson, who visited Boston in 1838, regarded Allston's American paintings as his most original and distinctive work.

This opinion is shared by Edgar Richardson, who argues that Allston's landscape reveries upon nature, done after his return to America, represent the aspect of his art most appealing to modern taste.

> As his art grew quieter the mood of his landscape changed: after the drama of the early works came in his old age a quieter reverie on the notes of wonder and solitude. To achieve this in pictures like *The Moonlit Landscape* (1819) or *The Flight of Florimell* (1819) . . . he developed a style of controlled luminosity and deep resonances of tone that set new standards of subtlety and atmospheric richness in American painting. . . . He thus found his own way to the new mode of perception which, between 1820 and 1830, became the problem of creation for the most advanced minds in painting—for Constable and Corot, Delacroix and Turner.
>
> . . . through the example of his work and through one of his early pupils, Samuel F. B. Morse, who became the first head of the National Academy of Design in New York City, his influence made itself felt. He was the pioneer of an art mood in America. The note of grave, brooding reverie which he struck became one of the characteristic tones of American painting in Page and Quidor, Rimmer and Fuller, La Farge and Vedder, it is heard throughout the nineteenth century. The vein of feeling opened by him proved to be a rich one.

Richardson argues that the very lack of an active professional tradition in America forced gifted artists to think out the meaning and purpose of their art. Some of them like Poe and Allston made fundamental discoveries in advance of European practice, as did Whitman at a later period. Certainly Allston freed himself from the academic, nineteenth-century theory based on neoclassicism that color and light were minor and unimportant; that only form counted. Just as Emerson, Thoreau, Hawthorne, and Melville went to Shakespeare and the seventeenth century for models of literary style, Allston had learned from Titian, Veronese, and Tintoretto "the poetry of color." It was this lesson he put to use in Cambridge.

Furthermore, during these later years he published verse and began a book on his theories of art. The five completed chapters were published in 1850 with the title *Lectures on Art and Poems*. His philosophical approach to the subject does much to justify Coleridge's estimate of Allston in 1818 as a man of "high and rare genius . . . whether I contemplate him in the character of a Poet, a Painter, or a philosophic Analyst." Certainly the legend fostered by Story and Henry James, and repeated by Van Wyck Brooks, that in the unsympathetic atmosphere Allston's mind "rotted away" is obviously false. All the evidence points to the conclusion that he found the American atmosphere congenial and that he did his best work after repatriation.

Unlike Allston, who stoutly maintained his faith in America, Samuel Morse continually found fault with his native land. Possibly influenced by his association with Cooper, Morse on his return to America in 1841 complained bitterly of the drive for money. He told a pupil that a housedog lived better than a painter in America. The irony was that Morse himself was infected with the desire to get rich. With his brother he had invented a fire-engine pump; he pioneered in experiments with the daguerreotype process (Matthew Brady was a pupil) and devoted his mature years to promoting his invention of the telegraph, engaging in a long series of quarrels and lawsuits. There was enough money for all in the development of the new invention, but those involved fought like hogs in a trough.

It was not repatriation which embittered Morse; he had also taken a sour view of Europe. Brought up in a pious household, he found much in Europe to disgust him. His mother had been loath to let him go abroad for she believed that all Americans in Europe except West and Allston were "dissipated infidels." In Europe Morse would not travel on the Sabbath and refused to take off his hat at religious processions. He found Catholic chants "monstrous." Thinking that "man is led astray by his imagination more than by any other faculties," he argued that it was "dangerous to his best interests" to have paintings in churches. In his view America did not need theaters; it had so many other topics of conversation. Italy, he believed, was rotten to the core. These were not the opinions of a young man on his first visit; they were those of a man of thirty-eight who was studying in Europe for a second time.

On his first return to America Morse's difficulties as a painter were more than a little due to his failure to understand the conditions and needs of the young nation. As Edgar Richardson puts it:

> Samuel F. B. Morse (1791–1872), like Vanderlyn, illustrates the tragedy of an observer, a realist by temperament, who was carried away by the theory of ideal art. Morse brought back from his years in London an excellent coloristic technique; yet he wandered unhappily from city to city, up and down the Atlantic coast, in search of portrait commissions. . . . He was tormented by the feeling that the only work worthy of a true artist was to create great imaginative compositions. No one ordered such pictures, however; nor did they come out of Morse's own mind. He had time and opportunity, during the intervals between portraits, to paint whatever he wished. Instead of pouring forth a stream of imaginative compositions he sat idle, and felt unhappy.

It is worth noting that in one year of portrait painting in Charleston Morse made $9000 above expenses.

Even imaginative painting could be profitable. Rembrandt Peale's huge picture, "The Court of Death" (11 feet 6 inches by 23 feet 5 inches), painted in 1820, was exhibited in various cities and brought in admission returns of $8000. There were no ducal palaces to house such a picture, but there was an interested public. Even to a modern critic like Richardson, it "is by no means an inconsiderable painting; it is monumental, graceful in detail, subtle in its chiaroscuro."

Perhaps more important, these painters trained in Europe helped to train a younger generation of American painters of considerable importance. Charles Willson Peale after two abortive attempts to establish an art school helped to found the Academy of the Fine Arts in Philadelphia. Here were trained artists who learned to use the American scene, men like Thomas Doughty (1793–1850) and Caleb Bingham (1811–1879). William Sidney Mount (1807–1868) studied at the National Academy of Design, founded by Morse. And the sculptor Horatio Greenough acknowledged his debt to Washington Allston.

Far from being the artistic wasteland described by later critics, America in the 1820's and '30's was enthusiastic about painting and engravings made from paintings. As Edgar Richardson puts it:

The generation that matured men like Lincoln and Emerson cannot be said to have failed to meet the challenge to create a new imaginative life in the vast new land which was growing increasingly remote from European traditions of culture. The country poured its energies into painting, to such a degree that the English critic, Mrs. Anna Jameson, traveling here in 1837–1838, found painters literally everywhere.

In 1834 William Dunlap was able to produce a two-volume work, *A History of the Rise and Progress of the Arts of Design in the United States.* Horatio Greenough, writing in 1843, said of America: "Artists have arisen in numbers; the public gives its attentions to their productions; their labors are liberally rewarded."

Like Cooper and Irving a number of these painters, even those such as Thomas Cole (1801–1848), who studied in Europe, discovered the American landscape and the frontier. On the one hand was the "Hudson River School," including Cole and Doughty, who put Washington Irving's country onto canvas; on the other were painters like Mount and Bingham, who discovered the landscape and the human types of the region beyond the Alleghenies. James Audubon went far beyond the earlier painters of American birds: William Bartram and James Wilson. And a Philadelphia portrait painter, George Catlin, became the great recorder of the American Indian.

Nineteenth-century America was enthusiastic not only about painting but also about sculpture. As Albert Gardner in *Yankee Stonecutters* has pointed out, the Revolution and the War of 1812 produced the symbolic heroes of the republic and the example of Greece and Rome furnished a precedent for memorializing these heroes in marble. The classical education then in vogue may have contributed to this taste: the history and legend of Greece and Rome were more familiar to Americans than were the Middle Ages or the Renaissance. American place names, the Romes, Athenses, Troys, Syracuses, Ithacas, are testimony to this veneration for the ancient world. Furthermore plaster casts of famous busts and statues were imported. Most Americans had to get their ideas of famous paintings from prints or poor copies, but they could early see respectable copies of Greek statues or busts by Houdon. And a print or a drawing can give a better idea of the Elgin marbles or of the Venus de Milo than of a Titian or a Rubens.

As a result state legislatures and the Congress appropriated large sums for sculpture to adorn the state and national capitol buildings. As early as 1817 the state of North Carolina commissioned the Italian sculptor, Canova, to do a huge statue of Washington for the State House at Raleigh. At a time when the budget was $90,000 a year, the state paid $11,000 for the statue. This figure in Roman armor was unveiled four years later in a capital city with a population of two thousand.

However, by 1832 when Congress appropriated money for a statue of Washington for the Rotunda of the national Capitol, the commission was given to an American, Horatio Greenough. As Gardner says, "From that time forward political figures enter as an important factor in deciding and forwarding the careers of almost every American sculptor. These happy artists, once their reputations were established, had powerful statesmen to push them forward. They reveled in incredibly lush commissions from cities, states, and nation." Powers received $19,000 for a monument to Webster in Boston; Story was paid $40,000 for one to Chief Justice Marshall. And so it went: Randolph Rogers received $50,000 for a Civil War monument in Rhode Island and $75,000 for one in Michigan.

Despite these commissions at home the sculptors tended to become expatriates. For this there was an economic reason. The nineteenth-century sculptor modeled his figures in clay or plaster, then turned them over to stonecutters who carved them in marble. By the use of proportional compasses the workmen could make the figure any desired size. Powers told a visitor that he paid his poorest Italian workmen $0.50 and his finest $4 a day; whereas in New York a man could earn twice the latter sum for carving weeping willows on tombstones. Powers' total bill for workmen came to $15 a day; another American, Harriet Hosmer, kept twenty stone-cutters at work reproducing her designs. And as Powers told a visitor, he could maintain a family in Florence at much less than in the United States.

Then there was the problem of models. For some reason, nineteenth-century taste dictated that statues should be undraped, whereas figures in paintings should be clothed. Thus West and his imitators turned out biblical and historical paintings, and Leslie set a fashion for scenes from literature. On the other hand the sculptors turned out a succession of Venuses, Eves, nymphs, Greek slaves, white captives, etc. The statuary room of the staid Boston Athenaeum between 1850 and 1860 bore a striking resemblance to a night in the harem.

This sculptural emphasis on nudity very early ran afoul of American puritan prejudices, but it also helped to make sculpture a matter of public interest. One of the earliest American sculptors to be both the victim and beneficiary of this puritan prurience was Horatio Greenough. Greenough was not by temperament an expatriate. In many ways his functional theories of art and architecture give him a place in cultural history similar to that of his friend Emerson. Both emphasised the American vernacular tradition.

Born in 1805 of a well-to-do Boston family, Greenough became interested in sculpture through a marble figure of Phocion in his father's garden. He tried carving in chalk and later in plaster. A neighbor sent him to William S. Shaw, director of the Boston Athenaeum, who, recognizing the boy's talent, allowed him to make plaster casts in the fine arts room. M. Binon, a French sculptor then in Boston, let Greenough work at his side, and Alpheus Carey, a stonecutter, showed him how to carve in marble.

On his father's insistence he entered Harvard at the time when Everett, Ticknor, Cogswell, and Bancroft were on the faculty. Cogswell had brought back casts and valuable drawings, some of which he lent to Greenough, who later said that Cogswell more than anyone else helped him to fix his purpose to become a sculptor. In his sophomore year Greenough took up the study of anatomy. In his junior year he was introduced to Washington Allston, then fifty-five. Greenough attended those evenings when Allston benignly presided in his studio or on a moonlit piazza, and where he met Edmund T. and Richard Henry Dana, Sr. In later years Greenough said, "Allston was to me father in what concerned my progress of every kind. He taught me first how to discriminate, how to think, how to feel."

However, it was of course necessary for a sculptor to study abroad. The Harvard authorities permitted Greenough to sail in 1825 before the end of his last year, sending him his diploma later.

From France he wrote enthusiastically to his brother Henry, saying that he had seen an Andrea del Sarto, a Rembrandt, a Bernini, and a Murillo—artists who had been familiar names, but only names. He planned to enquire for situations that would suit Henry, for "you should be an artist." In Rome Horatio was helped by Thorwaldsen, to whom he had letters of introduction. However, within the year he contracted malaria and had to return home.

In America he associated with Morse, Allston, Gulian Verplanck, William Dunlap, Thomas Cole, and William Cullen Bryant. In 1828 he was elected an honorary member of the American Academy of Fine Arts, and from 1829 to 1838 held the title of Professor of Sculpture. At a levee at the White House he met John Quincy Adams, who sat for a portrait bust. Although Adams did not especially care for the result, he asked Greenough to do one of John Adams. Greenough also modeled Chief Justice Marshall, who was sitting for the painter Harding. Robert Gilmore, a rich Baltimore merchant, who owned one of the best art collections in the country, commissioned Greenough to do busts of himself and his wife.

Nevertheless, Greenough complained that there was no atmosphere for art and wished that Allston would return to England. Greenough himself went back to Italy in 1828, financed by a loan of $1000 furnished by Boston merchants. Although it was then the custom for sculptors to model in clay and hire stonecutters to translate the design into marble, Greenough spent three months in the quarries at Carrara learning to work in stone. He was determined to follow the example of the Greeks and of Michelangelo. Even when he entrusted the blocking out to workmen, he put the finishing touches on his own statues.

Greenough's experience in Italy is a good example of the dilemma of the expatriate artist of the nineteenth century. Naturally the works of art in Italy delighted him. Florence was "the most inspiring place in the world." When his brother Henry came over in 1829, Horatio wrote to him in quarantine: "The Carnival will be in its glory when you arrive. I've engaged for a large masked ball at Lord Barghersh's on the sixteenth. We'll teach you, my boy, how to combine the *utili* with the *dulci*." However, he did not care for contemporary Italian art, and by 1831 was speaking of "this beautiful but unhappy country." On the one hand were "those gigantic structures born of the wealth of Europe and of Florentine genius and will"; but why had three centuries of regular government ended "in a dwindled population, *political* nullity and social corruption"?

He was proud of the work of his fellow Americans. At the Academy of Fine Arts he had studied with Morse, Cole, John Cranch, John Gore, and other compatriots. In the spring and summer of 1831, these men and the two Greenoughs took a house together. To Allston he wrote asking for a painting to demonstrate "how nobly *we American apples swim.*" He regarded himself as "a pioneer of a band which I doubt not will hereafter enrich and beautify the cities of the Republic."

In 1831, six years before Emerson declared that "we have listened too long to the courtly muses of Europe," Greenough wrote a letter, published in the *New York Mirror*, in which he said that American scholars "have looked so much abroad for salvation in letters arts and manners that they have not only overlooked home but unfitted all under their influence for judging impartially of anything American."

When Cooper came to Florence, Horatio asked permission to make a bust. This proved so successful that Cooper commissioned a group in marble—"Chanting Cherubs." As has been noted (p. 81) Cooper believed that he was promoting the cause of American sculpture. Greenough in turn was very grateful for the much needed commission. "Fenimore Cooper saved me from despair," he wrote. "He employed me as I wished to be employed; with a commission for original work and has, up to this moment, been a father to me in kindness."

When the Cherubs reached Boston, Allston praised the work, but a number of people and some newspapers expressed the view that their nakedness was immoral. For a brief time aprons were tied on them, but were removed after newspaper ridicule. George Ticknor sent a present of $1200. In New York the Cherubs caused less commotion but some disappointment. A friend of the sculptor wrote

> The Cherubs failed here, owing it is said to their name. Our literal folk actually supposed that they were to sing, and when the man turned them round in order to exhibit them in a different position they exclaimed, "Ah, he is going to wind them up: we shall hear them now."

The writer added: "I wish the scene of my story lay anywhere but in New York, but it cannot be helped, and I must continue to consider my townsmen as a race of cheating, lying, money-getting blockheads."

At Cooper's suggestion Greenough spent the winter of 1831 in Paris, where Cooper persuaded Lafayette to sit for a portrait bust. Two years later Greenough began his most famous piece of work, the immense statue of George Washington. Allston, hearing that Congress was about to appropriate money for such a project, had urged Webster to award the commission to Greenough. Cooper also used his influence.

This project on which he worked for eight years brought Greenough face to face with the dilemma of the expatriate who loves his homeland. Early in 1833 he wrote to Cooper, who had just returned to America:

> Still I see many obstacles to study and exercise of my arts in the States. The choice of a country in this case amounts to a choice of life. Like the ass between 2 bundles of hay I cast my eye from continent to continent and sigh that I can't plant one foot in the States and the other on the boot—chisel here with one hand and hold up to the christening font there with the other.

Greenough was definitely homesick. Not only had Cooper left, but so had Morse and Cole. Emerson visited Florence in that year and Greenough introduced him to Landor, but despite a stream of British and American visitors to his studio, Greenough wrote to Allston: "I beg you will pity me as a sojourner in a land of strangers. I am a poor land-bird at sea . . . a few years and I shall I trust sit by you and smoak and look out of a window at the trees and sky of Cambridge." On a visit home in 1836 he found everything in America more to his mind than he had expected, and even thought of settling down and dreaming "no more of foreign lands, or of any advantages not enjoyed here."

But he still had several more years of work to do on his "Washington." The Congressional appropriation had been $20,000, and although Greenough sometimes complained of delayed payments, he was able to live in some style. At a total cost of $1 a day he kept two horses and a groom. In 1837 his fortunes further improved through his marriage to the wealthy Elizabeth Gore, a sister of the painter John Gore, who had been one of Greenough's early companions in Rome. "She is my only comfort in this exile, apart from my profession," wrote Greenough.

In 1840 he received another government commission for a large group, "The Rescue," which now stands on the east stair of the Capitol. In three years, in addition to his work on Washington, he put into marble or clay some thirty-three pieces, and finished three others. When Hiram Powers came to Florence, Greenough introduced him to the chief artists and lent him workmen and marble.

When in 1841 the "Washington" was finished, Cooper, with his low view of native culture, warned:

As respects your statue, talk not, touch not, think not. You are in a country in which every man swaggers and talks, knowledge or no knowledge; brains or no brains; taste or no taste. They are all *ex nato* connoisseurs, politicians, religionists, and every man's equal, and all men's betters. In short you are to expect your own matured and classical thoughts will be estimated by the same rules they estimate pork, and rum, and cotton. Luckily you get a pretty good sum, and the statue that has cost them $20,000 may stand some chance. Alas! my good Greenough, this is no region of poets, so sell your wares and shut your ears.

Cooper's prophecy was partly fulfilled. Although the newspapers were generally favorable, the public did not approve of the "Washington." Morse liked it, and Emerson called it "simple and grand . . . it greatly contents me." However, jokers suggested that Washington's upraised hand was pointing to the Patent Office, where his clothes were. In the past Washington had been sculptured in a Roman toga by Canova for North Carolina and by Chantry for Boston. The latter had been derided by such a connoisseur as Davy Crockett, who preferred the buff and blue of a statue at Richmond.

Part of the trouble was that the light in the Rotunda was bad. When Greenough saw it in 1842 he said he felt like a man who had left his child blooming in the evening, and found it the next day pinched and worn with disease. He suggested moving the statue outside and building a temporary shed over it. His idea was to try out various designs for housing the work. One evening before the move was made, he experimented with illuminating the figure by torchlight in the presence of a group which included Calhoun and Emerson. The latter, who found it an exhilarating spectacle, advised against removing the statue from the Rotunda. Nevertheless, Greenough, with the help of John Quincy Adams, got Congressional approval for the move and had himself named to supervise the operation. For three years there was a temporary shelter; then the statue stood outside until 1908, when it was moved to the Smithsonian, a building Greenough had deplored because of its medieval confusions.

The nudity of the statue of Washington was not a neoclassic imitation like Canova's "Napoleon"; rather it exemplified Greenough's home-grown theory of functionalism in art and architecture. Greenough was far and away the most original thinker among nineteenth-century American artists. Calling himself a Yankee stonecutter, he wrote his "Stonecutter's Creed"

> By beauty I mean the promise of function.
> By action I mean the presence of function.
> By character I mean the record of function.

Like his friend Emerson, who sought transcendental meanings in the meal in the firkin, the milk in the pan, Greenough wrote: "There are threads of relation which lead me from my specialty to the specialties of other men. . . . I lay my artistic dogma at the feet of science; I test it by the traditional lore of handicraft . . . ." His practice and theory were both in sharp contrast to the current sentimentalized imitation of the baroque in art and of pseudo-medievalism in architecture. His Washington, whatever its faults, is strong and austere. There is none of the softness and sentimentality of Powers' more famous "Greek Slave," none of the fussy quality of Story's "Cleopatra." There is a kind of archaic vigor in the "Washington," the kind of thing characteristic of American folk art.

But Greenough was not a folk artist; instead, along with Emerson and Thoreau, he tried to fuse the things of everyday life into a transcendental philosophy. Like the designers of the New England meeting house and the clipper ship he scorned embellishment. He wrote:

> I understand, therefore, by embellishment, THE INSTINCTIVE EFFORT TO DISGUISE ITS INCOMPLETENESS, EVEN AS GOD'S COMPLETENESS IS TO INFANT SCIENCE DISGUISED . . . .
>
> I base my opinion of embellishment upon the hypothesis that there is not one truth in religion, another in mathematics, and a third in physics and in art; but that there is one truth, even as one God, and that organization is his utterance . . . .
>
> The normal development of beauty is through action to completeness. The invariable development of embellishment and decoration is more embellishment and more decoration . . . but where is the first downward step? I maintain that the first downward step was *the introduction of the first inorganic, non-functional element, whether of shape or color.* If I be told that such a system as mine would produce *nakedness,* I accept the omen. In nakedness I behold the majesty of the essential, instead of the trappings of pretension.

Like Emerson he found the laws of God in the world around him.

> There is no conceivable function which does not obey an absolute law. The approximation to that law in material, in parts, in their form, color and relations, is the measure of freedom of obedience to God in life . . . .
>
> I call, therefore, upon science in all its branches, to arrest the tide of sensuous and arbitrary embellishment . . . . The craving for completeness will then obtain in its normal food in results, not the opiate and deadening stimulus of decoration. Then will structure and its dependent sister arts emerge from the stand-still of *ipse dixit* and, like the ship, the team, the steam-engine, proceed through phases of development towards a response to need.

It may well be, as Greenough's biographer suggests, that the limitation of his "Washington" as a work of art is that it is an intellectualized rather than a plastic conception. It is important to note that the artistic theories on which the work is based are not borrowed European concepts, but are characteristically American doctrines stemming from Allston and Emerson.

It is also important that, despite the jibes of the uninformed, the American government in the 1830's and '40's commissioned the work, paid $20,000 for it, and tried to house it appropriately. That same government commissioned and paid for Greenough's "The Rescue." In 1840 the Boston Athenaeum showed seven of Greenough's works. In the same year he was unanimously elected to the faculty of the Academy of Fine Arts in Florence, with the honorary rank of Associate Professor of Sculpture. In Boston he was elected a Fellow of the American Academy of Arts and Sciences. The American apple was swimming pretty well on both sides of the Atlantic.

Back in Europe the Greenoughs underwent a series of hydropathic treatments, a system of therapy which assumed that nature was the only curative agency—a theory which appealed to Horatio. "Nature," he wrote "is merely another word for *God in Creation*." In February 1846 he published in the *United States Magazine and Democratic Review* four essays on art and politics. The fourth of these, "By Their Fruits Ye Shall Know Them," contrasted the beneficial social effects of republics with the tyranny of empires.

In 1851 he finally left Florence to settle in America, declaring that democratic institutions were "more favorable to a natural, healthful growth of art than any hotbed culture whatever." He had left in disgust after some Austrian troops were quartered in his house. His appeal to the American consul had got them out but the incident reinforced his patriotism. He also believed that conditions were becoming more favorable for the artist in the United States. To Bryant he wrote:

> I thank God from the bottom of my heart that I have once more put foot on my own, my native soil and I hope though now arrived at the "mezzo del cammin di nostra vita" to be of some use here both in illustrative art and in structure for here I mean now to stay.

Yet he had the expatriate's characteristic ambivalence. That same year he wrote, "I have not yet given up all thoughts of remaining in America. If I go away it will be to enjoy my leisure and my books."

One of his projects if he stayed was an imposing monument to James Fenimore Cooper. Irving was chairman of the committee. However, during a series of lectures in Boston Greenough was stricken with "brain fever" and died at the age of forty-seven. The *Home Journal* memorialized him as "the highest artistic authority in the country."

Greenough's theory and practice were too far ahead of his time to please the more sentimental nineteenth-century taste. The sculptor who best satisfied that taste on both sides of the Atlantic was Hiram Powers, a self-taught mechanic from the frontier town of Cincinnati, Ohio. For one thing he made by far the most famous statue of the period—"The Greek Slave." It was the sensation of the Great Crystal Palace exhibition of 1851. Queen Victoria and Prince Albert admired it and Elizabeth Barrett Browning wrote a sonnet apostrophizing the "fair stone." Powers made six copies of this very naked lady, with slight alterations in the position of the chain, and sold them for prices averaging $4000 each. On a tour of the United States the original grossed $23,500 from admissions charges. The debate over the morality of the work did not injure its fame. In Cincinnati a committee of clergymen gave their approval for its exhibition.

Edward Everett wrote, ". . . our country has much to boast of in Mr. Powers; we hope he will have as much to be grateful for to his country." Hawthorne in his *Italian Notebooks* devoted much space to Powers, and the sculptor Kenyon's studio in *The Marble Faun* is drawn partly from that of Powers, partly from W. W. Story's.

When Hawthorne met Powers in 1858, he described the sculptor as "very American in character." This estimate is almost an understatement. Powers had been born in 1805 in Woodstock, Vermont. When he was fourteen, his family took a flatboat down the Ohio to Cincinnati, where they started to farm. When his father died of a fever, Hiram got a job in a produce store, then one in an organ factory. While there he made toys and devised a machine to cut clock wheels twice as fast as those made in Connecticut. In a museum he saw a cast of Houdon's bust of Washington—the first work of art he had ever seen. He went home and made a bust in beeswax. When a Frenchman opened a museum in Cincinnati, Powers helped to repair some damaged busts. He took home one of the evangelist, Lorenzo Dow, and converted him into a cannibal king. In true Mark Twain style, the Frenchman added a body; the concoction was then advertised as the embalmed body of a maneater from the South Seas, secured at immense expense. Powers also worked out an inferno patterned after Dante's description, and, dressed as the Devil, he gave bystanders a shock with a homemade electrical wand—thus anticipating an American Legionnaire at a convention.

Nicholas Longworth, seeing the display, offered to buy the museum, or to send Powers to Europe to study art, or to Washington for the purpose of doing busts of public figures. Powers accepted the last alternative. In Washington he modeled busts of Jackson, John Quincy Adams, Calhoun, Van Buren, Marshall, and others. Jackson was at first reluctant to pose, for he remembered that a sculptor had nearly smothered Jefferson while making a life mask. However, Powers assured him that posing would involve no such hazards. Jackson insisted on stark realism:

> Make me as I am, Mr. Powers, and be true to nature always, and in everything. It's the only safe rule to follow. I have no desire to *look* young as long as I *feel* old: and then it seems to me, although I do not know much about sculpture, that the only object in making a bust is to get a representation of the man who sits, that it be as nearly as possible a perfect likeness. If he has no teeth why then make him with teeth?

Senator Preston of South Carolina, impressed with the young man's work, presented $10,000 to send him to Europe for study. Powers took with him the clay bust of Jackson and set about carving it in marble. Although Powers later claimed that he carved four of the busts of

American statesmen, some authorities think the one of Jackson the only one entirely by his own hand. In any case it is perhaps his best piece of work.

Powers was thirty-two when he sailed for Europe. The voyage was an exciting one. In a letter home he reported sighting a sea serpent, which proved to be the skeleton of a ship. Then his own ship caught fire from an overturned candle in a stateroom, and it leaked so much that constant pumping was necessary. In Paris his wife—for like a good American he had already married—caught varioloid smallpox. Nevertheless he got to Florence, where Horatio Greenough gave him a hand.

Powers had arrived in the heyday of American sculptors in Florence. Between the time of his arrival and Greenough's departure in 1851, thirteen others followed: Clivenger, Brown, Ives, Mozier, Stephenson, Story, Galt, Randolph Rogers, Hart, Richard Greenough, Akers, Barbee, and Bartholomew. Thomas Crawford was settled in Rome.

Powers soon proved to be a shrewd businessman of the type that gave Yankees a rather unsavory reputation among Europeans. When customers did not pay for work Powers put their busts on a shelf marked "Delinquents." When one man refused to pay for a bust on the grounds that it was not a good likeness, Powers put it in a cardboard prison with the legend "For Debt." The head was so good a likeness that everyone recognized the sitter—who was shamed into paying up.

Less admirable were his dealings with Miner K. Kellog, who claimed that he had lent money to Powers during his early years in Florence. Later on Kellog managed the American tour of "The Greek Slave." When the time came to settle up, Powers, like some of his customers, was so slow in paying that Kellog threatened suit. Powers asked to examine the books and papers; then refused to give them up because as he admitted before witnesses he "did not wish a paper to get before the world in which he acknowledged his indebtedness for his success in any way to Mr. Kellog." According to Gardner the threat of a law suit was a factor which prevented his return to the United States. There was, of course, an additional reason for remaining in Europe; like other sculptors of the time, Powers depended entirely upon Italian workmen for stone carving.

In any case he considered himself very much an American. H. W. Bellows, who interviewed him in 1869, wrote:

> Thirty years away from home have not affected his patriotism or his New England homeliness. He is every inch an American, and

perpetual converse with other nationalities, and with all schools of art, has not shaken him from his native style, or the well-considered home-brewed notions of his vocation he brought abroad with him. His manners, his accent, his expression are thoroughly unartificialized.

When Hawthorne met him in 1858 Powers was bearded like an Old Testament prophet. He was, of course, already famous for "The Greek Slave" and was at work on an equally naked Eve. To Sophia Hawthorne Eve looked "primal. There is not one hour's experience in her new soul, beaming out of her large innocent eyes." Nathaniel was more critical. For his part he would have all the Venuses, Greek Slaves, and Eves burnt into quicklime, leaving only the Venus di Medici. Untrained as he was in art, Hawthorne had glimpsed the machine-made quality of much nineteenth-century sculpture and he recognized its derivative nature. A character in *The Marble Faun* says:

> There are not, as you will own, more than half a dozen original statues or groups in the world, and these few are of immemorial antiquity. A person familiar with the Vatican, the Uffizi Gallery, the Naples Gallery, and the Louvre, will at once refer any modern production to its antique prototype, which, moreover, had begun to get out of fashion, even in old Roman days. . . . Fairly own to me, my friend . . . that you sculptors are of necessity, the greatest plagiarists in the world.

Nevertheless Hawthorne found Powers a fascinating conversationalist—or possibly a monologuist, for he spoke of the millstream of Powers' talk. He had seldom felt so inclined to write down a man's conversation: Powers' ideas were so "square, solid, and tangible." Unlike Hawthorne, the sculptor did not speculate on the mysteries of the universe.

Nor did he seem to recognize any mysteries in works of art. Some of his square, tangible ideas are preserved in the journals of both Nathaniel and Sophia. The latter recorded:

> He told us that the skin about the mouth was knitted over the lips in its own cunning way, separating the roseate color from the white cuticle. This he found in nature, but never found it imitated in sculpture till he did it himself. The ear, also, he said was generally

neglected, while it was a very beautiful part, when well formed; and the ears of his own heads proved how exquisite it could be.

Secure in such knowledge Powers was able to point out the faults of the Venus di Medici, which he hardly classed as equal to his own "Greek Slave." The Venus had the face of an idiot. "It is a rather bold thing to say, isn't it," he remarked "that the sculptor of the Venus di Medici did not know what he was about."

In fact Powers had opinions on everything from airplanes, which he regarded as the future mode of travel as soon as adequate power was developed, and the Atlantic cable, which he said would have worked if his plan for it had been followed. He showed the Hawthornes machines of his invention for the carving of marble. One of them particularly interested Sophia—a self-cleaning file which was also "first rate for culinary purposes," as well as for grating his clay models. No wonder Powers described himself as a bit of a Yankee. Like Hawthorne, Powers was something of a puritan, albeit of a Swedenborgian variety. As he told a later visitor, he employed only professional models as he did not wish to take the responsibility for introducing young girls into such a dangerous profession.

Hawthorne was especially interested in the effect of expatriation on Powers, who, like many of his kind, tended to rationalize his residence abroad. In *The Marble Faun* Hawthorne pictured the fraternity of artists in Rome as refugees from "the unsympathizing cities of their native land." But in *The Italian Notebooks* he wrote of Powers:

> He said that it would make him very unhappy to believe that he should never return thither [to America]; but it seems to me that he has no such definite purpose of return as would be certain to bring itself to pass. It makes a very unsatisfactory life, thus to spend the greater part of it in exile. In such a case we are always deferring the reality of life till a future moment and, by and by, we have deferred it till there are no future moments; or if we do go back, we find that life has shifted whatever of reality it had to the country where we deemed ourselves only living temporarily; and so between two stools we come to the ground, and make ourselves a part of one or the other only by laying our bones in its soil. It is particularly a pity in Powers's case, because he is so very American in character, and the only convenience for him of his Italian residence is, that here he can

supply himself with marble, and with workmen to chisel it according to his designs.

Certainly Powers was comfortable in Florence. A later visitor described his brick and stone villa, in an enclosed acre of ground, which Powers said cost him $16,000 in gold to build. So many other American artists had homes in Florence that they had much of the home feeling and character. To another visitor of the same period, Powers said that the money-getting propensities and social rivalries of America tended to harden human character, and to bring out a severe selfishness which was offensive.

As for bringing up children abroad there were advantages and disadvantages. He thought that except for music and languages education was better at home, but that abroad there were fewer temptations to vice, and less exposure to the American habit of hard drinking among young men. But foreign residence did not develop manly, energetic, self-relying characteristics as well as did America.

What Powers of course never realized was that residence abroad was debilitating to his art. Gardner remarks on the look of sameness in the work of different sculptors, an impersonal quality, a monotony of surface—all of which were due to the marble polisher. "In the busy studios of American sculptors the Carrara blocks were pulverized under the hands of Italian artisans whose familiarity with marble seemed to produce a cold contempt for the material, which they belabored and abraded with a truly monstrous facility." Hawthorne noticed the superiority of the clay models to the finished products. He tended to agree with Mrs. Anna B. Jameson that American sculptors were "men of no high aims, no worthy conception of the purposes of art, men who were desecrating marble by the things they wrought in it." Hawthorne's account of Powers' conversation suggests that the sculptor thought almost entirely in terms of technique.

This led to another great weakness of the work of such men as Crawford, Powers, and Story—an imitative classicism—the sort of thing which caused Hawthorne to call sculptors the greatest plagiarists in the world. Gardner states that their uncritical acceptance of all Greek and Roman sculpture in the galleries of Rome led them to piece together their "creations" by stealing a head here, a torso there, bits of drapery and stage props from another antique statue or relief. Story even put together bits from different periods. Powers was especially famous for his soft Praxitelean texture—the result of the special tools he had invented.

Greenough had come nearer an understanding of the underlying principles of Greek art than did any of the others. Powers, like Copely before him, lost his native American vigor—the vigor of folk art—and imitated the surface qualities of European art. He had none of the sensual vitality of the Greeks or the men of the Renaissance. Like other American sculptors of the time he had a puritan heritage which caused him, in Gardner's words, to cast "an antiseptic moral air over any subject represented—rendering even female nudity acceptable in a morbidly squeamish age."

Hawthorne, who had faced the problem of expatriation in his own life, had also noted how the native vigor of American sculptors died out in Italy.

It was Hawthorne, that most perceptive of observers, who alone of all the visiting Americans saw that William Wetmore Story was not happy as an expatriate. The others were so dazzled by Story's conversation, his achievements as a lawyer, essayist, poet, sculptor, bon vivant that they pictured him as the most fortunate of men. Mrs. Lew Wallace went into ecstasies over the happy married life of the poet-sculptor.

Story had been born in 1819, in Hawthorne's town of Salem. His father became an Associate Justice of the Supreme Court in 1811, the youngest man ever appointed to that office. At ten Story was taken to Cambridge, Massachusetts, where his friends included James Russell Lowell, Charles Sumner, and Thomas Wentworth Higginson. After graduating from Harvard and Harvard Law School he entered a Boston law firm. At twenty-three he married into a society which Henry James described as one of Arcadian innocence, a society in which a friend of Lowell's counted seventy-five puns in twenty minutes.

At Harvard he became interested in music, literature, painting, and sculpture. When in 1845 his father died, William was chosen to make a portrait statue of him for the memorial chapel in Mount Auburn Cemetery. To prepare himself for this he went to Italy in 1847, despite the objections of his friends and family. His mother's comment was, "Well, William, I've known in my life many a fool, but I've never known so great a one." Story did finish a second volume on contracts, and a two-volume life of his father, but he was haunted by dreams of art.

Story brought some of his puritan prejudices with him to Italy. To

Lowell he wrote that Holy Week in Rome seemed to him "a series of the most consummate humbugs that it has been my fortune to witness." But he was not immune to the aesthetic pull of the Church. Guglielmi's *Miserere* in St. Peter's was "no humbug," but a deeply affecting and beautiful experience. Then, again, in the illumination of St. Peter's the architecture seemed as if traced with a pencil of fire in the blue firmament. Like Hawthorne he was faced with the expatriate's dilemma:

> How shall I ever again endure the restraint and bondage of Boston? Still there are a great many things which Italy has not and which are great and good! There is life, and thought, and progress of ideas and political liberty!

Lowell replied with an ironic letter about the glories of America.

Henry James, writing of Story, spoke of the young Americans for whom the Europe of that day meant culture and culture meant romantic sentiment. But for Story that was only part of the appeal of Europe: it fed his need for sensuous experience. Of Venice he wrote:

> 'And now I am in Venice'—the thought trembles livingly in my heart even as the quivering lights reflected in the canal while we rowed home at dusk. All my memories were a confused cluster of splendours and horrors, as the twisted globes of Venice glass. . . . I cannot tell what I thought, but I felt strange feelings.

Three years after he went abroad he told Lowell that of all places in the world Rome was the place he and his wife loved best. It haunted his dreams; whereas "the thought of New England life cuts across me like a knife."

The note of aesthetic enjoyment runs throughout the letters. Unlike Powers, Story was wealthy enough so that he did not have to depend upon his work as a sculptor. At times, before his work became famous, he thought of returning to Boston and the practice of law. But he told Lowell that every day in Italy made life in America seem less and less satisfactory:

> Such a summer as we have had I have never passed and never believed in before. Sea and mountain breezes all the time, thundershowers varying with light and shade the Campagna, donkey rides and rambles numberless—a long, lazy, luxurious *far niente* of a summer. . . .

He went on to describe picturesque processions, and scenes of wild dancing to thumping tamborellas—the laughter, gaiety, and screaming, which he saw were reviving.

A year later he wrote "we are leading the most *dolce far niente* of our lives." The Storys were then living near the Brownings, whom they saw almost daily. There were rambles, picnics, drives every evening. Elizabeth Browning described Mrs. Story as "a sympathetic, graceful woman, fresh and innocent in face and thought." As James describes the life, there was always an excursion to some church, a feast, some curiosity, some new find in an excavated site or some clever chap's studio to visit, some singer, for sixpence singing an old opera, or some evening entertainment in a palace.

James says that "the whip in the sky, the lash cracked by the New England Jehovah" was "blissfully absent." But was it? Story's constant railings against New England—such as his description of Allston starving spiritually in "fearful Cambridgeport"—suggest a man trying to assuage a sense of guilt. He delighted in finding incidents suggesting moral turpitude in America. After telling one such, he said, "I disbelieve in the superior honesty of the Americans. They have too little blood and few unusual temptations, but they do not resist what temptations they have." The tone of Story's letters is reflected in a reply by Lowell:

> As to what you say about Boston, I will drink up Essel and eat a crocodile with you on that subject any day—you can't scold worse about it than I would. I know that the finest political institutions in the world don't make a country pleasant to live in. . . . I would gladly subscribe toward *offering* (a judicious phrase) a handsome reward to anybody who will find a cure for the (small-) potato-disease with which Boston is fearfully infected. . . .

In 1856 the Storys sent an announcement to their friends saying that they were settling permanently in Rome. Here they rented, for $250 a year, the second story of the Palazzo Barberini. A friend described their apartment enthusiastically as original, some portions resembling an oriental bazaar, others so classical as to suggest the atrium of a Roman patrician. Story filled it with works of art, bric-a-brac, bits of classical remains, and with his own sculpture. Mrs. Story had one of the largest rooms made into a theater, complete with footlights and scenery. This, too, was ornate with lounges upholstered in silk and with tapestries on the walls. Here the Storys and their friends gave amateur productions in English, Italian, and French. Story himself was considered an excellent actor. On one occasion Sir Edward Mallet's *The Ordeal* was given with Sir Edward taking a part. In addition many musical compositions were here given their first performances.

The Storys entertained lavishly. Here Protestant clergymen mingled with prelates of the Catholic Church. The guest list included most of the notables who came to Rome: British prime ministers, General Grant, Leigh Hunt, Joseph Severn, Tennyson, Thackeray, Hawthorne, and many others. The Brownings continued to be especially close friends. Story was regarded as a fascinating conversationalist. Mrs. Gaskell spoke happily of the many puns he got off. But Hawthorne saw the shadow beneath the surface:

> Mr. Story is the most variously accomplished and brilliant person, the fullest of social life and fire, whom I have ever met . . . . he kept us amused and entertained the whole day long. . . . Still though he bubbled and brimmed over with fun, he left the impression on one . . . that there is a pain and care, bred it may be out of the very richness of his gifts and the abundance of his outward prosperity.

On the other hand it was the charm of Story's life in Italy which struck his fellow Bostonian, Charles Sumner. Following the brutal beating by Congressman Brooks, Sumner went to Europe for his health. In Italy he visited the Storys, at whose home he met Hawthorne and John Lothrop Motley, and was introduced to the Brownings. On his way to Genoa aboard the vessel *Lombardo*, Sumner wrote in appreciation of Story's hospitality:

> What I have left undone at Rome haunts me more than all that I enjoyed. . . . Why did I not press you to go with me to the Capitol and the Vatican? . . . Rome now, as when I first saw it, touches me more than any other place. Then I have been happy with you. Perhaps it will be long before we meet again; but I cannot forget these latter delicious days.

Three months later from the Bains Frasceti near Le Havre he wrote in praise of Story's guide book *Roba di Roma*:

I do love Italy, and wish that I were there, to lap myself in its Elysium. But I shall be in another place, in scenes very different, amidst tobacco-spitting, swearing slave drivers, abased by the press, insulted so far as is possible, pained and racked by insensibility about me to human rights and the dreams of human nature.

Back in America Sumner sent Story money for bronze castings of a head of Plato, a Demosthenes, and a Minerva from the Vatican Museum. He also ordered reproductions in marble of the "Psyche of Venice" and a Roman statue of Young Augustus. But "What a difference between this place and Rome! I feel it keenly. And yet there is a delight here which you have not. It is the standing up for Truth and Liberty." In May of 1860 he again wrote to Story:

A walk in the streets of Rome—a stroll on the Pincian—a visit to the Vatican—a sight of St. Peter's—Oh! for an hour—of any of these. And better still a talk with you. I have so much to say on art—and on our politics here, which have none of the refinements of art.

When the war came, Story forgot the refinements of art sufficiently to write several articles for the London press, based on Sumner's letters about the irony of a nation which supported Southern slaveocracy while opposing slavery. Some authorities argue that Americans abroad like Story, Motley, and Thurlow Weed did much to clarify European opinion about the issues in the Civil War. However, the war years were increasingly lonely for Story. Elizabeth Browning died in 1861, and Robert left Italy. Story wrote to Norton that there was no one like Sumner with whom he would walk the higher ranges of art and philosophy. The Roman artists had brains about an inch deep.

In a depressed state of mind Story had about decided to give up sculpture when in 1862 his "Cleopatra" and "Libyan Sybil" became the sensations of the London International Exposition. They had been sent there at the expense of Pope Pius IX. Hawthorne's *Marble Faun* helped to spread the fame of the "Cleopatra." In his *Notebooks* Hawthorne described this as "a work of genuine thought and energy, representing a terribly dangerous woman; quiet enough for the moment, but very likely to spring upon you like a tigress." James wrote that the special turn of Story's imagination in his Medeas, Judiths, Cleopatras, etc. was "the note of passion let loose." On the other hand a modern critic sees them as lacking in sufficient vitality to stand upright. ". . . they recline, heavily draped against their self-generated cold, in elegant chairs of classic design." In fact Cleopatra looks like nothing so much as a woman who, after a long day of ironing and looking after the youngsters, has sat down and loosened her bra.

Story's poem "Cleopatra" contains some of the fire which the statue lacks. In verse Cleopatra muses about the time "aeons of thought away" when she was "a smooth and velvety tiger." When her mate appeared:

> Then like a storm he seized me,
> With a wild triumphant cry,
> And we met, as two clouds in heaven
> When thunders before them fly.
> We grappled and struggled together,
> For his love like his rage was rude;
> And his teeth in the swelling folds of my neck
> At times, in our play, drew blood.
> Often another suitor—
> For I was flexible and fair—
> Fought for me in the moonlight,
> Where I lay crouching there,
> Till his blood was drained in the desert;
> And ruffled with triumph and power,
> He licked me and lay beside me
> To breathe him a vast half hour.

With such memories she cries:

> Come to my arms, my hero,
> The shadows of twilight grow,
> And the tiger's ancient fierceness
> In my veins begins to flow.
> Come not with cringing to sue me!
> Take me with triumph and power,
> As a warrior storms a fortress!
> I will not shrink or cower.
> Come as you came in the desert,
> Ere we were women and men,
> When the tiger passions were in us,
> And love as you loved me then!

This indeed seems as far removed from nineteenth-century Boston as the expatriate Bayard Taylor's *Bedouin Love Song* seems distant from his Quaker background in Chester County. But like Taylor, Story complained of American puritanism while sharing many of its views. Thus in *Conversations in A Studio* Story could deplore the portrayal in French novels of illicit love affairs. And of Zola's *Nana*, "What is this but the literature of the brothel? If this is what we are to come to with our 'Realism,' as it is called, for Heaven's sake let us be as unreal as possible." And Offenbach and his school were in the same way degrading music. "The Maenads carry the day with riot and indecency and vulgarity. We are all going the way of the old Romans."

Thus, like Hawthorne, Story seems to have been an ambivalent puritan. It is hard to reconcile Story's attacks on the "restraint of bondage of Boston" with his moralistic sentiments. Similarly his rather hedonistic life in Italy was lived within the limits of the strictest propriety. Like Hiram Powers he was extremely critical of the moral failings of America. This seeming paradox: the attack upon puritan narrowness by persons who are essentially puritans, is characteristic of American expatriates from Fenimore Cooper to Edith Wharton. Story's life may shed some light on the whys and wherefores of this paradox. Certainly the widely held theory that the expatriates were refugees from puritan morality is not supported by the evidence drawn from the lives of nineteenth-century Americans in Europe.

The other theory holds that these men and women were driven out by a crass, money-mad society. For instance when Story returned home for a visit after the Civil War he wrote to his daughter from Newport: "All the talk here is about dollars, how much money this one or that one has got, and a dreary and monotonous thing it is to hear it so constantly." But in Boston Story was feted at the Saturday Club, where Longfellow, Lowell, and Norton joined in welcoming him—hardly a group of dollar-chasers. In fact the intellectual Bostonian circle into which Story had been taken seems to have been much less money-conscious than was Henry James. Money plays a key role in novel after novel by James; it is almost absent from the writings of Emerson, Longfellow, and Lowell. Holmes mentions it as a means of obtaining leisure, culture and the good things of life, but for him money is never an end in itself. Story's fellow expatriate, Hiram Powers, was more money-minded than were the Boston Brahmins.

If literature is a reflection of social values, English writers in the nineteenth century were far more concerned with money than were the Americans. One need only cite Jane Austen, George Eliot, Dickens, Thackeray, and Meredith as compared with Poe, Hawthorne, and Melville. Tennyson's *Locksley Hall* was bitter on the subject of wealth; Walt Whitman had almost no interest in the subject. Carlyle, Matthew Arnold, and Ruskin were preoccupied with economic questions; whereas Emerson was serenely oblivious of them, and Thoreau compared the inheritance of a farm to a sentence in the county jail.

There can be little doubt that Americans of the business classes talked about money, but so too did the Englishmen encountered by Hawthorne. The Europeans pictured by James are far more avaricious than his Americans like Christopher Newman or Lambert Strether. More to the point is the fact that in America such men as Hawthorne, James, and Story had access to, and were by inheritance a part of, an intellectual society which had little interest in money.

Manners were something else. At the Harvard commencement of 1865 Story walked arm in arm with Lowell. But Mrs. Story wrote to her daughter:

> Fancy the musty old professors dressed not in the academic robe of former days, but according to the caprice of individual New England taste, than which nothing is more eccentric. Consider the motley group upon the stage, some dressed in light tweeds others in linen slacks, with straw hats and boots uncleaned.

Of lesser interest to her was the fact that Emerson spoke and "James Lowell read a very fine poem." This was of course the "Harvard Commemoration Ode." A few days later Story wrote to his daughter that he had seen an advertisement for overstrung pianos: ". . . the Overstrung Piano struck me as thoroughly American. Isn't everything here overstrung?"

In other words America lacked the *dolce far niente* quality Story enjoyed in Italy. Nearly twenty years of his life there antedated the Franco-Prussian War, which Henry James called "the hitherward limit of the liveable era."

Story also felt that America did not appreciate him. Despite the fact that his rather antiquarian essays on Rome, the *Roba di Roma*, were published in the *Atlantic* he felt that they did not receive the attention they deserved. Sumner tried, and failed, to get Congress to commission a statue of Lincoln by Story. But when he visited America in 1877 he made a triumphal tour. At that time in testimony before a Senate committee he proposed a new design for the unfinished Washington monument. He wanted to encase the existing part in colored marble and turn it into a tower with a portico at its base. There he would place a colossal statue of Washington faced by a statue of Liberty. On the bronze doors there would be portraits of Revolutionary heroes. The tower was to be crowned with a statue of Fame in gilt bronze, "the spiritual essence of life" as the Washington at the base represented "the corporeal presence." It would seem that expatriation did not necessarily improve artistic taste.

He returned to America in 1884 to supervise the placing of his colossal statue of John Marshall. President Arthur invited him to dine at the White House, but he found the capital a lonely place without Sumner, who had died ten years before. Mrs. Story reported to their daughter that "Papa" was anxious to get on shipboard for a return to Italy.

The fact was that Story had become completely the expatriate. But ironically his fame was largely due to Americans, especially to Hawthorne's *Marble Faun*. Lowell dedicated *Fireside Travels* to Story, and while Minister to England used his influence to have Oxford grant an honorary degree. In later years Story's commissions came from America: the John Marshall, a statue of Ezra Cornell, and a colossal one of William Cullen Bryant, modeled but never executed in marble.

But Americans were also the ones who recognized Story's limitations—not American philistines, but Hawthorne, Mrs. Henry Adams, and Henry James. Hawthorne had been impressed by the "grand seated figure" of Cleopatra, but he had glimpsed the hollowness behind the glittering facade of Story's life. He had seen how American artists abroad became men wandering between two worlds. Mrs. Henry Adams, after a visit to Rome, wrote:

> We went to Mr. Story's studio, and oh! how he does spoil nice blocks of white marble. Nothing but Sibyls on all sides, sitting, standing, legs crossed, legs uncrossed, and all with the same expression as if they smelt something wrong. Call him a genius! I don't see it.

It is of course not given to every artist to be a genius, and expatriation was not necessarily the reason for Story's limitations as a sculptor. But even Henry James saw that expatriation was an element in a life that was somehow tragic. He spoke of Story's "beautiful sacrifice to a noble mistake . . . the mistake . . . of the frank consent to be beguiled . . . [the] danger in consciously planning for happiness."

> In London, in Boston, he would have *had* to live with his conception, there being nothing else about him of the same colour or quality. In Rome, Florence, Siena, there was too much—too much, that is, for a man for whom, otherwise dedicated it had not been in question to become a second Gregorius.

Story died in 1895 in his daughter's villa at Vallombrosa. He was a forerunner of the expatriated Americans of inherited wealth and cultivated tastes who found Europe more comfortable than America and who justified themselves by condemning their countrymen for the pursuit of money. Story basked in a world where starving peasants were picturesque, where the well-to-do could afford palaces and numerous servants. Life was not always *dolce far niente,* but the picnics, the excursions to picturesque ruins, the amateur theatricals were possible because of cheap servants, cheap carriages, guides eager for a few pennies—an economic order where money from America bought more than it did at home—in James's phrase "the celestial cheapness" of Europe.

Unlike Henry James, who had been partly brought up in Europe, or James NcNeil Whistler, who never saw America until he was twenty, Story had deep roots in his native land. His father had been, next to John Marshall, the leading interpreter of the American Constitution. But the self-exiled sculptor sent his sons to Eton; his daughter made her debut in Europe and married the Marquis Simone Peruzzi di Medici.

A number of earlier expatriates had tried to bring back to America the fruits of European culture; those after 1860 often tried to be Europeans. Charles Willson Peale, Washington Allston, Horatio Greenough are typical of the earlier group; Story of those after the Civil War.

ESCAPE FROM BOSTON

MARGARET FULLER

Margaret Fuller began preparing for Europe in her childhood. No other expatriate with the exception of Henry James had such an intense longing to go abroad. In fact her longings and repeated frustrations foreshadowed those of Caroline Spencer in James's story "Four Meetings." Unlike Caroline, Margaret finally had her European experience, an experience which transformed her life.

Sarah Margaret Fuller was born at Cambridgeport in 1810, the daughter of Timothy Fuller, a lawyer who later became a Congressman. A man well read in French and English literature, he tried to make Margaret the heir of all he knew. As a small child she was often kept up late so that her father could hear her recite her lessons of the day.

At six she began the study of Latin. Soon the thoughts and lives of the great Romans became her daily food. In her fragmentary autobiography she devoted several pages to a discussion of the magic she found in Roman history and literature. In addition Ovid gave her a glimpse into "the enchanted gardens of Greek mythology." Always a person whose responses were intense, she carried the early vision of Greece and Rome throughout her life. It may well be that her early emotional identification with things Roman had much to do with her intense love of the city when she finally got there.

She took up the study of French and Italian with enthusiasm. By the time she was fifteen she was reading both languages easily. The following year it seemed as if her dream of Europe was to be realized. Her father, having given up his seat in Congress, hoped for a diplomatic post from President Adams, whose election he had worked for. But an expensive dinner party for the President was a bitter disappointment. Adams, who was unwell, stayed only briefly. And the appointment never materialized.

Margaret next took up the study of German with the same energy she had devoted to other languages. After three months she was reading with ease, and within a year had read Goethe's *Faust, Tasso, Iphigenia, Hermann and Dorothea, Elective Affinities,* and *Memoirs,** Tieck's *William Lovel, Prince Zenobia,* and other works. She began to plan a biography

* Probably *Dichtung und Warheit*

of Goethe. But she mourned, "How am I to get the information I want unless I go to Europe?"

Her professed ambition was self-culture. *"Very early I knew that the only object in life was to grow."* (The italics are hers.) This ambition was hindered by the family's removal to Groton. Later she was to write bitterly of the move. She was torn from the more congenial intellectual atmosphere of Cambridge and Boston; her mother's health was impaired, and her own "destroyed." Always a sufferer from headaches, she believed that early overstudy had been the cause. There are indications of psychosomatic illness, the causes of which she herself glimpsed. She had a feeling of being too intense about life.

Apparently with the understanding that her father would pay her way to Europe she took over the education of the four younger children, Arthur, Ellen, Richard, and Lloyd. Five days a week she gave lessons in three languages and geography and history. She herself studied the geography and history of modern Europe, the elements of architecture, the historical and critical works of Goethe, and the outlines of the history of her own country.

Then in 1835 the dream of Europe seemed to be near realization. On a visit to Cambridge she met Harriet Martineau at the house of Mr. and Mrs. John Farrar. Margaret had longed for an intellectual guide and Miss Martineau seemed to be what she was seeking. Miss Martineau approved the plan for a life of Goethe, but pointed out the necessity of research in Europe. The Farrars were sailing the following summer; why should not Margaret accompany them and be Harriet's house guest in London before going on to Germany, France, and Italy? Timothy Fuller said no.

Back at Groton, shortly after receiving Miss Martineau's letter, Margaret became dangerously ill. For nine days she lay in agony. Perhaps she had a touch of Asiatic cholera. Her mother nursed her "like an angel." One morning her father came to her room and after a few minutes of conversation, said, "My dear, I have been thinking of you in the night, and I cannot remember that you have any *faults*. You have defects, of course, as all mortals have, but I do not know that you have a single fault." These were some of the few words of praise she ever remembered from him. A few days later Timothy Fuller lay dead of Asiatic cholera.

At first it seemed as if there might be enough money in the estate to enable her to accept the renewed invitation to join the Farrars and Miss

Martineau in the trip to Europe. But it soon appeared that there was only $20,000, not enough to support the family.

Margaret Fuller experienced a bitter period. In her journal for January 1, 1836, she wrote: "The New-year opens upon me under circumstances inexpressibly sad. I must make the last great sacrifice. . . ." But she continued to hope and plan. Writing to her eldest sister at the end of the month, she said:

> I was a great deal with Miss Martineau, while in Cambridge, and love her more than ever. She is to stay till August, and go to England with Mr. and Mrs. Farrar. If I should accompany them, I shall be with her while in London, and see the best literary society. If I should go, you will be with mother the while, will you not? Oh, dear E——, you know not how I fear and tremble to come to a decision. My temporal all seems hanging upon it, and the prospect is most alluring. A few thousand dollars would make it all so easy, so safe. As it is, I cannot tell what is coming to us, for the estate will not be settled when I go. I pray to God ceaselessly, that I may decide wisely.

By April she realized that she could not go:

> If I am not to go with you I shall be obliged to tear my heart, by a violent effort, from its present objects and natural desires. But I shall feel the necessity, and will do it if the life-blood flows through the rent.

She could not even bear the thought of corresponding with Harriet in Europe. Late in May she knew there was no longer an *if:*

> Circumstances have decided that I must not go to Europe, and shut upon me the door, as I think, forever, to the scenes I could have loved. Let me try now to forget myself, and act for others' sakes. What I can do with my pen, I know not. At present, I feel no confidence or hope.

Her health suffered, and she spent her time devouring book after book. Groton, despite its beauty, reminded her chiefly of the "hours of anguish as great as I am capable of suffering."

Before leaving for England, Harriet Martineau told Emerson of Margaret's plight. Emerson, who had come back from Europe more than ever satisfied with America, found it hard to sympathize with Margaret's longing to go abroad. But because of Miss Martineau's enthusiasm about the girl, the Emersons invited her to Concord. It was perhaps the best thing that could have happened to her. Emerson, only seven years her senior, went with her on walks around Concord and took her ideas seriously. True, Emerson was a little wary; Margaret made him laugh at her satiric wit oftener than he wanted to. Not only was Emerson's calm optimism healing, he also offered practical help by inviting Bronson Alcott out to Concord. Alcott, who had lost Elizabeth Peabody as an assistant, hired Margaret to teach in his experimental school, the Institute of Spiritual Culture in Boston—usually referred to as the Temple school.

Here she taught French, Italian, German, and Latin. Within three months her classes were reading twenty pages of German for a single lesson. Emerson thought that she was better acquainted with foreign authors than with English literature. He noted that she showed a preference for Italian genius. Nor did he approve of her belief in omens, ciphers, talismans, coincidences, birthdays, and fate. She chose a male carbuncle as her own stone, and wore a ring or bracelet of certain stones when she wrote to friends whom she connected with those stones.

The Temple school closed within the year, the victim of the depression of 1837 and of Boston's puritan prejudices. Alcott, who had dared to introduce the subject of sex into discussions with his pupils and his *Conversations on the Gospels*, was attacked by Andrews Norton, "the Unitarian Pope," as "one-third absurd, one-third blasphemous and one-third obscene." Margaret herself was later to suffer similar charges against her book *Woman in the Nineteenth Century*.

Next she took a job at $1000 a year in the Greene Street School in Providence. She had hoped to find time for writing, but discovered that the responsibility for a hundred pupils left her little time. She did, however, complete her translation of Eckermann's *Conversations with Goethe*. After two years in Providence she returned to Boston and began conducting her "Conversation" classes there and in Cambridge, a series which lasted five years. This was a project for the education of women, whose opportunities for formal learning she regarded as deficient. The project started off well with twenty-five subscribers at $20 for the winter quarter and another $20 for the spring quarter. On the whole she was pleased with her class, although one squeamish lady protested the choice of Greek mythology as the subject for the first conversations.

The tone was, of course, transcendental: Jupiter represented the will, Mercury the understanding, Apollo terrene inspiration, and Bacchus the abandonment of genius. One lady insisted upon taking care that Christianity and morality were not forgotten.

The discussion of mythology led in later sessions to a consideration of art, for Margaret had become increasingly interested in sculpture and painting. In 1823 the Boston Athenaeum had opened a museum of antique sculpture in plaster, selected, Emerson believed, by Canova. To the reproductions of antique sculpture there were soon added busts by Horatio Greenough and the "Night and Day" of Michelangelo. Inspired perhaps by Goethe, Margaret became an enthusiastic admirer of these works and went on to read everything she could find about Michelangelo and Raphael. Others shared this enthusiasm, and Emerson reported that in 1839 and 1840 people covered their walls with prints of the great Italians. As it had been with literature, art for Margaret also pointed in the direction of Europe.

During the years of her "Conversations," she was associated with the transcendentalist group: Emerson, Alcott, Elizabeth Peabody, Frederic Hedge, and James Freeman Clarke. With the encouragement of Emerson she became in 1840 the first editor of *Dial*. When she could no longer afford to continue without pay, Emerson took over the editorship. In 1841 she visited the Brook Farm community. At first she did not sympathize with the socialistic ideas of the more radical members of the colony:

> Utopia is impossible to build up. I accept the limitations of human nature and believe a wise acknowledgement of them a condition of progress. Yet every noble scheme, every poetic dream foreshadows man's eventual destiny. It is on this ground that I sympathize with the transcendental party.

But when Brook Farm became a Fourieristic phalanx she went along with the left wing. Fourier's ideas were to influence her when she went to Rome.

In the summer of 1843 she made her first extended journey, this one to Illinois and Wisconsin with James and Sarah Clarke. The party traveled from Buffalo to Chicago by steamboat and then hired a large covered wagon for a tour of the prairies. As a preparation for this Margaret read various books on the region, including Irving's *A Tour on the Prairies,* the only one which did not have a secondhand air about it. She had been prepared to dislike the West because "go ahead" was its only motto and there was no mellowing from long settlement. Her ideal was essentially English: "In older countries the house of a son grew from that of the father, as naturally as new joints on a bough, and the cathedral crowned the whole as naturally as the leafy summit of a tree."

On the whole, however, she liked the West despite what seemed to her "the general dullness that broods over this land where so little genius flows." People were kindly and hospitable, and in the Rock River region of Illinois she found beautifully landscaped estates. Again she was reminded of the England she had seen only through books. "The villas and castles seem to have been burnt," she wrote ironically, "but the velvet lawns, the flower-gardens, the stately parks, scattered at graceful intervals by the decorous hand of art, the frequent deer, and the peaceful herd" were all in evidence.

Her account of the trip, *Summer on the Lakes,* was published the following year. In it her style for the first time adumbrates that of her later writing on Italy. Except at times, *Summer on the Lakes* is free from the exclamatory, sentimentalized writing she was prone to. There are clear, straightforward narrative passages and good sketches of persons and places. As a humanitarian she was much interested in the Indians, whom she championed. Seeing the site of a former Indian village, she could not believe that a people who chose such a beautiful place to live were ignoble. She visited an Indian village and spent much time talking with the women by signs. In wigwams she noted scenes of conjugal and parental love which could give lessons to the whites. But she was not blind to the degradation and drunkenness of this dispossessed people.

To a degree her journey gave her good training in the observation of social and economic conditions. She was especially interested in the lot of women, whether Indian or white. On the whole she found the white women ill prepared for life in a new country. The overworked wives of the poorer settlers became slatterns; the wealthier class had been taught to dance, draw, and speak French, but could not ride, drive, or row alone. Accustomed to the pavements of Broadway, they feared to walk in the woods because of rattlesnakes. And much as she longed for Europe she had absorbed enough of Emerson's doctrines to comment: "Everywhere the fatal spirit of imitation, of reference to European standards, penetrates and threatens to blight whatever of original growth might adorn the soil."

Back in New York she met Horace and Mary Greeley, friends of William Henry Channing. Greeley was editor and publisher of the crusading *Tribune,* and Mary shared Margaret's interest in George Sand and women's rights. Greeley was familiar with *The Dial,* which he called the "most original work yet published in America." Margaret dined with the Greeleys, where she met Albert Brisbane, a socialist who had studied with Fourier in Paris. She also dined with Henry James, Sr., then about to sail for Europe with his wife and small sons. James liked Margaret so much that he told Emerson that he hated to leave just as he had "come to talk with the dear noble woman."

Margaret returned to New England, where Brook Farm was being reorganized as a Fourieristic phalanx. She spent the summer writing *Summer on the Lakes.* Greeley liked it so much that he gave it much space in the *Tribune* and offered Margaret a job as his assistant. He also urged her to expand her essay on women's rights, "The Great Lawsuit," into a book. He said that the *Tribune* would publish it if Emerson would write an introduction. Emerson at first agreed but found that his sentiments and Margaret's were too far apart for him to carry out the assignment. Happy in his marriage and the birth of a son, he particularly disagreed with Margaret's insistence on the need for virginity in those women who would represent their sex. "No married woman can represent the female world," she wrote, "for she belongs to her husband."

When *Woman in the Nineteenth Century* appeared in 1845 it created something of a stir. Poe commented that it was "a book which few women in the country could have written, and no woman in the country would have published, with the exception of Miss Fuller." Horace Greeley wrote to Rufus Griswold, "It is not elegantly written, but every line talks." Early in the book she throws down the gauntlet: "We would have every barrier thrown down. We would have every path laid open to Woman as freely as to Man." Not only did this idea disturb people in the nineteenth century, there was a guarded discussion of prostitution, a topic which upset the squeamish puritanism of many readers.

For modern taste *Woman* is much too transcendental and high flown. After the temporary ferment of woman's emancipation had subsided, Margaret believed:

. . . we should see crystallizations more pure and of more various beauty. We believe the divine energy would pervade nature to a degree unknown in the history of former ages, and that no discordant collision but a ravishing harmony of the spheres would ensue.

Readers living in a time when woman has been given most of the opportunities Margaret demanded are less likely to share this dithyrambic vision. Ironically enough her view of woman was one little calculated to recommend her as a candidate for business or political office. She declared her "faith that the feminine side, the side of love, of beauty, of holiness," was now to have its full chance.

Despite masculine jeers, *Woman in the Nineteenth Century* established Margaret Fuller as a serious writer. When a year and a half later she went to London, she wrote home: "I have been received here with a warmth that surprised me; it is chiefly to *Woman in the 19th Century* that I am indebted for this; that little volume has been read and prized by many."

Greeley, who had urged her to do the book, now helped to make possible her longed-for trip to Europe. Her friends Marcus and Rebecca Spring invited her to accompany them, asking only that she help to look after their youngster. The Springs, wealthy and philanthropic, had befriended Margaret when she first came to New York. Like Greeley, Marcus Spring was deeply interested in the North American Phalanx, a Fourieristic colony near Red Bank, New Jersey. From the sales of her books Margaret had saved a thousand dollars—not quite enough for the trip. Therefore she asked her old friend Sam Ward to lend her five hundred dollars, reminding him that ten years before she had been compelled to abandon her trip to Europe with him and the Ferrars. Sam, now a partner in his father's banking firm, furnished the money. So it was that in August 1846 she sailed with the Springs on the steamship *Cambria*.

Margaret Fuller's longing for Europe was not motivated by any rejection of America. Like such earlier expatriates as Ticknor and Bancroft she was interested in furthering her education. There was the attraction of the art and antiquities of Europe and the desire to broaden her experience. Certainly she was not a refugee from either American culture or American puritanism. As *Woman in the Nineteenth Century* showed, she shared many of the puritan views about morality. In *Papers on Literature and Art* she dealt respectfully with such writers as Irving, Cooper, Prescott, and Bancroft; she was enthusiastic about Hawthorne and Emerson. Throughout her writing her only serious quarrel with her own country was over the American mania for money—what Irving had called the Almighty Dollar.

What set Margaret Fuller apart from other American expatriates except Hawthorne was her interest in social and economic conditions. But whereas Hawthorne had refused to become involved, even emotionally, Margaret became deeply committed to the cause of reform. In her first letter to the *Tribune* she deplored the honor paid by both the English and Americans on board to the wife of the Governor of Nova Scotia, the illegitimate daughter of William IV. And on landing she had "a foretaste of the delights of living under an aristocratical government" when the baggage of Lord and Lady Falkland was given priority over that of other passengers.

Liverpool immediately impressed her with the difference between England and America;

> . . . we felt ourselves in a slower, solider, and not on that account less truly active, state of things than at home. . . . There is not as we travel that rushing, tearing, and swearing, that snatching of baggage, that prodigality of shoe-leather and lungs, which attend the course of a traveller in the United States; but we do not lose our "goods," we do not miss our car. The dinner, if ordered in time, is cooked properly, and served punctually, and at the end of the day more that is permanent seems to have come of it than on the full-drive system.

But she also noted the shameless beggars, the coarse mill girls walking the streets, the women in gin palaces, "too dull to carouse."

> The homes of England! their sweetness is melting into fable; only the new Spirit in its holiest power can restore to those homes their boasted security of "each man's castle," for Woman, the warder, is driven into the street, and has let fall the keys in her plight.

In her early letters to the *Tribune* Margaret is a jumpy writer: she describes with enthusiasm a Mechanics Institute where for a small fee students could take mathematics, French, German, fine arts, etc.; deplores the state of women in Liverpool; and marvels at the romantic beauties of Chester—all within a few pages. She visited Wordsworth, then seventy-six in "a florid, fair old age," and her friend Harriet Martineau. Within a few paragraphs she comments on Wordsworth, fuschias, Wordsworth's views on the Corn Laws, the landlady's praise of Wordsworth, Dr. Arnold, Miss Martineau, and Langdale (the scene of the *Excursion*). But it was Burns, not Wordsworth, who received Margaret's highest praise: "Since Adam, there has been none that approached nearer fitness to stand up before God and angels in the naked majesty of manhood than Robert Burns."

She visited Abbotsford, where she noted that five hundred Americans a year signed the porter's book. Back in the Lake Country she spent two hours listening to DeQuincey, whom she found charming. On a stagecoach ride to Perth she sat on top in a heavy rain. She was glad she got the chance before the era of the stagecoach was over. But in Perth she was appalled by the dirty women and even dirtier children. "To the horrors and sorrows of the streets of such places as Liverpool, Glasgow, and, above all, London, one has to grow insensible or die daily." The streets of Glasgow reminded her of the *Inferno*. Like Hawthorne she commented that poverty was a worse ill in England or Scotland than in warmer climates; it made people fierce or stupid; they took refuge in drink. Poverty in England had terrors she never dreamed of at home.

She climbed Ben Lomand, where she got separated from her companion and had to spend the night. Because of the cold she kept walking until shepherds found her in the morning. Her hunger for experience led her to go down into a coal mine at Newcastle. Then she went on to York where she described the Minster as "that dream of beauty realized." She mourned that the Puritans had destroyed the windows and statues: "Such a church is ruined by Protestantism."

As a sample of her headlong pace, her insatiable curiosity, and her catch-all style, there is the chapter head for her Letter IX to the *Tribune*:

Writing at night.—London.—National Gallery.—Murillo.—The Flower Girl.—Nursery-Maids and Workingmen.—Hampton Court.—Zoological Gardens.—Kew Gardens.—The Great Cactus.—The Reform Club House.—Men Cooks.—Orderly Kitchen. —A Gilpin Excursion.—The Bell at Edmonton.—Omnibus.—Cheapside.—English Slowness.—Freiligrath.—Arcadia.—Italian School.

—Mazzini.—Italy.—Italian Refugees.—Correggio.—Hope and Italians.—Addresses.—Supper.—Carlyle, his Appearance, Conversation etc.

Because of her experience with England and Scotland she approached Carlyle with increased reverence, for she had learned

> to appreciate the strength and height of that wall of shams and conventions which he more than any other man, or thousand men,—indeed, he almost alone,—has begun to throw down. . . . He has torn off the veils from hideous facts. . . .

During her several meetings with Carlyle she found that he did not converse; he harangued. He was arrogant and overbearing, but his arrogance had no littleness or self-love; it was "the arrogance of some Scandinavian conqueror." He was the Siegfried of England, the dragon killer, but she saw that he lacked constructive ability.

It was at Carlyle's house that she met Mazzini. Later she visited a school for poor Italian boys maintained and taught by Mazzini and other exiles. "Mazzini, one of those noble refugees, is not only one of the heroic, the courageous, and the faithful,—Italy boasts many such,—but he is also one of the wise. . . ." She found that he preached liberty not only for Italy but for Europe at large. In praising Mazzini she launched into a poem to Italy which with a fine disregard for history and linguistics she hailed as "the mother of our language and our laws, our greatest benefactress in the gifts of genius, the garden of the world" but over "whose bowers now hangs a perpetual veil of sadness, and whose noblest plants are doomed to removal."

Margaret Fuller was not alone among American expatriates in her enthusiasm for Italy. Nineteenth-century education with its emphasis upon Latin and the history of Rome had given an exaggerated idea of the place of these in English history and the language. Also the recent importation of reproductions of Italian art had made educated Americans aware of the immense contribution of the Italian Renaissance. What set Margaret apart from her fellow expatriates was her political and social conscience. Most Americans gloried in the scenery, the art and architecture of Italy, but accepted the political system along with the fleas and beggars and malaria as part of the local color. Insofar as they thought about the political system they compared it unfavorably with that of their homeland. Margaret, on the other hand, shared Mazzini's vision of a new Italy.

It is not strange that she was drawn to him. Not only was he a "beauteous" creature, he was also an intellectual. Five years her senior, he too had had a precocious childhood. His father was a university professor, and Mazzini himself read Dante, Shakespeare, Goethe, and Schiller. He could speak both English and French. At sixteen he had joined the Carbonari. Imprisoned for six months on suspicion, he had spent the time reading the Bible, Tacitus, and Byron. After his release he had gone to France, where he and others edited the *Journal of Young Italy,* which was smuggled into his own country. When Metternich's police broke up the revolutionary group in Italy, Mazzini went to Geneva and later to England. Thus by the time Margaret met him, he had led a life of adventure; he had like Margaret suffered a broken love affair. The lady was a fellow refugee in Geneva, the widow of a nobleman, but she refused to leave with him for England.

Margaret's love had been a neurotic young Jew, James Nathan, with whom she had taken walks and held tortured conversations in New York. There were frequent misunderstandings; his letters were filled with accusations, and hers with contrition and forgiveness. Nathan had left for Europe before she did. While she was in Scotland she learned that he was to be married. She wrote asking for the return of her love letters, but he wrote a refusal filled with new accusations of falsehood and saying that she had insulted him. The friendship was at an end, but her letters to Nathan were published in 1903 by Julia Ward Howe as *The Love-Letters of Margaret Fuller.*

Before leaving England she visited a model prison at Pentonville and establishments where the poor could bathe and wash clothes. She noted that a woman could in three hours get through an amount of washing and ironing which ordinarily would take three or four days. She hoped to see similar facilities established in American cities. Later on in Paris she visited day nurseries where poor working women could leave their children. Characteristically she lumped the English prison, the bath houses, the washing establishment, and the Paris *crèches* into a single account, followed by one of London theaters, opera, and the theaters of Paris. Like so many other Americans she was fascinated by the acting of Mlle Rachel. Here was "a true genius, absolutely the diamond." Margaret saw her seven or eight times and wrote about her at length. Despite the exasperating quality of her flealike jumps of subject Margaret often reveals facts of Europe unreported by other travelers. Characteristically she gave a full account of a visit to a school for mentally retarded children, and made only a passing reference to a court ball she attended. Only Hawthorne had so keen an eye for the sociological scene.

In Paris the person she most wanted to meet was George Sand. Margaret's attitude toward the novelist was ambivalent: she admired her as a symbol of women's independence, but there was the question of her morals. Carlyle had refused to let George Sand's name be mentioned under his roof. Margaret hoped that the tales of Sand's lovers were exaggerated, but found that they were true. Yet many women considered it an honor to visit her; even some Americans spoke of her with esteem. Margaret noted too that Mme Sand, as she was called in Paris, had subscribed twenty thousand francs for the relief of the poor—five thousand more than she was paid for a novel.

Margaret had a letter of introduction from Mazzini, as was the custom, and went to call. A servant mangled the name of Fuller, and Mme Sand sent word that she did not know the caller, although Margaret had written earlier. Then George Sand herself, dressed in a robe of violet silk with a black mantle, opened a door and said, "C'est vous." They went into the study to talk. "I loved, shall always love her," wrote Margaret to Elizabeth Hoar. Despite the fact that George Sand was very busy preparing copy for the printer, she spent most of the day with her visitor. Margaret's puritan prejudices broke down. To Elizabeth she wrote:

> She needs no defense, but only to be understood, for she has bravely acted out her nature and always with good intentions. She might have loved one man permanently, if she could have found one contemporary with her who could interest and command with her throughout her range; but there was hardly a possibility of that, for such a person.

Margaret even took it in her stride that Mme Sand smoked cigarettes.

Later Margaret heard Chopin play especially for her. She speculated that he needed the relationship with George Sand because he needed her care. But then the puritan asserted itself: ". . . you cannot know much about anything in France, except what you see with your two eyes. Lying is ingrained in *la grande nation.*"

The other person she wanted to see was the poet Béranger, whom she regarded as an apostle of democracy. She had the luck to meet him during a call upon La Mennais. The three had a pleasant conversation in the latter's study. These men were "the true kings, the theocratic kings, the judges in Israel."

Because she discovered that her French accent was poor she took lessons in pronunciation. While in Paris she had a tooth pulled under ether, but the pain lingered for several days until one night it suddenly disappeared while she was listening to *Don Giovanni*. Like Hawthorne she foreshadowed something of what is now called psychosomatic medicine: "Ah! if physicians only understood the influence of the mind over the body, instead of treating, as they so often do, their patients like machines. . . ."

Another step in her European education came with her meeting with Adam Mickiewicz, the exiled Polish poet. Like Mazzini, Mickiewicz had abandoned literature for revolutionary politics. Like Margaret he preached the equality of the sexes. Margaret, having read his lectures and his interpretation of Emerson, sent him Emerson's poems and invited him to call. According to his son, Mickiewicz so moved her by his eloquence on their first meeting that she fainted on the sofa. It is obvious from his letters to her that she made a deep impression on him. In his first he said

> Your spirit is linked with the history of Poland, of France and is beginning to link itself with the history of America.
>
> You belong to the second generation of spirits.
>
> Your mission is to contribute to the deliverance of Polish, French and American womanhood.

However, he raised questions about her virginity:

> You have acquired the right to know and to maintain the rights and the obligations, the hopes and the exigencies of virginity. For you the first step of your deliverance and of the deliverance of your sex (of a certain class) is to know, whether you are permitted to remain a virgin.

He signed himself, "Thy brother A——."

When she went to Italy his letters to her continued to exhort her to live more fully. In March he advised: "Learn to appreciate yourself as a beauty, and after having admired the women of Rome, say, 'And as for

me, why I am beautiful!' " In April: "Try to bring away from Italy what
you will be able to take of it in joy and health." In August:

> I tried to make you understand that you should not confine your life
> to books and reveries. You have pleaded the liberty of woman in a
> masculine and frank style. Live and act as you write. . . .

> I saw you, with all your knowledge and your imagination and your
> literary reputation, living in bondage worse than that of a servant.
> You were obligated to everybody. You have persuaded yourself that
> all you need is to express ideas and feelings in books. You existed
> like a ghost that whispers to the living its plans and desires, no
> longer able to realize them itself.

Margaret thought the letter harsh, but Mickiewicz replied in the same
vein, "try to get this inner life lodged and established in all your body.
You still live spiritually in the society of Shakespeare, Schiller, Byron.
Literature is not the whole of life." He suggested that she spend less time
with her traveling companions. Much of this advice came at the precise
moment in her life when she had an opportunity to put it into practice.

She left Paris in February for Marseilles, where she took a steamer to
Italy. Genoa failed to charm. Between Leghorn and Naples her boat was
rammed by another and she barely escaped drowning. But at Naples her
dreams were realized:

> I could not realize that I had actually touched those shores to which
> I had looked forward all my life, where it seemed that the heart
> would expand and the whole nature be turned to delight. . . . Only
> at Naples have I found *my* Italy.

Yet there was an ambivalence of response: Naples was "priest-ridden,
misgoverned, full of dirty, degraded men and women, yet still most lovely
Naples." She visited the Grotto of Pausilippo, Cuma, Baiae, Capri, and
climbed Vesuvius, all of them "with a charm unhackneyed, unhackney-
able, which the boots of English dandies cannot trample out, nor the
raptures of sentimental tourists fade or daub."

She liked the Italians but regarded the traveling English as "the most
unseeing of all possible animals:"

> What is the vulgarity expressed in our tobacco-chewing and way
> of eating eggs, compared to that which elbows the Greek marbles,

guidebook in hand—chatters and sneers through the Miserere of the Sistine Chapel . . . praises St. Peter's as "nice"—talks of *"managing"* the Colosseum by moonlight,—and snatches *"bits"* for a *"sketch"* from the sublime silence of the Campagna.

In Rome she visited the studios of American painters and sculptors. The workrooms of Gott held her longest, for she found his spaniels far better than most of the marble nymphs and muses of other sculptors. But she also admired the work of Crawford. She was pleased that he had joined the Italian National Guard. In the museums she learned to appreciate most the paintings of Domenichino and Titian. But sightseeing soon became boring. She visited the Colosseum by moonlight and remarked that the owls hooting there spoke more to the purpose than any voice she had heard on the subject. To William Henry Channing she wrote:

> Art is not important to me now. . . . I take interest in the state of the people, their manners, the state of the race in them. I see the future dawning; it is in important aspects Fourier's future. But I like no Fourierites; they are terribly wearisome here in Europe. . . .

Margaret had another interest which she did not write about to Boston. One April evening coming out of St. Peter's she got separated from the Springs. A polite young Roman offered to help her find a carriage. When they failed, he walked with her from St. Peter's to the Corso. Despite her halting Italian the two were greatly attracted to each other, and the young man, the Marquis Giovanni Ossoli, began calling on Margaret. Mrs. Story, who met him frequently in Margaret's rooms, described him as tall and slender, with quiet manners and a melancholy expression.

When Pope Pius IX seemed ready to grant long overdue reforms, the Romans held a torchlight procession. Ossoli marched in it and Margaret watched from her window. On their walks together she talked to him of Mazzini and won him over as a convert to the revolutionary movement. When she wrote to Mickiewicz about her new friend, he replied, "Do not leave lightly those who would like to remain near you." He followed this up with the advice already quoted about the danger of living vicariously. Ossoli suggested marriage, but there were difficulties. He was only twenty-eight and she thirty-seven. His family was traditionally in the service of the Pope and marriage to a Protestant would endanger his small patrimony. Sometime during that summer or autumn they became lovers.

Late in the summer she made a journey with the Springs to Switzerland. The Springs went on to Germany and Margaret visited Florence, which she found she did not like. For one thing she became so ill for three weeks that she might have died had not a banker's family looked after her. In Florence she met Horatio Greenough and Hiram Powers, whose Greek Salve at first entranced her, but later seemed merely "a form of simple and sweet beauty" lacking in ideal beauty or plastic power. Greenough interested her for another reason: he was one of the few Americans living in Italy who took the pains to know whether it was alive or dead, who could penetrate beneath the cheats of the tradesmen and the cunning of a people corrupted by centuries of oppression. She complained that many Americans talked about the Italians as they did about the slaves at home: because people were degraded by bad institutions, it was assumed that they were not fit for better ones.

There were, she found, three classes of touring Americans: "the servile," who came to spend money; "the conceited," who bristled with national pride; and "the thinking American," who valued his own country but wished to carry back and plant the seeds of European culture. Nevertheless, "The American in Europe, of a thinking mind, can only become more American."

Her Italian experience led her to a re-evaluation of her own country, its virtues and its defects. She could take pride in the freedom of the press, in the quality of many men in public life. But part of the earlier American dream was sullied by "the boundless lust of gain" and especially by slavery. It pleased her to think of the abolitionists despite their tediousness and narrowness. There were also among American youth, ardent souls who would help to "give soul to the huge, over-fed, too hastily grown-up body." She wondered if the idealistic young people she had found in England, France, and Italy would have the courage and purity to fight for a better day.

At first, like many liberals, she had been enthusiastic about Pope Pius IX, who seemed friendly to the cause of Italian unification and more democratic government. In September 1847 Mazzini in London wrote a letter to the Pope calling upon him to lead the movement for unification. Margaret reported it in full to the *Tribune*.

In October she returned to Rome, where she took an apartment in the Corso. She hoped to keep her expenses down to $400 for six months. She was, she felt, no longer a staring, sight-seeing stranger. On Monday evenings she received friends, chief among them the Christopher Cranches and the Storys. Not since her childhood had she felt so well. "Italy has been glorious to me," she told Emerson, "and there have been hours in which I received the full benefit of the vision. . . . I find how true was the lure that always drew me towards Europe. It was no false instinct that said I might find an atmosphere to develop me in ways I need." Too much of her life, she thought, had been wasted in abstractions because she did not grow in the right soil.

Abstractions were indeed not her problem: she was pregnant. Just when she and Ossoli were secretly married is not known. Mrs. Story, as an afterthought, suggested that it was in December, but she may have been charitably counting backwards from the birth of Margaret's child. There is some evidence that the marriage took place in April 1848.

As if this were not enough, Margaret was soon plunged into the exciting events of 1848. Revolution in France had been followed by uprisings in the Italian states, which declared their independence from Austria. Rome was in a ferment of revolution. Ossoli joined the Civic Guard. Margaret's letters to the *Tribune* became an excellent running account of the exciting events. To Emerson she wrote:

> It is a time such as I always dreamed of, and for long secretly hoped to see. I rejoice to be in Europe at this time, and I shall return possessed of a great history. Perhaps I shall be called to act. At present, I know not where to go, what to do. War is everywhere.

In a letter to the *Tribune* she pled that America should learn the real meaning of the words *Fraternity, Equality,* that the country would learn to guard "the true aristocracy of a nation, the only really nobles—THE LABORING CLASSES." She excoriated the kind of tourist who regarded the revolution as a nuisance:

> The rich English traveller, fearing to see the Prince Borghese stripped of one of his palaces for a hospital or some such low use, thinks of his own twenty-mile park and the crowded village of beggars at his gate, and muses; "I hope to see them all shot yet, the rascally republicans."

However, she found time during the carnival to attend a German artists' ball and the Italian masked ball. Mickiewicz came from France and visited her frequently. In April she rejoiced that Italy was free, independent, and unified, but prophetically remarked that it seemed too good, too speedy a realization of hope.

Then came the defection of the Pope. Asked to declare war on Austria he called a consistory and then declared that he had intended only local reforms; the war was offensive to the spirit of religion. Despite her belief that a republican form of government would eventually prevail in the civilized world, Margaret was enough of a realist to suggest that Italy might not be ripe for it.

In May she went to Rieti in the Umbrian Apennines to await the birth of her child. Ossoli visited her weekly, bringing mail and news. She had told no one in Boston of her pregnancy and marriage. The Storys, apparently also unaware of the situation, urged her to visit them in their villa at Sorrento. Much of the time she devoted to writing her European experiences. The situation would have been idyllic, for as she told Emerson she loved the peasants, and they found her *simpatica,* but she was plagued by the lack of money. For some reason none came from the *Tribune* and none from home. At times it seemed as if she had no friends. Later to her sister she revealed that the peasants of whom she had written so glowingly to Emerson were "ferocious and mercenary." Believing her to be a rich, ignorant *Inglese* they had tried to plunder her.

For a time it seemed as if Ossoli would have to go to the frontier with the Civic Guard, but the Pope suspended the departure of the troops. Ossoli was with her when their child was born on September 5. It was baptized Angelo Eugene Philip. The village priest gave a Latin document certifying that Angelo was the legal heir to Ossoli's title and share of the estate.

In November she returned to Rome with Ossoli, leaving the child with a nurse. Her reasons were threefold: to help in the struggle for liberty, to earn money by writing, and to preserve the secrecy of her marriage. At the sight of the city her heart welled even to tears and she echoed Bryon's cry: "O, Rome, *my* country, city of the soul!" Something of her tortured state of mind appears in a letter to her mother:

> Of other circumstances which complicate my position I cannot write. Were you here, I would confide in you fully. . . . In earlier days I dreamed of doing and being much, but now am content with the Magdalen to rest my plea hereon, *"She has loved much."*

Her choice of allusion suggests the Boston heritage of a sense of guilt.

Greeley wrote asking her to resume the letters to the *Tribune* and raising the price from $8 to $10. He was indeed getting a bargain, for the letters run to ten or fifteen printed pages. The earlier exclamatory style was largely replaced by straightforward narrative. The letters from Rome are no longer those of a schoolgirl but of a mature, thoughtful woman. To a large degree she kept her own sufferings out of them. In fact she began to write like a trained war correspondent. Europe had indeed proved to be a maturing experience.

In February 1849 the Roman Republic was proclaimed. The Pope left Rome and excommunicated the revolutionists. Mazzini returned to Italy and called upon Margaret by night to avoid public demonstrations upon his appearance on the streets. She went twice to the Assembly to hear him speak. For a time it was hoped that France would intervene on the side of the revolution, but Louis Napoleon was not the friend of liberty he had been thought. A French army was sent to put down the uprising.

When the siege of Rome began, Margaret was made *Regolatrice* of the Hospital of the *Fate-Bene Fratelli.* Soon she learned the terrible effect of gunshot wounds. She saw men with amputated arms and legs. From her slender means she gave generously—Mrs. Story never knew anyone so generous. Ossoli, stationed near the Vatican, was in a post of danger. Daily Margaret dreaded that she would see him brought bleeding into the hospital.

Almost all other Americans fled the city. Before the Storys left, Margaret confided to Emelyn Story the secret of her marriage, and exacted a promise that should she and Ossoli be killed the Storys would look after Angelo and take him to Mrs. Fuller in America. Margaret left with Mrs. Story her autobiographical manuscript and the document attesting to Angelo's right to his father's title.

To Emerson she wrote that she had received his letter amid the din of cannonade and musketry. It grieved her that the beautiful oaks and villas were being destroyed. From her balcony she could see the progress of the fighting. A French rocket had exploded in the courtyard of the hospital just as she was arriving. After the French victory she visited the scene of the heaviest fighting and was impressed by the difference between the military installations of a professional army and those of the Roman volunteers.

To Emerson she expressed doubt that she should ever get home. But she no longer wished to live in Rome. "O Rome, *my* country! could I imagine that the triumph of what I held dear was to heap such desolation on thy head!" She told Channing, "I have played for a new stake and lost it. Life looks too difficult." The stake was not only her hopes for Italian liberty but the possibility that Ossoli would obtain a post under the new government and that he could acknowledge his marriage.

She returned to Rieti only to find that the nurse had neglected Angelo and that he was near death. It required incessant nursing to bring the child back to health. Prophetically she wrote: "But I could not let him go, unless I went with him; and I do hope that the cruel law of my life will, at least, not oblige us to be separated." The Ossolis took the child to Perugia, where with careful nursing he became well and strong.

At long last Margaret wrote to her mother telling of her marriage and a year-old child. She told Mrs. Fuller to write in the family Bible, "Angelo Ossoli, born September 5, 1848. God grant he may live to see you, and may prove worthy of your love." She and Ossoli planned to spend the winter in Florence and then come to the United States. But there were the old self-doubts. After praising her husband Margaret added: "I do not know whether he will always love me so well, for I am the elder, and the difference will become, in a few years, more perceptible than now. But life is so uncertain, and it is necessary to take good things with their limitations."

Mrs. Fuller answered with an affectionate letter which only stirred up Margaret's New England conscience the more. "It is only since I have had my own child that I have known how much I always failed to do what I might have done for the happiness of you both. . . ."

Margaret told her mother that she was sad at the prospect of leaving Italy, but that Ossoli, like all young Italians, thought of America as the land of liberty. However, he hoped that in a few years a new revolution would make possible his return to Italy.

In Florence Mrs. Story noted that she had rarely seen such a tender, unselfish love as Ossoli showed his wife. "It made green her days and gave her an expression of peace and serenity which before was a stranger to her." Margaret herself spoke of an interval of peace, but she thought of it as the "halcyon prelude to the storm." The police gave them leave to stay and they felt safe in their little apartment.

What then was the storm she feared? For despite Mrs. Story's picture of serene days such as Margaret had rarely known, the letters home show an undercurrent of foreboding.

> "Do not you die, my beloved mother;—let us together have some halcyon moments, again, with God, with nature, with sweet childhood, with the remembrance of pure trust and good intent; away from perfidy and care, and the blight of noble designs."

Margaret had seen much in Europe to destroy her earlier illusions. The Pope, whom she had first admired, had turned against liberal ideals; the French had become the champions of reaction. And there were private betrayals. Angelo's first nurse had been seduced and had to be discharged; his second one, after taking Margaret's money, had let him nearly die from neglect. The girl the Ossolis brought with them from Rieti tried to stab another lodger with whom she had a feud. Margaret had intervened as she had done more than once before to head off Italian violence. Mrs. Story told several anecdotes of Margaret's peace-making abilities at country inns.

She wanted to go home but she dreaded the Boston "social inquisition," the prying into all the details of her life. As she told Emelyn Story:

> If my mother is content; if Ossoli and I are content; if the child, when grown up, shall be content; that is enough. You and I know enough of the United States to be sure that many persons there will blame whatever is peculiar. The lower-minded persons, everywhere, are sure to think that whatever is mysterious must be bad.

It was Fenimore Cooper's complaint all over again.

Through her letters runs a sense of foreboding. Ten months before she sailed she wrote to her sister:

> The journey home seems so long, so difficult, so expensive. I should really like to lie down here, and sleep my way into another sphere of existence, if I could take with me one or two that I love and need me, and was sure of a good haven for them on the other side.
>
> The world seems to go so strangely wrong. The bad side triumphs; the blood and tears of the generous flow in vain. . . . Eternity is with us, but there is much darkness and bitterness in this portion of

it. A baleful star rose on my birth, and its hostility, I fear, will never be disarmed while I walk below.

It was of course natural that she should be unhappy over the defeat of the cause to which she had devoted so much thought and energy, but she was happy in her marriage and in her child. Her letters are filled with praise of both. It would seem that the dread of Boston puritanism was a fearful thing.

Her last letter from Europe to her mother almost suggests precognition:

> Should anything hinder our meeting upon earth, think of your daughter, as one who always wished, at least, to do her duty, and who always cherished you, according as her mind opened to discover excellence. . . . I hope we shall be able to pass some time together in this world. But if God decrees otherwise,—here and HEREAFTER, my dearest mother,

> > Your loving child,
> > Margaret

Because they could not afford steamer passage the Ossolis sailed in May in the brig *Elizabeth*. Already in debt to Sam Ward, Mme Visconti, and others, Margaret borrowed from Marcus Spring for the voyage. She instructed her brother how to pay the bill "in case of accident." Soon after they left Gibraltar the captain died of smallpox. After a stay in quarantine they sailed under the command of the first mate. Two days later Angelo came down with smallpox. The parents treated him with cooling drinks and wet applications to the skin. The child recovered and Margaret went back to work on her book on Italy. Ossoli and Horace Sumner exchanged lessons in Italian and English.

On July 18 the ship ran into heavy weather. The officer in command believed himself to be between Cape May and Barnegat. Then the hurricane struck and the ship, close-reefed, drove ahead faster than was calculated. On the morning of the nineteenth it struck a sand bar on Fire Island. The boats were swamped or carried away.

When the cabin seemed about to break up, the mate, Davis, called on the sailors to help the passengers across the deck to the forecastle. Angelo was carried in a sling. Three times the mate made the perilous journey to retrieve belongings of the passengers. Margaret did not have the heart to ask him to make a fourth trip for her precious manuscript of the Italian revolution.

It was now discovered that the shore was only a few hundred yards away. A sailor with a life preserver and another with a spar managed to reach shore. Sumner tried it, but was drowned. Then Davis got Mrs. Hasty to the beach on a plank although once they were overturned. Now it was Margaret's turn. But she refused to be separated from Ossoli and Angelo. There was still some hope that Davis could get hold of a boat and return to the ship. However, when a boat was finally found, there was no attempt to launch it. As the storm had lulled somewhat, the commanding officer again tried to induce Margaret to try to escape. He would himself take Angelo and the sailors were to go with Ossoli and the maid Celeste. Margaret again refused, and the order was given to the sailors to save themselves.

Several of them made it safely. Only four seamen remained on the ship. At last the steward took Angelo in his arms just as a heavy wave struck the forecastle, bringing down the mast. Twenty minutes later the steward and Angelo were washed ashore, both dead. Margaret and Ossoli were caught in the rigging and drowned. When last seen she had been seen seated at the foot of the foremast, clad in her white nightdress, with her hair fallen upon her shoulders. Her death wish was realized; she did not have to face the social inquisition of Boston which she had so much dreaded.

THE AMBIVALENT PURITAN
NATHANIEL HAWTHORNE

When Nathaniel Hawthorne went to Liverpool as consul in 1853 he had already written *The Scarlet Letter, The House of the Seven Gables,* and most of his best short stories. It was six years before he began *The Marble Faun,* based upon his Italian visit. This was the only work of fiction he completed during his seven-year stay abroad. True, he had filled his notebooks with impressions of England, France, and Italy—the English notebooks alone running to 200,000 words—but he could not seem to get down to creative work.

The *English* and *Italian Notebooks* are filled with impressions of places and people, but unlike the *American Notebooks* they contain few jottings of ideas for stories. In fact, despite their often perceptive comments, they show small evidence of an original, creative mind. Page after page is devoted to guidebook descriptions of cathedrals, ruined abbeys, quaint towns, and all the other tourist attractions. On several occasions Hawthorne mentions his plan for an English romance, but he could never seem to get his teeth into it.

His lack of productivity during his years in Europe is not to be entirely explained by his duties as consul. As far back as 1847 he had written to Longfellow, saying that his mornings in the Salem custom house knocked out of his head the ideas of the night before for stories. On another occasion he had complained of his lack of materials due to his limited knowledge of the world. Yet despite his complaints he had managed to write. In Europe, as his letters and notebooks show, he saw a great deal of the world, and as consul had to listen to tales of woe and adventure poured out by hundreds of his countrymen. There was the rich and varied European scene. At first his duties as consul were heavy, but as time went on, he spent much time away from the office—on one occasion three weeks in London. And he found time for the almost daily stint of writing long entries in his notebooks.

Part of the explanation of his lack of creativity may lie in the ambivalence of his response to the Old World. It would be difficult to cite such conflicting emotions on the part of any other expatriate before Henry James. Irving, throughout most of his years abroad, had largely accepted

Europe on its own terms; Cooper had remained the American in Europe, viewing everything from certain well-established points of view, as to a considerable degree had Ticknor, Bancroft, and Cogswell. The sculptors Greenough, Powers, and Story were part of an American colony in Italy. But for over four years Hawthorne was very much a participant in English life; he even thought of settling in England. With his letters and the Notebooks before us we can follow some of the convolutions of his conflicting responses to Europe.

When the Hawthornes sailed for Liverpool in the summer of 1853 they took along their three children: Una aged nine; Julian, seven; and Rose (whom Nathaniel called "Rosebud"), only two. At first Nathaniel seems to have given little thought to the effect of expatriation upon the children, but as will appear, it became a matter of increasing concern. At first the family stayed at Mrs. Blodgett's boarding house, but within a month moved to a house at Rockferry, the first of many residences they were to occupy in England. They paid £160 a year for a place with shrubbery and gardens such as only the very rich could enjoy in America.

At the time Hawthorne was appointed consul, the remuneration was in the form of fees which he hoped would amount to at least $10,000 a year. Later on when Congress proposed a flat salary of $7,500 he talked of giving up the post. There were numerous expenses connected with the job, and Americans who got into difficulties made constant appeals for loans. His fellow countrymen were, he thought, the most vagabond people on earth. It seemed to him that nothing was more common than for a young American deliberately to spend all his resources in an aesthetic peregrination of Europe, returning with pockets empty "to begin the world in earnest." His letters and journals are filled with references to money lent to fellow citizens—a number of whom he considered bad risks. For others he arranged a passage home as seamen, despite "pathetic appeals from painters and musicians, touching the damage which their artistic fingers were likely to incur from handling the ropes."

As consul Hawthorne saw much of the ugly side of American life. Because of the brutal conditions on American ships he was constantly called upon to visit law courts, hospitals, and undertaking establishments. He took depositions from dying men, he sent their effects home, he helped to bury them, and he sent back reports to authorities at home. On one occasion he found evidence that a man who brought a trunk aboard a ship had been kidnaped, compelled to serve, brutally treated, and left to die in England—"a strange thing to happen in the United States," he commented.

After seeing much of this kind of thing he wrote in his journal, "There is a most dreadful state of things aboard our ships. Hell itself can be no worse than some of them; and I do pray that some New Englander with an itch of reform in him, will turn his thoughts this way." Two years later he wrote to William Ticknor, his friend and publisher, ". . . there is nothing in this world so much like hell as the interior of an American ship." He said that he had made repeated statements on this to government officials and had pled with Charles Sumner to bring the matter before Congress. "Had he busied himself about this instead of Abolitionism, he would have done good service to his country and have escaped Brooks's cudgel."

Hawthorne was not a reformer or a sentimentalist. He believed that philanthropy had overshot itself by prohibiting flogging, with the result that captains unable to inflict "solemn punishment" were forced to let the mates "make devils of themselves by habitual (and hardly avoidable) ill-treatment of the seamen." At the start of a voyage all the men were drunk, some with delirium tremens. Sailors on American ships were a particularly brutal class of men. On one occasion he got an alcoholic captain to sign a pledge of abstinence; then, pleased with himself, Hawthorne took too much wine and suffered a hangover. On another he had to deal with a clergyman from New Orleans who had gone on a spree and spent a week in a brothel. Hawthorne read the man such a lecture that he shook in his shoes. "Not knowing whether I should ever have another opportunity of preaching to a Doctor of Divinity (an orthodox man, too) I laid it on without mercy."

But street scenes in Liverpool were uglier than anything he had seen at home. Almost the first things he noted were the spirit vaults every few steps with their sinister advertisement of "Beds" for the drunks. On the streets "with dreadful faces thronged" he saw such squalor as he had never imagined. In a charity school the children were stupid and animal-like: "All America could not show the like." In December there were barefoot women and children on the streets. Later when he visited Scotland he found the poorer classes of Glasgow even more drunken than those of Liverpool. The Scotch seemed to get drunk at very unreasonable hours.

In contrast to the wretched poor the middle classes seemed bloated and overfed, especially the women. At Lord Mayor's banquets he had ample opportunity to see the gluttonous feeding of the well-to-do. After a civic banquet where he ate turtle soup, salmon, woodcock, oyster patties, and could have eaten twenty other things, he saw a large throng of poor lined up waiting for a handout of soup: "there does seem to be an insolence of riches and prosperity, which one day or another will have a downfall." One result of the rich English diet was that

> The women of England are capable of being more atrociously ugly than any other human beings. . . . As a general rule, they are not very desirable objects in youth and, in many instances, become perfectly grotesque after middle age; so massive, not seemingly with pure fat, but with solid beef making an awful ponderosity of frame. You think of them as composed of sirloins, and with broad thick steaks on their immense rears.

(It is perhaps understandable that Sophia Hawthorne inked out certain passages in her husband's journals and bowdlerized the selections she published.)

A year later after a soirée given by the Mayor he made even more vitriolic notes in his journal:

> . . . my experience is, that an English lady of forty or fifty is apt to become the most hideous animal that ever pretended to human shape. No caricature could do justice to some of their figures and features; so puffed out, so huge, so without limit, with such hanging dewlaps, and all manner of fleshly abomination—dressed, too, in a way to show all these points to the worst advantage. . . . They are gross, gross, gross. Who would not shrink from such a mother! Who would not abhor such a wife! I really pitied the respectable elderly gentlemen whom I saw walking about with such atrocities hanging on their arms—the grim, red-faced monsters! Surely a man would be justified in murdering them—. . . .

As he frequently did, he went on to say that he preferred his own countrywomen although he felt it a shame that one had to choose between "a greasy animal and an anxious skeleton."

Before he had been in England a year he wrote Ticknor that he was getting to look John Bullish on roast beef, brown stout, port, and sherry. "I never felt better in my life. England is certainly the country to eat in and drink in." That was in May; late in June he was complaining of the detestable climate which forced them to keep fires. The whole family, including himself, had whooping cough. In July he planned to take the children to Wales for a change of air, but he felt that one week of his Concord hillside would do the whole family more good than all the English air that was ever breathed.

However, he added that things were in such a "confounded mess" in the United States that they might never come home. He could not read American newspapers without being ashamed of his country. It was no wonder, he said, that Englishmen hated and despised Americans.

Hawthorne's letters and journals are filled with pendulum-like swings from liking to revulsion—both for his own country and for England. Part of the reason was that he consciously attempted to see everything with fresh eyes: ". . . all past affairs, all home-conclusions, all people whom I have known in America, and meet again here, are strangely compelled to undergo a new trial." These things did not necessarily suffer from a comparison with English life, customs, and people, but he felt that being free of his old surroundings and the inevitable prejudices of home he could "decide upon them absolutely." Some of his swings of emotion can be accounted for by the accidents of everyday life, like the whooping cough and a cold June. Thus his praise of English food turns to a complaint about its monotony when they had to pay as he said, like nabobs, during a trip to the Lake Country.

But much of his ambivalence about foreign things and about his own country grow out of conflicts within the man himself. One of the most obvious themes in his journals is the pull between his love of good food and drink and his Puritan distrust of such pleasure. Thus he alternates between comments upon the thick-wittedness of a people devoted to beef, mutton, ale, and port and a kind of admiration for such simple enjoyments. For instance, after deploring the amount of liquor consumed by the English at Christmas he added, "They are still a nation of beastly eaters and beastly drinkers." Yet three months later he mused benignly upon a group of white headed men eating dinner:

> There is a satisfaction in seeing Englishmen eat and drink, they do it so heartily, and on the whole so wisely—trusting so entirely that there is no harm in good beef and mutton, and a reasonable quantity of good liquor; and these three hale and hearty old men, who acted

on this wholesome faith for ever so long, were proofs that it is well, on earth, to live like earthly creatures. In America, what squeamishness, what delicacy, what stomachic apprehensions, would there not be among three stomachs of sixty or seventy years' experience!

The moral implications of the enjoyment of food become of even more concern to him in France.

> . . . I doubt whether English cookery, for the very reason that it is so simple, is not better for men's moral and spiritual nature than French. In the former case, you know that you are gratifying your animal needs and propensities, and are duly ashamed of it. . . .

Yet only four days later he noted that it was thwarting Providence to treat food as the English do: producing from better materials than those available to the French "nothing but sirloins, joints, joints, steaks, steaks, steaks, chops, chops, chops, chops, chops!" After describing the fine French meal he concluded: "It was all very good, and we respected ourselves far more than if we had eaten a quantity of red roast beef; but I am not quite sure that we were right. . . ."

It is ironic that Hawthorne, puritanically concerned about the pleasures of the table, wrote more about food and drink than did any of the other expatriates, including such gourmets as Henry James and Edith Wharton. It would seem that Hawthorne could not eat a chop or drink a glass of ale—both of which he enjoyed for lunch—without noting it down.

Certainly he was no prohibitionist. Even before he went abroad he wrote from Concord to William Ticknor saying that thanks to gifts from friends he had claret, sauterne, champagne, and sherry, and he had laid in a supply of first-rate brandy on his own hook: "so I hope to keep myself pretty jolly, in spite of the Maine law." In England he customarily had ale with his lunch and when traveling often stopped in for a refreshing mug. Nor was he unfamiliar with a drink before lunch: ship captains entertaining guests usually offered brandy, and Hawthorne accepted it. At public dinners where he was called upon to speak he found it was quite painless if he were "pot valiant with champagne." After one such speech he complained to Ticknor that the papers had misquoted him. "I was about half seas over when I got up to speak; but I swear I spoke a devilish sight better than that." Despite the fact that another of his after-dinner speeches was well received, it seemed to him that "it is altogether a ridiculous custom to talk in one's cups."

Hawthorne's feelings about England and the English were even more mixed than his emotions about food and drink. During his first year in Liverpool he confided to his notebook, "I think I have been happier this Christmas, than ever before,—by our own fireside, and with my wife and children about me." In June of 1855 he wrote to Ticknor, "Massachusetts must be a very uncomfortable place, just now, with your liquor laws and other nonsense. I wish we could annex this island to the Union, and that I could have an estate here in Warwickshire." A month later he noted that the papers from home had made him sick of America, and that he had been bothered with his own countrymen and their "troublesome peculiarities." "I need a residence of two or three years on the Continent, to give me a sense of freedom."

Shortly after this when some Americans stayed in his boarding-house he noted: "My mind has been considerably enlivened, and my sense of American superiority renewed, by intercourse with these people; and there is no danger of one's intellect becoming a standing pool, and a scum gathering over it in such society." In October he told Ticknor that he loved England so much that he wanted to annex it, "and it is by no means beyond the scope of possibility that we may do so, though hardly in my time." But in a letter two weeks later he said: "I HATE England, though I love some Englishmen, and like them generally, in fact." By December he was writing in his notebook:

> There are some English whom I like—one or two for whom, I might almost say, I have an affection;—but still there is not the same union between us, as if they were Americans . . . . in this foreign land, I can never forget the distinction between English and American.

Only about a year later he told Ticknor that he would be well content to spend the remainder of his days in England—"though certainly not in the office of Liverpool Consul." And in April of 1857 he said that he was leaving England with regret, "and if I were rich enough, I doubt whether I should ever leave it for a permanent residence elsewhere."

When he finally returned to America, he tried to assess his feelings toward England in *Our Old Home:*

After all these bloody wars and vindictive animosities, we have still an unspeakable yearning towards England. When our forefathers left the old home, they pulled up many of their roots, but trailed along with them others, which never snapped asunder. . . . It has required nothing less than the boorishness, the stolidity, the self-sufficiency, the contemptuous jealousy . . . that characterize this strange people, to compel us to be a great nation in our own right, instead of continuing virtually, if not in name, a province of their small island. What pains did they take to shake us off, and have ever since taken to keep us apart from them.

Many Americans, including those who have governed our foreign policy, have felt ambivalent towards England, but few individuals have shown more violent swings of emotion than Hawthorne. In fact, his letters and journals suggest a manic-depressive personality.

Like any manic-depressive Hawthorne could find objective reasons for his swings of emotion: a bad day at the office could make Americans unpleasant; an incident in the street—such as seeing women pick up fresh horse dung in their hands—could disgust him with the English. In the same letter he could deplore the necessity of making after-dinner speeches as the most unpleasant chore of his office, and could rejoice at his sense of power when on his feet. He approached such occasions as Lord Mayor's dinners with dread, but after a quantity of champagne, found that he enjoyed public speaking.

More important than all his ambivalence is the fact that Hawthorne was a perceptive observer of English life. Thus although his observations are colored by his temperament and by his moods, they are often extremely vivid. And even in his alternation between attacks on England and on America there is a kind of unity—the point of view of the transcendentalist for whom the affairs of everyday life fall short of the ideal. Apropos of English businessmen he wrote: "I have been quite impressed to find that our respectable merchants have a higher moral standard than the same class of men here. We Americans are the best people in the world,—but it is a poor world at that."

Granting Hawthorne's own ambivalence, his revulsion against a world which fell short of his transcendental ideal, there were a number of very down-to-earth reasons for his mental conflicts about American and English values. Like almost all American expatriates in the 1850's he was unhappy about affairs at home. Unlike most of his New England compatriots at home and abroad he was not an abolitionist. In so far as he took any position in the matter of slavery it was that of his classmate at Bowdoin, Franklin Pierce. In 1860 this caused him some difficulty and disrepute in New England. On the whole, however, his attitude was "a plague on both your houses." Thus in 1857 he wrote to Ticknor apropos of affairs in France:

> But there seems to be no stormier prospect any where, than in our own country; and I find myself less and less inclined to come back, with every budget of news that comes from thence. I sympathize with no party, but hate them all—free soilers, pro-slavery men, and whatever else—all alike. In fact I have no country, or only just enough of one to be ashamed of; and I can tell you, an American finds it difficult to hold up his head, on this side of the water, in these days. The English expect to see the republic crumble to pieces, and are chuckling over the anticipation. This is all nonsense, of course; but it grinds me, nevertheless.

On the other hand there was a coarseness in English life which frequently led him to make comparisons favorable to his own country. His remarks on the grossness of English women have already been quoted. Holiday crowds had an evil odor. At home everyone had work clothes and a holiday suit and was "occasionally as fresh as a rose"; whereas English people on a holiday wore their work clothes. The girls at a fair were plump and homely, most unlike the trim little damsels of his native land.

As a rule Englishmen scoffed at the idea of chastity among the women of the lower classes. The English cottage girl held a social position analogous to that of a Negro girl in the Southern states. England was, he felt, still the "unscrupulous old England of Tom Jones and Joseph Andrews, Humphrey Clinker and Roderick Random."

Running through Hawthorne's commentary is indignation at the social injustices he observed. The dirt of a poverty-stricken street was "a monstrosity unknown on our side of the Atlantic." He saw children carrying home gin in shaving mugs and broken teapots. In Manchester he saw a mass wedding of pauper couples, then a wealthy bride and groom married by a bishop and three or four clergymen. He visualized the fine home they would enjoy.

Is, or is not, the system wrong that gives one married pair so immense a superfluity of luxurious home, and shuts out a million others from any home whatever? One day or another, safe as they deem themselves, and safe as the hereditary temper of the people tends to make them, the gentlemen of England will be compelled to face the question.

On another occasion after going from a workhouse to a wealthy home he mused, "I wonder how many people live and die in the workhouse, having no other house, because other people have a great deal more home than enough!"

Sophia Hawthorne was more naïve as a social observer: "We saw some ugly small manufacturing towns in Lancashire," she wrote, "in which I do not understand how any one can consent to live."

Nathaniel's tastes, he found, were becoming "woefully aristocratic." When he was invited out to dinner, he was conscious of a certain disgust if the house had a small entrance hall and narrow staircase or a parlor with chintz curtains.

Like a number of other expatriates he worried about the effect on the children of long residence abroad.

I sometimes doubt whether this European residence will be good for us, in the long run. All of us will come back with altered habits, accustomed to many things we shall not find at home; and as for the children (though they imagine that they love America above all the rest of the world) they will really belong on this side of the water, rather than on that.

After three years abroad he told Ticknor that he questioned whether he should ever return to America were it not for the children. He loved his country but found that he could live more pleasantly elsewhere. Julian, however, did not share his father's views. He came home one day with a black eye got in a fight with some English boys who, he said, had abused his country, but his father thought the quarrel began with Julian's statement that his highest ambition was to kill an Englishman. It is characteristic of expatriated children to develop an exaggerated loyalty to their homeland. For one thing other children are likely to make fun of the manners and speech of foreigners and to sneer at other lands. As many expatriates, including Irving, Cooper, and Hawthorne, noted, there was considerable anti-American sentiment in England. Certainly the children must have encountered this from English children uninhibited by the polite reticences of adult life.

And like the elder Henry James, the Hawthornes never settled down in one place. During his years as consul the family moved from one residence to another. At one point Hawthorne was commuting twenty miles a day to and from Liverpool. Because of her ill health Mrs. Hawthorne spent the winter of 1855–1856 in Lisbon with the two girls while Nathaniel and Julian stayed in England. And both Sophia and Nathaniel were inveterate sightseers, as a rule taking the children with them through churches, art galleries, and ruins. Sometimes Nathaniel would be away from his office for a week or two, at times on business outside of Liverpool, at others simply touring. "It is a strange, vagabond life this that we are leading," he noted. And again, "What sort of character will it form in the children, this unsettled, shifting, vagrant life, with no central home to turn to except what we carry in ourselves?"

Fortunately the home they carried within themselves was a happy one. In the evening Hawthorne would read aloud from such books as *Robinson Crusoe, Don Quixote,* and *The Lady of the Lake* or would improvise imaginative tales. He taught the children to make paper boats, and Julian's bureau was covered with intricately folded models. They played battledore and shuttlecock and blindman's buff. Because of Julian's interest in natural history, his father took him to zoos and museums of science. On sightseeing tours Julian and Una took along fishing rods, and at least once Una caught a perch. Julian collected bugs, toads, and frogs.

Both Nathaniel and Sophia filled their notebooks with descriptions of scenery and antiquities. Because Chester was not far from Liverpool, Hawthorne visited it often, despite his frequent comments on the evil smell of the place. He walked the ancient city walls and the covered galleries lined with shops; he marveled at the cathedral. As time went on he became increasingly enthusiastic about the great churches. At Lichfield he mused, ". . . it seems to me a Gothic Cathedral may be the greatest work man has yet achieved—a great stone poem." York Minster at first seemed cold and forbidding, but on subsequent visits he became enthusiastic about it. And after seeing Salisbury he wrote, "Cathedrals are almost the only things (if even those) that have quite filled out my ideal, here in the old world. . . ." It was Westminster Abbey which lured him back most often. He never went to London without visiting it at least once. This was the spot which he "had dreamed about more reverently from my childhood upward, than any other in the world." In the Poets' Corner he felt the appropriate emotions but described them less picturesquely than had Cooper and Irving.

Mrs. Hawthorne reveled in the picturesque and wrote of it in a style which may have had something to do with Nathaniel's contempt for female writers. In her journals as published after her husband's death she made such comments on ruined abbeys as: "Thomas à Kempis might here have written his divine sentences, each one so like a translucent drop of that singing, shining fall—including also the infinite serenity of the lawns, and the slumbering sunshine of dim gold." And a few pages later: "Certainly beauty seems to haunt these old abbeys, and to place her magic finger, in especial love, where decay encroaches."

With his characteristic ambivalence Nathaniel was torn between the charm of ancient things and his sense of the stagnation of society. Often in visiting villages and old churches he had a strange sense of having been there before, whether because of his reading, or because of some ancestral memory in his blood, he could not tell. Of one such church he wrote:

> . . . it thrills you with strange emotion to think that this little church of Whitenash, humble as it seems, stood for ages under Catholic faith, and has not materially changed since Wickliffe's days, and that it looked as gray now as in Bloody Mary's time, and that Cromwell's troopers broke off the stone noses of the same gargoyles that are now grinning in your face.

As his Notebooks show, his first reaction to the inherited ways of village life was that "it is rather pleasant to know that such things are." But when in America he reworked some of this description into *Our Old Home*, his opinion was unfavorable:

> Life is there fossilized in its greenest leaf. The man who died yesterday or ever so long ago walks the village street today, and chooses the same wife that he married a hundred years since, and must be buried again tomorrow under the same kindred dust that has already covered him half a score of times. . . . Better than this is the lot of our restless countrymen, whose modern instinct bids them tend always towards "fresh woods and pastures new." Rather than such a monotony of sluggish ages, loitering on a village green,

toiling in hereditary fields, listening to the parson's drone length-
ened through centuries in the gray Norman church, let us welcome
whatever change may come—change of place, social customs, political institutions, modes of worship—trusting that, if all present
things shall vanish, they will make room for better systems, for a
higher type of man to clothe his life in them. . . .

This is of course good transcendental doctrine. Emerson had said,
"Give me insight into today and you may have the antique and future
worlds." Early in his manhood Hawthorne had jotted down as one of his
rules of life: "Break off old customs." In fact he carried this rejection of
the past so far as to wish that the Elgin Marbles were burnt into lime and
the granite Egyptian statues hewn into building blocks. "The present
is burthened too much with the past. We have not time, in our earthly
existence, to appreciate what is warm with life."

Hawthorne had his greatest difficulty with the art of the past. Here his
Puritan heritage kept getting in the way. On first visiting the National
Gallery he felt that with a little attention to the subject he might develop a
taste. But a Venus was "naked and asleep in a most lascivious posture."
(Mrs. Hawthorne inked out the *naked*.) From the Gallery he walked to
St. Paul's, where, after looking at all the monuments, he concluded that
there was nothing very wonderful in any of them and he wished that
English warriors had not usually gone into battle stark naked.

His patriotism did cause him to defend a cast of Hiram Powers'
celebrated Greek Slave which he saw at a country estate. His English
friends criticized the nude figure as too thin and meager, but Hawthorne
agreed that the lady was done in accordance with American ideas of
feminine beauty. Neither party to the discussion apparently noticed that
the work was simply bad art.

When the Hawthornes had been in England four years all of them,
including little Rose and the nurse, visited an exhibition at Old Trafford
of works of famous painters. With the exception of Julian, who escaped to
the Botanical Gardens, they spent the day there, and Nathaniel went back
several times later, alone and with Una. He was, he decided, at last
developing a taste for pictures. In particular he liked the old Dutch
masters, who seemed to him "the most wonderful set of men that ever
handled a brush. . . . Even the photograph cannot equal these miracles."
But he became "weary of naked goddesses, who never had any real life

and warmth in the painter's imagination—or, if so, it was the impure warmth of the unchaste women who sat or sprawled for them."

On one visit to this exhibition Nathaniel caught a glimpse of Tennyson, but not having been introduced, he was too shy to speak to the poet. Instead he hunted up Sophia and the girls so that they might catch a glimpse of "this one poet of our day," a somewhat difficult feat because Tennyson was passing from one picture to another with considerable haste.

An earlier generation of American expatriates met the great poets of the day, Wordsworth and Coleridge, as well as many lesser literary figures. Hawthorne's more limited circle of literary acquaintance was in part no doubt due to his own shyness. It is also probable that the post of Liverpool Consul was not conducive to the meeting of important people. But perhaps the most important element in the situation was that times had changed. Americans in Europe were no longer a novelty. Irving and Cogswell had been guests of Scott at Abbottsford; Cooper had known him well. By the time the Hawthornes visited Abbottsford, the visitors' book contained more names of Americans than of any other people in the world, including those from Great Britain. In the Lake District gardeners and sextons showed Hawthorne the homes and graves of Southey and Wordsworth.

Had he wished, Hawthorne could have exploited his literary reputation, for his work was well known in England. Going to Evans's supper rooms with a friend he was introduced to the manager, a Mr. Green, who gave an enthusiastic welcome. Now that he had had Hawthorne as a guest he felt that it needed only Emerson, Channing, and Longfellow to fulfil the dream of his life. In his notebook Hawthorne remarked dryly that Channing was dead. A Mrs. Hall told him it had been the dream of her life to see Longfellow and himself. "Good heavens! What an object to live for!"

From Surrey, Martin Tupper, author of the immensely popular *Proverbial Philosophy*, sent an invitation, asking Hawthorne to visit his home. With Francis Bennock, a mutual friend, Hawthorne went to Surrey. On the village street they encountered Tupper, a short-legged, round little man, who extended his arms to Bennock and then greeted Hawthorne with "Oh, Great Scarlet Letter." Hawthorne's reaction was characteristic:

> I did not know what the devil to say unless it were, "Oh wondrous Man of Proverbs!—or, "Oh wiser Solomon!"—and as I was afraid

to say either of these, I rather think I held my tongue. I felt in an instant that Tupper was a good soul, but a fussy little man, of a kind that always takes me entirely aback.

Although Hawthorne and Bennock had already breakfasted on two chops apiece, they sat down with the Tuppers and their seven children to a second breakfast. Tupper was a man who could hardly sit down, and even sitting gave the effect of bustling about. He claimed that his house had seven gables although Hawthorne counted eight or nine. He showed six fine lithographs of the Queen's children, pictures presented by Victoria herself in appreciation for *Proverbial Philosophy*, a copy of which she gave to each of her children at an appropriate age. (This may help to explain the behavior of Edward VII.) Hawthorne's comment in his notebook was not very reverent: the pictures showed each child at the same age "so that they would appear to have been littered at one birth, like kittens." He found Tupper's vanity amusing but inoffensive: "I liked him, and laughed in my sleeve at him, and was utterly weary of him."

Hawthorne's association with Monckton Milnes, whom he met on several occasions, was more pleasant. Milnes reminded him of Longfellow, a little thicker in build and "not quite so polished in address" as the American. On one occasion he was invited by Milnes to a ten-o'clock breakfast. Fortifying himself with cold beef and coffee, Hawthorne went sightseeing in Cheapside. After viewing the Guildhall he got lost and arrived fifty minutes late for the breakfast. Here he found George Ticknor—grayer than he had been in Boston, but "in good preservation." Milnes introduced him to Mrs. Browning, "a small delicate woman, with ringlets of black hair (I think they were ringlets, and am sure they were black)." He found her more youthful and pretty than he had supposed. Also present was Mrs. Nightingale, the mother of Florence.

Mrs. Browning was the kind of responsive woman with whom he could talk more easily than with men. She was, he noted, a vegetarian. They talked of spiritualism, a great interest of hers, and of Delia Bacon, whose book on Shakespeare Hawthorne had helped to promote, of Margaret Fuller and of William Story. Margaret had spent her last night in Italy with the Brownings. Hawthorne had been an intimate friend of hers and apparently was not at this point so bitter about her as he became later on. As for spiritualism, he could not understand how a woman of Mrs. Browning's intelligence could be so taken in by it. After breakfast he had a chat in the library with Browning and a gentleman who admired the *Blithedale Romance*. All the guests at the breakfast were people of high rank or remarkable intellect. "An Englishman," he noted, "can hardly be a gentleman unless he enjoys one or the other of these advantages; and perhaps the surest way to give him good manners is, to make a lord of him—or rather, of his grandfather, or great-grandfather."

Another Englishman who impressed Hawthorne as having un-English characteristics was Leigh Hunt, whose home he had visited. Barry Cornwall had written a note of introduction.

> He is a beautiful man. I never saw a finer face. . . . I saw that he was old, his long hair being quite white and his wrinkles many. . . . I have never met an Englishman whose manners pleased me so well. . . . There is not an English trait in him, from head to foot, nor either intellectually or physically; no beef, no ale or stout; and this is the reason that the English have appreciated him no better, and that they leave this sweet and delicate poet poor, and with scanty laurels, in his old age. It is his American blood (his mother was a Pennsylvanian) that gives him whatever excellence he has—the fineness, subtlety, and grace that characterize him—and his person, too, is thoroughly American.

American friends occasionally turned up at the consulate. In November 1856 Melville appeared with a small bundle containing a night shirt and a toothbrush. Hawthorne invited him to stay with the family at Southport, where he remained from Tuesday to Thursday. He noted that Melville was very gentlemanly despite his heterodoxy in the matter of clean linen. The two men took a walk and sat down in the sand to smoke. It was not Europe or America they talked of, but of transcendental matters. Wrote Hawthorne:

> Melville, as he always does, began to reason of Providence and futurity, and of everything that lies beyond human ken. . . . He can neither believe, nor be comfortable in his unbelief; and he is too honest and courageous not to try to do one or the other.

The day after Melville departed, Henry Bright came to the office, and Hawthorne took him sightseeing. On Saturday Hawthorne and Melville went to Chester, which Hawthorne liked; it was the one place near

Liverpool which possessed "an English interest." The two men made a very thorough job of their sightseeing expedition. On Monday Melville came to say goodbye before starting his travels. He said he already felt much better in England than in America, but that he did not much look forward to his rambles: the spirit of adventure had gone.

The friend Hawthorne saw most often was the English merchant, Francis Bennock. Whenever the Hawthornes were in London, Bennock entertained them and took them sightseeing. When Bennock's business failed, Hawthorne was greatly distressed. Realizing the difficulty of a businessman re-establishing himself in England, Hawthorne suggested a new start in America. However, he did not push the matter, for he realized that Bennock was probably too English to succeed in the New World.

Bennock's failure occurred just before the Hawthornes were to go to Italy. This trip was one they had long planned. Sophia was especially eager to see the ancient world she had read so much about. Possibly Margaret Fuller and George Ticknor had helped to stimulate her enthusiasm. In any event she was not disappointed; despite dirt, beggars, and illness she kept journals filled with enthusiastic descriptions of ruins, paintings, and natural scenery.

The Hawthornes had been in England nearly five years and Nathaniel was tired of the consulship. He realized that his income would not pay the expenses of the trip, and decided to draw upon his savings. He told Ticknor that in Italy he hoped to become literary again: in fact he felt the symptoms already. In this hope he was not mistaken. As he had done in England he kept voluminous notebooks, but he also got started on *The Marble Faun*. Europe had at last stimulated his creative imagination. If it were not for the children, who pined for home, he doubted if he would ever come back; he considered himself a citizen of the world.

Before leaving England the Hawthornes engaged Miss Ada Shepard as a governess for the children. Hawthorne had tried English governesses and found them ignorant and inefficient; whereas Miss Shepard was a graduate of "Mr. Mann's College at Antioch." As such she was an early proof of the value of coeducation. Women's institutions doing genuine collegiate work had yet to be founded, so that it was only at Oberlin and Antioch that a woman could get an education equal to a man's. Miss Shepard, a girl of twenty-one, gave instruction in reading, spelling, writing, composition, Latin, Greek, German, French, Italian, arithmetic, alge-bra, geography, and chronology to the Hawthorne children and to other expatriate youngsters who joined her school from time to time.

So proficient was she in French that when Hawthorne, who could read it, but could not understand the rapid speech of the customs officials, became hopelessly bewildered, Miss Shepard acted as interpreter. To her fiancé, Clay Badger, she wrote "As they cannot afford a courier, I do not know what would become of them and their baggage if they were left to themselves."

During the short stay in Paris Hawthorne admired the architecture and the lack of smoke and soot, but felt that Parisian life was too artificial. Always concerned with the moral implications of whatever he saw, he noted, "Nothing really thrives here; man and vegetables have but an artificial life, like flowers stuck in a little mould, but never taking root." Furthermore the weather was frigid and Nathaniel had a severe cold which he could not throw off.

After a week's stay the party, now including the astronomer Maria Mitchell, set out for Italy on January 12, 1858. From the railway carriage en route to Marseilles, Hawthorne saw, for the first time since leaving America, a brilliant sunset. When it got dark, the stars were brighter than any ever seen in England. Miss Mitchell identified some of them for the children. But what chiefly impressed Hawthorne in Marseilles was the filth of the water closet in the hotel, and the lack of privacy in public toilets.

The party took a boat to Civitavecchia, then hired a four-horse car-riage to transport them and their mountain of luggage to Rome. The forty-mile trip took almost ten hours, and part of the road was known to be infested with bandits.

It was still cold when they reached Rome. Julian's first memory was of sliding on the ice in a fountain near St. Peter's. But Mrs. Hawthorne was ecstatic; to her sister she wrote: "I am in Rome, Rome, *Rome!* I have stood in the Forum and beneath the Arch of Titus, at the end of the Sacra Via. I have wandered about the Colosseum the stupendous grandeur of which equals my dream and hope." The list goes on and on. As she wrote in her notebook: "How I like to write down all the illustrious names of what I have all my life long so much desired to see! I cluster them together like jewels, and exult over them." Nathaniel was more sardonic.

In *The Marble Faun* he referred to a party of Americans in the Colosseum, "paying the inevitable visit by moonlight, and exalting themselves with raptures that were Byron's, not their own."

At first Hawthorne was uncomfortable. For the first three months he was hardly ever free from a cold, and the lodgings they had taken—a suite of ten rooms—could not be properly heated; it would take, Hawthorne said, the logs from a New England forest. With a rent of $100 a month for the apartment, living was about as expensive as in England. But by April he wrote to Ticknor:

> Rome struck me very disagreeably at first, but rather improves upon acquaintance, and has a sort of fascination which will make me reluctant to take a final leave of it. I wish I were a little more patriotic; but to confess the truth, I had rather be a sojourner in any other country than return to my own. The United States are fit for many excellent purposes, but they are certainly not fit to live in.

A year later he estimated that there were fifteen hundred Americans in Rome.

That same year produced changes in his own attitudes. In 1858 he had viewed the carnival coldly; only the young enjoyed it. But the following year after saying that the young people found it great fun, he added, "To say the truth, so do I."

During that year he had made a determined effort to understand something about art: he had studied the paintings in museums and had spent much time in the studios of American sculptors such as Thomas Crawford, W. W. Story, Maria Louise Lander, Harriet Hosmer, and Hiram Powers. The results of this interest, as well as his ambivalent response, run throughout *The Marble Faun*. As Miss Lander was a Salem girl, Hawthorne allowed her to make a portrait bust. The American painter, Cephas Giovanni Thompson, had already painted Hawthorne's portrait in Boston. In Rome, after a visit to Thompson's studio, Hawthorne wrote that he did not think there was a better painter alive, at least among Americans, none so religious in their worship of art.

Nathaniel was somewhat put off by the mannish dress of Miss Hosmer, but generously added, "I give her leave to wear what may suit her best." Sophia after a more detailed description of the sculptor's costume, concluded, "I liked her at once, she was so frank and cheerful, independent, honest, and sincere—wide awake, energetic, yet not ungentle." Miss

Lander pleased Nathaniel better, but both girls furnished details for the portrait of Hilda in *The Marble Faun*. However, the description of Hilda as "a dove" hardly fits the independent Miss Hosmer, who shocked the Romans by going about unchaperoned and by riding horseback astride.

The Hawthornes were not alone in finding her interesting. In fact her unusual characteristics attracted to her studio almost every royal visitor who came to Rome. When the Prince of Wales purchased her "Puck," she soon had orders for thirty copies at a thousand dollars each. At one point she had so many commissions that she employed twenty marble workers.

Miss Hosmer, however, had much less influence on *The Marble Faun* than did William Wetmore Story, whose Cleopatra is the same one attributed to Kenyon in the novel. In addition, Greenough and Crawford are mentioned by name in the story. All of the fraternity of artists in Rome are pictured as refugees from "the unsympathizing cities of their native land." Rome had special advantages:

> One of the chief causes that made Rome the favorite residence of artists—their ideal home which they sigh for in advance, and are loathe to migrate from, after once breathing its enchanted air—is, doubtless, that they find themselves in force, and are numerous enough to create a congenial atmosphere. In every other clime they are isolated strangers; in this land of art, they are free citizens.

But Hawthorne also noted the jealousies and petty animosities among the sculptors—animosities he said that modern poets had thrown aside. He attributed the difference to the fact that a literary man had potentially a large audience; whereas a sculptor's market was limited to a small body of wealthy patrons. Thus the success of even a gifted artist became an affair of intrigue, and each one hesitated to speak favorably of a rival's work. Nevertheless they shared a kind of social warmth. But they paid the price of expatriation: "they linger year after year in Italy, while their originality dies out of them, or is polished away as a barbarism." One thinks of the vigorous bust of Jackson done by Hiram Powers in America and of his sentimentalized Eves and Greek Slaves done in Italy.

Elsewhere in *The Marble Faun* Hawthorne mused:

> The years, after all, have a kind of emptiness when we spend too many of them on a foreign shore. We defer the reality of life, in such cases, until a future moment, when we shall again breathe our native

air; but by and by there are no future moments; or if we do return, we find that the native air has lost its invigorating quality, and that life has shifted its reality to the spot where we have deemed ourselves only temporary residents. Thus between two countries we have none at all, or only that little space of either in which we finally lay down our discontented bones. It is wise therefore to come back betimes, or never.

But Hawthorne himself was still the Puritan. In both his Journal and in *The Marble Faun* he deplored the fact that sculptors did not do the stone cutting themselves but employed common workmen to translate their clay models into marble. Nor had he got over his prejudice against nudity. After visiting the studio of the American, E. S. Bartholamew, he commented, "I do not altogether see the necessity of ever sculpturing another nakedness. Man is no longer a naked animal; his clothes are as natural to him as his skin, and sculptors have no more right to undress him than to flay him"—an idea repeated in *The Marble Faun,* which also contains the phrase "guilty glimpses of hired models." He tended to agree with the art historian, Mrs. Anna B. Jameson, that the American sculptors in Rome were men of no high aims, no worthy conception of the purposes of art, men who were "desecrating marble by the things they wrought in it." This view was not entirely Puritan moralizing. He had been much impressed by Michalangelo's paintings and Greek sculpture. "I am partly sensible that some unwritten rules of taste are making their way into my mind; that all this Greek beauty has done something towards refining one, though I am still, however, a very sturdy Goth."

In May, after four months in Rome, the Hawthornes went to Florence, where the sculptor, Hiram Powers, got them a furnished house for $50 a month. Chiefly because of his statue, "The Greek Slave," Powers was perhaps the most famous sculptor of his time. Both Nathaniel and Sophia were fascinated by his conversation and his views on art. But Hawthorne was no slavish disciple. For his part he would have all the Venuses, Greek Slaves, and Eves burnt to quicklime, leaving only Venus di Medici. There were mysteries in art that Powers did not recognize. "Classic statues escape you with their slippery beauty, as if they were made of ice." Powers seemed to regard technique as the essence of art; Hawthorne considered it from the point of view of a moralist. Thus the Venus di Medici seemed "tender and chaste"; whereas a painted Venus by Titian was "naked and lustful." And after seeing Titian's painting of Magdalen, Hawthorne decided that "Titian must have been a very good-for-nothing old man." He could not understand how after painting one of his Virgins, Raphael could be so sensual as to paint "such a brazen trollop" as the Fornarina in the Barberini Palace.

Italy was a sensuous experience which the New England moralist tried desperately to deal with. It was too hallowed by history and tradition to be rejected out of hand. At his side Sophia reveled in the delights she encountered. At Casa Guidi, Robert Browning and his son Pennini played sonatas. Later when Browning talked, he was "full of vivid life, like a rushing river," and Mrs. Browning was "a seraph in her flaming worship of heart."

The summer of 1858 was, Julian believed, the happiest of his father's life. After spending June and July in the city, the family rented the Villa Montauto, within walking distance of the city. This was so large that each member of the family could have a suite to himself. It was richly orna- mented, Una's chamber having a vaulted ceiling; there was a grand salon—used as a schoolroom—and a little oratory decorated with sacred prints, crucifixes, etc. A battlemented square medieval tower became Hilda's tower of *The Marble Faun*. In the evening the family would climb to the top to watch dusk fall over the roofs of the city and toward the Apennines in the distance. After the family had descended, Hawthorne liked to remain, smoking a cigar and meditating. "I hardly think there can be a place in the world where life is more delicious for its own simple sake than here."

But as always for Hawthorne there were ethical problems in paradise. In Rome he had been concerned about Una's fervor for the city. "We shall have done the child no good office, in bringing her here, if the rest of her life is to be a dream of this 'city of the soul,' and an unsatisfied longing to come back to it." Characteristically he added an ambivalent note: "On the other hand, nothing elevating and refining can really be injurious."

With Powers he had also discussed expatriation. When Powers held forth on the moral deterioration of America, Hawthorne found himself defending his homeland.

> His long absence from our country has made him think worse of us
> than we deserve; and it is an effect of what I myself am sensible, in

my shorter exile: the most piercing shriek, the wildest yell, and the ugly sounds of popular turmoil, inseparable from the life of a republic, being a million times more audible than the peaceful hum of prosperity and content which is going on all the while.

Despite the sculptor's talk of going home, Hawthorne doubted that he would ever do so. "Like most exiles of twenty years, he has lost his native country without finding another." Hawthorne, who often questioned his own return, nevertheless recognized the price of expatriation.

As has been shown, Hawthorne shared a number of the puritan prejudices of his countrymen, but he also detested the village morality of America. In *The Scarlet Letter* he had represented the homeliest women of the town as the most violent of Hester's accusers. And in *The Marble Faun* he wrote, "Rome is not like one of our New England villages, where we need permission of each individual neighbor for every act that we do, every word that we utter, and every friend that we make or keep." On an occasion in England when he had smoked a cigar on the street, he noted that no Northern gentleman in America could do this. The puritan Hawthorne often found the puritans of his homeland hard to endure.

Another source of soul searching was the conflict between his Puritan inheritance and the emotional attraction of the Catholic Church. In France he had attended a service which impressed him as "a superb work of art, or perhaps a true growth of man's religious nature. . . . Being of another parish he looked coldly, but not irreverently." Protestantism, he felt, needed a new apostle to convert it to something positive.

The ambivalence of his response is reflected in *The Marble Faun*. At one point Italy is referred to as priest ridden, and "a monk . . . is inevitably a beast." Yet a little further on there is the observation, "Whatever may be said of the papal system, it was wise and lovely sentiment that set up the frequent shrine and cross along the roadside." When Hilda is tortured by her knowledge of Donatello's crime, Hawthorne comments that had the Jesuits known of her troubled heart, "her inheritance of New England Puritanism would hardly have protected her from the pious strategy of those good fathers." He went on to speak of the skill of Catholicism in dealing with the human heart. "Its mighty machinery was forged and put together, not on middle earth, but either above or below." This uncertainty about the ancestry of Catholicism led him to handle the scene of Hilda's confession with mixed feelings. When she confesses to an English-speaking priest, she experiences a powerful spiritual catharsis, but the priest immediately reprimands her for availing herself of the offices of a church she will not accept. For a time he is pictured as something of a bigot; then he turns into the understanding father. It is as if Hawthorne were not sure of what role the man should play. Even as far back as *The Scarlet Letter* Hawthorne had thought of having the Reverend Arthur Dimmesdale confess to a Catholic priest; in *The Marble Faun* Hilda's confession is one of the key incidents in the story.

Julian Hawthorne quotes his father on the subject:

> Saint Peter's offers itself as a place of worship and religious comfort for the whole human race; and in one of the transepts I found a range of confessionals, where the penitent might tell his sins in the tongue of his own country, whether French, German, Polish, English, or what not. If I had a murder on my conscience or any other great sin, I think I should have been inclined to kneel down there and pour it into the safe secrecy of the confessional. What an institution that is! Man needs it so, that it seems as if God must have ordained it. The popish religion certainly does apply itself most closely and comfortably to human occasions, and I cannot but think that a great many people find their spiritual advantage in it, who would find none at all in our formless mode of worship.

Like Hilda, Hawthorne had too much Puritan inheritance to become a Catholic, but he obviously found that the Church answered certain aesthetic and psychological needs better than the New England meetinghouse did. Unlike the New Englanders, the Italians did not pride themselves "upon sharing in the counsels of Providence and kindly helping out its otherwise impractical designs." After seeing the stained glass in an Italian church he wrote a glowing description of the colors, like rubies, sapphires, emeralds, and topazes, "bright in themselves, but dim with tenderness and reverence because God himself was shining through them." Characteristically he added, "I hate what I have said." Mrs. Hawthorne was less disturbed by her aesthetic delight. "In Italy," she wrote, "architecture, painting, music, all do their utmost. Thousands of Gothic pinnacles and arches point to heaven."

It is significant that in *The Marble Faun* the chief villain is a Capuchin monk, and that the two other characters who sin are a Jewess and an

Italian. The American sculptor, Kenyon, is little more than an observer
and the American girl, Hilda, suffers vicariously for the sins of the
characters from the old world. It is generally recognized that Hilda, with
her horror of moral evil, is an idealized portrait of Sophia Hawthorne.
But if the characters who share in the guilt are Europeans, the problem is
straight out of New England Calvinism: What is sin and what is its place
in the universe? In a number of ways *The Marble Faun* is a reworking of
the theme of the *Scarlet Letter*. Because of her sin and atonement Hester
had risen to a higher moral level than that of her original innocence. In a
similar way Donatello's crime awakened his soul from its state of pagan
innocence. As Kenyon puts it:

> Sin has educated Donatello, and elevated him. Is sin, then,—which
> we deem such a dreadful blackness in the universe,—is it, like
> sorrow, merely an element of human education, through which we
> struggle to a higher and purer state than we could otherwise have
> attained? Did Adam fall, that we might ultimately rise to a far
> loftier paradise than his?

Thus the summing up of Hawthorne's Italian story could apply word for
word to the one he had laid in seventeenth-century Massachusetts.

It is not strange therefore that the European characters have a certain
unreality. Donatello, the Faun, is drawn less from an earthly Italian
pagan than from a creature of legend—Hawthorne's attempt to translate
the Faun of Praxiteles into a human being. Miriam is drawn from a
Jewess Hawthorne met at a Lord Mayor's dinner in Liverpool. Despite
her beauty he felt a slight repugnance:

> I doubt not she could have slain a man, in good cause—what
> Bathsheba was; only she seemed to have no sin in her—perhaps
> what Eve was, though one could hardly think her weak enough to eat
> the apple.

It would seem that Hawthorne paid less attention to the lady as a person
than as a Biblical character.

This tendency to approach the contemporary Italian scene through the
art and literature of the past appears in the whole treatment of Miriam in
The Marble Faun. Several critics have suggested that her relationship
with the mysterious Capuchin was incestuous—a reworking of the Beatrice Cenci story. Certainly both Nathaniel and Sophia were fascinated by

Beatrice Cenci. Again and again Hawthorne went back to look at her portrait by Guido Reni. In her journal Sophia wrote:

> And now we sat down before Beatrice Cenci! at last, at last! after so many years' hoping and wishing. . . . She is a spotless lily of Eden, trailed over by a serpent, and unable to understand the desecration, yet struck with a fatal blight.

It seems that the Hawthornes were more familiar with Shelley than with Italians.

The Americans, Kenyon and Hilda, as expatriate artists may seem equally unreal to twentieth-century readers familiar with the extracurricular activities of American expatriates of the 1920's, but the evidence suggests that Hawthorne was drawing a true picture. The Storys lived lavishly but not dionysiacally, and such artists as Harriet Hosmer and Hiram Powers were rather puritanic. *The Marble Faun* is therefore an extremely American book. Its descriptions of Florence and Rome made it almost a guidebook to Hawthorne's compatriots. However, it is not a story about Italians, about the mores and sensibility of the old world, but one about the mores and sensibility of New Englanders when faced with Italy.

In October 1858 the Hawthornes left Florence, taking the train to Siena, where they again visited the Storys for a day. They wandered through a vineyard, and at evening sat looking down an avenue of cypresses. There was even a comet. In his journal Nathaniel gave a picture of the vivacious Mrs. Story and the happy life of the family. Had it not been for the wildness of the winter climate he would have been tempted to buy a villa in Siena. He wrote:

> . . . if I could take root anywhere, I know not but it could be as well here as in another place. It would be only a kind of despair, however, that would ever make me dream of finding a home in Italy; a sense that I had lost my country through absence or incongruity, and that earth is not an abiding place. I wonder that we Americans love our country at all, it having no limits and no oneness; and when you try to make it a matter of heart, everything falls away except one's native State. . . .

From Siena they took a *vettura* to Rome. Their driver (*vetturino*) took them to good hotels where they feasted on the best. Of one dinner where they had Montefiascone wine, "the Est, Est, Est," Mrs. Hawthorne noted, "I do not know how to describe its etherial fire, unless I say it was like dissolved diamonds. . . ." As they drew near Rome, Nathaniel wrote, "Rome certainly does draw in to itself my heart, as I think even London, or even little Concord itself, or old sleepy Salem, never did and never will."

The plan was to spend six months in Rome and then return to America. But by October 23 Nathaniel's "home-feeling" had evaporated. Then in November Una came down with Roman fever, attributed to a sketching expedition to the Colosseum. She seemed to recover, then for a period of six months had relapses. Mrs. Hawthorne was ill in December, Ada Shepard in January, and Nathaniel in February. By the end of February all were well enough to attend the carnival, where Nathaniel threw confetti. Then in April Una had a relapse which seemed likely to prove fatal.

During the crisis, which lasted about two weeks, Mrs. Browning brought broth, and other friends came with flowers. Mrs. Hawthorne wrote to her sister Elizabeth that on one day in particular "there seemed to be a cloud of good spirits in the drawing-room, Mrs. Ward, Mrs. Browning, Mrs. Story. . . . The American Minister constantly called. Mrs. Aubrey de Vere came. Everyone who had seen Una in society came to ask." A most welcome visitor was ex-President Franklin Pierce, with whom Nathaniel spent much time. General Pierce, as Hawthorne called him, seemed very happy and more like what he had been in youth. Sophia felt that her husband almost owed his life to Pierce during this difficult time.

In May 1859 the Hawthornes set out for England, where they planned to stay until July. They left three trunks filled with clothes, curios, and works of art at Marseilles. At LeHavre Miss Shepard left to sail for America after having been with them for nearly two years. In London Francis Bennock found rooms for them. Soon they were involved in an active social life. The Motleys were there and James T. Fields and his new wife. It was Fields who caused the Hawthornes to change their plans about going home. He arranged with the London publishers Smith and Elder for a payment of £600 for the romance Hawthorne had written in Italy. To be near his publishers and to insure the British copyright, Hawthorne decided to stay in England while he revised the first draft of the story.

Certainly he was in no great hurry to get home. In May he had written to Ticknor from Rome, saying he was not particularly happy at the thought of his return. To get away from the distractions of London and to let Mrs. Hawthorne rest and Una recuperate he took the family to Redcar on the North Sea for the summer. In October they moved to Leamington because of its milder climate. At both Redcar and Leamington he kept to a nine-to-three schedule of writing and revising. His continued ambivalence about going home is reflected in his letters to Ticknor. In October he said that he thought he could never be content to settle down in one place, and besides the Concord house was too small and hardly worth repairing. Then, during a dull winter in which Mrs. Hawthorne suffered from bronchitis, he wrote, "I shall really be glad to get home, although I do not doubt that I shall be tortured with life-long wishes to cross the sea again. I fear I have lost the capacity of living contentedly in any one place." Three weeks later he longed to be home but dreaded the approaching crisis. New England, he had concluded, was the healthiest country in the world. In England people always had something wrong with them.

An important reason for his hesitation about going home was that he knew his political opinions were unpopular in New England: he favored a dissolution of the Union and hoped that the abolitionists would push matters to that extremity. And although he had held political jobs in Salem and Liverpool he detested politics. As he told Ticknor:

> All the advantages of residing in England are concentrated in London. Leave out that, and I would rather be in America—that is to say, if Presidential elections and other political turmoil could be done away with—and if I could but be deprived of my political rights and left to my individual freedom. The sweetest thing connected with a foreign residence is, that you have no rights and no duties, and can live your own life without interference of any kind. I shall never again be so free as I have been in England and Italy.

Perhaps no other expatriate has so clearly stated the lure of expatriation.

In April he wrote that all his homesickness had fallen on him at once and that Julian was scarcely more anxious to get home than he himself. On June 16, 1860, along with the James T. Fields, who had spent a year abroad, they boarded the steamer for home. They had been away almost exactly seven years.

As with James Fenimore Cooper, life abroad had given Hawthorne a taste for a larger and more luxurious home than he had had in America.

He at once set about enlarging Wayside and Mrs. Hawthorne undertook its redecoration. As is customary, the cost ran far above the estimate— $2000 as against $500.

Old friends welcomed them home. Emerson gave a party at which the other guests were Thoreau, Alcott, Frank Sanborn, and W. M. Hunt. The young people plunged into American life: picnics, dances, and masquerades at the town hall. In June 1861 the Hawthornes gave a dance at Wayside for forty young people. In 1859 Hawthorne had been made a member of the Saturday Club, which met at the Parker House once a month. Here gathered Agassiz, Emerson, Lowell, Motley, Whipple, Holmes, Prescott, Whittier, Norton, Samuel Gridley Howe, and Longfellow. It was on the whole a more distinguished company than Hawthorne had associated with abroad. In Europe he had met prominent literary figures, but had not been a part of a literary group. The artists he had known abroad were chiefly Americans.

As he had been in Europe, he was often restless. In 1861 he spent two weeks at the shore with Julian; in 1862 father and son took a trip to Maine, where they fished, swam, rowed, and had chowder on the beach. Hawthorne found himself at home with farmers, country lawyers, village editors, and lumbermen.

During these last four years of his life he tried to get back to creative writing, but his powers were failing. At his death in 1864 he left in manuscript *Septimus Felton* and *Dr. Grimshaw's Secret, The Ancestral Footstep*, and three chapters of *The Dolliver Romance*. None of these is important in the Hawthorne canon. To support himself he had contributed to *The Atlantic* a series of sketches of English life, which in 1863 were collected in *Our Old Home*.

The return to American life had not stimulated his imagination, but ironically it was American politics which gave prominence to *Our Old Home*. It was dedicated to his lifelong friend Franklin Pierce, and on the day of its publication the *New York Evening Post* and other papers printed a letter from Pierce to Jefferson Davis, in which Pierce blamed the abolitionists for breaking up the Union and predicted fighting in the streets of Northern cities. Hawthorne, who did not agree with all of Pierce's views, was accused of supporting a copperhead. But the furor helped the sale of his book.

Apparently neither Hawthorne's long expatriation nor his repatriation was a factor in the lack of creativity of his last years; rather the evidence points to failing physical and mental powers. Julian attributed his father's death to a failure of the will to live.

Few American expatriates have been keener observers of the European scene, but it cannot be said that expatriation gave Hawthorne particularly keen insights into the strength and weakness of his homeland. He falls far below Cooper as a social critic of the United States. Hawthorne's quarrel was less with America than with a world which failed to reach his transcendental ideal. Whether he laid a story in Massachusetts or in Italy, his basic preoccupation was with the nature of evil: Was it a chimera of man's own creation, or a basic quality of the universe, or was it a necessary part of man's education? Like Blake he tended to reject the innocence of Eden in favor of the organized innocence, in which experience triumphs over evil. For Hawthorne, Europe and America were only different stages for the enacting of mankind's spiritual drama. Like Melville's Queequeg, "Thought he, it's a wicked world in all meridians."

THE CORK-LINED ROOM

HENRY JAMES

Henry James has long been a kind of symbol of the plight of the artist in the United States. It has become a cliché to say that he was forced to flee the America of the Gilded Age, that there was no place in his own country for so fine and sensitive a literary artist. This idea has long been popular among those artists and critics who feel themselves not fully appreciated at home. The comment of Wright Morris in 1957 has already been cited (p. vii). Ezra Pound had expressed much the same idea with more wit in 1913: "America of today is the sort of country that loses Henry James and retains to its appreciative bosom a certain Henry Van Dyke."

The view that James fled a hostile America was especially popular in the 1920's when so many literary people were in revolt against the values of the Harding-Coolidge era. Those writers who contributed to Harold Stearns's *Civilization in the United States* (1921) almost to a man pictured the country as a cultural wasteland. Their culture heroes became such expatriates as Henry James, Ezra Pound, Gertrude Stein, and T. S. Eliot. Oddly enough, it was William Dean Howells, that whipping boy of the young rebels, who in his last essay in 1920 stated the case:

> America was never kind to Henry James. It was rude and harsh, unworthily and stupidly so, as we must more and more own, if we are to be true to ourselves. We ought to be ashamed of our part in this; . . . from the people conscious of culture throughout New England, especially the women, he had sometimes outright insult.

Van Wyck Brooks in *The Pilgrimage of Henry James* (1925) took up the theme that James fled a country hostile to culture. In support of this view he quoted a letter of 1913 from Henry to Mrs. William James:

> When I think of how little Boston and Cambridge were of old ever *my* affair, or anything but an accident, for me, of the parental life there to which I occasionally and painfully and losingly sacrificed, I have a superstitious terror of seeing them at the end of time again stretch out strange and inevitable tentacles to draw me back and destroy me.

Brooks interprets this as evidence that James believed, "The American artist in the American aim is a doomed man;" pitfalls surrounded him on every side.

In the first place, this statement was made late in James's life, when as this chapter will attempt to show, James had altered his views of America. Also a close reading of the statement suggests that it was "parental" shackles that he feared. This will become clearer in the light of evidence cited below.

It is perhaps worthwhile, therefore, to examine what did happen to Henry James. Why did he spend most of his adult life abroad? There is a revealing passage in *The Middle Years*, in which nearly fifty years after the event James recalled a breakfast at the old Adelphi Hotel in Liverpool. The twenty-seven-year-old novelist had just landed in England after spending nine years in America.

> I was again and again in the aftertime to win back the homeliest notes of the impression, the damp and darksome light washed in from the steep, black bricky street, the crackle of the strong draught of the British "sea-coal" fire, much more confident of its function, I thought, than the fires I had left, the rustle of the thick, stiff, loudly unfolded and refolded "Times," the incomparable truth to type of the waiter, truth to history, to literature, to poetry, to Dickens, to Thackeray, positively to Smollett and to Hogarth, to every connection that could help me to appropriate him and his setting, an arrangement to things hanging together with a romantic rightness that had the force of a revelation.

This memory, which in 1914 was for him, "To return . . . across the years to the gates of paradise. . . ."

Obviously it is not the scene itself which is glamorous, not the black, bricky street, the damp and darksome light: the glamour is read into the scene from Dickens, Thackeray, Smollett, and Hogarth. Even the fire is somehow better, more sure of itself than an American fire. The pathetic fallacy—the attributing of human emotions to things—is a part of this subjectivity. The fact that the pathetic fallacy is one of the distinguishing marks of James's later manner, whether he was writing of Europe or America, is an indication that in his search for relation James read his own feelings into what he observed. Even the landlord at the paradisiacal Liverpool hotel was "a feudal retainer."

If this dithyrambic account of the glamour of Liverpool had been only the reaction of a young American to his first taste of a foreign land, it would be little more significant than the romantic emotions of Irving, Cooper, or Longfellow. But there is an important difference. The others experienced such feelings when confronted with such genuine marvels as Westminster Abbey, Rouen Cathedral, or St. Mark's in Venice; James had his orgasm on a damp day in Liverpool. A smelly sea-coal fire opened the gates of paradise which had remained closed in front of a hickory-wood fire in New England.

To understand the imagined Europe of Henry James, one must know something of his history. His earliest memory was of a great, stately square in Paris, surrounded by high-roofed houses, and having in its center a glorious column, which he later learned was the Colonne Vendome. Henry was not yet two when the incident took place, but the picture was so clear that he was later able to convince his parents that he remembered it.

Henry had been six months old when his father first took the family abroad for a two-year-stay. Henry James, Sr., was a transcendentalist, a friend of Emerson's, a searcher for ideal systems of education. He was less an expatriate from America than an expatriate from the world in general. Over the years he put his boys in a variety of schools at home and abroad, but none of them ever measured up to his ideal academy. Like Fenimore Cooper, he was an ardent patriot abroad and uncomfortable at home. In 1849 he decided to enlarge his town house in New York and take a place in the country because his four stout boys lacked play space within doors and imported "shocking bad manners from the street." In fact it might be better to take them abroad for a few years "to absorb French and German and get a better sensuous education than they are likely to get here." A sensuous education was not a usual part of the transcendental curriculum. Six years later, when Henry, Jr., was thirteen and William fifteen, the family did go to Europe for a three-year stay.

Henry James, Sr., was able to engage upon this and subsequent quests for the ideal environment because his father, an immigrant from Ireland, had made $3,000,000 in America. As Henry, Jr., put it, "The rupture with my grandfather's tradition and attitude was complete; we were never in a single case, I think, for two generations, guilty of a stroke of business. . . ." This lack of guilt did not, however, prevent the novelist from complaining throughout his life of the public's failure to buy his books to the extent that he desired.

Even in New York the boys were conditioned for their European experience. Governesses and tutors were selected for the purity of their French accents. Because Henry found boys difficult to play with, he saturated himself in books, especially Dickens and Thackeray. And as he later wrote, there was *Punch*: "*Punch* was England; *Punch* was London and England and London were at that time words of multifarious suggestion to the small American child." In passing it may be noted that bookishness is a frequent characteristic of the expatriate. To reinforce Dickens and *Punch* there was Henry's aunt Kate Walsh, an ardent Anglophile. And the one boy he got on well with was the transplanted Louis de Coppet: "he opened vistas." To Coppet, James attributes part of the fascination that foreign lands held: Coppet was "the pointed prefigurement of the manners of Europe."

At thirteen the shy, stammering, bookish Henry was again taken abroad. First he and William were put in a school in Geneva. When after three months, this failed to come up to his father's ideal, they were transferred to one in England, which also proved to be less than utopian. Next they were exposed to schools in France. Thus the sensuous education of the boys failed to include the kind of companionship possible only when there is an opportunity to make friends. During the family's residence in Berkeley Square, Henry and William in their top hats "and other neatnesses" took long walks along Baker Street. At home they painted. As James remembered the life, they "endlessly walked and endlessly daubed." They knew no boys at all, and glimpsed only rude ones on the streets. The London of Dickens was often brutal. From his seat in a carriage, young Henry saw a man fell a woman with a blow of his fist.

The family moved on to Paris, but Henry James, Sr., began to tire of Europe. In 1856 he wrote of his dislike of the English, who he said were abject slaves to routine. "American disorder is sweet beside European order; it is so full of promise."

What Henry James, Sr., regarded as the insufferable manners of the English impressed his son also, but more with envy than dislike. Four years before in his father's library at home, Thackeray had addressed him with, "Come here, little boy and show me your extraordinary jacket!" Inspecting the shrinking boy through his spectacles the large man stated that such a jacket in England would cause him to be addressed as "Buttons." Instead of resenting Thackeray's boorishness, Henry felt ashamed of his jacket: his sense of it "became from that hour a heavy one. . . . It had been revealed to me thus in a flash that we were somehow queer."

Before going home, the James family moved from Paris to Bologna, where Henry, Jr., nearly died of typhoid. Then in 1858 the family returned to settle in Newport, but only for a year. In 1859 they were again in Europe. The elder James had a theory that American travel abroad was the dawn of a new international civilization. Also he had grown discouraged with American education and dreaded the habits of extravagance and insubordination which he believed it encouraged. With the expatriate's characteristic ambivalence he wrote to Sam Ward: "I am a good patriot, but my patriotism is even livelier on the other side of the water."

Believing that Henry was too much addicted to novel reading, his father put him in a Geneva school specializing in science and mathematics. The boy found these subjects incomprehensible. In Newport there had been congenial friends; in Geneva none of the fellows showed a desire to be friends. After a few months James, Sr., recognized the uselessness of his experiment, and permitted Henry, Jr., to study literature. The new *Cornhill Magazine* opened up "the vales of Arcady" for the boy.

The next stop on the educational pilgrimage was Bonn, Germany. Young Henry's subjective approach to new scenes in Europe was in contrast to his younger brother Wilky's outgoing response. Henry was keenly aware of the contrast:

> Life meanwhile I had a good deal of at my side in the person of my brother Wilky, who, as I have had occasion elsewhere to say, continued in those years to live, or to have the appearance of so doing, with an immediacy that left me far in the lurch.

On the other hand Henry dreamed romantic dreams. For him the beeches and poplars across the Rhine "gothically rustled and murmured":

> I fancied their saying perpetually "We are German woods, we are German woods—which makes us very wonderful, do you know? and unlike others; don't you feel the spell at the very sound of us and of

the beautiful words, 'Old German woods, old German woods,' even if you can't tell why?"

To Henry the murmur of the woods and the magic name of the Rhine brought a message of his destiny:

> You shall suffer, yes, indeed you *are* doing so (stick up for your right to!) in your sense of form; which however is quite compatible with culture, is really one of the finest parts of it, and may decidedly prove, that you are getting it.

Granted that this was written long after the event, and that James's preoccupation with form, suffering, and culture may have intensified over the years, all the evidence points to his early sense of his own purpose and destiny. Certainly the vision of Europe came early, the tendency to hear its streets and groves speak to him of romance and culture.

Oddly enough it was Henry, Jr., who began to question the family's expatriation. To a friend in Newport he wrote, "I think that if we are to live in America it is about time we boys should take up our abode there; and the more I see of this estrangement of American youngsters from the land of our birth, the less I believe in it." William also wanted to return; he planned to study painting with William Morris Hunt in Newport. Henry, Sr., turned another of his mental somersaults. He was glad, he said, to have come abroad for the last time; otherwise he would have always felt that something better could have been done for the boys.

> As it is we go home profoundly persuaded that no wilder hallucination exists, at least in reference to boys who are destined to grow up into American men. America is "the lost Paradise restored" to boys and girls both, and it is only our paltry cowardice and absurd ducking to old world conventionalities that hinder our realizing it as such at once.

Henry James, Sr., never went abroad again, nor did the younger boys, Wilky and Bob. William was to return for a year's study, and Alice toward the end of her life. Thus it was only Henry, Jr., who, despite a ten-year attempt to do so, could not learn to feel at home in America. A year after his return the elder James made a spread-eagle, Fourth-of-July address on the superiority of America to Europe. The difference was spiritual: our Constitution bound us to disallow privilege and legislate

only for the common good. Henry, Jr., on the other hand, found that
Newport fed his American consciousness but thinly:

> Newport, with its operaglass turned for ever across the sea—for
> Newport, at least *our* Newport, even during the War, lived mainly,
> and quite visibly, by the opera glass—was comparatively, and in its
> degree incurably cosmopolite. . . .

But neither the experience of Europe nor the Newport opera glass is
enough to explain Henry James's failure to establish a relation with his
native land. Neither his older brother William, his younger brothers
Wilky and Bob, nor his sister Alice seems to have been troubled by what
Henry called "the aftertaste of Europe," which would not leave him, and
had "to be desperately dealt with." It seems clear that the answer is to be
found not in externals: Newport, America, Europe, but in the psyche of
Henry James.

In the molding of that psyche many things besides expatriation played
a part. One of these was his shyness, to which his tendency to stammer
was related. Also there was his lack of physical vigor. His father had
spoken of "our four stout boys," but Henry never engaged in the activities of a stout boy. As has been noted, his avid novel reading had become
a matter of concern to his scholarly father. The boy's bookish tendencies
had, of course, been reinforced by his frequent lack of playmates—a lack
which seems to have left William, and especially Wilky and Bob, little
affected.

There was, in addition, the injury to which Henry continued to refer
throughout his life, an injury to which he attributed, among other things,
his stomach ailments and constipation. There was also his failure to
participate in the Civil War. On the surface this last is largely the result
of his injury. But the picture as a whole inevitably suggests psychological
problems and psychosomatic illness.

Certainly, except possibly to a chiropractor, the injury itself seems an
inadequate explanation of a lifelong series of sequelae. In the spring of
1860 in Newport Henry uncharacteristically answered a fire alarm. Along
with the other young men he took his turn at the brakes—that is helped to
pump the hand engine. It is probably that he was awkward at the
unaccustomed physical exercise. In any case he received what he later
described as "a horrid even if obscure hurt."

Reading that, one would assume that the injury was at least a hernia,

but Henry James, Sr., took his son to an eminent surgeon, who diagnosed
the injury as a sprained back, which with proper rest, would shortly heal.
It is possible that a nineteenth-century specialist had made an inaccurate
diagnosis, but there are other possibilities. After all, by 1861 qualified
surgeons were, as their record in the Civil War proved, thoroughly
capable of diagnosing and treating serious injuries. Sprained backs are
no medical novelty. And Henry's alleged symptoms never suggest a
slipped disk. They were digestive troubles, a notoriously psychosomatic
ailment. Most of James's acquaintances testify to his lifelong worry over
his health. Edith Wharton says that he followed the dietary fad of
Fletcherizing, which she thought led to intestinal atrophy.

The psychosomatic overtones are present in James's own account of his
injury. It kept him out of participation in the Civil War. It is significant
that he ties up the account of his mishap with the firing on Fort
Sumter:

> Scarce at all to be stated, to begin with, the queer fusion or confu-
> sion established in my consciousness during the soft spring of '61 by
> the firing on Fort Sumter, Mr. Lincoln's instant first call for volun-
> teers and a physical mishap, already referred to as having overtaken
> me at the same dark hour, and the effects of which were to draw
> themselves out incalculably and intolerably. Beyond all present nota-
> tion the interlaced, undivided way in which what had happened to
> me, by a turn of fortune's hand, in twenty odious minutes, kept
> company of the most unnatural—I can call it nothing less—with my
> view of what was happening, with what might still happen, to every-
> one about me, to the country at large: it so made of these disparities
> a single visitation.

This strange linking of his own misfortune with the national tragedy is
characteristic of Henry's introspective, self-centered approach to life.
This appears again in relation to an experience early in the war. At the
age of twenty he visited an army camp at Portsmouth Grove, near
Newport. Writing about the experience fifty years later James stated that
the memory overtopped others of its class. Here for the first time he saw
the American soldier "in his multitude"—"the most amusing figure of
romance conceivable." Henry felt that in several cases he had "established . . . a relation." To some of the men he gave money.

In retrospect it seemed to him that he could rejoice in having to some extent anticipated "dear old Walt." He also remembered the return trip on the steamboat, and the "acute consciousness of paying physically for my excursion—which hadn't answered the least little bit for my impaired state." Yet even this gave him a "strange rapture," a sense of "measuring wounds against wounds." Through such devices, giving money to soldiers, and suffering a stomach ache, James sought for "a relation" to the war.

At the time of the Battle of Gettysburg Henry found himself "getting furiously American. . . . It was as if one's sense of 'Europe,' sufficiently sure of itself to risk the strategic retreat, had backed away on tiptoe."

Wilky and Bob enlisted, and in 1863 Wilky came home with a severe foot wound. Meanwhile William and Henry had gone to Harvard. For some strange reason Henry entered the Law School, an experiment which terminated when he attempted to argue a case with a fellow student. Although the audience consisted of a few fellow students, the awful glare of publicity remained "a black little memory."

During his year at Harvard, Henry felt that Boston and Cambridge were "literally the American feast." He boarded at Miss Upham's, which he saw through the eyes of Balzac: the *maison* Upham seemed an American version of the Maison Vanquer in *Le Père Goriot*. Among the boarders was Professor Francis Child, an authority on Chaucer and later the compiler of the great collection of folk ballads. Child, a delightful, humorous man, was an excellent talker. William and Henry sat just across the table from Child, in whom, as Henry saw him,

> . . . *there* was the American spirit—since I was "after" it—of a quality deeply inbred, beautifully adjusted to all extensions of knowledge and taste and, as it seemed to me, quite sublimely quickened by everything that was at that time so tremendously in question.

Translated out of the private idiom of James, this seems to mean that he found it interesting to hear an intelligent American talk about literature and the Civil War.

The following year Henry remained at home while William went back to Harvard. Then, in the spring of 1864, the James family moved to Boston, where Henry, Sr., found the intellectual climate stimulating. The elder James was a famous talker, much in demand by hostesses like Mrs. James T. Fields, and at the Saturday Club. Henry, Jr., found it more to his taste to walk over to the office of Charles Eliot Norton, who seemed to him the symbol of a "positive consecration of letters." Norton had the sort of tastes which appealed to young James: a distaste for the contemporary world and an enthusiasm for the art and literature of the European past.

As the new editor of the *North American Review* Norton accepted Henry's first published article, a review of W. Senior's *Essays on Fiction*. Within the next five years Norton published more than twenty reviews by James. James T. Fields of the *Atlantic* and Edwin L. Godkin of the *Nation*—both friends of Henry James, Sr.—also opened their pages to stories and reviews by Henry, Jr. For it was during the Boston years that young James settled down to the task of becoming a writer.

On the surface, the years immediately following the Civil War seem to have been happy and rewarding ones. There were summer visits to Swampscott and Newport, to John La Farge, the painter, and to the Edmund Tweedys', whose house was almost a second summer home for the Jameses. At Newport also were the Temple girls, one of whom, Minnie Temple, became the painter's model for Isabel Archer and Milly Theale. Biographers of James would have it that Henry fell in love with Minnie Temple. In the winter there was the stimulating intellectual life of Boston and Cambridge. In 1866 the Jameses moved to Quincy Street just behind Harvard Yard. And friendly editors of America's best magazines were publishing Henry's reviews and stories.

But for James the American scene lacked the kind of materials he thought necessary for fiction. He found the scene around him was less vivid than the glimpses of Europe such as those he found at Shady Hill, Norton's Cambridge home. In his pilgrimages to this shrine he found himself among the "spoils of Europe": pictures, books, drawings and medals, memories and anecdotes, things of a remote but charming reference, *very much the effect of a sudden rise into a finer clearer air and of a stop-gap against one's own coveted renewal of the more direct experience.*

What he found lacking in America is described in his famous passage on Hawthorne:

> . . . one might enumerate the items of high civilization, as it exists in other countries, which are absent from the texture of American life, until it should become a wonder to know what was left. No State, in the European sense of the word, and indeed barely a

specific national name. No sovereign, no court, no personal loyalty, no aristocracy, no church, no clergy, no army, no diplomatic service, no country gentlemen, no palaces, no castles, nor manors, nor old country houses, nor parsonages, nor thatched cottages, nor ivied ruins; no cathedrals, nor abbeys, nor little Norman churches; no great Universities nor public schools—no Oxford, nor Eton, nor Harrow; no literature, no novels, no museums, no pictures, no political society, no sporting class—no Epsom nor Ascot!

As Van Wyck Brooks noted, most of the items James enumerated were then equally absent from the texture of Russian and Scandinavian as from American life—which did not prevent the emergence in Russia and Scandinavia of a fiction entirely comparable with that of England or France. The tone of James's book was patronizing. Hawthorne was "on his limited scale a master of expression"; his stature was augmented by "the absence of competitors in his own line, and from the general flatness of the literary field that surrounds him." This "flat" field was of course the one that included Emerson, Thoreau, Melville, and Whitman.

Maxwell Geismar argues that James felt the need to denigrate Hawthorne to justify his own obsession with Europe. It is ironic that James called Hawthorne's *Our Old Home* the work "of an outsider, of a stranger, of a man who remains to the end a mere spectator. . . ."

This is precisely the charge that can be made against James. His famous catalogue of the materials lacking in American life is noteworthy for the things it leaves out of European life. It is a list of the romantic features of Europe, especially of the European past and its legacy of architectural and pictorial qualities. There is nothing of the England of the Industrial Revolution, the London of Dickens, the Paris of Balzac. In a discussion James once argued that *Madame Bovary* was a less important book than *Anna Karenina* because it dealt with lower-class characters. Despite his later long residence in England James remained outside of much of the social world he sought in his imagination to penetrate. As Percy Lubbock puts it:

It remained true, none the less, that with much that is common ground among educated people of our time and place he was never really in touch. One has only to think of the part played, in the England he frequented, by the school and college, by country-homes, by church and politics and professions, to understand how much of the ordinary consciousness was closed to him.

In both America and Europe James thought of himself as the observer, the *flaneur*. He believed that by means of the imagination, the artist could create the essence by observing the surface. In *The Art of Fiction* he tells of an English woman of genius who wrote a tale of the nature and way of life of French Protestant youth on the basis of having in Paris passed an open doorway through which she glimpsed the household of a *pasteur*. To James this represented the triumph of the imagination, a refutation of the creed of the realists. But it also suggests his subjective approach to the world around him. In any case it is clear that during his nine years in America he never felt himself a part of his world, despite the fact that he was surrounded by a cultivated, intellectual society. Whatever else he fled, he was not a refugee from a crass business environment.

Nor was he "exiled" by a country unappreciative of his talents. In 1865, ten years before Henry's first novel, William Dean Howells stated in *The Atlantic*, "He has already made his public." (James was then only twenty-two.) Two years later *The Nation* said, "Within the somewhat narrow limits to which he confines himself, Mr. James is . . . the best writer of short stories in America."

Among the reasons which sent him abroad in 1869 were his own health and his sense of the thinness of the American scene. But two other factors may have been even more important. One was his sense of inferiority to young men like John Jay Chapman and Oliver Wendell Holmes, newly returned from the Civil War. The young veterans had competed for the attention of Minnie Temple. Earlier he had felt a sense of inferiority to soldiers when he visited his brother Wilky at camp. He could only gape "as at shining revels. . . . I couldn't do things." In 1865 he wrote the "very smell of having served in the war [seemed] an emanation the most masculine." He felt swamped by "a quantity of military life" and "images of military experience."

Henry James was not a person who easily accepted a secondary position. In social life he felt inferior to the young veterans; at home he resented his status as a second son, and as Henry James, Jr. Almost his first act upon the death of his father was to write his publisher asking that the "Jr." be left off his name. Leon Edel has cited a considerable body of evidence to show that Henry had the habit of making second sons the heroes of his stories. Thus the letter quoted by Brooks takes on added meaning. James was not so much fleeing America as he was an inferior status as Son and Brother—the title is significant.

His emotions upon reaching the refuge of England have been reported at the beginning of this chapter. Almost immediately he dined with the Nortons, and with Norton's friend Ruskin, received a visit from Leslie Stephen, was taken to call on William Morris, whose designs he found entrancing. And Mrs. Morris might have stepped out of a missal, or out of a picture by Rossetti or Hunt—James apparently was unable to distinguish between medieval and pre-Raphaelite painting. In France soon after this he was to find the impressionists less interesting than the pre-Raphaelites. Even as late as 1898 he described Burne-Jones as "one of the greatest boons to our most vulgar of ages."

In conversation with Englishmen he was surprised to learn that "there were things of interest taking place in America, and I had had, in this absurd manner, to come to England to learn it." For instance, people asked him about General Grant's cabinet appointments.

Englishmen of the past were delightful, but those of the present were often disappointing. Breakfasting at the Half-Moon "was association at a jump with the ghosts of Byron and Scott and Sheridan and Scott and Moore, and Lockhart and Rogers . . . as well as the exciting note of a social order in which everyone wasn't hurled straight with the momentum rising, upon an office or a store." But he quickly found that "the face of things here throws a sensitive American back on himself—on his prejudices and national passions." A year later he wrote to his brother William:

> Plenty of gentle emotions from the scenery, etc.; but only man is vile. Among my fellow-patients here I find no intellectual companionship. Never from a single Englishman of them all have I heard the first word of appreciation and enjoyment of the things here I find delightful. . . . As for the women, I give 'em up in advance. I am tired of their plainness and stiffness and tastelessness—their dowdy beads and their lindsey woolsey trains.

In the meantime he had been to Rome where he went "moaning thro' the streets in a fever of enjoyment." Back in England he was homesick, and the news of Minnie Temple's death in March 1870 was a great blow.

Many pages of his reminiscences are devoted to her, and as has been mentioned, she sat for the portraits of Isabel Archer and Milly Theale.

That James would have ever married her is doubtful. His valetudinarianism, his lack of self-confidence, his preoccupation with renunciation all weigh in the scales. One of the most recurrent themes in his stories and novels is non-consummation of an attachment. A considerable number of Jamesian women marry unhappily: Mme de Mauves, Isabel Archer, Mme de Vionnet, Maggie Verver. It is notorious that James was incapable of portraying a passionate relationship between a man and a woman, that his love affairs are of the drawing room rather than of the bedroom, but it is perhaps more remarkable that he drew almost no picture of a warm, happy marriage or family relationship. His own parents were greatly devoted to each other and to their children; the children, despite strong sibling rivalries, were fond of each other. But always James writes as the outsider in love or marriage. His warmest sentiments about Minnie Temple were expressed after her death.

Also there is a curious ambivalence in James's attitude toward the American girl. Most critics emphasize his preoccupation with her innocence and integrity. But R. P. Blackmur has noted another quality, that of *La Belle Dame Sans Merci*. When Daisy Miller accuses Winterbourne of being mean to her just after he has dashed from Geneva to Rome on her account, "He remembered that a cynical compatriot had once told him that American women—the pretty ones, and this gave a largeness to the axiom—were the most exacting in the world and the least endowed with a sense of indebtedness." And of Gertrude Wentworth in *The Europeans*, Blackmur says, "Gertrude is a woman the prudent would run from. . . ." As Felix Young, who loves her, says of her nature, "But it pulls—it pulls—like a runaway horse. Now I like the feeling of a runaway horse; and if I'm thrown out of the vehicle it is no great matter." After leaving her wooer and benefactor Mr. Brand, she bursts into tears briefly. "But they presently passed away. There was something a little hard about Gertrude and she never wept again."

One of James's characters in *The Passionate Pilgrim* volume is Euphemia, who as an American schoolgirl in France, "dreamed of marrying a title . . . because she had a romantic belief that the best birth is a guarantee of an ideal delicacy of feeling." In her idealistic innocence she marries the charming de Mauves, who turns out to be consistently unfaithful. However, she rejects her sister-in-law's suggestion that she console herself with her American admirer, Longmore. When de Mauves repents and on his knees tells her he is desperately in love with her, "She was stone, she was ice, she was outraged virtue." When her rejected husband blows out his brains, Longmore was at first moved to return immediately to Europe. But he did not. "The truth is that in the midst of all the ardent tenderness of his memory of Madame de Mauves, he has become conscious of a singular feeling—a feeling for which awe would be hardly too strong a name."

Like Longmore, James seems to have had mixed feelings about the American girl. Even his sympathetic treatment of Isabel Archer, who was based in part on Minnie Temple, shows some of this ambivalence. It was not until comparatively late in life that James could draw such wholly sympathetic portraits of the American girl as Millie Theale and Maggie Verver. By that time Minnie Temple had become a sentimental memory. Like Winterbourne and Longmore, he remained the cautious observer.

It was not only in America that James felt himself unable to participate. After four years abroad he wrote to Howells from Berne, "What is the meaning of this destiny of desperate exile—this dreary necessity of having month after month to do without friends for the sake of this arrogant Europe which so little befriends us?" Six months later he told Grace Norton that he belonged much more to America than to Europe: he felt that Europe held him at arm's length, and condemned one to a meager scraping of the surface. After nearly a year in Italy he had talked to almost no one except washerwomen and waiters. Yet his own country seemed poor and bare; whereas England and Italy were the lands for "happiness and self-oblivion."

The last phrase is revealing. Europe was for James the Proustian cork-lined room. He was homesick but he dreaded the return: he had a prevision that he would not find life *"simpatico,"* and that it would even hinder literary work. America seemed a "great unendowed, unfurnished, unentertained and unentertaining continent." But he could not face another year of British solitude. Obviously after nearly five years abroad he had not been able to establish "a relation."

During his year at home the *Atlantic* ran *Roderick Hudson,* an international novel. Here James introduced the theme he was to use in so many stories and novels: the naïve American destroyed by the corrupt world of Europe. A minor theme also foreshadowed *Portrait of a Lady,* that of the impecunious individual given an opportunity to develop by means of money from a wealthy benefactor. And Rowland's unselfish generosity to his rival in love adumbrates Milly Theale's bequest to Densher so that he may marry her rival. In many ways *Roderick Hudson* is an overture to James's later novels.

In barest outline it is the story of an American sculptor who is enabled to go abroad by the generosity of a wealthy young man, Mr. Rowland Mallet. Instead of developing as an artist Roderick Hudson develops as a heel. When his American fiancée, Mary Garland, comes to Europe, he borrows money from her in order to court the glamorous Christina Light. The avuncular Mallet—a kind of younger Strether—looks after Mary and Roderick's clinging-vine mother. In the end Christina marries Prince Casamassima, and Mary goes home heartbroken. As a typical Jamesian character she prefers the memory of her faithless lover to marriage to Rowland.

The flaw in the picture is that Roderick Hudson is not really corrupted by Europe—that is merely the scene of his selfish, caddish behavior. Hudson was already the spoiled mama's darling before he went abroad. He would have been a cad in any country. It is clear, however, that James wanted his story to carry international overtones. Rowland has James's own ambivalence about Europe:

> It's a wretched business, this virtual quarrel of ours with our own country, this everlasting impatience that so many of us feel to get out of it. Can there be no battle then, and is one's only safety in flight? This is an American day, an American landscape, an American atmosphere. It certainly has its merits, some day when I'm shivering with the ague in Italy, I shall accuse myself of having slighted them.

This is obviously the dilemma of James himself. Later there will be a comment on James's identification with the Mallet-Strether type, but the identification with Rowland's point of view is clear. Later he has Rowland tell the beautiful Miss Light: "For better or worse you seem to me to belong both by character and by destiny to what is called the world, the great, the dangerous, the delightful world."

This outsider's, child-at-the-store-window view of the great world colors much of James's work. The extent to which he felt himself the outsider is revealed in his letters from France and Italy. After his year in America he had gone to Paris in the autumn of 1875. Here he began *The American* and contributed a series of letters on France to the *New York Tribune*. He became acquainted with Turgenev, and through him with Flaubert, Edmond de Goncourt, Daudet, de Maupassant, and Zola. It amazed James to see the enthusiasm with which Turgenev acted in charades. "Fancy Longfellow, Lowell, or Charles Norton doing the like, and every Sunday evening!" he told his father.

However, by spring he reported to Howells that he was seeing almost nothing of the literary group: "I don't like their wares, and they don't like any others; and, besides, they are not *accueillants*. Turgenev is worth the whole heap of them. . . ." James associated with other expatriates: "Of pure Parisianism I see absolutely nothing."

This outsider's view may account for the basic unreality of *The American*. On a literal level the reader is asked to believe that an American manufacturer of washtubs should meet and fall in love with a Frenchwoman of the tight-knit royalist circle, and that she should fall in love with him. Certainly Christopher Newman bears little resemblance to any other successful American businessman. James had absolutely no conception of what makes a businessman tick—of the problems and triumphs which are part of his sensibility. The real Christopher Newman would have been married to a home-town girl and have been raising a family; the Jamesian Newman is simply a man of leisure, a *flaneur*, who is able to indulge his tastes because of his successful operation of a washtub factory. The Frenchwoman, Claire de Cintré, is a first draft of the aristocratic European lady, most fully developed in Mme de Vionnet of *The Ambassadors*. She was in the eyes of Christopher Newman–James, "a kind of historical formation."

Like so much of James's later work, *The American* has to be read on the symbolic level. For although he has been called a realist, James is really the novelist of the psyche—frequently of his own psyche. The name Christopher Newman is obviously symbolic—the American, the new man who, like Columbus, is a discoverer. James was undoubtedly aware of the ironic implications of this new Columbus exploring the old world. One must not push this matter of names too far, but *cintre*—a curve or bend—suggests certain elements in the portrait of Claire de Cintré, that most graceful woman, who at the last, bends to the will of her family.

That the novel as a whole represents a conflict of values, of two societies, rather than a drama of individuals is clear. Newman is in character as well as in name the naïve, idealistic American; Claire de Cintré is the charming product of an ancient, complex, and corrupt social order. She herself is not corrupt, but the members of her family, in various ways, are. But with the grace of a disciplined member of an aristocratic society she accommodates herself to the demands of that society. It is to her unthinkable that she should marry without her elder brother's consent, and when he goes back on his word, she enters a convent. In the end the code of her class triumphs. Newman, who has been bilked, tears up the evidence of a crime committed by her brother instead of using it as a weapon to get the woman he loves. Faced with the corruption of old Europe, Claire de Cintré submits; Christopher Newman makes the magnanimous, grand gesture.

The point is that James, in portraying Claire de Cintré, is less interested in her complexities as a woman than in her as the symbol of the "impenetrabilities" of Europe. And Christopher Newman is the symbol of American idealism confronted with the ambivalences of Europe. Europe is glamour and romance, but it is also treachery and moral decay. Christopher Newman's dilemma was not that of an American businessman but of Henry James.

James's role as the outsider fascinated by a world he cannot penetrate continued when he went to England in 1876. He had, he told William, got nothing important out of Paris and was done with the French forever; now he intended to feed on English life and the contact with English minds. In London he met Thomas Huxley and dined with Lord Houghton, Gladstone, Tennyson, and Dr. Schliemann. Tennyson surprised him: here was a man of strange, rustic accent, swarthy and scraggy, who drank a whole bottle of port. He seemed to James "a creature of some primordial English stock, a thousand miles away from American manufacture." Like Turgenev with his charades the European reality was interesting but a bit repellent to the fastidious American. A year later he told Grace Norton that he had talked with a considerable number of people, but had become intimate with none. At thirty-four he believed himself past the age to form friendships. He should not want to marry an English wife. "So my interest in London is chiefly that of an observer in a place where there is most in the world to observe."

Nevertheless, he said London was the place in which he felt most at home despite the fact that English people seemed vulgar minded and superficial. This last observation may grow out of the fact that during the winter he dined out 107 times. Certainly it has bearing upon the kind of materials he used in his novels. To Howells he argued that "It is on manners, customs, usages, habits, forms, upon all these things matured and established, that a novelist lives—they are the very stuff his work is made of. . . ." The omission of people—of their quirks and passions—is significant. *Daisy Miller* and *The Europeans*, written during this period, are much more significant as illustrations of manners, customs, usages, and forms than as studies of people. In fact *Daisy Miller* is a tragedy growing out of the conflict of these things. It is a drama of conflicting mores, those of the naïve, high-spirited American girl whose free and easy manners cause the loss of good reputation among the sophisticated and rather cynical Europeans. As the American, Winterbourne, who also misjudged her says at the end, "I was booked to make a mistake. I have lived too long in foreign parts."

In *The Europeans* James transfers the conflict to New England. Some rather down-at-the-heel Europeans come to America to look up some wealthy relatives. To keep the story going, there are a couple of love affairs: the playboy Felix wins Gertrude, who is in revolt against New England primness, and Mr. Brand, sought by the Baroness, marries the American Charlotte. But the main themes of the novel are the conflicts of mores and values: European enjoyment of life versus New England seriousness: European corruption of morals (here lightly touched) against American purity and probity.

As writers on James have frequently noted, he was a good bit of a puritan. In Paris he regarded the Variétés as merely a pretext for bad jokes and undressed *figurantes*. It will be remembered that in *The Ambassadors* that most unpleasant American, Jim Pocock, headed at once for the Variétés. For James a masked ball at the opera begot "a pestilent congregation of vapors." At a watering place he was amazed by the skill with which French women swam, but he felt that Mlle X's somersault from a diving board was "an impropriety." He was puzzled by the logic of this: white and black were divided by a hair, but "virtue is on one side of the hair and vice on the other." After seeing Daudet, Goncourt, and Zola, he commented on their handling of "unclean things." It is not surprising therefore that the unsophisticated Americans in James's stories usually emerge as superior, more admirable than the Europeans they encounter. It is only necessary to mention the Wentworth family in *The Europeans;* Daisy Miller, Isabel Archer, Mme de Mauves, and above all, Milly Theale.

As the years went on, James visited Paris less often, but he usually spent part of the year in Italy. London and Rye were his real homes. By 1877 he told Grace Norton that he felt more at home in London than anywhere else in the world. To this he added a curious note: "I have taken a great fancy to the place; I won't say to the people and things; and yet these must have a part in it." Eight years later he was saying much the same thing: he was attached to England despite its sometimes exasperating people. This tendency to separate a place from its inhabitants, to look at it as a spectacle, a composition, had its most complete expression long after this in *The American Scene,* where not a single person appears on the landscape.

It is not surprising, therefore, that *The Portrait of a Lady* (1881) should be a picture of national types: Isabel Archer, the American girl personified—beautiful, self-confident, out to conquer the world; Caspar Goodwood, the energetic American businessman (a reworking of Christopher Newman); Lord Warburton, the British parliamentarian; the Europeanized Americans Gilbert Osmond and Mme Merle with their continental polish; and Henrietta Stackpole, the American career woman. Henrietta, who has many fine qualities, is nevertheless the one character who is caricatured, at times almost lampooned. James did not like writers for newspapers.

Isabel Archer is almost invariably referred to as having been drawn from Minnie Temple. James himself said this view was partly right, partly wrong; he had Minnie in mind, but she had died essentially incomplete, whereas Isabel Archer was more rounded, more finished. As Leon Edel suggests, the description of Isabel early in the book could have been applied to Minnie: "her meagre knowledge, her inflated ideals, her confidence at once innocent and dogmatic, her temper at once exacting and indulgent, her mixture of curiosity and fastidiousness, of vivacity and indifference, her determination to try, to know. . . ."

It is these qualities which make Isabel Archer stand out as a memorable portrait—qualities drawn from a real woman. But there are other elements in the picture which do not quite fit. At some point along the way Minnie Temple becomes Henry James, filled with fears, retreating from sex, overawed by connoisseurship, and in the end making an ideal of renunciation. For despite a number of memorable characters, this is a novel based less upon life than upon intellectual concepts. James regarded it as second only to *The Ambassadors* as his best proportioned novel. In many ways it has the careful design of a laboratory experiment.

Leon Edel speaks of the fairy-tale quality of much of the plot. Certainly it is unreal enough. Isabel Archer, the flamelike American girl from the starved aesthetic background of Albany, New York, comes to Europe, where she visits her wealthy relatives the Touchetts. In passing it may be said that Mr. and Mrs. Touchett are vividly drawn as expatriate types. Isabel's invalid cousin Ralph falls in love with her and in a splendid renunciatory gesture persuades his aged father to leave £70,000 to Isabel so that she may try her wings.

Isabel is offered three choices of marriage as stylized as the three caskets offered to Bassanio. There is Lord Warburton, active in Parliament, and with 50,000 acres; there is Caspar Goodwood—the surname is descriptive—the American owner of a cotton factory; and Gilbert Osmond, the Italianate American. The middle-aged Osmond devotes himself to connoisseurship: his ideal is "the old, the consecrated, the transmitted." His alleged charm is visible only to Henry James.

Leon Edel has compared Isabel Archer with the fictional portraits of Emma Bovary, Becky Sharp, and Anna Karenina, but with the difference that she "is a new kind of heroine, given all the freedom and innocence of the New World and made to confront the worldly-wise, the urbane, the civilized, but also the deeply corrupt, life of the old." This American innocent is a kind of James stereotype, perhaps with a certain basis of reality, but none the less a stereotype. But, more important, Isabel's motivations are obscure. Those of Emma Bovary, Becky Sharp, Anna Karenina are clear enough: boredom, ambition, sex—but Isabel's are understandable only in terms of James himself. As an American she lacks the practical common sense of her breed. She is almost entirely lacking in sex drive, in ambition, in respect for achievement, in democratic ideals. She shows no distaste for Osmond's boast that he has never earned a penny. Her great and unexpected legacy suggests to her nothing more than a sexless hedonism of travel and visiting in wealthy homes.

Although the ardently American Miss Stackpole hopes that Isabel will not marry a "fell European," Isabel accepts Osmond. Osmond quickly shows his true colors: he married Isabel only for her money. From here on he treats her with contempt. When her cousin Ralph, who had sacrificed his fortune for her, is dying, Osmond refuses to let her visit him. When Isabel tries to argue, Osmond turns from her contemptuously to study some prints he had been examining. In fact Osmond is one of the most repulsive characters James ever drew.

That Osmond should have attracted Isabel in the first place is incomprehensible on a realistic level. But as a symbol he represents the attraction of European culture—which James tends to confuse with connoisseurship. Even after Osmond proves to be a cold-blooded, sadistic character who despises Isabel, she is still offered choices. Lord Warburton and Caspar Goodwood both turn up once more. For these are Jamesian men, not an active member of Parliament and the owner of a cotton factory. They have time and inclination to cherish hopeless love.

Despite the fact that Isabel has become cynical about marriage—"Did all women have lovers?" she asked herself—she still believed in such things as "chastity and even decency." When the importunate Goodwood kisses her—the only kiss in the book

> His kiss was like white lightning, a flash that spread, and spread again, and stayed; and it was extraordinarily as if, while she took it, she felt each thing in his hard manhood that had least pleased her. . . .

In other words her rejection of Goodwood is the Jamesian rejection of sex.

Another characteristically Jamesian reaction is revealed earlier. In her musing about her fate she considers:

> It couldn't be she was to live only to suffer; she was still young, after all, and a great many things might happen to her yet. To live only to suffer—only to feel the injury of life repeated and enlarged—it seemed to her that she was too valuable, too capable for that. Then she wondered if it were vain and stupid to think so well of herself. When had it ever been a guarantee to be valuable? Wasn't history full of the destruction of precious things? Wasn't it much more probable that if one were fine one would suffer?

So it is that she decides to return to Osmond and his daughter Pansy, though it is clear that he despises her and that she can do nothing for Pansy, whose probable fate is to enter a convent.

This is not the place to analyze Henry James's ethical system, or the skill with which he has told his story. Both of these have been the subject of extended comment. The point here is that like much of James's fiction, *The Portrait of a Lady* is not so much the representation of Americans or Europeans as of the psyche of Henry James. The unlikely series of events in the story becomes comprehensible in the light of his own dilemmas and solutions.

As for the three suitors, they represent in a clearly symbolic form the vigorous business life of America, the English country-house society, and the ambivalences of Continental life—the mixture of old world charm and corruption. These are the three worlds which pulled at Henry James. As has been indicated, James was by no means oblivious to the pull of the bare, vigorous, moral life of America, symbolized in the novel by Caspar Goodwood. And of English country-house society he had written to Grace Norton: "the British country-house has at moments an insuperable flatness. On the other hand, to do it justice, there is no doubt of its being one of the ripest fruits of time. . . ." This might also be a thumbnail sketch of Lord Warburton. And throughout James's letters runs the ambivalence about France and Italy. The Old World charm brought him back time after time, and his Puritan conscience as often revolted.

The Portrait first appeared serially in *Macmillan's Magazine* of London and *The Atlantic* in Boston. Each paid him exactly the same amount—$250—for each of the fourteen installments—a considerable sum for the time. When he sent off the final installment in the fall of 1881, he set sail for the United States. Leon Edel points out that James believed it would further his literary career to be at home when *The Portrait* appeared in book form, when Houghton Mifflin published it late that year.

Certainly he did not come back as an unappreciated writer. His first volume of short stories had appeared in 1875. Richard Foley, who made a study of the American criticism of James, states, "No other American writer published his first book with the critical recognition James enjoyed when he published *A Passionate Pilgrim and Other Tales*. He had already gained not only the attention of a small but devoted group of readers but also the respect of influential reviewers."

Similarly, *The Portrait* had considerable success in the United States, and provoked much critical discussion. There were complaints that such a perceptive woman as Isabel would not have been taken in by so transparent a cheat and dilettante as Osmond, but such then important critics as Horace Scudder, J. H. Morse, and W. C. Brownell wrote perceptive discussions of the originality of James's technique. In fact Brownell argued that in showing the development of character James surpassed George Eliot. Few writers in any country could have asked for a more enthusiastic discussion of their work than that by Howells in *The Century* for November 1882. In it he argued:

> . . . the art of fiction has, in fact, become a finer art in our day than it was with Dickens and Thackeray. . . . This school, which is so largely of the future as well as the present, finds its chief exemplar in Mr. James: it is he who is shaping and directing American fiction, at least. It is the ambition of the younger contributors to write like him; he has his following more distinctly recognizable than that of any other English-writing novelist.

Even James confessed to having enjoyed "a certain success." But the death of his mother that year cut a home tie. It was a blow which his friend Percy Lubbock described as "the deepest stroke he had ever received." In any event his return to Europe in 1882 was not the often alleged flight from an unappreciative homeland. Rather it was a retreat to the cork-lined room. A summer in London was followed by an excursion to Touraine and Provence, which led to the book *A Little Tour in France*. The illness of his father brought him again to America in 1883, too late to see the elder James alive. He went back to England, not to return to America for another twenty years. In 1884 his sister Alice joined him in London and later at Bournemouth, not far from his home at Rye. Always a man of warm family feeling, James enjoyed the association with his active-minded sister during the few years which remained to her.

The years between 1883 and 1898 were filled with social life in London and occasional trips to France and Italy. Creatively they represent an interlude between the periods of his greatest work. He produced such works as *The Princess Casamassima, The Reverberator, The Tragic Muse, The Lesson of the Master, The Real Thing and Other Tales, The Death of the Lion,* etc. and *The Spoils of Poynton.* Only his short stories and *The Bostonians* (1886) stand out—this last perhaps a conspicuous exception, for it shows James still fascinated by American themes. Indeed the vitality of *The Bostonians* suggests that much of James's deepest emotional experience was American. But it also shows his distaste for the American, especially Bostonian, zeal for causes. These are also the years of his unhappy attempts to succeed as a writer for the theater. That so subjective an artist as James failed as a dramatist should surprise no one, although James himself found it incomprehensible and deeply frustrating.

Edmund Gosse gives a picture of him during these years, "sitting like a beneficent deity, a sort of bearded Buddha," or taking sauntering walks. This was on an occasion when James had joined a group summering in Worcestershire: Gosse and the American artists Frank Millet, Edwin Abbey, John S. Sargent, Frederick Barnard, and others.

In 1898 James gave up his London residence to settle permanently at Lamb House in Rye. Here with occasional interruptions for entertaining he could work undisturbed. Eventually, however, he found the winters lonely and took rooms in London at the Reform Club, of which he had long been a member. In fact the character Lord Warburton of *The Portrait of a Lady* may be a kind of composite of the English gentlemen he met at the club. *The Awkward Age* (1899) is his chief attempt to represent British society.

Then came a period of major works. *The Sacred Fount* (1901), *The Wings of the Dove* (1902), *The Ambassadors* (1903), and *The Golden Bowl* (1904). He also did a biographical memoir and edition of the letters of another expatriate: *William Wetmore Story and His Friends* (1903).

The limits of the present account do not permit an analysis of all of the important work of James, but two novels have especial bearing on James the expatriate—*The Wings of the Dove* and especially *The Ambassadors*.

The Wings of the Dove is only partially on the "international theme," but it contains the memorable portrait of Milly Theale. In many ways she seems to be more like her model, Minnie Temple, than was Isabel Archer. The novel as a whole has overtones that go beyond the international theme. Quentin Anderson (*Henry James*, 1957) argues that it is a symbolic rendering of the ethical system of Henry James, Sr. Be that as it may, it contains a vivid picture of the overfed, overstuffed upper-class society of the late Victorian era.

The story concerns a love affair between an impecunious English newspaper man, Merton Densher, and Kate Croy—her name suggests a predatory bird. Kate's wealthy Aunt Maude takes her under her wing with the stipulation that Kate shall see nothing of her raffish father. Aunt Maude Lowder (another suggestive name) likes Densher, but disapproves of him as a suitor. (It is in the picture of Aunt Maude and her lavish house at Lancaster Gate that James gives an illusioned picture of late Victorian crass opulence. Anderson regards the house as a symbol of greed.)

Into this situation comes the ailing American heiress, Milly Theale.

Milly's companion, the self-sacrificing Mrs. Stringham, had once gone to school with Maude Lowder, and during an assignment in America, Densher had met Milly and Mrs. Stringham. Like Isabel Archer, Milly is avid for life. Her London physician, Sir Luke Street (another symbolic name), suggests that living fully may cure her. Milly has fallen in love with Densher, but she is wooed by Lord Mark, who she suspects is after her vast wealth.

The scene shifts to Italy, where Milly has gone for her health, and where Mrs. Lowder, Kate, and Densher follow. Kate conceives the idea of having Densher woo the probably dying Milly. He agrees to this if Kate will come to his rooms for an afternoon of lovemaking. (Anderson regards Milly's palace as symbolic as the house of the dove; Densher's rooms as the house of lust.)

Densher half heartedly goes through his role, then in disgust with himself goes back to England. After Milly's death, he receives a document which both he and Kate are sure represents a bequest to him of Milly's fortune. Half in love with the memory of Milly and in disgust at his role, he burns the document unread. Milly's unselfish act, for she knew about his engagement to Kate, regenerates him.

Here again, then, are the Jamesian themes of sex as evil, of renunciation, and of the essential goodness of American character: Mrs. Stringham has sacrificed herself to Milly, and Milly to her love for Densher. Once again James has been less interested in observed life than in an ethical drama representing certain qualities of Europe and America, in this case the materialism of the British upper class versus the naïve idealism of Americans.

Thus the shift of point of view in *The Ambassadors* is all the more remarkable. For over thirty years James had in his novels represented Americans as morally superior to Europeans. Caroline Spencer, Daisy Miller, Mme de Mauves, Christopher Newman, Isabel Archer, and Milly Theale had all suffered from the moral corruption of Europe. Yet only a year after *The Wings of the Dove* James wrote a novel satirizing America and American morals.

This may be in part a delayed result of his increasing identification with the European and especially the English environment. The Spanish-American War had made him "want to curl up more closely in this old world corner," but he regarded the Boer War as necessary, things "really had to be taken in hand."

Another possibility, although it may be merely a coincidence is that his friendship with Edith Wharton, that acid critic of American life, seems to have begun about this time. Their two meetings in the eighties and early nineties made little impression on him, but in the early 1900's they became close friends and were often guests in each other's houses. There are of course other explanations for James's changing view of America. As his letters show, he had come to feel increasingly at home in Europe. And among his friends were a number of American expatriates like Sargent and Whistler, who were at times undoubtedly critical of their compatriots. Furthermore, the two most savage portraits, those of Jim and Sarah Pocock, are pictures of American plutocratic tourists who made such a nuisance of themselves around the turn of the century. It must be remembered that Daisy Miller, Isabel Archer, and Milly Theale are essentially contemporaries of Minnie Temple.

The realistic rather than symbolic nature of the story is also significant. James had a theory of point of view: everything in a story, he believed, should come into it through the perceptions of one of the characters. As has been suggested, such central characters as Christopher Newman and Isabel Archer have essentially Jamesian sensibility despite the unsuitability of this to their ages and condition. Perhaps it was this disparity between the youthful character and the Jamesian sensibility which so often led to a symbolic rather than a realistic presentation.

In *The Ambassadors* none of this applies. The central character, Lambert Strether, despite certain surface resemblances to Howells, has long been recognized as a projection of many of James's own characteristics. With no other character in a novel has James so successfully identified. (Some of the characters in short stories are, of course, obviously Jamesian in their sensibility). Even Strether's age, reported variously in the novel as fifty and fifty-five, was close to that of James at the time of writing.

Strether, the editor of a literary review subsidized by Mrs. Newsome, is sent by her to France to rescue her son Chad from the supposed clutches of some European hussy. She and the town of Woollett, Massachusetts, can think of no other explanation for Chad's continued stay abroad. At once Strether encounters Maria Gostrey, a charming Europeanized American girl. At a candlelit dinner in a restaurant Strether is aware that neither the situation nor Miss Gostrey's modest décolleté would have been possible with Mrs. Newsome.

Using the old school-friend device from *The American* and *The Wings of the Dove*, James represents Miss Gostrey as an intimate of Chad's friend and mentor, Mme de Vionnet, who proves to be the apotheosis of European charm. She is all that Woollett, Massachusetts is not. And when Chad appears on the scene he is no longer the crass, crude American young man, but a person of polish and charm. Strether realizes that Mme de Vionnet has done much for the young man.

Back in Woollett, Mrs. Newsome begins to detect in Strether's letters a weakening of his purpose to "rescue" Chad. She promptly dispatches two other ambassadors, Sarah and Jim Pocock, her daughter and son-in-law.

In some beautifully managed social comedy James confronts the brash, self-righteous Sarah with Mme de Vionnet. Then the "moral" Americans plunge into European life: Jim hunts up the Variétés and Sarah conducts a flirtation with a bored American tourist, Waymarsh. Meantime Strether, who has assumed that the relationship between Chad and Mme de Vionnet is platonic, discovers them in a rendezvous in the country.

Through delicate stages, James has shown Strether's growing acceptance of European mores—a process accelerated by the advent of Jim and Sarah. On discovering that Chad and Mme de Vionnet are lovers, Strether goes through some soul searching, but entranced by the lady and realizing her genuine love for Chad, he ends by pleading with Chad not to desert her.

Then having abdicated from his ambassadorship, and therefore having lost his chance to marry the wealthy Mrs. Newsome, Strether makes a typically Jamesian gesture. Miss Gostrey has fallen in love with him and he with her, but he backs out on the grounds that he must get nothing out of his mission for himself. It is typical of James that this renunciation is presented as being a moral triumph—however Miss Gostrey may have regarded it.

As always in James's major works this is essentially a drama of moral choices. Although the characters to some degree symbolize national types, it is essentially a drama on a realistic level. Mrs. Newsome, Strether, Jim and Sarah Pocock, Mme de Vionnet, as well as the minor characters are all superbly individualized. But the ethical thesis—if this is not too dogmatic a term for a subtle social drama—which emerges is that European mores with all their faults are superior to the hypocritical standards of Woollett, Massachusetts. As a moral being, Mme de Vionnet is superior to Jim and Sarah Pocock.

The flaw in the picture is the defect of James's social ideal. A deeply moral man, in fact a moralist, he tended to confuse manners with other values. James, the expatriate, skilfully showed the crudities of Waymarsh and Jim Pocock, the American businessmen in Paris. Through Strether he approves Chad's decision to remain abroad instead of going back to help to run the corporation dominated by his family. The implication is that Chad would become another Jim Pocock, who is described as "awful." But Chad's fate in Europe is adumbrated. In a subtle bit of drama between Strether and Chad, Strether recognizes that Chad's recent visit to England has been to see a woman. For although Chad enjoys the association with creative artists, which he could not have at home, he himself is a *flaneur*. In Europe he will almost certainly become a cultured playboy. James has no notion of the creative side of an American business executive.

Edith Wharton put her finger on this limitation of James in *A Backward Glance*:

> The truth is that he belonged irrevocably to the old America out of which I also came, and of which—almost—it might paradoxically be said that to follow up its last traces one had to come to Europe. . . . Henry James was essentially a novelist of manners, and the manners he was qualified by nature and situation to observe were those of a little vanishing group of people among whom he had grown up, or their more picturesque prototypes in older societies.

She failed, of course, to see the deeper preoccupations of James, his concern with morals, but her statement helps to explain why James could admire an Isabel Archer or a Milly Theale and regard Jim Pocock as merely "awful." It apparently never occurred to him to consider the parasitical characteristics of Isabel and Milly, with their vast unearned wealth, nor the productive side of a Waymarsh or a Pocock.

In *The Golden Bowl* James drew another rich American businessman, Adam Verver, but as usual presented him not in a business setting but as a man of leisure in Europe. The international theme, however, is less important here than are the moral choices involved. And these in turn are clouded by the Freudian overtones of Maggie Verver's overattachment to her father and Verver's marriage to a much younger woman. Thus when Maggie's husband, Prince Amerigo, is unfaithful to her, it is not so much because he is a European as that Maggie has been giving her chief devotion to her father. Thus the novel, like some of James's later short stories, is more of a psychological than a social drama. It therefore has less relevance to a discussion of James as a social critic than do his other major works of the period.

The limits of his social vision are especially apparent in *The American Scene* (1907), the result of an eleven months' visit to his native land. His letters show that after an absence of twenty years he looked forward to the trip with enthusiasm. He was especially happy at the prospect of a reunion with his brother's family. In his stay of less than a year he tried to take the continent at a gulp—New York, New England, Philadelphia, Baltimore, Florida, Chicago, California; in fact he hoped to visit Mexico.

The account of his travels written immediately upon his return to England tells less than the whole story. He quickly found that he had too much material for one book, so *The American Scene* is confined to the Eastern seaboard. And as his letters show, he pulled his punches. Thus the published version of his impressions of New York City are less pungent than such comments to his correspondents as "New York is appalling, fantastically charmless and elaborately dire," or "that altogether unspeakable city."

A less understandable omission is that of people: James's pictures of the American scene are the snapshots of a tourist with an eye for landscape and architecture. After a day at Harvard

> It was after all in the great hall of the Union perhaps (to come back to that day's delicate end) that the actual vibration of response seemed most to turn to audible music—repeated with all its suggestiveness, on another occasion or two.

Now this was the Harvard in which William James was a famous professor, and where Henry must have certainly met some of the other greats like Charles W. Eliot, or perhaps Kittredge, or Copeland, or Dean Briggs.

In Philadelphia he met such celebrities as the flamboyant Dr. J. William White, who fought the last duel in Philadelphia, and the novelist-psychiatrist S. Weir Mitchell. Mitchell was a friend of William James and had had some correspondence with Henry. Perhaps no other American novelist of the period had come so near to James's own psychological probing. But *The American Scene* contains no mention of White or Mitchell.

Even more remarkable is the absence of figures in the Washington scene. In a letter James mentions meeting the "extraordinary and rather personally-fascinating President—who was kind to me." In the book James talks about the Washington Monument but not the President, although in 1904 Theodore Roosevelt was a more remarkable feature of the scene than was the stone obelisk.

James has some interesting comments on American hotels, Pullman cars, and country clubs—all of which he admired—and he even found Grant's Tomb praiseworthy, but when he tried to deal with New York skyscrapers he was lost. He saw nothing beautiful in them and he was nervous about elevators. But perhaps the most revealing note is his comment on the tall buildings. They were "a huge, continuous fifty-floored conspiracy against the very idea of ancient graces." The "aesthetic view is invariably blighted" by their many windows which spoke of "the economic idea." "Doesn't it take in fact acres of window-glass to help even an expert New Yorker to get the better of another expert one, or to see that the other expert one doesn't get the better of *him?*" On the other hand "the comparatively windowless bell-tower of Giotto in Florence, looks supremely serene in its beauty."

Throughout his journey, despite much that interested him, his letters speak of his homesickness for Lamb House, the "tight anchorage, *a definite little downward burrow, in the ancient world* [italics inserted] —a secret consciousness that I clink in my pocket as if it were a fortune in a handful of silver." In Florida, "In the heart of golden orange groves [he] yearned for the shade of the old L[amb] H[ouse] mulberry tree." Nearly two years later he wrote to Paul Harvey: "I found my native land, after so many years, interesting, formidable, fearsome, and fatiguing, and much more difficult to see and deal with in any extended and various way than I had supposed."

In America Henry received a doctorate from Harvard, and on his return to England one from Oxford. But the novel he had planned on America would not go forward. Instead he turned to the volumes of reminiscence of his boyhood and young manhood: *A Small Boy and Others, Notes of a Son and Brother,* and *The Middle Years.* As the excerpts from these, referred to earlier, suggest, James explored both his American and his early European experience. To some extent they are an apologia.

One thing becomes abundantly clear: in his later life James re-examined his life, particularly in relation to his expatriation. All the evidence suggests that like so many other expatriates he had conflicting emotions about Europe and about his homeland.

Edith Wharton asserts flatly:

> As for the nonsense talked by critics of a later generation, who never knew James, much less the world he grew up in, about his having thwarted his genius by living in Europe, and having understood his mistake too late . . . I can affirm that he was never really happy or at home there [in America].

Mrs. Wharton may have been reading some of her own feelings into Henry James. It would seem that he was never really happy anywhere. And it was not only critics of a later generation who commented on James's uneasy expatriation; there is testimony from his intimates. Ford Maddox Hueffer wrote:

> Indeed I know that, towards the end of his life, he came to think that the society of early, self-conscious New England, with its circumscribed horizon and want of exterior decoration or furnishings, was a spiritually finer thing than the mannered Europeanism that had so taken him to its bosom. . . . When I first knew him you could have imagined no oak more firmly planted in European soil. But, little by little, when he talked about America there would come into his tones a slight tremulousness that grew with the months. . . . Occasionally he would burst out at me with furious irritation if I ventured to have any opinions about the United States.

Then there is the testimony of Hamlin Garland who reported a conversation with James in 1900:

> "If I were to live my life over again," he said in a low voice, and fixing upon me a sombre glance, "I would be an American. I would steep myself in America, I would know no other land. I would study its beautiful side. The mixture of Europe and America which you see has proved disastrous. It has made me a man who is neither American nor European. I have lost touch with my own people, and I live here alone. My neighbors are friendly, but they are not of my blood, except remotely. . . ."

James's long-time friend, Howells, asserted that the cause of his long expatriation was his health, he was "less a sufferer in Europe than in America. The climate was kinder to him than ours. . . ."

Two of James's most subtle short stories may shed light upon his inner life: "The Jolly Corner," and "The Beast in the Jungle," both published in 1903, the year in which *The Ambassadors* came out. Both are highly symbolic, but it seems clear that "The Jolly Corner" deals with the question of his expatriation. The protagonist, Spencer Brydon, returns to his vacant mansion in New York. Near by is the new skyscraper built on land he once owned. Brydon had been twenty-three when he left New York; now he is fifty-six. Alone he prowls through the home of his youth. Soon he becomes aware that there is a ghost in the building, his alter ego. Night after night Brydon pursues this apparition, gradually working down from the upper floors to the vestibule with its remembered "marble squares of his childhood." There he catches a glimpse of the spectral figure, "a man of his own substance and stature." But the stranger was "evil, odious, blatant, vulgar." In Brydon's dialogue with Alice Staverton, it becomes clear that she would have accepted the alter ego, with his million a year, but prefers Brydon, monocle and all.

This along with *The Ambassadors* of the same date would suggest that just before his return to America James had re-examined his homeland and had asked himself what would have been his fate there. Just as Chad might have become another Jim Pocock, so Spencer Brydon might have become his blatant, vulgar alter ego.

But it was not as simple as all that. In one of the most vivid scenes in *The Ambassadors,* James's other alter ego Strether says to Little Bilham

> "All the same, don't forget that you're young—blessedly young; be glad of it on the contrary, and live up to it. Live all you can; it's a mistake not to. It doesn't so much matter what you do in particular, so long as you have your life. If you haven't had that, what have you had?"

Dupee reports that James, during a party at Whistler's said almost the same thing to a young friend, adding, "I see it now. I haven't done so—and now I'm old. It's too late. It has gone past me—I've lost it. You have time. You are young. Live!"

This sense of not having lived appears again in a story of terrible revelation, vividly named "The Beast in the Jungle." As a young man, John Marcher has confided to May Bartram (the names of the months embodied here suggest their temperaments) his sense of some important fate in store for himself. Over the years he keeps assuring her that it has never come. The story involves her increasing awareness of the real situation and his blindness to it. As she is dying she tells him that the destined thing has happened to him. Tantalized by her cryptic statements he visits her grave. At a nearby grave he observes a middle-aged man ravaged by grief. Suddenly the terrible revelation comes to him about himself:

> No passion had ever touched him, for this was what passion meant; he had survived and maundered and pined, but where had been *his* deep ravage? . . .
>
> The escape would have been to love her; then, *then* he would have lived. *She* had lived—who could say now with what passion?—since she had loved him for himself; whereas he had never thought of her (ah how it hugely glared at him!) but in the chill of his egotism and the light of her use. . . . The Beast had lurked indeed, and the Beast, at its hour, had sprung. . . .

It is of course possible to read into this a sense of guilt over Minny Temple, dead for thirty-odd years. In the light of the many pages he was to devote to her in his reminiscences this is a tempting explanation. Or the story may reflect a feeling of guilt over Constance Fenimore Woolson, with whom James had a long platonic friendship, although her letters suggest a warmer feeling on her part. In any case she jumped or fell from her Venice apartment. However, in the context of his remarks about never having lived, about his sense of not having appreciated the beauties of his own country, it is more likely that *The Beast in the Jungle* deals not with a single situation but with his sense of not having committed himself to anything. Early in life he had accepted the role of the observer who would translate his observations into art. Of his commitment to the artistic career there can be no doubt: it runs through his letters, his critical work, and his stories. In that commitment he saw his destiny.

But the stories, novels, his picture of *The American Scene,* and his volumes of reminiscence all suggest a search for relation to places and to people. Throughout all of them runs a note of loneliness, of bafflement. Despite a host of social engagements, especially in England, he continued to feel himself an outsider. Certainly he felt himself the outsider when he returned home in 1904–05. Chiefly in the hotel, the Pullman car, the country club could he establish a sense of relation. As has been said, there are no people in the expatriate's America: the human beings are all in his books of childhood and youth.

This search of a lonely man for an emotional commitment, a relation, would help to explain his action when in 1915 he became a British subject in protest against the failure of the United States to make common cause with the Allies. This act has been variously interpreted as a rather childish protest and as the logical culmination of James's expatriation. However, it must be remembered that long before this James had stated his theory that both England and America were parts of Anglo-Saxon civilization. When the war came he felt that this civilization was under attack by "two infamous autocrats," the Emperors of Germany and Austria. In his young manhood he had pathetically tried to establish a relation to the Civil War through a sense of common suffering; in later years through an identification with "Dear old Walt." It is perhaps significant that Edith Wharton remembered James's superb reading aloud of "When Lilacs Last in the Dooryard Bloom'd." Possibly his quixotic declaration of loyalty to England was a last desperate effort to make a commitment to life, to establish a relation. His act was triggered by the fact that he had to register as an alien. Even so, he told his nephew Henry, Jr., that he would not have taken the step if America had done more for England.

Whatever the implications of this renunciation of America, it seems clear that James the expatriate was a lonely man. How much of this was due to expatriation and how much to the psyche of the man is not easy to determine, but the evidence suggests that James would have been lonely in any country. His often used theme of suffering is that of a personal ache; it is not the result of sacrifice to a person or a cause. Isabel Archer, Christopher Newman, and Lambert Strether all accept suffering because of commitment to a personal ideal—not because their self-sacrifice can benefit anyone else.

Even in his style James is a man without a country. Several critics have remarked that his idiom is neither British nor American. Unlike Mark Twain, he had no ear for localized speech. For instance in *The Wings of the Dove*, Mrs. Lowder speaks in typically Jamesian parentheses:

> "Dear Susan tells me that you saw in America Mr. Densher—whom I've never till now, as you may have noticed, asked you about. But do you mind at last, in connection with him, doing something for me?"

And the English girl Kate Croy and the American Milly Theale sound alike, that is like Henry James:

Kate: "You'll extraordinarily like her."

Milly: "Didn't he awfully like you?"

James: "It made him helplessly gaze."

This odd unidiomatic placing of the adverb—often the adverb *beautifully*
is almost a trademark of James.

Examples could be multiplied ad infinitum. Certainly James's "third
manner" has been widely discussed. It is clear that its complicated
structure, its parentheses, reflect not anything he had ever heard, but his
own style of conversation, what Van Wyck Brooks calls "the evasiveness,
the hesitancy, the scrupulosity of an habitually embarrassed man." Edith
Wharton once invited James to dinner with Mr. Dooley, who commented
mournfully, "What a pity it takes him so long to say anything! Everything he said was so splendid—but I felt like telling him all the time:
"Just 'pit it right into Popper's hand.' "

The point is that James carried his private vision—yes even his search
for relation—from his conversation into his novels. Even in the language
of the characters one hears not a variety of individuals but Henry James.

The theory that James the sensitive artist was the victim of an uncul-
tured America has a number of flaws. In the first place he regularly
achieved publication in the United States, frequently in both magazine
and book form. Even so difficult a novel as *The Golden Bowl* went
through four editions in America during its first year. Of course he was
subjected to adverse criticism by Americans, but Europeans also have
made derogatory remarks. His friend H. G. Wells caricatured him in
Boon and spoke of "the elaborate, copious emptiness of the whole Henry
James exploit." E. M. Forster wrote: "James has a very short list of
characters and besides being few in number, they are constructed on
personal lines. They are incapable of fun, of rapid motion, of carnality,
and of nine-tenths of heroism. Their clothes will not take off. . . ."
André Gide, while recognizing the importance of James, complained that
"he dominates his narrative from too great a height; he does not commit
himself to it. . . . So much dressing and distinction, I am satiated with it
in advance; he surpasses us in our own faults."

It is worth noting that James himself in his picture of a crass society
which destroys the artist laid the scene of his most bitter picture of this
situation in England, i.e. "The Death of the Lion." The fact remains that
few writers who have been so subtle, so wilfully obscure, have received so

much respectful attention in their own lifetimes on both sides of the Atlantic. It would be hard to find a critic contemporaneous with James who so consistently insisted on his importance as did the American William Dean Howells. In so far as James's picture of the artist as the victim of society has validity, it is a universal picture of both Europe and America in the nineteenth century—what he called "our most vulgar of ages."

The fact is that James, like Gilbert Osmond, preferred "the old, the consecrated, the transmitted." In his biography of Story he spoke of an idyllic past which they had shared:

> The celestial cheapness of the early times made up for many a *train de luxe* and many an electric bell. The old letters are full of it—it made even *them*, the old wanderers marvel; it was in particular the last cloying sweet in the rich feast of Italy; it could add grace even to the grace of Florence, and a thrill even to the thrill of Rome.

In contrast he had written in 1890 of the new age:

> . . . the deluge of people, the insane movement for movement, the ruin of thought, of life, the negation of work, of literature, the swelling, roaring crowds . . . the age of Mrs. Jack [Gardner], the figure of Mrs. Jack, the American, the nightmare—the individual consciousness—the mad, ghastly climax . . . the American looming up—dim, vast, portentous—in their millions—the gathering waves—the barbarians of the Roman Empire.

His cork-lined room was being invaded.

Much of the evidence suggests that Henry James was not an exile from America but a refugee from his era in both Europe and America. In fact he regarded the date of the Franco-Prussian war as "the hitherward limit of the *liveable* era."

The limitations of James as a delineator of his contemporary European scene are especially obvious when his observations are compared to those of such people as Cooper, Hawthorne, Margaret Fuller, and George Ticknor. They examined and compared the social, political, economic and educational systems of England and America; they discussed these matters with prominent Europeans. It has often been remarked that the Europe of Henry James is that of the drawing room and country house. It is also worth noting that his Americans are largely representative of the well-to-do expatriate class, and their visiting relatives, a class which had gone to Europe in search of inexpensive leisure in picturesque surroundings. In London, Paris, and especially in Florence, Rome, and Venice James spent many hours with these leisured expatriates—a class which had cut its roots in America and which struck down no new ones in the functioning life of Europe. Their daughters frequently married Europeans, often, according to James, with unfortunate results. On the whole it was a class uncommitted to anything but the kind of puritanical hedonism engaged in by the Storys. Isabel Archer's choice of the dilettante Osmond over the American businessman and the English parliamentarian is symbolic of the type of American James pictured.

The industrial revolution, the business civilization of England and America were both unpleasant to him. He found plutocracy distasteful—whether of the British Maude Lowder or of the American Jim Pocock. But, as has been indicated, the inherited amenities of the old European order had for him become corrupt. With all their naïveté and crassness, his American characters come off best. In fact, his most vivid characters are usually Americans. In his concern with ethics and questions of morals, James is very much the American. It would be difficult, perhaps impossible, to cite another writer who has so consistently dwelt upon the moral corruption of Europeans. Even the charming Mme de Vionnet is tainted with dishonesty. It is scarcely too much to say that the moral corruption of Europe is an obsession with James. Thus in his deepest emotional commitments Henry James was very much an American. For him, like so many other Americans of the nineteenth century, the appeal of Europe was its cultural past. And for James it was also the cork-lined room which partially shut out the noise of the modern world.

THE FLAMBOYANT AMERICAN
HAROLD FREDERIC

It is difficult to imagine two American writers more different than Henry James and Harold Frederic. Frederic was an outgoing, even bumptious man who dominated the conversation in his London clubs, a man who had three children by his wife and three by a mistress. In fact he supported two households in England simultaneously. As a newspaper man he had worked for the election of Cleveland as governor of New York and maintained a friendship during the latter's terms as President. In London he covered Parliamentary debates for the New York *Times*, became intimate with leading political figures, and informed himself on economic and sociological questions. Of James he once remarked, "Henry James is an effeminate old donkey who lives with a herd of other donkeys around him and insists on being treated as if he were the Pope. He has licked the dust from the floor of every third-rate hostess in England." Yet like James, Frederic spent most of his mature life abroad and wrote his novels there. Like James he was a keen observer of the social order on both sides of the Atlantic.

Harold Frederic's masterpiece, *The Damnation of Theron Ware* (1896), is only one of the six or seven novels* he wrote in his brief life of forty-two years. In addition he poured out newspaper and magazine articles and stories for the New York *Times, The Fortnightly Review, The Idler, The English Illustrated Magazine, The Bookman, Pall Mall Gazette, The Saturday Review* [London], *Cosmopolitan, Harper's New Monthly Magazine, The Youth's Companion, Scribner's Magazine, The Saturday Evening Post*, and others.

Published in England under the title of *Illumination* (1896), *The Damnation of Theron Ware* was compared by *The Spectator* to *The Scarlet Letter. The Daily Chronicle* said, "Mr. Frederic is winning his way by sure steps to the foremost ranks of writers of fiction." *The Westminster Gazette* and *The Manchester Guardian* joined in praise, the latter saying that Frederic had gained a front rank among living novelists

---

* One of these, *Mrs. Albert Grundy*, could be classed as a group of satirical sketches.

and that *Illumination* was a rarity: a book of genuine importance. Gladstone thought it a masterpiece of character drawing. By comparison the British response to Henry James was tepid.

In America *Theron Ware* provoked a brief spurt of favorable criticism, especially from Howells, but as his biographers O'Donnell and Franchere sum it up, "With few exceptions, American critics have over the past seventy-five years neglected Harold Frederic. . . ." Only two novels, *Seth's Brother's Wife* and *Theron Ware*, have received much attention. Yet the fact is that Frederic was one of the most perceptive commentators in our literature on both America and England.

Born in Utica, New York, in 1856, the son of a freight conductor on the New York Central, Harold Frederic graduated from the Advanced School of his native city. He worked on the Utica *Morning Herald* and the *Observer*, of which he became editor at the age of twenty-four. He then went to the Albany *Evening Journal*. When it was sold in 1884, he was given the post of London correspondent for the New York *Times*. Except for three short visits to the United States he lived in England for the last fourteen years of his life.

In characteristic American fashion he had married early. He was twenty-one when he took as a wife Grace Williams, the granddaughter of Beriah Green, a famous abolitionist. Grace remained a Utica girl all her life, refusing to become a part of his London life except for dutifully entertaining his new and important friends. But she did not go with him to their parties. His mistress, Kate Lyon, was also an upstate New York Girl, from Oswego, whom he probably met at the British Museum in 1890. He lived openly with her at "Homefield," fifteen miles south of London, while spending weekends with his legal family in London.

The important thing is not, however, Frederic's unconventional love life but his response to expatriation. In the year he reached England (1884), sponsored by Aaron Watson and supported by the personal recommendation of Grover Cleveland, he joined the Savage Club. A year later he was elected to the National Liberal Club, although he did not become active for another year. Here he met Gladstone, Lloyd George, Parnell, and became a friend of a number of British Parliamentarians. In 1889 he became active in the Ghouls Club, whose membership included James Barrie, W. E. Henley, Joseph Pennell, Conan Doyle, and Bernard Partridge, the cartoonist for *Punch*. At the club's meetings in Signor

Roma's restaurant he ordered the menu and dominated the conversation. Frank Harris remembered Frederic as "the best of boon companions and a storyteller of the rarest."

Frederic, who had a photographic memory for details, collected an immense fund of information; he familiarized himself with the ranks, relationships, and marriages of the British aristocracy. In a pre-Gallup era he had at the time of a General Election a notebook crammed with statistics on the political situation.

A friend writing a reminiscence just after Frederic's death said that on arrival in England

> He was, of course, American, patriotically and flamboyantly so, and like a good American he was ready to point out our faults, and failings, and contrast them with the full-orbed perfection of the other hemisphere.

The two men, who were the same age, spent hours together over drinks while they argued politics, especially the Irish question. At such times, said the friend, "the self-assertive American journalist entirely disappeared, and the real Frederic, intensely curious about the movements and forces at work in Europe came to the front."

This curiosity had manifested itself immediately. He had left New York in June; by July 27 he had sent the *Times* "Down among the Dead Men," an account of a five-day tour of the cholera-stricken cities of Toulon, Marseilles, and Arles. This made him something of a hero to his colleagues and brought him an international reputation.

During his first eight years in Europe Frederic traveled extensively—to Ireland, Berlin, Paris, Brussels, and elsewhere. In Germany he collected enough information to write a biography of William II: *The Young Emperor* (1891). That same year he traveled to Russia to report on a Jewish pogrom then raging. His news stories, collected under the title *The New Exodus,* were published in book form in both London and New York. On the way back from Russia he visited Buda Pesth, Vienna, Munich, and Frankfort. In 1892 he was back in Germany making another tour.

Because Frederic's social criticism of American and European life is chiefly embodied in his novels, the following discussion will be concerned with them. It was to his American experience that he first turned when he began writing fiction. His first three novels: *Seth's Brother's Wife*

(1887), *In the Valley* (1890), and *The Lawton Girl* (1890), are all laid in upstate New York, the scene of the later *Theron Ware*. All three were published in both England and America.

Because all of these except *In the Valley*, which is a historical romance, deal realistically with village and rural life, Frederic is usually classified along with E. W. Howe and Hamlin Garland as a pioneer of the revolt against the American small town. Parrington described *Seth's Brother's Wife* as

> . . . a drab tale of farm life in upper New York State, as bitter as any tale of the western border. It is a story of defeat, a flight from country to town. The blight of failure is upon the farming community—a blight that embitters old and young: and the sketches of country louts, of soured lives, of broken men and women, do not make pleasant reading.

This, as will appear, represents almost a complete misreading of the novel. Yet in *The Literary History of The United States* (1948) Walter F. Taylor wrote: "Frederic's first novel, *Seth's Brother's Wife* . . . anticipates Garland's *Main Travelled Roads* in its removal of false glamour with which the romantic era had invested rural life. . . ."

Frederic himself, however, described the novel to Daniel Lamont, Cleveland's secretary, as dealing with "farm-life, politics, and newspaper work in a provincial city" during the campaign of 1882. "The whole thing is between the good and bad in politics." And in the novel the good triumphs. In briefest outline it is the story of Seth Fairchild's development in emotional maturity and success as a newspaper man during a political campaign. His old brother, Albert, a wealthy New York lawyer married to a silly young wife, comes back to the farm to establish a residence from which to run for Congress. His bored wife conducts a flirtation with Seth, who works on a small-city newspaper. In an attempt to buy the nomination Albert is murdered for the money by a brutish countryman he has used as a go-between. The honest newspaper owner, Beekman, and the honest politician, Andsell, refuse to be bought and carry the day. It is true that Frederic gives some of the drabness of rural life, but the characters who come off worst are the citified lawyer Albert and his silly wife Isabel. Some of the criticism of rural life is put in her mouth.

Essentially this novel and the two which followed it are dramatizations

of Frederic's democratic philosophy. *Seth* shows the triumph of good
government during the Cleveland campaign for governor; *In the Valley*
pictures the class war of the 1770's between the Tories and their democratic neighbors. *The Lawton Girl* is the story of an attempt by a group of
dog-eat-dog businessmen to capture the iron works which are the chief
industry of Thessaly, New York. As O'Donnell and Franchere point out,
the novel is Frederic's dramatization of the conflict between the social
Darwinism of William Graham Sumner and the melioristic sociology of
Lester Ward and E. L. Godkin. As they sum up the three novels:

> In *Seth's Brother's Wife*, this same region had triumphed over
> political corruption; in *In the Valley* it had destroyed the threat of
> class tyranny; now in *The Lawton Girl*, the region wins again—this
> time over economic despotism of the kind Frederic saw to be inher-
> ent in the belief of social Darwinists like William Graham Sumner.
> . . . And all three victories had been achieved under the leadership
> of men who were themselves able and intelligent products of the
> region.

Thus during his first six years in England Frederic's sensibilities were
very much those of an American patriot. He was by no means rejecting
his homeland. Nor was he in his first novel laid outside the United States,
The Return of O'Mahony (1892). It can best be described as a romp—a
mixture of farce, caricature, and melodrama with a hearts-and-flowers
ending. Obviously it was done for fun, but even so it contains some
shrewd, even biting, social criticism.

The plot would do for a movie comedy. A veteran of the Union Army
gets hold of some papers which enable him to masquerade as the heir to a
broken-down Irish estate. In short order the bogus O'Mahony becomes a
kind of Yankee at King Arthur's court: he reduces rents, abolishes feudal
levies, starts a lobster cannery, reopens some copper mines, and puts the
estate on a paying basis.

All this upsets the resident bard, O'Daly, who asks what good is it if

> ". . . ye've no ancesthral pride, no love and reverence for ancient
> family thraditions, no devout desoire to walk in the paths your
> forefather's trod?"
>
> "Faith, thim same forefathers trod thim with a highly unsteady
> step, thin, bechune oursilves," commented Mrs. Fergus.

"But their souls were filled with blessid piety," said Mother Agnes
gravely. . . .

Mother Agnes is one of three elderly nuns attached to the family convent
of the order of the Ladies of the Hostage's Tears, founded 1191. When
O'Mahony finds that seven-year-old Kate, whom he calls Skeezucks, is destined to become a nun, he tells her, "Now don't you fret your gizzard,
siss . . . you needn't be a nun for one solitary darned minute, if you don't
want to be." He suggests that she would rather be "climbin' trees and
huntin' eggs . . . than go into partnership with grandma . . . in the nun
business."

Obviously, Frederic, despite his affection for Ireland, where he spent
his holidays, has little of James's longing for the old, the consecrated, the
received. Frederic's sensibility, even his prejudices, are thoroughly American. This vein continues in the second half of the novel. O'Mahony
unwisely gets mixed up with a Fenian attack on the British and is forced
to disappear. O'Daly takes over the management of the estate, restores
the high rents and the feudal charges, and embezzles the royalties from
the mines. In midwinter he evicts some delinquent tenants by having the
roofs taken off their cottages. Frederic comments, "a gloomy spectacle,
familiar enough elsewhere throughout Ireland."

Twelve years after O'Mahony's disappearance an Irish-American mining engineer Bernard O'Mahony, the real heir to the estate, turns up and
woos Kate. He finds that the convent is no longer recognized by the
church, and thus she is free of her promise to enter it. He excoriates those
who have let O'Daly usurp the estate:

> "That's the worst of your fellows. . . . You take flight like a flock
> of sheep. What the deuce are you afraid of?"
> ". . . Ah, sir," said Jerry, "It isn't like in Ameriky, where every
> man's free to do what plases him:"
> "There's the whole trouble in a nutshell," said Bernard. "Every-
> body talks and nobody does anything."

The young O'Mahony is described as answering to the villagers' *"conception of what a man from America should be like.* [Italics inserted.] He
was young, fresh-faced and elastic of step—with square shoulders, a lithe,
vigorous frame and eyes which looked with frank and cheerful shrewd-
ness at all men and things. . . . There was a delightful absence of reserve
in this young man from America."

The British appear only briefly in the story, and not to their advantage. An English magistrate uses a brutal tone with some prisoners:

"Bernard, as he heard it, felt himself newly informed as to the spirit in which India was governed. Perhaps it was necessary there; but it made him grind his teeth to think of its use in Ireland."

While *O'Mahony* was in the process of publication Frederic wrote for the *National Observer* a series of satirical articles called "Observations in Philistia." All but two of these were later collected under the title *Mrs. Albert Grundy*. The satire, done with a broad brush, is directed chiefly against the prejudices of the British upper middle class: their hypocritical prudishness, their social pretensions, their ignorance about art, their anti-Americanism, and their muddle-headedness. The scene is Mrs. Grundy's villa near the South Kensington museum.

For instance, Mrs. Grundy locks away from her daughters a novel which she describes thus: "Respectable people were only incidentally mentioned in it. Really it was quite *too* low. The chief figure was a farmgirl who for the most part skimmed milk or cut swedes in a field and often at other times behaved in a manner positively unmentionable." Mrs. Grundy cannot understand why some critic had hailed it as "a tragic work of the noblest and highest order." The novel is obviously Hardy's *Tess*, published the year before.

Another character, Mr. Hump, says that one of the joys of living in England is that one can always enjoy delicious game, whereas Americans live chiefly on fried salt-pork. The narrator assures Mr. Hump that in America one could enjoy eighteen edible varieties of wild birds for every one in England. At which "Mrs. Grundy whispered . . . warningly that Mr. Hump had made America his special subject, and wrote most vigorous comminatory articles about it almost every week." Similarly, on the authority of an Englishman who had spent nearly three weeks in the United States, Mr. Hump says that it is extremely rare to meet an adult American who has not been divorced at least once.

As the ladies leave the room after an especially inane dinner-table conversation, Mrs. Grundy's brother, Uncle Dudley, reaches for the port and remarks, "Gad, . . . I don't wonder that the pick of our young fellows go in for marrying American girls."

Especially amusing to Frederic are the British views on art. All that Uncle Dudley knows about Whistler is that he was once mixed up in some sort of law suit. Mrs. Grundy clarifies the matter:

"I was under the same impression till Lady Wallaby set me right. It seems that was another man altogether—some foreign adventurer who pretended to paint and imposed upon people—don't you recall how *The Tarradiddle* exposed him—and Mr. Burnt-Jones had him arrested or something."

At an art exhibit Miss Timby-Hucks remarks that "foreigners are so sensitive about the superiority of British Art. . . . They have nothing at all on the Continent like our Royal Academy. . . ."

"A safe statement . . . ," I assured her. "You might go further and assert that no other country at any stage of its history has had anything like the Royal Academy. It is the unique blossom of British civilization."

Miss Timby-Hucks attributes this to "the diffusion of Christian principles among us, our high standard of national morality and the sanctity of the English home."

It is obvious that eight years of expatriation had not turned Frederic into a complete Anglophile. As will appear, his two posthumously published novels, although not satirical, do not glamorize English life. Thus his masterpiece, *The Damnation of Theron Ware* (1896), must be considered within the context of Frederic's social criticism as a whole. There can be no question that this novel presents a disillusioned view of certain aspects of American life: small-town intolerance, narrow religion, hypocrisy—especially that of businessmen. Although it is a far better book than *Elmer Gantry,* the two are often compared.

The fact that *Theron Ware* is one of the truly great American novels has tended to obscure Frederic's stance as a social critic. Most readers who know of him at all have read only this one book.

Theron Ware is laid in Octavia, New York, a Methodist stronghold. When Theron brings his bride to his new charge, he is quickly informed by the elders of the church that he may not have milk delivered on the Sabbath and that his wife must take the flowers off her bonnet. When he tries to reduce the 7 per cent interest on the church's debt, two elders who hold the mortgages talk of the sacredness of contracts. Like Seth of the earlier novel, Theron is an American Adam tempted by a more sophisticated Eve—in this case the rich Celia Madden, Celia describes herself thus:

"I am a Catholic. . . . But I should explain that I am a Catholic only in the sense that its symbolism is pleasant to me. You remember what Schopenhauer said—you cannot have the water by itself; you may also have the jug it is in. Very well, the Catholic religion is my jug. I put into it the things I like."

In her room she has nude statues and pictures of the Virgin. Celia's cynical sophistication is matched by those of the learned and agnostic Father Forbes and the atheistic scientist, Dr. Ledsmar. Father Forbes explains to the naïve pastor that biblical history is largely based on archetypal myth. On another occasion, Theron is faced with the contrast between a dour Methodist camp meeting and a happy, beer-drinking, baseball-playing Catholic picnic.

Then his church undertakes a money-raising campaign led by two imported professionals, Brother and Sister Soulsby. As characteristically American types the Soulsbys rival the King and the Duke of *Huckleberry Finn*. Although supposedly husband and wife, they are probably not married, and they have a background of the road show, fortunetelling, and lectures on phrenology and female diseases. In a money-raising session Sister Soulsby locks the church doors, puts on an excellent act, and gets the congregation to bid against one another in offering pledges. When two of the elders later welch on their pledges, Sister Soulsby gives Ware a lecture on the cynical management of such matters.

Theron, disillusioned about primitive Methodism and having been nearly seduced by Celia, follows her and Father Forbes to the city. She recognizes him and tells him she is bored with him. He goes on a spree and hunts up Sister Soulsby, who tells him some of her life story and gets him back on his feet.

Certainly few novels have given a more disillusioned picture of American Protestantism.

It is probably a mistake, however, to see the novel, as does John Henry Raleigh, as "concerned with the relationship of America to Europe." In Raleigh's view Celia "bears the stamp of late nineteenth century English culture and brings up memories of the Pre-Raphaelites and *The Yellow Book*. . . ." However, *The Yellow Book* was founded by an American, and the aesthete with his incense, private altars and nude statues, missals and erotica flourished at Harvard as well as at Oxford. Celia's real-life counterpart would be someone like Mrs. Jack Gardner of Boston. And as for Raleigh's emphasis, the contrast between Irish Catholicism and American Protestantism, it is not the Irish of *The Return of the O'Mahony* who appear in *Theron Ware* but the Irish-Americans of Utica, New York—playing baseball and drinking German beer. Father Forbes says that "the lager-drinking Irishman in a few generations will be a new type of humanity. He will be *the* American." Even the atheistic German scientist, Dr. Ledsmar, was a type who had become familiar in the United States. Insofar as *Theron Ware* presents a contrast of cultures, it is not that of Europe versus America, but is the kind which Crèvecoeur had noted in America as far back as the 1770's. As Celia in a later novel says of the making of a gentleman, "We do it more simply in America. One generation makes the fortune, and leaves it to the next generation to put on the frills." Her own father, for instance, never altered the habits he had formed as a poor workingman in Ireland. In other words, Celia recognizes herself as a characteristically second-generation American.

Before Frederic is pigeonholed as an expatriate who became disillusioned with the United States one must consider his last two novels, both dealing with the English scene. These lack some of the blood-and-bone reality of *Theron Ware*, but Frederic is never dull; he never lost his ability to create vivid people and a sense of place. Always he is the social critic. For the purposes of this study his views of the European scene are perhaps more important than his novels of the Mohawk Valley.

In many ways *Gloria Mundi*, published posthumously in 1898, is a conventional romantic novel of the nineties. But it is more than that. The story opens when a young man, Christian Tower, bound for England, boards a train at Rouen. In the compartment is a girl who mistakenly believes she has an exclusive reservation. He recognizes that "she was above all things English. . . . From this fact alone would be inferred a towering personal pride, and an implacable resentment towards those who no matter how accidentally, offered injury to that pride." Sure enough when he offers her his seat with the better view, she declines, saying, "I should be obliged if you would take the view that conversation is not necessary."

Finally he does get into conversation with her and tells her that he has been summoned home by his relatives, the Torrs. (His black-sheep father had changed the name.) She knows something of the family and tells him that because of the accidental deaths of two of his cousins he will be the next Earl of Glastonbury when his ailing grandfather dies. Christian and the girl, Frances Bailey, part on good terms. In the end he will marry her.

From here on the novel becomes the story of a rather naïve young man, who has never been in England, being introduced to the realities of the British aristocracy. Just as Theron Ware found the corruption behind the façade of organized religion, Christian discovers the brutalities of wealth and privilege.

Because of mismanagement the huge estate—80,000 acres—would have been bankrupt except for the fortune brought by the Jewish wife of Lord Julius, an uncle of Christian's. As Lord Julius says of the dying old man, "He has been a duke nearly eighty years . . . but he has been an ass still longer than that." When Christian is taken to meet the Duke, the old man rants against a tenant who has put up a barbed wire fence: "A good hearty cut across the face is what'd teach the swine" and "no gentleman would listen to his evidence for a minute."

As Lord Julius says, "In the Almanach de Gotha he is classed among the princes, but what he dwells upon most fondly among his public duties is the kicking of tenant-farmers in the stomach when they try to save their crops from being ruined by the hunters."

Julius's son Emmanuel remarks, "We have an immense deal to make up to the people about us, and to humanity in general, have we Torrs." Proudly Emmanuel explains his "System" for managing his own estate—a paternalistic one based on Carlyle's ideas. Emmanuel believes "that the feudal stage had offered mankind its greatest opportunities for happiness and the higher life."

In his discussion of *Gloria Mundi* in *American Fiction,* Arthur Quinn is almost certainly wrong when he says, "Frederic represented the strength and weakness of the English patrician system and the materialistic basis of its social structure, but as a contrast to the truer democracy of the Middle Ages." The rather naïve Christian has some doubts about the System, but it is Frances Bailey who later correctly describes it as one "which exalts the few and keeps the many in subjection." Emmanuel had admitted to Christian that the greatest difficulty was fitting women into his System. "It is not so much a matter of evil natures as of inferior brains." Again Frances puts her finger on the real trouble: ". . . the corner-stone of the System is the perpetual enslavement of women."

Thus Frederic, who in *The Lawton Girl* had rejected the social Darwinism of William Graham Sumner, obviously finds the aristocratic paternalism of Carlyle equally distasteful. In fact Frederic's first three novels laid in upper New York state had shown the forces of democracy triumphing over Tories and plutocrats.

Certainly he had small respect for the British aristocracy. Lady Cressage, the widow of the deceased heir presumptive, speaks of Christian's cousins Edward and Augustine. "You saw those two young men this morning. They are not up to much certainly; their uncle Porlock and his sons averaged, perhaps, even a shade lower . . . but when all is said and done, they are not remarkably worse than other men of their class." Lady Cressage feels that she was sold into marriage. But as one character remarks, Lady Cressage had married Christian's cousin knowing that he was a "violent, ignorant, low minded fellow"—but the heir to a dukedom. In a quietly ironic vein Frederic shows the naïve Christian wondering if his cousin Edward would not be better suited to a dukedom than himself: "Should the duke not be a rough, hard sportsman, a man with a passion for horses and dogs and gunpowder saturating his veins. One who loved the country for its rude, out-of-door sports, and who liked best in town the primitive amusements of the natural man?"

Certainly there is little gracious living in what Lord Julius calls "that criminal old coal-mine of a castle." The food is very bad. Christian reflects that since his arrival in England he has not encountered a tolerable dish. "Vegetables and fish half raw, meats tasteless and without sauce or seasoning, bread heavy and sour, coffee unrecognizable." Perhaps it was this graceless and repellent diet which made the English such physical and temperamental masters of the world.

The importance of *Gloria Mundi* for the purposes of this study is that it strips the Jamesian glamour from British aristocracy. Here are no story-book noblemen like Lord Warburton who, as Frederic may have remembered, had 50,000 acres, but who in *Portrait of a Lady* never struck tenants, drank, went to prizefights, or took mistresses. Instead of spending his time in the hunting field he divided his energies between a Parliamentary career and a courtly wooing of the empty-headed Isabel Archer. Even more important, *Gloria Mundi* shows that for the expatriated Frederic the culture of an English castle is not notably superior to that of an upstate New York parsonage. If *Theron Ware* shows a bleak society, *Gloria Mundi* shows a brutal one.

Nor does British society appear to better advantage in Frederic's last novel, *The Market Place* (1899). It presents a contrast between an effete aristocracy and a ruthless British entrepreneur Joel Stormont Thorpe. If

Theron Ware was the prototype for Elmer Gantry, Thorpe might be the model for Dreiser's Frank Cowperwood. And just as Ware is a more complex person than Gantry, so Thorpe is a more fully rounded character than Cowperwood. Frederic's novel has emotional subtleties and intellectual complexities beyond Dreiser's reach. But as a picture of the world of business and finance *The Market Place* presents a London as cynically corrupt as Cowperwood's Philadelphia and Chicago.

Thorpe, the son of a London bookseller, returns to England after fifteen years of knocking about the world in search of riches—"A passion to reap where others had sown." As the owner of a nearly worthless rubber concession in Mexico he organizes a corporation and floats a stock issue of "Rubber Consols." To obtain a respectable front for the corporation he secures a number of men of title for his board of directors, the most important being Lord Plowden, Lord Chaldon, and General Kervic. As Thorpe's broker, Semple, tells him, the only way such men know how to get money is to let their names be used in this way. With the tacit consent of his directors, Thorpe manages to get a group of financiers to sell Rubber Consols short; then he corners the market and runs the prices up from £1 to £15, then £25 a share.

Thorpe, in gratitude for Plowden's help, has promised him a quarter of the shares. Plowden, although somewhat dubious about Thorpe's social skills, invites him to his mother's country house. Thorpe is puzzled over the contrast between Plowden's talk of poverty and the lavishness of an estate with scores of servants. Here Thorpe meets Lady Edith Cressage (who appeared in *Gloria Mundi*) and her friend Celia Madden (of *Theron Ware*). Celia has been much chastened by life. She says that once she used her wealth and power only to produce misery for others. The widowed Lady Cressage, it develops, is General Kervic's daughter, a woman who greatly attracts Thorpe.

A key incident during the visit is a pheasant-shooting expedition. For Thorpe—and apparently for Frederic—it symbolizes the attitudes of the British upper class. Lord Plowden's brother Balder, who does nothing but hunt and fish, goes out early by himself; Plowden lets Thorpe wait around until noon, then has a servant bring a folding chair for himself but none for his guest. After the shoot, Plowden somewhat contemptuously asks if Thorpe has bagged anything. It turns out he has killed more birds than the others put together.

Despite Plowden's rather contemptuous attitude toward his guest, he in effect offers to let Thorpe marry his sister in order to bring the illgotten fortune into the family. However, the hunting incident has so angered Thorpe that he gives Plowden shares of less value than had been implied. Lord Plowden then embarks upon a scheme to blackmail Thorpe by bringing from Mexico a drunken geologist, Tavender, who can expose the worthlessness of the rubber concession. Thorpe sees the man first and orders General Kervic to get him drunk and keep him out of sight so that the man cannot appear before a committee of the Exchange. Kervic overdoes his assignment and the man dies of drink. When Lord Chaldron hears disquieting rumors, Thorpe buys him off by a promise of a substantial share in the profits.

It is in his relationships with Chaldron, Plowden, and the General that Thorpe shows his complete contempt for their class. On one occasion the General complains that his daughter, Lady Cressage, did not provide adequately for him: "I secured for her the greatest marriage in England [but] instead of being the grandfather of a Duke, I have a childless widow thrust back upon my hands."

To this Thorpe responds, "I don't want to hear you abuse your daughter. . . . Why should you expect her to support you . . . ? No sit still! Listen to me! . . . You don't want to have any row with me. You can't afford it. Just think that over to yourself—you—can't—afford—it."

Thorpe had "learned what he wanted to know about this veteran. If he had the fierce meanness of a famished dog, he had a dog's awe of the stick." Shortly after this Kervic writes to tell Thorpe where he can see Lady Cressage. Thorpe meditates, "These beautiful women, trained from childhood for the conquest of a rich husband, must have cultivated an extraordinary delicacy of consciousness in such matters."

As for Plowden, Thorpe gets him to sign an incriminating agreement, then taunts him for his incompetence in the matter of the geologist.

All this might suggest that Thorpe is a completely heartless man, that there is little to choose between the buccaneer and the aristocrats. Not so. Thorpe can be impulsively generous. When he finds that one of the shorts will have to sacrifice his daughter's marriage portion, Thorpe sells the man's shares at a loss to himself of £10,000. He even arranges to have Semple put Lord Plowden on the board of the reorganized company. However Semple later has to get rid of the nobleman as "a parasite." Nor is Thorpe represented as being worse than other speculators. The men he had squeezed were known in financial circles as "wreckers," men who strangled weak enterprises. The newspapers are presented as completely venal, accepting pay-offs for printing slanted financial news.

After he has made his fortune, Thorpe marries Lady Cressage and buys a country estate. She was attracted to him by his swashbuckling qualities; she says it was the sort of appeal that Bothwell had for Marie Stuart. Highborn ladies and gentlemen now fawn on him, but "It was impossible to get a sense of companionship from people who cringed to him and swallowed his affronts and cackled at his jokes with equal docility." He and his wife rent a house for the London season, but for both of them "it was one endless procession of stupid and tiresome calls and dinners and parties." To his sister, who has stubbornly held onto the family bookshop, he tells of his boredom with country life. His sister says that Lady Cressage, a customer of hers, is equally bored, that her endless gardening is to keep her from dying of loneliness. Other ladies from country families tell her the same story. She suggests that Thorpe devote some attention to the awful conditions of the London poor.

This talk with his sister gives Thorpe a new insight into his wife's feelings. He discovers that because of her rank he has been a little afraid of her. In a long *aufklärung* he breaks through Edith's reserve and woos her as a lover, a wooing to which she happily responds. With regained sense of power he tells the Duke of Glastonbury (the hero of *Gloria Mundi*) of his plans for political and philanthropic activity, and suggests that he too join in. The Duke has a sense of futility: "Ah, the terms and forms survive . . . after the substance has disappeared. The nobleman, the prince, was a great person in the times when he monopolized wealth. The barriers are down now. Everything which used to be exclusively the nobleman's is now within everybody's reach, including the sins."

Thorpe refuses to be discouraged: "All the same," he declares roundly, "I'm going to do the trick. London has been waiting for an organizer—a leader for a hundred years. The right kind of man, going the right way to work, can stand London on its head, as surely as I can burn this cigar. And I'm going to have a try at it."

O'Donnell and Franchere point out that in the portrait of Thorpe Frederic is almost certainly representing the Nietzschean superman. And in a passage of subtle irony, Frederic lets Thorpe make the discovery that in the contemporary world, philanthropy is a sure road to power. It is Celia Madden who pronounces the last line of the novel, "I shall always insist, just the same, that crime was his true vocation."

This outline of the story of necessity omits some of the subtleties of psychological portraiture, but it should make clear Frederic's view that the British aristocracy had become effete and enervated. For instance, he has Lord Plowden's mother deplore the disappearance of the old purchase system for commissions in the Army. There was Balder, for instance, a gentleman just made to be a soldier, but he couldn't get into Sandhurst: "The poor boy will never pass those examinations in the world. . . . All over England there are young gentlemen like that—the very pick of the hunting fields. . . ."

Obviously Frederic was looking at England through American eyes up to the time of his death. Thorpe is of course not an American, but because of his long residence in the United States and in Australia he seems very American to Lord Plowden, who several times remarks on this. Certainly Thorpe bears a striking resemblance to the type of American financier later portrayed by Dreiser. And just as the American Zeke in *The Return of O'Mahony* brought new life to a decayed Irish estate, so Thorpe is a vital, if not an admirable, force in a decadent society.

Whatever their merits as literature, and they are considerable, Frederic's novels point up the limitations of James as a social critic. James had viewed English life from the terrace; Frederic, with his newspaperman's eye and ear, knew what went on behind the scenes. More important he had pondered deeply about social and political forces. His biographers present evidence that he had read widely on those subjects. They suggest that he foresaw the loss of the Empire; certainly he recognized that the playing fields were no longer an adequate training for a ruling class.

To the end of his life James had been preoccupied with the private lives of his character, never realizing that at least for a man, his political, business, or professional life is a part of his psyche. Therefore just as Lord Warburton seems unreal as a Parliamentarian, so Christopher Newman seems unreal as a self-made millionaire who has knocked about in mining camps and plunged in the stock market. In *The American* he is a pretty tame drawing-room character, whereas Joel Stormont Thorpe is entirely believable as a ruthless moneymaker. Both writers picture the cultural poverty of up-state New York cities: James in "Four Meetings" and Frederic in *Seth's Brother's Wife, The Lawton Girl*, and *Theron Ware*. But a spinster schoolteacher mooning over an album of European photographs is pretty thin stuff compared to Frederic's picture of a Methodist convention. James's ladies are pastels beside Celia Madden and Lady Cressage, both of whom are fully sexed. As a reviewer said in *The Bookman*, September 1899, *"The Market Place* is one of the few men's novels . . . as a Romance of the City it has no equal in modern fiction."

It should be clear also that Frederic cannot be pigeonholed as a mere delineator of the drab American scene. As Thorpe discovered, nothing could be more monotonous and intellectually sterile than life on an English country estate. The fact is that Frederic was a wide-ranging social critic of considerable stature. He is not primarily a propagandist, but whether he is writing of America, Ireland, or England, his point of view is essentially the melioristic one of American progressivism.

Two years before his death he wrote for *The English Illustrated Magazine* an article on the War of 1812. As is usual in whatever he wrote, this is packed with factual information, but as in his novels Frederic throws barbs into the British lion. The Americans are pictured as "strangely supine for years under . . . provocations to wrath." English prison ships were floating hells. Frederic contrasts the harsh conditions in the British navy and merchant marine with the vastly better conditions on American ships. Thus the British sailors seized by press gangs performed far less well in battle than did the volunteer Americans. The American clipper ships were "the most beautiful flying model the world has ever seen."

Obviously after a dozen years of expatriation Frederic was still "flamboyantly" American.

A MOTOR FLIGHT FROM SOCIAL CHANGE
EDITH WHARTON

Edith Wharton was one of Henry James's American women come to life. However, the reality differed somewhat from the fictional portraits. "Why must Mrs. Wharton be treated as royalty?" asked her British hostesses. No one quite knew why, but they were all conscious of the implied demand. The only way to approach her, wrote her English friend, Percy Lubbock, was "up a red carpet, so to speak in a strong light. . . . I had never seen a writer in our old world who kept such a state as she did. . . ."

Edith Newbold Jones was not born to royalty. But the New York society of her birth and upbringing had the same consciousness of superiority, of being a closed caste as that of the English or French aristocracy. This feeling comes out in such of her novels as *The House of Mirth* and *The Age of Innocence* and in her autobiography, *A Backward Glance*. In this last she boasted in Jamesian fashion that only one of her near relatives and not one of her husband's was in business. The money came from inherited real estate, which in rapidly growing New York continued to appreciate in value. Both in her novels and in *A Backward Glance* Mrs. Wharton was especially contemptuous of the new plutocracy which built mansions and skyscrapers. She never seemed to consider that it was this activity which made possible the moneyed leisure of her own class.

Edith Jones was born in 1862. Like James she was taken to Europe as a child—not because of her father's search for culture but because the depreciation of American currency after the Civil War made it cheaper to live abroad. Her father let his town and country houses for six years "to some of the profiteers of the day." "Happy misfortune," she wrote, "which gave me, for the rest of my life, that background of beauty and old-established order! I did not know how deeply I had felt the nobility and harmony of the great European cities till our steamer was docked in New York." Her memories of New York of the 1870's were of "mean, monotonous streets, without great churches or palaces, or any visible memorials of an historic past. . . . One of the most depressing impressions of my childhood is my recollections of the intolerable ugliness of New York."

Behind the brownstone fronts of well-to-do New Yorkers there was little provision for the life of the imagination. "Beauty, passion, and danger were automatically excluded." The ladies understood only two artistic productions: lace and fans, both of which they collected in quantity. Such a life with its "tepid sameness of moral atmosphere resulted in a prolonged immaturity of mind." All this she realized much later, but even as a child she longed for a return to Europe. After eight years at home she got her wish when the family again went abroad, this time because of her father's ill health.

At twenty-three she married Edward Wharton of Boston, apparently a pleasant, easy-going man who was more at home in America than in Europe. One of the memories of her early married life was the week-day luncheons where the men, not tied to offices, were as numerous as the women. It was a closed circle where people saw each other almost daily. This was one of her criteria for pleasant society. However, it was a society which had almost no intellectual interests. Before her birth, Washington Irving had been a friend of her parents, but he was such a gentleman that he was accepted despite the fact that he wrote. Madeira was a more important topic than books: her father's and uncle's cellars were famous for madeira which had rounded the Cape.

Each February she and her husband went abroad for four months. In 1888 they decided to spend a year's income on a four-months' yacht trip in the Mediterranean. She always believed that one's itinerary should be governed by the sound of place names. This criterion apparently did not apply to their selection of a summer house at Lenox, Massachusetts. Here and at Newport she occupied herself with social life and gardening. Among their friends was Charles Eliot Norton, one of her earliest literary mentors.

But despite Edith Wharton's friendship with Norton and other Bostonians and her realization of the intellectual sterility of her New York circle she was always somewhat contemptuous of Boston. In her autobiography she told the anecdote of a Bostonian returning in a carriage from his wedding who remarked, "And now, my dear, there is nothing before us but Mount Auburn." She contrasted New Yorkers hurrying to board ocean liners with Bostonians "too lacking in intellectual curiosity to have any desire to see the world"—a remark which in view of the almost notorious passion of Bostonians for travel abroad may reveal something of her feeling towards her husband. For, as the earlier chapters of this book have shown, educated Bostonians were intensely curious about

Europe. But like Waymarsh in *The Ambassadors* Edward Wharton was at loose ends in France. He felt most at home in the country life at "The Mount" in Lenox.

Mrs. Wharton's remark about stay-at-home Bostonians might have applied to her husband, but it was certainly not appropriate to her friend Charles Eliot Norton, who had been a frequent pilgrim to Europe. Norton, more at home in Renaissance Italy than in his own America, had a summer home at Ashfield within motoring distance of "The Mount." Old and frail, he never ventured over to Lenox, but the Whartons went often to Ashfield. As Lubbock puts it, "He was indeed the one person to whom she *went*." In her account of him she spoke of his great influence on her generation of Americans: he was "supremely gifted as an awakener." But it was to the glories of the past that Norton awakened people. Along with Bernard Berenson, a friend of both Norton's and Mrs. Wharton's, he preached a culture which was connoisseurship—the kind of thing which flowered in Mrs. Jack Gardner's imported palace, "Fenway Court." Thus Norton could admire Mrs. Wharton's early historical novel *The Valley of Decision,* but became increasingly uneasy about the growing realism of her later work. As she put it, ". . . he would have been happier if I had never come any nearer to the nineteenth century than I did in *The Valley of Decision.*"

That Edith Wharton's artistic taste was not impeccable is suggested by her admiration for the work of Maxfield Parrish, whose idealized Italian landscapes were chosen by Scribners to illustrate her book *The Decoration of Houses.*

This first appeared serially, then in 1897 as her first published volume. Edith Wharton seems to have become a writer almost inadvertently. In later life she speculated as to whether an environment like her own in which the arts were nonexistent was not worse for the artist than active opposition. Certainly her earliest efforts were extremely tentative. One day she decided to send off three poems she had written—one each to *Scribner's, Harper's* and the *Century.* All three were accepted, but Edward Burlingame of *Scribner's* wanted to know what else she had written. She next wrote a few short stories, the best of which came out as a book in 1899. A year later she published a novelette, and in 1902 her first novel, *The Valley of Decision,* the scene of which is Italy in the eighteenth century. From that point on she became increasingly a professional writer, with the professional writer's interest in craftsmanship.

Until Edith Wharton's papers are opened to scholars, much of her life will remain obscure. In *A Backward Glance* she skims quickly over certain phases of her life such as her separation and divorce and her relationship with Walter Berry. She herself paid tribute to Berry as her guide and literary mentor. "He alone not only encouraged me to write, as others had already done, but had the patience and the intelligence to teach me how. Others praised, some flattered—he alone took the trouble to analyze and criticise." But it was more than that: "his character, his deepest personality, were interwoven with mine."

Walter Van Rensselaer Berry was born in Paris in 1859. He graduated from Harvard and was admitted to the New York bar. Between 1908 and 1911 he was Judge of the International Tribunals in Egypt, and from 1916 to 1923 President of the American Chamber of Commerce in Paris. Proust dedicated *A l'Ombre des Jeunes Filles en Fleurs* to him. Caresse Crosby, whose husband Harry was Berry's cousin and heir, remembered him in his later years as "the epitome of elegance in the Jamesian manner." In fact she claimed that "Cousin Walter was James' pattern for manners. . . . His speech was witty, and his knowledge worldly; his manner with women was most gallant and wicked; and to me he was utterly delightful." In addition to Berry's accomplishments as a gallant, he was one of the most widely read men Edith Wharton ever knew. He also had a refined taste in architecture and painting. On his walls hung modern paintings, including one or more by Picasso. In Paris his apartment at 53 rue de Varenne had, according to Mrs. Crosby, a secret stair connecting with Edith Wharton's *pied à terre* in the same building.

After Edith Wharton's divorce, people expected her to marry Berry, but he had taken to amusing himself with younger women. At his bedside during an illness the physician in attendance was Dr. Voronoff, famous for his attempts to rejuvenate elderly men with monkey glands.

Much as Berry may have influenced Edith Wharton's writing, he was not the primary reason for it. Edmund Wilson asserts that following a nervous breakdown she was advised by the psychiatrist S. Weir Mitchell to take up novel writing as a therapeutic measure. Although this is impossible to verify, it is a prescription quite characteristic of the novelist-physician who had himself turned to writing in times of personal troubles. And there is evidence that Mitchell was consulted about the mental illness of Edward Wharton.

Whether or not Edith Wharton was specifically advised to take up novel writing for her health, it is clear that she used it as an outlet for her fierce energy. She was a tremendously restless person. Henry James spoke of her pendulum-like crossings of the Atlantic. In England she could not fit into the easy social life of country estates; rather she enjoyed the stimulating conversation of Paris salons. Percy Lubbock says of her love of Paris: "She came . . . for talk—for more talk with more people, and with people as fearless of talk, as familiar with it, as, dependent on it, as herself."

The energy left over from her writing she put into gardening and house decoration. Her garden at Lenox was famous. Also she was an enthusiastic motorist; when Henry James visited America in 1904, she and her husband took him on motor tours of New England. Even before this the Whartons and James had motored together in Europe, but during a heat wave in Massachusetts when James suffered intensely "the only panacea was incessant motoring. Luckily by that time we had a car which would really go, and go we did, daily, incessantly, over miles and miles of lustrous landscape, lying motionless under the still glaze of heat. While we were moving he was refreshed and happy, his spirits rose, the twinkle returned to his lips and eyes. . . ."

But despite the motor car Edith Wharton was restless in America. In 1907 the Whartons settled permanently in France, allegedly because of Edward Wharton's health. Near Paris Edith established herself in the Pavilion Colombe. She had scarcely finished it to her taste when she fitted up Sainte-Claire le Chateau near Hyères in Provence. The menage included her secretary (formerly her governess), an English butler, a cook, a maid, and a chauffeur. Certain hours daily were devoted to writing, the rest to gardening and social life. Henry James spoke of the constant succession, "in our dear Edith's hospitality of succulent and corrupting meals." In her garden she made the rounds with the gardener at all hours, deep in conversation. Everything was done according to her strict orders. As Gaillard Lapsley said, "She never seemed to find leisure to be cosy and comfortable and confident with her brood."

She spoke French easily, but with a foreign intonation. Her habit was to change topics of conversation quickly, to get up and wander about, smoking endless cigarettes. Even in her reading she skimmed rapidly, tearing the meat out of a book. Henry James warned a friend, "You may find her difficult, but you will find nothing stupid in her and nothing small."

James knew whereof he spoke. In her periodic descents upon Europe before her settlement there she would arrive with her husband, her motor car, and her retinue. As Lubbock remembered these occasions, Henry James would be summoned from his house at Rye:

> It was magnificent, it was Napoleonic; but how little she understood the life of the literary hermit. . . .
>
> Here was America brilliantly flashing upon Europe; here was fine old New York, secure and decent, the right tradition, the real thing, and here upon that well-laid foundation, was her own skill, grace, intelligence, all of the best flashing across to meet this Europe on the highest terms, any terms she pleased—she had only to make her own.

After she settled in Europe, her scale of living was lavish. Her cooks were always excellent and the wines exceptionally choice. The appointments of her table were faultless, and in the decoration of her houses she made each room into a picture. This American precision and perfection of her home was not entirely attractive to Europeans. The Frenchwoman who helped with the translation of *The Age of Innocence* was somewhat chilled by the perfection of Mrs. Wharton's taste in the smallest details of house and garden—"something that exceeds measure." A French home might have a clock, a woolwork chair cover with sentimental associations, but not in good taste. In Mrs. Wharton's home there was a lack of spontaneous gaiety.

In Paris she was delighted to discover that the *salon* still existed. The one to which she was welcomed was presided over by Mme Rosa de Fitz-James, who entertained academicians, journalists, foreign secretaries. Distinguished transients like Count Keyserling were frequent visitors as were the Americans Henry James, Walter Berry, and Bernard Berenson. It was a social group in which the men outnumbered the women, and Edith Wharton preferred the conversation of men. Her friend Robert Sencourt says that although she knew many persons of importance in literature, and called the sons of princes by their first names, her closest friends were cultivated, but not distinguished, people.

But despite her frequent visits to England and the Continent before 1907 and her thirty-year residence in France after that date, she remained very much the American titaness—wealthy, brilliant, and dominating. Lubbock, who knew her well, says, "She never became, she had no call to become, any more of a European than she had been at first, but with Europe around her she had room, liberty, encouragement, to be what she was."

In her autobiography she stated that in her New York circle the subject of her novels was avoided as a kind of disgrace; whereas in London her writing would have opened many doors to her. There may be some rationalization in this, for like W. W. Story, Edith Wharton found it necessary to castigate America as a justification for expatriation. After all, the writing of stories and novels opened doors in America, as Irving, Henry James, and William Dean Howells had proved. James's novels had even opened the doors of the White House. Howells, the son of an Ohio printer, became the intimate of Boston Brahmins.

The fact is that Edith Wharton liked the glitter of a moneyed society. As she demonstrated in *The House of Mirth* (1905) and *The Age of Innocence* (1920), she was well aware of the limitations of the social elite of New York, but it is also clear that she shared much of their sensibility. It is for that reason these two novels are, along with two others, her best. Percy Lubbock says that she had no interest in people, no matter how talented, outside her circle. Thus in Boston, "her glittering plumage appeared misplaced; she was under suspicion there—not justly, but I am sure she did little to dispel it."

Edith Wharton's quarrel with her own country was a very personal quarrel. As a member of the old aristocracy of inherited wealth she recognized that, like the landed aristocracy of England, it had small interest in intellectual matters. Yet she was enough identified with it emotionally to resent fiercely the rise of a new moneyed class. Like Sir Fopling Flutter who said, "Beyond Hyde Park all is a desert," her class felt that about regions beyond the Hudson. With heavy-handed satire, she represented the Midwest as abounding in place names like Aeschylus, Lohengrin, Phalanx, Hallelujah, Euphoria, Pruneville.

Similarly she had no ear for the American idiom. Because the New York families of her childhood had employed teachers from England, she believed that she had been trained in "the best tradition of spoken English." This led her to reject and condemn American spellings in favor of *parlour, colour—even gaoler,* which the British themselves are abandoning. A particular *bête noire,* mentioned in several of her essays, was *a wood* or worse still *a woods* in place of *coppice, copse, spinney, covert, brake, holt, grove,* etc. She seemed to be unaware that a number of these had faded from British writing, or that she herself in 1908 had written, "The woods of this wonderful Bois de Vincennes are real woods. . . ." She probably did not know that four years before her most vigorous diatribe, Robert Frost had written a superb poem, "Stopping by Woods on a Snowy Evening." Not realizing that *gotten* was the survival of an older English usage she regarded it as an ignorant American attempt at cultured speech. In fact her attack on the poverty of American speech in "The Great American Novel" (1927) came eight years after the first edition of Mencken's *The American Language*.

Thus in her novels she can represent certain clichés of American speech like "hang it" and "chuck it," but none of its variety and vigor. In *Hudson River Bracketed* (1929), the Midwesterner, Vance Weston, is made to say "first rate" on inappropriate occasions—a locution which had already largely disappeared. For instance, after writing a short story for a high-brow magazine, Weston says apropos of a literary prize, ". . . of course I'd like that prize first rate." In the same novel she refers to an American radio as "a wireless." Mrs. Wharton's colloquial American speech tags were few, but she liked to work them often. Next to "first rate" she favored "I guess" in the sense of "I suppose." Undoubtedly she was unaware that this supposed barbarism, in exactly the same sense, went back to Chaucer and Shakespeare. Edith Wharton's frequent comments on the English language suggest the superficial learning of the salon rather than close study.

The same applies to her literary opinions. Although she considered herself an expert on Henry James, she only skimmed his novels. She regarded *Moby-Dick* as being an adventure story like *Treasure Island*. In her essay for the *Yale Review* on "The Great American Novel" she complained that to deserve the epithet "American" it must tell of persons so limited in education and opportunity that they live cut off from all the varied sources of culture which used to be considered the heritage of English-speaking people. The great American novel must always be about Main Street, "geographically, socially, and intellectually." However, she was also censorious of the new trend in English fiction. Possibly with Joyce in mind she had Vance Weston in *The Gods Arrive* comment that "The fishers in the turbid stream-of-consciousness had reduced their fictitious characters to a bundle of loosely tied instincts and habits borne along blindly on the current of existence."

The evidence suggests that Edith Wharton in rejecting America was, like James, rejecting the modern world. Lubbock says that the formality of French manners was agreeable to her, and Nevius argues that the French way of life "vindicated the notion of reality fostered by her own background and training. She found in them the same traits that were venerated in her youth." Writing of the institution of the *salon* she said, "This continuity of social relations was what particularly appealed to me." On reading *The Age of Innocence* as it came from her pen Walter Berry remarked, "We are the last people left who can remember New York and Newport as they were then." As her comment on James (p. 210) shows, she believed that both she and James had found in Europe the last traces of a world like the older America. It pleased her when French and English friends told her that before reading *The Age of Innocence* they had no idea New York life in the seventies had been so much like that of a big cathedral town or the French *ville de province* of the same date.

One thing is clear: despite her increasingly harsh criticisms of her own country her roots were in America. Henry James realized this as early as 1902 when, in a letter to Mrs. Cadwalader Jones thanking her for the gift of Edith's short stories and *The Valley of Decision,* he advised: "She *must* be tethered in native pastures, even if it reduces her to a back-yard in New York." This was three years before her first important novel, *The House of Mirth.* It gives a vivid picture of a girl, Lily Bart, without talent or money, losing out in an unequal struggle to hold her place in the New York aristocracy.

The novel is even more American than perhaps Edith Wharton realized. In her girlhood her mother had advised, "Never talk about money and think about it as little as possible." It is ironic that *The House of Mirth* is all about money. Of necessity Lily thinks about it all the time: expensive clothes, bridge games, and jewels are the price one has to pay to hold a place in her world. Because of her lack of money she is instantly suspect when seen in the company of a wealthy married man. Bachelors suspect her, not without justice, of fortune hunting. It is a tragedy of mores and money, and of the two, money is the more powerful force.

Edith Wharton argued that Europe offered better materials to the novelist because of "the dense European order, all compounded of differences and *nuances,* all interwoven with intensities and reticences, with passions and privacies, inconceivable to the millions brought up in a safe, shallow and shadowless world." The remarkable thing is that this dense

European order is almost entirely absent from her major novels. The theory about the poverty of American materials suggests rather the opinions of the dilettante circles she frequented. With the exception of Henry James, almost no one among her closest friends in Europe was a creative artist in any field.

Thus, although *The Reef* is laid in Europe, the characters are American. Even more important, the sensibility is American. Anna Summers had originally been attracted to the Europeanized Mr. Leath when he talked about France:

> Every word, every allusion, every note of his agreeable-modulated voice, gave Anna a glimpse of a society at once freer and finer, which observed the traditional forms but had discarded the underlying prejudices; whereas the world she knew had discarded many of the forms and kept almost all the prejudices.

Like Gilbert Osmond in *Portrait of a Lady*, such a man proves irresistible to an American girl. Some years after her marriage and her husband's death Anna Leath meets an old suitor, George Darrow, from America.

They fall in love, but while Anna delays a meeting in France, George has a casual affair with a discharged governess whom he has befriended. With Edith Wharton's love of coincidence, the girl turns up as the governess to Mrs. Leath's daughter. The governess, Sophy Viner, is quite a person—in fact perhaps the finest one in the novel. But Anna Leath's discovery of Sophy's brief affair with George causes her in the end to reject the marriage. If all this had happened in New York or Boston it would have been perhaps more believable, for George Darrow's sense of awful guilt and Anna's rejection of him grow out of their basic American mores and sensibility.

In one of her best novels, *Ethan Frome* (1911), she abandoned the European scene entirely. The novel is based upon her own recollections and those of Walter Berry of "the lives led in those half-deserted villages before the coming of motor and telephone." Again the past tense is significant—it was an earlier America which interested her. "In those days," she remembered, "the snow-bound villages of Western Massachusetts were still grim places, morally and physically: insanity, incest and slow mental and moral starvation were hidden away behind the paintless wooden house-fronts of the long village street, or in isolated farm-houses on the neighboring hills; and Emily Brontë would have found as savage tragedies in our remoter valleys as on her Yorkshire moors." The statement somewhat contradicts the one about a denser European scene.

Two years later she published her most bitter satire on American mores and values in *The Custom of the Country*. Although part of the story is laid in Europe, it is essentially the account of an opportunistic American girl, Undine Spragg, who divorces a series of husbands to gain what she considers social advantage. Most critics agree that the characters largely remain caricatured types and that Mrs. Wharton's bitterness against her own country led to a bad piece of writing. This caricature appears especially in a trick copied by Sinclair Lewis—the use of outlandish names: Undine Spragg, Mabel Blitch, Indiana Frusk, or New York hotels like the Stentorian, the Olympian, the Incandescent, the Ormolu. In New York those who have made money instead of inheriting it are referred to as "the Invaders."

It is significant that *The Custom of the Country* came out the same year that Edith Wharton got her divorce. As Sencourt points out, the subject which increasingly haunted her "was adultery or rather the moral struggle against passion when a marriage is unsatisfying." Undine Spragg is too self-centered a person to feel real passion: her series of marriages is more like a series of adulteries. Even before Undine's first marriage, she makes an unlikely statement which Mrs. Wharton represents as the Midwestern point of view circa 1912: "Out in Apex, if a girl marries a man who don't come up to what she expected, people consider it's to her credit to want to change [husbands]." Edith Wharton, planning her own divorce, used Undine Spragg as a scapegoat. In effect she is saying, "My divorce has nothing in common with the crude system of divorce in America." Thus, like Henry James, she exorcised her sense of personal failure by pointing to the limitations of America.

The artistic gap between *The Custom of the Country* and *The Age of Innocence* (1920) is immense. Along with *Ethan Frome* the latter represents her best work, and like *Ethan Frome* the scene is America. The only European in *The Age of Innocence* is Madame Olenska, who after an unhappy marriage, has been gingerly taken into the Newland clan in the New York of the 1870's. Half afraid of the attraction of the outsider, Newland Archer hastily marries the mild May Welland. When Archer is again attracted to Ellen Olenska, May pretends that she is pregnant. Not that this ruse was necessary, for Ellen also accepts American mores of the time. Newland asks her:

"Then what, exactly, is your plan for us?"

"For *us*? But there's no us in that sense! We're near each other only if we stay far from each other. Then we can be ourselves. Otherwise we're only Newland Archer, the husband of Ellen Olenska's cousin, and Ellen Olenska, the cousin of Newland Archer's wife, trying to be happy behind the backs of the people who trust them."

"Ah, I'm beyond that," he groaned.

"No you're not! You've never been beyond. And *I* have," she said in a strange voice, "and I know what it looks like there."

It is worth noting that in all three novels, *The Reef, Ethan Frome,* and *The Age of Innocence,* "the other woman"—Sophy Viner, Mattie Silver, and Ellen Olenska—always loses out, yet each one is a superior person when compared to her rival fiancée or wife.

In his study of Edith Wharton, Blake Nevius speaks of "a tendency in her later novels and short stories toward an almost ironclad rectitude in the treatment of ethical questions—a tendency in which a certain hardness and even a certain cruelty are involved and which is likely to outrage the sensibilities of a later, more tolerant generation." On the other hand there was her own divorce and her long association, platonic or otherwise, with Walter Berry. She frequently condemned Americans for hypocrisy in morals, for their puritan suspicion of pleasure or passion, but perhaps, as she wrote of George Eliot, "She never ceased to revere the law she transgressed." In any case, despite her somewhat clearer understanding of sex attraction, she is scarcely less puritanical than Henry James. To an even greater degree than with James, her sensibilities as revealed in her fiction were American. Her deepest prejudices and emotional attitudes remained those of the New York social group into which she was born.

This in part explains the increasing shrillness of her attacks upon America in her later novels and essays. Not only was her own country changing, but also there was her loss of roots. She had to look through the eyes of others. Thus it is hard to read *Hudson River Bracketed* and to some extent *The Gods Arrive* without hearing the voice of Sinclair Lewis. Vance Weston, the young novelist from Euphoria, Illinois, with his crudities and aspirations is a Martin Arrowsmith seen from the outside. There are also echoes of *Main Street* and *Elmer Gantry* in some of the portraits. Thus the novelist who, in *The Custom of the Country,* had anticipated certain of Lewis's devices, now seemed to be copying him. No longer was she writing of America from first-hand experience.

Both Lewis and Edith Wharton put something of their own sensibilities into their characters, but the difference is that Lewis knew what a Midwestern character felt, whereas Edith Wharton did not. Thus Vance Weston on seeing a Victorian Hudson River mansion, says: "You see, from the first day I set foot in this house I got that sense of continuity that we folks have missed out of our lives—out where I live, anyway. . . ." And in the same novel; "The mere discovery that there were people who had been born and died in the same house was romance and poetry to Vance." Or again, "The meagreness of his inherited experience, the way it had been torn off violently from everything which had gone before, again struck him with a pang of impoverishment."

It is obvious that this emphasis upon tradition is more characteristic of Edith Wharton than of her fictional character. The real meagreness of experience is the novelist's. As Lapsley says, "The fact is that she could neither do with contemporary America, nor do without it; she could neither forget nor forgive it. . . . her conscience was uneasy and her tongue sometimes bitter . . . . She had all too summarily cut her own roots. . . ."

Naturally, she tried to rationalize her expatriation. She was fond of quoting Kipling's line "How can they know England, that only England know?" And in an essay on Paul Bourget she wrote: "En effect, c'est seulement en ayant su d'autres pays, studié leurs moeurs, lu leurs livres, frequenté leurs habitants, que l'on peut situer son propre pays dans l'historie de la civilization." The irony is that, as most students of her work testify, she increasingly failed to understand her own country. Her friend Galliard Lapsley said "She did not realize and was not prepared to believe that there was much left in America she valued. . . ."

In a number of respects Edith Wharton represents a type of expatriate who flourished chiefly between the Civil War and World War I—people of inherited wealth who came from the Eastern states—the class which had kept its opera glass focused on Europe. Frequently these expatriates had received part of their education abroad. They might be characterized as the kind of people painted by John Singer Sargent. Only a few of them were important writers or artists. In that respect W. W. Story, Henry James, Mary Cassatt, and Edith Wharton are of course exceptions. Some of them such as Katherine De Kay Bronson and Mrs. Jack Gardner maintained houses in Venice and entertained celebrities like Henry James; others, including Logan Pearsall Smith and Bernard Berenson, were connected with the worlds of art and letters.

Looking back it is easy to see, as Story, James, and Edith Wharton saw, the graciousness of this world of palaces and servants and to contrast it with the crudities of post-Civil-War America. But they could not see, as Whitman did, the vitality of a nation which built the transcontinental railway, became the granary of the world, and opened its gates to the dispossessed of Europe. They could not recognize, as Horatio Greenough could have done, that the Brooklyn Bridge was a greater work of art than the Greek Slaves and Cleopatras of the expatriates. For them the democratic ideal produced bad servants and impertinent shop girls.

In large measure this class failure of social vision accounts for the decline of Edith Wharton's work after the superb achievement of *The House of Mirth, Ethan Frome,* and *The Age of Innocence.*

To a much greater degree than Henry James she was the novelist of observed surfaces. James, with his insight into the psyche, was closer to Dostoyevski and Chekhov; Edith Wharton's talent was more akin to Jane Austen's. Thus for her the cutting of roots was fatal. Her best novels were about a vanished America, one she had glimpsed in her youth.

As such books as *A Motor Flight Through France* (1908) and *French Ways and Their Meaning* (1919) show, her knowledge of France was superficial. The first was a tourist's picture of scenery and cathedrals. And like the typical tourist she told how much it rained. The second, when it was not castigating America, was a discussion of France as observed in the salon. In nothing she wrote did she get the density of old-world culture, the feeling for social nuances as had James in *The American, The Ambassadors,* and *The Wings of the Dove.* For all his private vision James was a far better observer of Europe than was Edith Wharton.

Her superficiality was not one of intellect: all of her acquaintances, including Henry James, testify to her brilliance. As *The House of Mirth* and *The Age of Innocence* demonstrated, she could be an excellent novelist of manners—one of the best that America has produced. Within the boundaries of her social class she could write superbly about the older America she had known, but she could not write about the Europe she had adopted nor the newer America she had abandoned.

AFTER THEY'VE SEEN PAREE
THE EXPATRIATES OF THE 1920'S

Nothing before or since has equaled the mass expatriation of Americans of the 1920's. It has almost the quality of the instinctive migration of the lemmings. As Malcolm Cowley says, ". . . the younger and footloose intellectuals went streaming up the longest gangplank in the world." And along with the intellectuals went the playboys, the recent college graduates, the art students, and the hangers on at the fringes of the intellectual world—everyone from Harry Crosby, who could have been a Morgan partner, to the girl from Iowa who wanted a free love life.

Some of them like Katherine Anne Porter and Stuart Chase went to Mexico; others like James Norman Hall, Charles Nordhoff, and Robert Dean Frisbee found refuge in Tahiti, but most of them went to France. Malcolm Cowley states it thus: "Indeed, to young writers like ourselves, a long sojourn in France was almost a pilgrimage to Holy Land." The forerunners they honored were Gertrude Stein, Ezra Pound, and T. S. Eliot. Gertrude Stein had settled in France in 1902; Pound had gone abroad in 1906 to gather material for a dissertation, and after a brief return to America, became a confirmed expatriate in 1908; Eliot had studied at the Sorbonne in 1911, returned to teach at Harvard, and then gone back on a fellowship in 1914. He married in England and decided to settle there. Thus three of the seminal figures in twentieth-century American literature were already established in Europe at a time when young writers fresh from the army or from college were beginning their careers.

Also in Paris were James Joyce and Igor Stravinsky, two of the culture heroes of American writers. Sylvia Beach mentions them along with Pound as figures who attracted the young Americans to Paris. Miss Beach, the daughter of a Princeton clergyman, had settled in Paris and opened her bookstore, Shakespeare and Company, in 1919. It quickly became a center for American expatriates, many of whom dropped in daily and had their mail delivered there. As she herself put it, "Every day someone whose work I had seen in *The Little Review* or *The Dial* would appear."

These two magazines were in part responsible for the enthusiasm for *avant garde* European literature, music, and art. Margaret Anderson's *Little Review* published *Ulysses* in installments until the magazine was seized by the postal authorities. Sylvia Beach said when she opened her bookshop she did not foresee that it was going to profit by the suppressions across the sea. For this was the era of Attorney General A. Mitchell Palmer, of Postmaster General Burleson, of John S. Sumner of the Society for the Suppression of Vice, and of the Watch and Ward Society in Boston. According to Miss Beach it was the atmosphere thus created which was in large part responsible for those "pilgrims of the twenties" who crossed the ocean and colonized the Left Bank of the Seine.

Whatever their reasons for coming to Paris most literary expatriates sought an introduction to Gertrude Stein. At her apartment at 21 rue de Fleurus they engaged in endless discussion of art, literature and America. For Miss Stein regarded herself as very much an American. America, she said, was what had made her: "America is my country and Paris is my home town." She gave as a reason for living in France: "And because France did produce all the painting that the nineteenth century produced those of us who had nothing to do with painting except to look at it lived in France." She added that "France was friendly and it let you alone." This was echoed by Robert McAlmon, the expatriate publisher, who said, "I prefer Europe, if you mean France to America because there is less interference with private life there."

This was obviously one of the reasons for the hegira of so many Americans in the 1920's. But it was far from being the only reason. The revolt against American puritanism was well underway before World War I. For at least a decade Greenwich Village had been in full flower. Speaking of the 1920's Harold Stearns commented that "at times in Montparnasse you could have sworn you were only in a transplanted Greenwich Village of the 1912–16 pre-war period." As biographies and autobiographies like those of Ben Hecht, Max Eastman, and Theodore Dreiser show, it was not necessary to cross the Atlantic for a free and easy love life. However, there may have been in Europe a more relaxed attitude about sex. Among the artistic and literary expatriates pairs of lovers were invited to parties as casually as were married couples. Hemingway later reported that in conversation Gertrude Stein defended lesbianism.

The revolt against middle-class mores was accompanied by a critical cult which blamed all the ills of the United States on the Puritan heritage, which, it was argued, was closely allied to the rise of industrialism. It was a doctrine preached by Van Wyck Brooks in *The Wine of the Puritans* (1908) and in *America's Coming of Age* (1915), by Randolph Bourne in *The Puritan's Will to Power* (1917), by Waldo Frank in *Our America* (1919), and especially by H. L. Mencken in *A Book of Prefaces* (1917), in his subsequent volumes of *Prejudices,* and after 1924 in *The American Mercury.* To prove their point that a puritan-industrial culture was hostile to the literary artist, the American past was pictured as a cultural waste-land in which wandered a few tragic pioneers: Poe, Whitman, Thoreau, Melville, Emily Dickinson, Twain, Henry James, Stephen Crane. Some-how or other Poe's alcoholism, Emerson's loss of memory in later life, Stephen Crane's death from tuberculosis, Frank Norris's from peritonitis, and Ambrose Bierce's, at seventy, at the hands of Mexican bandits all became examples of what America did to the literary artist. Even James McNeill Whistler and F. Marion Crawford, both brought up in Europe, were dragged in as examples of Americans who had to flee their own country. The publication in 1918 of *The Education of Henry Adams* gave a case history which seemed to confirm the thesis that the intellectual had no place in America. In 1921 Harold Stearns edited a survey: *Civiliza-tion in The United States, An Inquiry by Thirty Americans.* There were chapters on politics, education, the arts, the small town, sex, the family, business, advertising, and related topics. The writers were, on the whole, a distinguished group, including H. L. Mencken, Lewis Mumford, Robert Morss Lovett, Van Wyck Brooks, George Jean Nathan, H. W. Van Loon, and Katherine Anthony.

With few exceptions these thirty writers were dissatisfied with Ameri-can civilization. Deems Taylor found signs of health in American music, and Conrad Aiken in poetry. Much more typical are points of view represented by the following excerpts:

> To an extent almost incomprehensible to the peoples of older cultures, the things of the mind and the spirit have been given over, in America, into the almost exclusive custody of women. . . .
>
> Our intellectual life, when we judge it objectively on the side of vigour and diversity, too often seems like a democracy of mounte-banks.
>
> HAROLD STEARNS

[Of the average Congressman]

Examine him at leisure, and you will find that he is incompetent and imbecile, and not only incompetent and imbecile, but also incurably dishonest.

H. L. MENCKEN

[In the chapter on journalism]

As a citizen, a workman, a human being, the journalist is simply one of us, a victim of the conformity which has overwhelmed the American.

JOHN MACY

[Of scholarship]

What can we say . . . save that America has no scholarship because as yet it has a body but no soul.

J. E. SPINGARN

[Of the theatre]

In no civilized country in the world is there among playwrights so little fervour as in the United States.

GEORGE JEAN NATHAN

Malcolm Cowley suggests that the writers of *Civilization in the United States* were primarily concerned with one question: "Why was there, in America, no satisfying career open to talent?" Van Wyck Brooks in the essay "The Literary Life" gave a gloomy answer:

> . . . what immediately strikes one as one surveys the history of our literature during the last half century, is the singular impotence of its creative spirit. . . . one can count on one's two hands the American writers who are able to carry on the development and unfolding of their individualities, year in, year out, as every competent man of affairs carries on his business.

In the chapter "As an Irishman Sees It," Ernest Boyd sums it up: "It is now rare to find a young American who does not cry out against American civilization."

Harold Stearns, the editor of the symposium, left for Europe in 1921 for a stay of eleven years. In a book written largely during his stay in Paris (*In the American Grain*—1925) William Carlos Williams argued that the Puritan heritage had produced "a race incapable of flower." As a result America had "become 'the most lawless country in the civilized world,' a panorama of murders, perversions, a terrific unorganized strength, excusable only because of the beauty of its great machines. Today it is a generation of gross know-nothingism, of blackened churches where hymns groan like chants from stupefied jungles."

As Van Wyck Brooks later realized, the literary rebels of the early twenties knew little of the past of American writing. "They seldom read any American books but *Moby Dick* and *Huckleberry Finn*." One reason for this was that American literature was not regarded as a respectable college subject until after the 1920's. Barrett Wendell, who taught the subject at Harvard until 1921, is said to have told his classes, "Gentlemen, this is a course in American letters; there is no American literature." Speaking of the Harvard he knew from 1904 to 1907, Van Wyck Brooks said it was "up in all things European" but was no place for Americanism; there Americanism meant philistinism. He mentions that Henry Adams was unaware of Emily Dickinson and Stephen Crane, of Winslow Homer and Albert Ryder. Thus when in England Brooks wrote of the cultural deficiencies of his country in *America's Coming of Age*, he had not, as he later admitted, read much American poetry. The book reflected the impressions he had gathered at Harvard. When Brooks added together the tastes of his Harvard era: "the royalism and the classicism, the Anglo-Catholicism, the cults of Donne and Dante, the Sanskrit, the Elizabethan dramatists and the French symbolist poets, one arrived at T. S. Eliot, the quintessence of Harvard."

Brooks himself seriously considered expatriation and its possible effect on him as a writer. It took him twenty years and a long immersion in American life to get over a frequent homesickness for the European scene.

In addition to a considerable ignorance about the American cultural past the young writers rejected the literary establishment. "The most hopeful thing of intellectual promise in America today", wrote Harold Stearns, "is the contempt of the younger people for their elders; they are restless, uneasy, disaffected." It is interesting to contrast the respect of younger writers in the 1960's for such predecessors as Dreiser, Hemingway, Frost, Eliot, and Edmund Wilson with the contempt felt by the young intellectuals of the 1920's for such writers and critics as Howells, E. C. Stedman, and Paul Elmer Moore, and Hamilton Wright Mabie. This revolt against the literary standards of some of the reigning figures helps to explain the birth of the little magazines such as *Poetry, Broom, Secession, transition* and the *transatlantic review,* and the publication of Joyce by Sylvia Beach and of Hemingway by Robert McAlmon and by the Black Sun Press.

The established journals and publishers were wary of new writers. When the editor of *Outlook* asked Richard Aldington to write an article about young writers, he named Joyce, Eliot, Lawrence, Aldous Huxley, H. D., and Proust. The editor answered, "For God's sake, Richard, can't you think of somebody who has been heard of or is even likely to be heard of?" In the 1920's the literary establishment represented by *The Atlantic, Scribner's,* and *Harper's* continued to publish verse in the style of William Cullen Bryant and the work of such writers as Owen Wister, Henry Van Dyke, William Lyon Phelps, Katherine Lee Bates, Temple Bailey, and John Fox, Jr. (*The Century* under Glenn Frank was a little more adventurous.) William Carlos Williams complained of the "universal refusal to publish and pay for available new work by young poets." Little magazines like *Others,* which welcomed new work, died of financial malnutrition. Under Margaret Anderson and Jane Heap *The Little Review,* which appeared irregularly, published the new poets, but it could not afford to pay them. During much of the 1920's the chief home-based magazines which published and paid for experimental work were *The Dial* under Scofield Thayer and Marianne Moore, and Harriet Monroe's *Poetry.* It was these magazines which gave a hearing to Pound, Eliot, Masters, Sandburg, Lindsay, William Carlos Williams, Hart Crane, E. E. Cummings, Wallace Stevens, and numerous others neglected by the establishment.

The result was that much of the publication of new work became a major activity of expatriates. An important reason for this was economic. Because of the devaluation of European currencies, American dollars often brought a fantastic rate of exchange. At one time five hundred copies of *transition* could be printed in Vienna for $25. *Broom,* which monthly paid its contributors $300 to $400 and which maintained a New York office, was more expensive to produce. Its editor, Harold Loeb, estimated that it lost about $1000 a month. In Berlin typesetting and printing for three thousand copies cost only $150. Sylvia Beach's bookshop, Shakespeare and Co., undertook the publication and sale of *Ulysses.* True, there were numerous misprints because of the French printers' difficulties with the language of James Joyce. Like Harold Loeb, the

Crosbys—Harry and Caresse—had money to lose. Thus their Black Sun Press could go in for esoterica and erotica. But it could also afford to publish stories by Hemingway, who had not yet found a market in the United States.

Probably the most important expatriate press in Paris was the Contact Publishing Company of Robert McAlmon. Born in Kansas in 1896, McAlmon had joined the Air Force but had not been sent to Europe. After a stay in Greenwich Village he had gone to England, where he had married Annie Winifred Ellerman, who called herself "Bryher." Her father, Sir John Ellerman, a wealthy shipping magnate, presented McAlmon with £14,000. Through Hemingway, McAlmon met William Bird, who had started the Three Mountains Press in Paris about 1921. A year later Pound became the editor, and about the same time McAlmon joined with Bird to publish Contact Editions, which included books printed at the Three Mountains Press. Bird found a small office for Ford Maddox Ford to use while editing the *transatlantic review*. In 1926 Bird sold out his interest to McAlmon. William Carlos Williams, who saw much of McAlmon in 1924, remarked that the press had *Mons Veneris* to the fore.

Some idea of the importance of this publishing house can be gained from McAlmon's volume of 1925, entitled *Contact Collection of Contemporary Writers*. A selection of "works in progress," its contributors were: Djuna Barnes, Bryher, Mary Butts, Norman Douglas, Havelock Ellis, Ford Maddox Ford, Wallace Gould, Ernest Hemingway, Marsden Hartley, H. D., James Joyce, Mina Loy, Robert McAlmon, Ezra Pound, Dorothy Richardson, May Sinclair, Edith Sitwell, Gertrude Stein, and William Carlos Williams. Thus the expatriate presses and periodicals gave new writers a chance to be heard.*

Furthermore, struggling writers could live more cheaply in Europe. Malcolm Cowley and his wife left in 1921 with a fellowship of about $1000 for study in a French university. With the help of a few small checks from American magazines they managed to live in modest comfort, and even to travel. In *Exile's Return* Cowley gives a picture of the

---

* Before long, however, American book publishers began to catch up. Albert and Charles Boni, Alfred Harcourt, Horace Liveright, Alfred Knopf, and editors such as Maxwell Perkins of Scribner's brought out books by the rising generation of novelists, critics, and poets. By 1926 Pound, Eliot, Stevens, Cummings, and Hemingway had all appeared in book form in the United States.

chaotic state of European currencies which produced the kind of tourists called *Valutaschweine,* who wandered about seeking the cheapest prices. It was a state of affairs in which Americans could get a fine dinner in Hamburg for eight cents or a week's lodging in Vienna for the price of a pack of cigarettes. American students, artists, and writers could live abroad for a fraction of the cost of living at home. "Valuta" made it possible for expatriates to ignore the lure of advertising offices and slick-paper magazines in order to try to paint or write as they pleased. At home Hemingway had to devote his whole time to newspaper work; as a foreign correspondent in Europe he could live by sending home an occasional report while American magazines consistently rejected his stories.

Dissatisfaction with American civilization, expatriate publication, and favorable rates of exchange were not the only causes for the mass exodus. There was the impact of World War I. Most of the earlier writers who attacked American society did not become expatriates, although some of them went abroad as tourists. Thus the generation that produced Upton Sinclair, Robert Herrick, Carl Sandburg, Edgar Lee Masters, Sherwood Anderson, Theodore Dreiser, and H. L. Mencken remained largely home based. On the other hand, that generation born in the 1890's produced a high proportion of the expatriates of the 1920's. For one thing residence in Paris after the war became what a later generation would call an "in thing." Like the fox-trot and the Charleston, everyone was doing it. And tourist-class passage to Europe cost as little as $80. In a restless decade it was cheap and chic to become at least a temporary expatriate.

The restlessness of young writers is reflected in the number who had become ambulance or camion drivers for the Allies before the United States entered the war. In addition to himself, Malcolm Cowley lists Dos Passos, Hemingway, Julian Green, William Seabrook, E. E. Cummings, Slater Brown, Harry Crosby, John Howard Lawson, Sidney Howard, Louis Bromfield, Robert Hillyer, and Dashiell Hammett. As he puts it, "One might almost say that the ambulance corps and the French military transport were college-extension courses for a generation of writers." Many of them stayed in Europe or went back there after the war.

Hemingway's experience is typical. On his return from the war he got a job on the *Toronto Daily Star.* For it he did an essay on prohibition in which he showed his hostility to contemporary America. To his friends he talked often about his eagerness and determination to get back to Europe.

Almost every aspect of the United States was distasteful to him. Even what he had seen of American soldiers abroad had repelled him. For the paper he did articles on some of the more unsavory aspects of life in the states: gangland shootings and the Muscle Shoals scandal. He talked to Sherwood Anderson, who had just returned from a visit to Europe. Filled with memories of conversations with Gertrude Stein, Anderson was enthusiastic about the opportunities for literary and cultural enrichment which existed in Paris. In a similar vein, Ford Maddox Ford remarked, "There was never a day so gay for the arts as any twenty-four hours of the early 'twenties' in Paris."

In December 1921 Hemingway and his wife went to Paris, where he was to act as roving correspondent for the *Star*. But his real interest was in writing. As for newspaper work his biographer, Charles A. Fenton, quotes a friend of those years: "He didn't give a damn about it." He had a great admiration for Gertrude Stein, who gave him the phrase "You are all a lost generation." "We are just like brothers, and I see a lot of her," he wrote. For her he copied the manuscript of *The Making of Americans* and corrected the proofs. His debt to her is more than such obvious stylistic devices as the use of repetition; she helped him to discover what he was seeing and what to look for. At Sylvia Beach's bookshop he discovered Russian literature: Turgenev, Gogol, Chekhov, Dostoyevsky, Tolstoy. "To have come on all this new world of writing, with time to read in a city like Paris where there was a way of living well and working, no matter how poor you were, was like having a great treasure given to you." A generation earlier Henry James had become friendly with Turgenev, who introduced him to Flaubert, Edmond de Goucourt, Daudet, de Maupassant, and Zola. With the exception of Turgenev's he had disliked their work; they handled "unclean things." Howells, although an admirer of Tolstoy, shied off from *Anna Karenina* and was disgusted by French novelists. The point is that Hemingway's generation of Americans was the first to approach Europe without the blinders of puritanism.

In November 1923 Hemingway returned to Toronto because his wife was pregnant and they hoped to provide the child with a stable infancy. Their plan was to stay two years. But prohibition and the puritanism of Toronto disgusted him, so that after four months they returned to Europe. Part of the expatriate life he found there is reflected in his first full-length novel, *The Sun Also Rises*—a life of drifting from bar to bar, of sexual promiscuity, of going to Spain for bullfights. But there were other aspects. During the summer of 1925 the Hemingways spent a lot of time with the Fitzgeralds. Scott and Ernest met at lunch once a week with Dean Gauss of Princeton for a discussion of some serious topic.

Hemingway was also associated with the Crosbys, whose Black Sun Press published some of his stories. As Malcolm Cowley says, "Harry Crosby becomes a symbol" of the era. Perhaps it would be more accurate to say that Harry and Caresse Crosby became symbols. After their marriage in 1922 they left on the *Aquitania* for Europe. As she describes it, "Harry and I were actually escapists from the society in which we had been brought up and I wanted my children to be escapists too." Caresse, born Mary Phelps, was a niece of J. P. Morgan, had made her debut, and had married a Peabody of Boston. As a debutante she had symbolically invented and actually patented the brassiere as a gesture of revolt against the corsets then *de rigueur*. Her first marriage ended in divorce partly because of her husband's drinking and partly because she fell in love with Harry Crosby. When she met Harry in 1919 he was still wearing his shabby Field Service uniform. ". . . in his restless eyes I caught a look so completely *right* that from that moment I sensed my destiny."

Malcolm Cowley thinks that an incident in the war was the turning point in Harry's life. Caught in a bombardment, he underwent an experience which Crosby said led to "the violent metamorphose from boy into man." "There was indeed a violent metamorphosis," writes Cowley, "but not from boy to man: rather it was from life into death."

> Bodily he survived, and with a keener appetite for pleasure, but only to find something was dead inside him—his boyhood, Boston, St. Mark's, the Myopia Hunt, a respectable marriage, an assured future as a banker, everything that was supposed to lead him toward a responsible place in the world.

Back home Crosby entered Harvard, made good clubs, and took a position in a bank, but after a good bit of drinking, resigned. His mother got a position for him in the Bank of Paris. So it was that he and Caresse were able to go abroad. As she describes it:

> I became a rebel when I married Harry. By *that* act of emancipation and by the conquest of desire over obedience, opposing the code of a conformist upbringing, I, of my own volition, entered into a life of adventure . . . for life with Harry was a hedonistic adventure.

Hedonistic adventure it was, but like a number of their expatriate contemporaries the Crosbys mixed dissipation with intellectual interests. The remarkable thing is that Harry continued to work at the bank for five years. The Crosbys also had private incomes, and with the franc at about twenty to the dollar, were affluent by all normal standards. Unlike Zelda Fitzgerald, Caresse Crosby was not, at least according to her own account, a lavish spender. Nevertheless, by 1929 Harry was dipping into principal by selling stock. Partly as a gesture of defiance to Boston, Mary adopted the name Caresse to be used on the title page of a book of her poems. " 'Yes' and never 'no' was our answer to the fabulous twenties. We built a gossamer bridge from war to war, as unreal as it was fragile, a passionate *passerelle* between a rejected past and an impossible future."

Both Harry's diary, published under the title *Shadows of the Sun,* and the autobiography of Caresse, *The Passionate Years,* tell of the wild hedonism of their life abroad. Harry found in Baudelaire and Oscar Wilde the ideal he strove for. From *The Picture of Dorian Gray,* which he read twice, he quoted: "Every impulse that we strive to strangle broods in the mind and poisons us. The body sins once and is done with its sin, for action is a mode of purification." Harry experimented with alcohol, drugs, and sex. Annually they attended the Quatre Arts ball. Caresse tells of stepping over "the entwined bodies of couples rapturously climactic" and of her own triumph at being carried, nude to the waist and seated in a dragon's head, on the shoulders of ten handsome revelers. Back at the apartment she found Harry in the bathtub with three pretty girls. "That crazy night our bed slept seven." Apparently Caresse had come home with a cavalier, and an unknown man in a loin cloth—which he took off—joined them.

But as Cowley says, Harry could not get Massachusetts out of his blood. The morning after that Quatre Arts ball or another one he wrote, "Bed and no banking . . . and a vague *mal du pays* for Singing Beach and Myopia Links and Apple Trees in the Fog." Again, after he and Caresse went to a dive to see a naked little Arab girl do a *danse du ventre,* he ended his description of it with "O God when shall we ever cast off the chains of New England?"

He was also obsessed with the idea of death. Like Scott Fitzgerald, who set the date for his suicide at thirty (he later advanced it), Crosby had the time set. He had a tombstone made for himself and Caresse with the date October 31, 1942. They were to fly an airplane over a forest and jump out. In Syria they found a gold cup—"Our Chalice, the one for the October of our chosen year." They bought it for $2000.

In 1927 Harry gave up his job at the bank. "We had decided," wrote Caresse, "that life was too beautiful and days too short to devote three quarters of them to that unimaginative place." From their new life they banished newspapers and magazines except for the *Nouvelle Revue Française* and *transition.* A year later they started the Black Sun Press in order to publish a volume of poems by Harry. They also published English translations of French writers and the work of a number of Americans: Hemingway, Faulkner, Kay Boyle, Dorothy Parker, and others. Some of these were people Harry had met at Sylvia Beach's bookshop.

The reason for the choice of the name of the press was Harry's mystic obsession with the sun. He sunbathed for hours; he kept talking of the Sun Death; he called his mistresses the Lady of the Golden Horse, The Fire Princess, etc. On a trip to Egypt he got the brigandish crew of a sampan to take him out on the river at night where they tattooed the sun between his shoulder blades. After reading Lawrence's *The Plumed Serpent* he wrote to Lawrence about his belief in the Sun God and asked for a story about the sun to publish. Lawrence supplied one entitled *The Sun.*

Because of their wealth, charm, and family connections, the Crosbys associated with both Europeans and expatriates. Harry's cousin, Walter Berry, who had been a close friend of Proust, Henry James, and Edith Wharton, invited them to his cosmopolitan luncheons. When Berry died, Harry was executor of his estate, which included a fine library and two Picassos. This led to some controversies with Edith Wharton, who had been left the right to choose some of Berry's books. Harry was also associated with Eugène Jolas, the publisher of *transition,* which published some of his poems and prose. He helped the magazine financially and in 1929 became one of the advisory editors. He and Caresse were among the signers of the "Proclamation" of that year which set forth the symbolist and surrealist creed of the magazine. With liberal quotations from William Blake, especially "Damn braces! Bless relaxes," there were such statements as

> 3. Pure poetry is a lyrical absolute that seeks an a-priori reality within ourselves alone.

6. The literary creator has the right to disintegrate the primal matter of words imposed on him by textbooks and dictionaries.

10. Time is a tyranny to be abolished.

11. The writer expresses. He does not communicate.

12. The plain reader be damned.

In addition to the Crosbys the signers were Kay Boyle, Whit Burnett, Hart Crane, Martha Foley, Stuart Gilbert, A. L. Gillespie, Leigh Hoffman, Eugène Jolas, Elliot Paul, Douglas Rigby, Theodore Rutra, Robert Sage, Harold J. Salemson, and Lawrence Vail. Hart Crane later excused himself by saying that he was drunk when he signed.

Hart Crane was often drunk. Even among the tolerant bohemians in America his habit of breaking up furniture had made him a difficult guest. When the Crosbys agreed to publish *The Bridge*, Crane came to Paris to finish it. They put him up overnight in their apartment only to find in the morning that he had brought a chimney sweep home with him and that the wall paper and spread were covered with hundreds of black hand and footprints. After a number of such escapades the Crosbys in desperation took him to their week-end retreat, Le Moulin du Soleil, and shut him in the tower with writing paper and whiskey. Almost always they found that he had got into trouble: he had frightened the postman's daughter or insulted the baker's son; he moved some of the best furniture onto the roof. Eventually Crane got into a fight with the Paris police and spent a week in jail. Harry Crosby hired a lawyer for him, paid his fine, and gave him passage money home.

In a number of respects Crane's experience in Europe was typical of that of a number of the expatriates of the 1920's. Paris was just another place to continue the footloose lives they lived in America. In Greenwich Village and at the Connecticut homes of other writers Crane had engaged in the same wild drinking and homosexual adventures. Later he went to Mexico on a Guggenheim fellowship and on the way home committed suicide by jumping overboard from his ship.

The Crosbys came home in 1929 because Harry wanted to attend the Harvard-Yale game. In December they went to New York, where Hart Crane gave a party for them. A few days later Harry borrowed the key of a friend's apartment. There he and the young wife of a Harvard graduate student were found shot to death in what the medical examiner called a suicide compact. "I should like to have influence strong enough to lead a band of followers into the Sun Death," Harry had once written. Thus at thirty-one, rich, well-liked, and moderately successful as a writer he had sought and found the Sun Death thirteen years before the date he had planned to die with Caresse.

Among the expatriates who had known him, E. E. Cummings and John Wheelwright wrote poems on his death, and in *transition* Crane, Mac-Leish, Kay Boyle, Eugène Jolas, and Stuart Gilbert memorialized him. Malcolm Cowley argues that his death became a kind of symbol of the decay and suicide of a social order.

Scott Fitzgerald provided perhaps the best picture of the social order, or rather disorder, symbolized by Harry Crosby. Scott and Zelda first went to Europe in 1920 but stayed only three months. "What an overestimated place Europe is!," wrote Scott. In 1924 they went back determined to "live on practically nothing a year." In an article for the *Saturday Evening Post* Fitzgerald wrote, "We were going to the Old World to find a new rhythm for our lives, with a true conviction that we had left behind our old relics forever." He was mistaken.

At their villa at St. Raphael Zelda had a flirtation with a French aviator, an incident which caused a violent quarrel. They went on to Rome, where Scott got into a drunken fight with taxi drivers over the demand for an extravagant fare. He spent the rest of the night in jail. Like so much of his life this became part of his fiction. In *Tender is the Night* the incident is used as a milestone in Dick Diver's deterioration. Nevertheless, Fitzgerald finished *The Great Gatsby*, a novel so thoroughly American in setting, character, and mood that it bears no trace of European experience. (It is worth noting that Sinclair Lewis wrote *Babbitt* in Europe.) Perhaps Harold Stearns was right in arguing that expatriation was an irrelevant thing in a writer's work. Most Americans, he believed, would not have stayed ten weeks in Paris had there not been other compatriots there. Hemingway stated that Fitzgerald hated the French, the Italians, and sometimes the British. William Carlos Williams, who with his wife, was in Paris in 1924, said that "The Paris of the expatriate artist was our only world—day and night—and if bread is the staff of life, whiskey, as Bob [McAlmon] was fond of saying, is the staff of night life."

In May of 1925 the Fitzgeralds went to Paris for the rest of the year. That was the summer that Scott described as a thousand parties and no work. He would be drunk for a week or ten days at a time, and sober up in places like Brussels with no idea of how he got there. What Mizener describes as the nightmare quality of Paris nights is reflected in *Tender is the Night* and *Babylon Revisited*. In the novel there is a scene reworked from *The World's Fair* in which a party gets hold of the limousine belonging to the Shah of Persia and after riding about in state, end up by coming home in a farmer's wagon on top of a load of carrots. In *Babylon Revisited*, Charlie Wales remembers with amazement that he and Lorraine stole a butcher's tricycle and pedaled all over the Etoile between the small hours and dawn. "How many weeks or months of dissipation to arrive at that condition of utter irresponsibility."

Robert McAlmon told of being "poured off" a train in Venice, without any clear idea of how he got there. Someone checked him in at a hotel, whose name he promptly forgot because he went to an all-night party where he distinguished himself by surpassing various rivals in turning handsprings. He summed it up: "Those were the days of passion, love and intoxication."

The same note is echoed in Harold Stearns's account of the Americans working for the Paris edition of the *Tribune*. Someone was always absent on a spree; men turned up drunk for work; writers introduced obscene misprints into the paper. The editor accepted fantastic excuses because he had to. People talked about the intolerance and stupidity at home, but what they really wanted was "the freedom to be irresponsible." Remembering his own days at the race tracks, of drinking champagne until dawn, he commented, "It was a useless, silly life—and I have missed it every day since."

Fitzgerald's own escapades were as irresponsible as anything in his stories. At the Cap d' Antibes he told John Peale Bishop there was no one "except me, Zelda, the Valentinos, the Murphys, Mistinguett, Rex Ingram, Dos Passos, Alice Tarry, the MacLeishes, Charles Bracket, Maude Kahn, Esther Murphy, Marguerite Namara, E. Phillips Oppenheim, Mannes the violinist, Floyd Dell, Max and Crystal Eastman . . . just a real place to rough it and escape from the world. But we had a great time." At their villa various Americans turned up from time to time: Grace Moore, Alexander Woolcott, John Peale Bishop, Donald Ogden Stewart, and Charles MacArthur. MacArthur and Fitzgerald would write unprintable titles on Grace Moore's villa and then photograph them. One night they lured an orchestra from a hotel and locked them up with a bottle of whiskey, then settled down to listen to their old favorites. On another occasion they raided a small restaurant in Cannes, carried off all the silverware, and kidnaped the waiters. There was the ugly incident when Fitzgerald encountered an old woman selling nuts and candies, and kicked the tray out of her hands, scattering her wares. He began to be excluded from parties.

All this was not a result of expatriation: there had been similar escapades in New York like the one in which he and Zelda dived fully clothed into a fountain. And back in Hollywood Fitzgerald at a party collected watches and jewelry and boiled them in tomato soup. The point is that for many Americans in the 1920's Europe, and especially France, was just another playground. Hemingway's *The Sun Also Rises* represents the irresponsibility, the desperate escapism, but it misses the zest, the fun which Harold Stearns and Caresse Crosby remembered. Fitzgerald's *Babylon Revisited* is the morning after, but for a while it was a gay party, because "the snow of twenty-nine wasn't real snow. If you didn't want it to be snow, you just paid some money."

There is a more imaginative quality to the antics of Harry Crosby than to those of other expatriates. But he, like Fitzgerald and Stearns and Sinclair Lewis and others, often reveals a sophomoric quality. Every Christmas when Caresse arranged a celebration for her two children by her first marriage, Harry would pull out to spend the day or night with some other woman, always taking pains to inform Caresse of her rival's identity. Sinclair Lewis, according to his first wife, had an almost equal aversion to the responsibilities of parenthood. The hedonistic expatriate of the 1920's regarded children as a nuisance in a way characteristic of the British upper classes. But whereas the British pattern is reminiscent of the Spartan dedication of children to a social order, that of the American expatriates suggests a shrugging off of responsibility. An exception to this habit seems to have been the Fitzgeralds, who, until Zelda's breakdown, kept "Scottie" with them.

The distinction between the attitude toward children of Americans abroad in the 1920's and that of earlier generations is especially marked. Cooper and Hawthorne had made their children an integral part of their lives in Europe. Even the bachelor Irving had taken responsibility for his nephews. The more immature expatriates of the 1920's regarded children as pretty much of a nuisance, a hindrance to the hedonistic life. It is ironic that Sinclair Lewis, who disliked responsibility, represents Fran

Dodsworth as rejecting her role as grandmother. She demands that Sam shall not tell anyone about her daughter's child lest it interfere with her role as the glamorous siren. All this is not so much the result of expatriation as a reflection of the mood of the 1920's which led to expatriation as an escape from responsibilities of any kind.

The sophomoric quality of this group as contrasted with the urbanity of earlier expatriates is revealed in Sinclair Lewis's attempts to shock people he felt his social superiors and in the famous incident when Edith Wharton invited the Fitzgeralds for tea.

According to Arthur Mizener, Zelda, fearing that the urbane Mrs. Wharton would make them feel provincial, refused to go. There are some differing versions of what later happened, but there is evidence that Fitzgerald fortified himself for the meeting with several drinks. Theodore Chanler, who drove him to the Pavillon Colombe, and who was present at the tea, gave his version in 1959. Chanler's recollection was that Fitzgerald told a rather incoherent story about an American couple spending several days in a bordello under the impression that it was a hotel. Mrs. Wharton's response is variously reported as having been, "But Mr. Fitzgerald, you haven't told us what they did in the bordello," or "Mr. Fitzgerald, your story lacks data." In view of Chanler's theory that Mrs. Wharton's response was due to puzzlement rather than to an attempt to discomfort Fitzgerald, version number one seems more likely. Chanler did not think Scott was drunk, but reports that Gaillard Lapsley, who was also there, thought he was.

According to Mizener, when Scott got home, he first told Zelda the meeting had been a great success. Then after several drinks he put his head in his arms and began to pound the table with his fists. "They beat me," he said, "They beat me! They beat me! They *beat* me!" Whatever the exact details, the incident points up the difference between the urbanity of the older generation of expatriates and the callowness of a later one. In any case Mrs. Wharton wrote in her diary the word "horrible" beside Fitzgerald's name.

This sophomoric desire to impress, to shock may help to explain Hemingway's preoccupation with bull fighting. Here was a sport little known to most Americans, and one which was offensive to their sensibilities. It is hard to justify on artistic grounds the long technical account in *The Sun Also Rises.* In both the novel and in *Death in the Afternoon* there is the kind of showing off which led Max Eastman to describe the latter as *"Bull in the Afternoon."* Certainly Hemingway's lifelong flaunting of his masculinity has a sophomoric quality.

Fitzgerald gives some of this callowness to young Dick Diver when he first comes to Europe. Dr. Diver is subtly rebuked by the humbler Swiss physician, who after mentioning the great men buried near by, says, "I am continually confronted with a pantheon of heroes." In a scene reminiscent of Twain's badgering of a European guide, Sinclair Lewis gives a picture of Tub Pearson of Zenith trying to be funny at the expense of a waiter in a fine Parisian restaurant. It was this sort of thing which led Harold Stearns writing of his own years in Paris to speak of "the arrogance of being an American." William Carlos Williams praised the French for their willingness to permit such creatures "as we Americans, drunken, loud, often obscene, to exist in their city."

It is this callowness in many of the expatriates of the 1920's which sets them off from those of earlier generations. From Irving to Eliot most American writers and artists abroad had a certain urbanity. Even Cooper was at ease in aristocratic circles. As has been shown, Ticknor, Bancroft, Hawthorne, Margaret Fuller, Story, Edith Wharton, and James associated on equal terms with the prominent people in Europe. The same is true of others like Lowell, Motley, Norton, Logan Pearsall Smith, and Bernard Berenson. One could not imagine any one of them showing off like Scott Fitzgerald or Sinclair Lewis or the Crosbys. For instance Caresse Crosby sported a black whippet, "Narcasse Noir," which had a gold collar and gold laquered toe nails. The bar-flies like Harold Stearns, the Hemingway characters, the bohemians—Grace Hegger Lewis called them the "no goods on the Left Bank"—were all aspects of the twenties.

As the earlier chapters show, American expatriates before the 1920's were still committed to puritan views on sexual morality and the idea that life is a serious business. The hedonism of the expatriates of the twenties is part of the larger context of the era following World War I. Hemingway's Englishwoman, Lady Brett Ashley, is as lost as the Americans she associates with. The early novels of Aldous Huxley show the same kind of hedonistic, nihilistic people. Certainly hedonism is not entirely a postwar phenomenon. Upper-class European society in England and on the Continent had a long history of scandal and dissipation. The annals of Edwardian England and picture of prewar Europe in Briffault's

Europa are neither more nor less scandalous than the age of Byron or of Aldous Huxley.

The difference after World War I was that upper-class hedonism spread to the traditionally puritanical middle classes. The United States of course lacked a titled aristocracy, and until the 1880's or '90's had few idle rich of the kind pictured in *The Age of Innocence*. Therefore the American "aristocracy" were essentially equivalent to the British gentry and the upper middle class. It was this class of lawyers, clergymen, bankers, and merchants in the United States which had sent its sons and daughters abroad for travel and study. With few exceptions, Americans before 1920 represented in this account belonged to old Federalist gentry, to the Brahmin caste, or to the upper middle class. These groups were not distinct entities; they overlapped and intermarried.

Another thing which the nineteenth-century expatriates shared was that they were from the Atlantic states. For most of them this meant that they belonged to long-settled societies. Thus, Irving, Cooper, Greenough, Ticknor, Bancroft, Motley, Longfellow, Hawthorne, Lowell, Bayard Taylor, and Norton, among others, could step back into an established social order where their intellectual achievements were respected. William Wetmore Story and Henry James, although they did not choose to return, were acknowledged members of this social order. However, Edith Wharton claimed that New York society looked askance at a woman of her class who wrote. Certainly that would not have been true in her husband's city of Boston, and it was not true in New Haven, where Yale gave her an honorary degree. There is always a hint of rationalization in Edith Wharton's attacks upon American philistinism.

In contrast the expatriates of the 1920's tended to be rootless. Some of this was due to the war, some of it to the fluidity of American society. Like Van Wyck Brooks, Malcolm Cowley argued that the colleges with their emphasis upon the European past had failed to give a sense of American history and society. But this was not a new development in higher education; Emerson had attacked it as far back as 1837.

The mass expatriation of intellectuals in the 1920's was a symptom of a profound change that took place in American life beginning in the latter part of the nineteenth century, one which accelerated in the first decades of the twentieth. The intellectual became increasingly alienated from the rest of American society. One possible cause for this was the rapidity of social change, especially the shift from a rural to an urban society. In such a period the novelist and the social critic are likely to sense the change and adjust to it more quickly than do other members of society.

There is also some evidence of a lowering of the quality of American life, especially in the twenties. It is always easy to forget the harsher aspects of a distant past, but there seems to have been considerable justification for Pound's comment in 1920 that

> a tawdry cheapness
> Shall outlast our days.

In the nineteenth century politicians and professional men often took pride in their knowledge of literature. Rutherford B. Hayes built up an extensive private library; Grover Cleveland, who had to leave school in his teens, learned much of Shakespeare by heart and read extensively in Dryden, Pope, Prior, Cowper, Wordsworth, Shelley, and Keats; whereas Calvin Coolidge, who graduated *cum laude* from Amherst, confined his reading to the weekly magazines, Wells's *Outline of History*, and two or three trashy novels a year.

Throughout much of the nineteenth century the intellectuals had not felt alienated from political leaders. Arthur Schlesinger lists among the Jacksonians: Hawthorne, Bryant, Whitman, Cooper, Bancroft, Irving (for a time), Greenough, Powers, and numerous others. Van Buren, the son of a farmer and tavern-keeper, offered jobs to Bancroft, Hawthorne, Irving, Paulding, and Brownson. When Wilson entered the White House, the intellectuals thought they again had a champion, but by the twenties many of them had come to regard him as a betrayer. Certainly during the Harding-Coolidge-Hoover era scholars, writers and artists had no cause to feel welcome in the White House. The changed relation of poets to Presidents is reflected in Whitman's *When Lilacs Last in the Dooryard Bloom'd* and Cummings' epitaph on Harding, which begins:

> the first president to be loved by his
> bitterest enemies "is dead"
> the only man woman or child who wrote a simple
> declarative sentence with seven grammatical
> errors "is dead"
> beautiful Warren Gamaliel Harding "is" dead.

In the nineteenth century farmers and artisans had driven miles over muddy or frozen roads to hear Emerson lecture; in the 1920's they were reading Dr. Frank Crane's column. Until about the turn of the century the earlier Brahmins had maintained their prestige. A piece of Staffordshire china made about 1880 serves as a useful symbol. On it are the portraits of Emerson, Bryant, Poe, Longfellow, Whittier, Holmes, and Lowell. The fact that it was made and sold indicates the respect in which these men were held. One could not imagine a similar artifact in 1900. By 1913 Howells deplored the fact that in a recent magazine poll to determine the ten most useful living Americans, no poet, novelist, dramatist, actor, musician, artist, or architect came anywhere near the first ten. In the 1920's the *Saturday Evening Post* and the *American Magazine* were creating a pantheon of leaders of business and industry. Important writers of the twenties like Dreiser, Lewis, Dos Passos, Mencken, Hemingway, Sandburg, etc. were attacked as subversive and un-American. Many people regarded the awarding of the Nobel Prize to Sinclair Lewis in 1930 as a slap at the United States.

The hostility between the business community and the intellectual was reflected in the widespread dismissals of college professors for alleged radicalism. While he was vice-President, Calvin Coolidge wrote for a popular magazine a series of articles on the topic "Are the Reds Stalking our College Women?" On the whole he thought the leading women's colleges were dangerously radical. Never before in our history had the writer, the artist, and the intellectual been so alienated from the ruling caste of the country.

This alienation seems to have been felt most keenly by the writers from the Middle West. Howells had fled the region for Boston; a series of other writers—Garland, Dreiser, Sherwood Anderson, Sandburg, and Lewis—pictured it as a land of puritan intolerance, materialistic values, crudity of manners, emotional frustration, and contempt for culture. Edith Wharton, who did not know the region first hand, nevertheless used it as typical of the new America she hated.

The attempt to escape the Middle Western background is reflected in the experience of Ford Maddox Ford, who reported that as editor of *the transatlantic review* he received ten times more manuscripts from Chicago than from England. He added:

> . . . the real germ of the Middle Western literary movement is to be found in the Three Mountains Press, Paris, of Mr. William Bird who worked in conjunction with the Paris Contact Publishing Company

of Mr. Robert McAlmon. . . . These books were edited by Mr. Pound and were mostly American. McAlmon published a number of ugly wads of printing called "Contact Books." These were nearly all Middle Western in origin. . . .

Arthur Mizener has shown how deeply rooted the Middle West was in Scott Fitzgerald, how his sense of social inferiority was related to this background. In *The Great Gatsby*, Nick Carroway muses about the forces leading up to the tragedy on Long Island:

> I see now that this has been a story of the West, after all—Tom and Gatsby, Daisy and Jordan and I, were all Westerners, and perhaps we possessed some deficiency in common which made us subtly unadaptable to Eastern life.

This sense of alienation from one's background appears also in the picture of Dick and Maude Diver in *Tender is the Night*. Dick can neither become a European nor return to his American background. He wanders between two worlds as does Sam Dodsworth in the Sinclair Lewis novel. Sam is deeply committed to American values, yet after an evening of lively discussion in Europe, "He saw slowly that none of his prosperous industrialized friends in Zenith were very much interested in anything whatever." And on another occasion:

> He had been bored in Paris, yet he liked crepes susette better than flapjacks; he liked leaning over the bridges of the Seine better than walking on Sixth Avenue. . . . How was it that this America, which had been so surely and comfortable in his hand, had slipped away?

The account of Lewis's own years in Europe makes it almost certain that this was autobiographical. Van Wyck Brooks stated that "the question of expatriation was never out of Lewis's mind."

Malcolm Cowley gives a thumbnail sketch of the designers, stylists, editors, etc. who came flocking to Manhattan in the 1920's:

> Soon it became evident that all the younger members of this class had about the same experiences, the Midwestern background, the year in the army if they were men, the unhappy love affair that took its place if they were women, the long voyage to France; and it was evident too, that most of them were lost in their new environment and discontented . . . of course they couldn't go back: their own

country-side or Midwestern towns would offer no scope to their talents. . . .

This sense of rootlessness is reflected in MacLeish's "American Letter" (1930):

It is a strange thing—to be an American.
Neither an old house it is with the air
Tasting of hung herbs and the sun returning
Year after year to the same door and the churn
Making the same sound in the cool of the kitchen . . .

In contrast, Irving, over a century before, had given a nostalgic picture of just this kind of kitchen, not in Europe but in Sleepy Hollow, New York, Hawthorne's *Seven Gables* is a house haunted by ghosts of the past. Edith Wharton's *Hudson River Bracketed* is the story of the rootless Midwesterner, Vance Weston, discovering along the Hudson a society deeply rooted in tradition.

It is not surprising, therefore, that a significant proportion of the expatriates of the 1920's came from the Midwest, among them T. S. Eliot, Ernest Hemingway, Robert McAlmon, Hart Crane, Archibald MacLeish, Sinclair Lewis, Glenway Wescott, and Scott Fitzgerald. Malcolm Cowley, although born in Pennsylvania, came from west of the Alleghenies. Harold Stearns argues that Lewis was merely a tourist, but it is worth noting that one of Lewis's best novels, *Dodsworth,* is based upon his European experience. For all its crudities *Dodsworth* is in the tradition of Hawthorne and James: the attempt to contrast European and American values. The significant thing is that the fictionalized Americans of 1920 are pictured as less civilized persons than their prototypes in Hawthorne and James. For the earlier writers American culture might seem thin compared to the impenetrabilities of Europe, but in the person of Fran Dodsworth, Lewis pictured the phony elements in American culture: the women's club superficiality and false refinement. Fran Dodsworth was from the Middle West, unsure of itself as Boston had never been.

This shift toward philistinism is reflected in the changed status of returned expatriates. From Jefferson to Theodore Roosevelt, American Presidents had invited artists and intellectuals to the White House. Irving, Ticknor, Bancroft, Powers, Story, Lowell, Henry James, and Edith Wharton had all been received there. Theodore Roosevelt had greeted Mrs. Wharton with the remark, "Well, I *am* glad to welcome to the White

House some one to whom I can quote 'The Hunting of the Snark' without being asked what I mean!" He went on to discuss her novel *The Valley of Decision.* One could not imagine Harding discussing *Winesburg, Ohio* or Coolidge *The Great Gatsby,* much less *The Waste Land.*

In view of this divorce between the intellectual and the business and political leaders of the 1920's the remarkable thing is the slight impact of Europe. Never before had the expatriates tried so hard to shake off the dust of their native land; yet perhaps no group of expatriates were so thoroughly American. Harold Stearns argued that most of the expatriates in Paris would not have stayed ten weeks had there not been other Americans there to talk to. "Hemingway was no more Latin basically, than was Ring Lardner. Nor was Gertrude Stein, though she was a Paris institution." And it was Gertrude Stein who said that Hemingway was 90 per cent a Rotarian. She asserted that Cummings was the natural heir to the New England tradition. Symbolically George Gershwin's *An American in Paris,* written in Europe, is entirely in the American idiom.

Harold Loeb, the editor of *Broom,* with possibly a certain amount of hindsight, said that by living abroad he could better recognize the significant aspects of America by studying them from a distance. Somewhat diffidently he introduced into his editorials the theme that the new world was being forged in America. Similarly Robert McAlmon felt that compared to England, Italy or Germany, America was "an exciting, stimulating, imaginative country with the fresh imagination of youth and ignorance . . . I fail to discover fewer morons and bigotries in other countries than in the United States." Conrad Aiken, half English, half American, after living a time in England found it necessary to return periodically to Boston; "that pressing need for a kind of revitalizing in its more electric air, and for renewed draughts of its racier idioms . . ." The thought came to him that "the American scene itself, just now, at last, began to come to flower."

Malcolm Cowley argues that the young Americans abroad "had begun by discovering a crazy Europe in which the intellectuals of their own middle class were more defeated and demoralized than those at home." This may represent a certain amount of over-intellectualizing of the process. Harold Stearns may be closer to it in saying of expatriates:

> We cannot escape a dim feeling of uneasiness and insecurity, just as we are never certain how people, basically not like ourselves, will act

in the emergencies of life—whatever the civilized veneer. I mean, simply, we are homeless enough in this world under the best of circumstances without any special effort to test our capacity to be more so. . . . I have tried being homeless more than most people. And . . . I am ready to depose that it simply doesn't work.

It is significant that Malcolm Cowley called his book on expatriation, *Exile's Return.*

It is also significant that a number of the expatriates became identified with the rediscovery of America, particularly its history, literature and folklore, men like Cowley, Van Wyck Brooks, MacLeish, Cummings. Others like Hart Crane, Williams, Fitzgerald, and Lewis never lost their roots in America. Harold Stearns described the paradox:

> . . . an irony of history that our participation which many people hailed as an end of our "isolation" did in cold fact result in a greater nationalistic feeling than we had ever known before . . .
>
> And so today, when we go abroad we hear with a queer feeling of pride American music; we see copies of American paintings, a few bits of sculpture that would not be the same, had it not been for the "American" influence. . . . Not only is the Colonial period over, but even the highly self-conscious reaction of the Colonial period is over, also. We have long ceased to be perturbed about what Europeans do in the arts: today we no longer care tremendously what they think about them—least of all what they think about our own art, and music, and architecture. For—and this is the miracle that has taken place in my own lifetime—it *is* our own at last, without apology, without shame, without distrust. Even, increasingly, with something of wistful love, a curious surprised feeling that not all our children of the spirit are ugly ducklings.

Thus the 1920's, which saw the greatest mass expatriation of American intellectuals in our history—an expatriation motivated as never before by a rejection of native culture and values—ended in the rediscovery of America.

CONCLUSION

The announced objectives of this study were to consider three questions: What has the expatriate experience of a number of sensitive and thoughtful people revealed about the nature of American culture, especially as it contrasted with European culture? To what extent has the United States "exiled" its writers, artists, and intellectuals? And to what extent has expatriation been an important factor in the artistic and literary work of the expatriate? To a considerable degree these questions may have been answered in the accounts of the various people who have been discussed. However, a certain summing up may be in order.

It is obvious that throughout American history the pull of Europe has been powerful. For Hawthorne, England was "our old home," and Oliver Wendell Holmes remarked that "Good Americans when they die go to Paris." For at least a hundred years of our national existence Europe offered a kind of aesthetic and intellectual experience not available in the New World. During those years writers, artists, and scholars brought back the fruits of their years abroad—among them an insistence that art and literature were important.

There was, of course, always the danger that the imported cultural product would seem more valuable than that produced at home. It was this which Emerson warned against: "We have listened too long to the courtly muses of Europe." Boston perhaps needed the warning more than did the rest of America. Men like Ticknor, Longfellow, and Norton came back to teach the glories of European literature and art. As has been pointed out, English literature was a staple of the educated American's culture. In fact, as Van Wyck Brooks remembered Harvard before World War I, Americanism was equated with philistinism. The same view prevailed at other Ivy-League institutions. Dr. Coit, the headmaster of St. Paul's, permitted no games except cricket.

Magazines such as *The North American Review* and *The Atlantic* trained their opera glasses on Europe: the travel sketch was as customary a feature as the title page. Publishers in New York and Boston poured out an unending stream of books on the European experiences of tourists and expatriates. In fact most of the persons discussed in this study wrote one or more such books. In addition there were, of course many short stories and novels with a European setting.

The remarkable thing in our intellectual history, however, has been the strength of the native tradition. If one unifying element emerges from this study of representative expatriates it is that they remained American in their sensibilities and code of values. There were exceptions, of course, men like T. S. Eliot, who became essentially British. One need only compare his identification with the sensibility of the English as reflected in *The Family Reunion* and *The Cocktail Party* with the outsider's view of James, both in England and France. The latter knew in his bones and viscera how an American felt among the "impenetrabilities" of Europe—and the phrase, which was James's own, is significant. Certainly, however, no one could mistake the work of Cooper, Hawthorne, James, Frederic, Wharton, Howells, or Hemingway for that of an English or a French novelist. Scholars like Ticknor, Longfellow, Lowell, Bancroft, Motley, and Norton retained not only their American loyalties but often their prejudices. Norton is a case in point: for all his love of Italy he remained a bigoted hater of the Church of Rome. Howells, who wrote enthusiastic books on Venice and the Tuscan cities, was as puritanical in his views as a purely home-grown writer like Vachel Lindsay.

Perhaps even more important, most of the writers retained their emotional roots in America. *The Legend of Sleepy Hollow, Notions of the Americans, Washington Square, The Bostonians, The Damnation of Theron Ware, The Age of Innocence, The Great Gatsby*, and *Babbitt* were all written in Europe.

It is more difficult to generalize about the artists. West, Copley, Powers, Story, Sargent, and Mary Cassatt* all adopted styles that resembled those of their European contemporaries. This is understandable. There was no artistic tradition in America of comparable power to the native intellectual forces of democracy, puritanism, and transcendentalism. Hawthorne, Melville, Emerson, Whitman, Twain, Howells, Sinclair Lewis, and Faulkner, to mention only a few, have easily recognizable roots in the social, religious, economic, and political soil of America. There was no comparably rich artistic heritage. On both sides of the Atlantic painters and sculptors went to school to the artists of ancient Greece and of Renaissance Italy.

Even so a number of the artists, despite their study in Europe, could not be mistaken for Europeans—Charles Willson Peale, Horatio Greenough, Samuel F. B. Morse. Copley himself came to recognize that his

* However both in her way of life and in her painting Mary Cassatt remained the American puritan: There is for example none of Renoir's sensuality in her work.

earlier typically American work was superior to that done in Europe. It was after his return to America that Allston developed an original style, one that was a forerunner of the work of later painters. And as has been pointed out, sculptors like Powers and Story remained thoroughly American in their ideas and way of life.

Of course the expatriates found certain things distasteful in American life: the scramble for wealth, the materialistic values, the philistine views on art and literature. From the time Irving coined the phrase "the Almighty Dollar" and Cooper blasted the philistinism of his countrymen, these themes have, as we have seen, run through the writings of American expatriates. In the twentieth century puritanism became the *bête noire*. It must be remembered, however, that during the nineteenth century both British and American writers were complaining of these same things in England. Carlyle deplored "the cash nexus"; Tennyson thought that "the jingling of the guinea" governed foreign policy; Arnold gave the word *Philistine* its modern meaning; Ruskin and William Morris charged that human values were being destroyed by industrialism. As has been noted, Hawthorne had much to say about the bloated hoggishness of well-to-do Englishmen; the anglophile Henry James, writing to Charles Eliot Norton in 1886, compared the modern British upper class to "the same rotten and *collapsible* one as that of the French aristocracy before the revolution. . . . At all events English life is grossly materialistic and wants blood-letting." About the time that Bernard Shaw was beginning to satirize British puritanical hypocrisies, Harold Frederic was writing *Mrs. Albert Grundy* in London. James Joyce and D. H. Lawrence ran afoul of the same taboos on both sides of the Atlantic.

Before 1865 American expatriates were continually admonished about the evils of Negro slavery, but they discovered that the lot of the European peasant was often as bad as that of the American slave. Like Melville and Hawthorne they discovered that "it's a wicked world in all meridians." On the whole, however, the expatriates found higher standards of morality and social justice in America than in Europe.

As to the question of the "exile" of American artists and writers, it is obvious from the foregoing account that no one of them was driven out of his country as almost literally were Byron and Shelley, or at a later date were Freud and Thomas Mann, or more recently Russian and South African novelists. There is of course the possibility of a more subtle form of exile: the expatriation of a writer or artist who cannot get a hearing in his own country or is so unpopular there that his life is made miserable, for example James Joyce or Charlie Chaplin. All the evidence here examined supports the view that between 1783 and 1930 American writers, scholars, and artists were not disregarded at home nor made unwelcome there.

In fact the reverse is true: every one of the expatriates considered in this study was honored in his own country during his lifetime. Some like Irving, Cooper, and James were attacked by xenophobes, but certainly suffered no more violent attacks than European writers experienced from their own reviewers. One could call the roll of Wordsworth, Coleridge, Byron, Keats, Shelley, Flaubert, Ibsen, Hardy, Wells, D. H. Lawrence—all of whom were the subject of especially hostile criticism in their own times.

The case of that key figure, Henry James, here examined at length, did not in the light of the evidence support the contention that he was either "exiled" or disregarded. In fact expatriated American writers from Irving to Hemingway—and including James—have received at least as much recognition in their homeland as they did abroad. Some like Margaret Fuller, George Bancroft, Edith Wharton, and F. Scott Fitzgerald were probably better known at home than in Europe. Certainly this was true of E. E. Cummings, Archibald MacLeish, and Hart Crane. This is not merely a matter of critical acclaim but also of wide circulation. *The Atlantic Monthly*, which often published James, paid him the same price for *Portrait of a Lady* as did *Macmillan's Magazine* of London. In the year of its publication Edith Wharton's *House of Mirth* led the best-seller list in the United States. Three of Harold Frederic's novels were first serialized in *Scribner's Magazine,* one in *The Cosmopolitan,* and *The Market Place* in *The Saturday Evening Post.* The *Post,* that *bête noire* of the intellectuals, regularly published Fitzgerald before the professors discovered him.

The expatriate artists mentioned in this study often received more recognition both at home and abroad than they deserved. The scholars were given important university posts or, if they wanted them, diplomatic assignments. Irving was Minister to Spain, Lowell to England, Bancroft to Austria, and Motley to Germany—in other words they held the most important diplomatic posts offered by the United States. No one of the important expatriates before 1920 can be said to have been neglected or ignored by his own country. Those of the twenties often had at first a harder time. As confessed rebels and mavericks they were less readily accepted. Like the home-based writers of their time, they suffered because of the crassness of their era. George F. Babbitt and Calvin Coolidge symbolized the ruling forces. Even in the Gilded Age, the intellectuals had not been so much under attack.

Yet, despite the attacks of alarmed conservatives, the writers who had deplored so many features of American life came to be recognized during their own lifetimes as important. Their books often became best sellers and before long were studied in college classrooms. The intellectuals who had fled their country came back to take important editorial posts and university professorships. Thirty years after the mass hegira of the twenties a number of former expatriates like Van Wyck Brooks, Cummings, Hemingway, Fitzgerald, MacLeish, and Cowley were respected figures in American letters. Their expatriation, like that of Cooper or Hawthorne, becomes little more than a footnote in a critique of their writings. Even the eternally wandering Hemingway is everywhere thought of as an American writer—almost as an archetype of the American. In fact the only two major American expatriate writers who, like Joseph Conrad, are claimed as part of another national literature are James and Eliot. But as has been argued in this study, James is far more American than British.

Thus the evidence derived from this examination of the lives and work of representative artists, scholars, and writers from the time of Irving to 1929 leads to the conclusion that the artist and intellectual has not been rejected by his own country nor has he as a rule become a spiritual expatriate.

NOTES AND INDEX

NOTES

As a rule quotations from works of fiction (which often exist in several editions) will not be footnoted.

PROLOGUE

Page

4 James Fenimore Cooper stated . . . , James Fenimore Cooper, *Gleanings in Europe*, ed. Robert W. Spiller (New York, 1930), II, 377.

5 Copley's comment on his American work, James Thomas Flexner, *America's Old Masters, First Artists of the New World* (New York, 1939), p. 166.

According to Rembrandt Peale . . . , Rembrandt Peale, *Notes on Italy* (Philadelphia, 1831), p. 4.

"It is not indeed the fine arts . . . ," *Familiar Letters of John Adams and his Wife, Abigail Adams, during the Revolution*, ed. Charles Francis Adams (Boston, 1875), p. 381.

West on the fine arts in America . . . , MS letter, Sept. 8, 1805. Simon Gratz Collection, Historical Soc. of Pa.

6 Copley: ". . . it is a pleasing reflection . . . ," John Singleton Copley, *Letters and Papers of John Singleton Copley and Henry Pelham, 1739–1776* (Boston, 1914), p. 301.

7 "There the Italian pictures . . . , Peale, *Notes on Italy*, p. 4.

7–8 "On these bleak climes . . . ," Philip Freneau, "To an Author."

8 Emerson said that "from 1790 . . . ," Quoted, Russel B. Nye, *George Bancroft, Brahmin Rebel* (New York, 1944), p. 4.

9 "No village bell . . . ," Frances Trollope, *Domestic Manners of the Americans*, ed. Donald Smalley (New York, 1949), p. 50.

Secure in a belief in beef . . . , *ibid.*, p. 297.

In like manner Fanny Butler . . . , Frances Anne (Kemble) Butler, *Journal* (Philadelphia, 1835), I, 176–177.

9 Captain Basil Hall, a much more judicious observer . . . , Captain Basil Hall, *Travels in North America* (Edinburgh, 1829), I, 47.

9–10 "No foreigner of that day . . . ," Henry Adams, *History of the United States during the First Administration of Thomas Jefferson* (New York, 1889), I, 166.

10 "I am induced, ere I conclude . . . ," Trollope, pp. 354–355.

Young George Ticknor wrote . . . , George Ticknor, *Life, Letters, and Journals of George Ticknor*, ed. George S. Hillard (Boston, 1876), I, 85.

Cooper was irritated . . . , Cooper, *Gleanings*, II, 71–72.

"England can't like America . . . ," James Russell Lowell, *Letters*, ed. Charles Eliot Norton (Cambridge, Mass., 1904), II, 118.

10–11 "Well, you know, what can be expected . . . ," *ibid.*, II, 232.

11 "But you're an American . . . ," Conrad Aiken, *Ushant* (New York, 1962), p. 173.

"The most prominent character . . . ," Stanley T. Williams, *The Life of Washington Irving* (New York, 1935), I, 220.

12 Adams advised against it . . . , Nye, p. 31.

"All Americans in Europe . . . ," Carleton Mabee, *American Leonardo* (New York, 1943), p. 37.

Hiram Powers, whose nude Greek Slave . . . , H. W. Bellows, "Seven Sittings with Powers the Sculptor," *Appletons' Journal*, I, No. 13 (June 26, 1869), 402–404.

AT EASE IN ZION

13 When Napoleon III was crowned . . . , Letter to Mrs. Storrow, March 28, 1853, Pierre M. Irving, *The Life and Letters of Washington Irving* (New York, 1862), IV, 138.

Ladies in New York once displayed . . . , Stanley T. Williams, *The Life of Washington Irving* (New York, 1935), I, 54.

13–14 "These lascivious exhibitions . . . ," *ibid.*

14 In Sicily he engaged . . . , *ibid.*, I, 57, 62.

"Compared with other American men of letters . . . ," *ibid.*, I, 67.

He often expressed a wish . . . , *ibid.*, I, 69.

There is no country . . . , *Life and Letters*, I, 129.

15 Through Allston he met Coleridge . . . , Jared B. Flagg, *The Life and Letters of Washington Allston* (New York, 1892), p. 64.

Allston, a modest man . . . , *ibid.*, p. 87.

"He was to reside . . . ," *Life and Letters*, I, 131–132.

"Of all the places I have seen in Europe . . . , *ibid.*, I, 149–150.

16 No city in Europe . . . , Williams, I, 75.

He told Kemble . . . , *ibid.*, I, 77.

"I shook hands with the mob . . . ," *Life and Letters*, I, 187.

Three years later . . . , Williams, I, 95.

Travelling to Palermo . . . , *Life and Letters*, 107, 116.

"I am wearied and heartsick . . . ," *ibid.*, III, 343.

17 But for the most part . . . , Williams, I, 151.

18 Visit to Scott, *Life and Letters*, I, 381–385.

Be that as it may, Scott wrote . . . , *ibid.*, I, 387.

Arthur's seat is perfect . . . , *ibid.*, I, 378–379.

20 Holland House, Lloyd Sanders, *The Holland House Circle* (London, 1908), pp. 16–31, *et passim*.

21 "To carry this into better effect . . . ," *Life and Letters* I, 412–414.

22 "If the American public wish . . . ," *ibid.*, I, 429.

23 Scott made him an offer . . . , *ibid.*, I, 439–440.

"The success of my writings . . . ," *ibid.*, II, 81.

And on another occasion he proudly told . . . , *ibid.*, II, 37.

Murray, who had rejected . . . , Williams, I, 259.

When *Bracebridge Hall* was ready . . . , *Life and Letters*, II, 72.

24 "But I shall return home . . . ," *ibid.*, I, 463.

"I am endeavoring to serve my country . . . ," *ibid.*, II, 36–37.

24–25 ". . . a world of people living at their ease . . . ," *ibid.*, II, 84–85.

25 Moore reported that in Paris . . . , *ibid.*, II, 38.

26 "Sweet tempered, gentle . . . ," *ibid.*, II, 128.

He realized that this was . . . , *ibid.*, II, 165.

"How many an hour of hard labor . . . ," *ibid.*, II, 234.

27 Strangely enough this thin concoction . . . , Williams, I, 276.
To Irving familiar with . . . , Sanders, pp. 233–237.
What may have hurt him . . . , Williams, I, 277.
"I look forward to my return . . . ," *ibid.*, II, 259.
28 "Here, then, I am nestled . . . ," *ibid.*, II, 385–386.
Irving's biographer argues . . . , Williams, I, 377.
29 "Never shall I meet on earth . . . ," *Life and Letters*, II, 408.
Like many of his countrymen . . . , Williams, II, 4–5.
30 Attacks by American newspapers, *ibid.*, II, 13, 19, and *Life and Letters*, III, 103–110.
Even Van Buren . . . , Williams, II, 11.
Before he left, he took Van Buren . . . , *ibid.*, II, 25.
"Can I be content . . . ," *Life and Letters*, II, 490.
31 "The mode of living . . . ," *ibid.*, III, 14.
To Fanny Kemble he deplored . . . , Williams, II, 27.
"Certainly official life in Washington . . . ," *Life and Letters*, III, 23.
Once he got out of cities . . . , *ibid.*, III, 27–31.
32 After camping out . . . , *ibid.*, III, 40–42.
"It is a sort of sentimental journey . . . ," *ibid.*, III, 67.
"The more I see of political life . . . ," *ibid.*, III, 64.
In 1836 he was deploring . . . , *ibid.*, III, 77, 91, 153.
At this cottage . . . , Williams, II, 47.
"Neither Spanish nor Italian skies . . . ," *Life and Letters*, III, 155.
33 *The Spectator* called it . . . , Williams, II, 85–87.
When Van Buren became President . . . , *ibid.*, II, 68.
"It will be a severe trial . . . ," *Life and Letters*, III, 177.
"How strange it seems . . . ," *ibid.*, III, 197–198.
34 "My visit to Europe . . . ," *ibid.*, III, 204–205.
After only two years in Spain . . . , *ibid.*, III, 343.
"The charm was broken . . . ," *ibid.*, III, 254.
36 ". . . the doubts which her ladyship has heard . . . ," *ibid.*, II, 22.
37 "I feared some humiliating blow . . . ," *ibid.*, III, 389.
"A rancorous prejudice . . . ," *ibid.*, III, 390.
"every political change is a military convulsion," *ibid.*, IV, 100.
37 "I was present at the going out . . . ," *ibid.*, IV, 139–140.
"frank, manly, and unaffected . . . ," *ibid.*, I, 338.

THE SCHOLARS

38 "I have grown quite estranged . . . ," Russel B. Nye, *George Bancroft, Brahmin Rebel* (New York, 1944), p. 60.
39 Samuel Eliot endows a professorship, *ibid.*, p. 21.
40 Harvard graduates, 1766–1776, Henry Adams, *History of the United States of America during the First Administration of Thomas Jefferson* (New York, 1889), I, 77.
He borrowed a grammar from Everett . . . , *Life, Letters, and Journals of George Ticknor*, ed. George S. Hillard (Boston, 1876), I, 11–12.
At last in Jamaica Plains . . . , *ibid.*, I, 11.
When the learned friends . . . , *ibid.*, I, 11.
41 "The truth is, Dear Charles, . . ." *ibid.*, I, 24.

42 "I think I have received more kindness . . . ," *ibid.*, I, 73.
". . . what a mortifying distance . . . ," *ibid.*, I, 73.
However he remarked that at Göttingen . . . , *ibid.*, I, 85.
The high point of the journey . . . , *ibid.*, I, 113–114.
42–43 Cogswell brings offer from Harvard, *ibid.*, I, 116.
43 Visit to Paris, *ibid.*, I, 137ff.
Mme de Staël, although very ill . . . , *ibid.*, I, 126–130.
44 On one occasion he became involved in a discussion . . . , *ibid.*, I, 148–149.
"With Rome I feel every day . . . ," *ibid.*, I, 172.
On a billboard he saw a decree . . . , *ibid.*, I, 193.
45 He went to the Lake District . . . , *ibid.*, I, 287–288.
Back in London Ticknor met . . . , *ibid.*, I, 294.
Jefferson tried to get him to come . . . , *ibid.*, I, 303.
. . . the Harvard library . . . , *ibid.*, I, 72n.
46 American colleges before 1870, Ernest Earnest, *Academic Procession: An Informal History of the American College, 1636–1953* (New York, 1953), p. 25.
47 The first principles of religion seemed to be unknown . . . , *Life of Joseph Green Cogswell as Sketched in His Letters*, ed. Anna Eliot Ticknor (Cambridge, Mass., 1874), pp. 18–19.
Longfellow on Paris . . . , Samuel Langfellow, *Life of Henry Wadsworth Longfellow, with Extracts from His Journals and Correspondence* (Boston, 1886), I, 79.
"It is time for Cambridge . . . ," Cogswell, *Life*, p. 44.
48 For instance as a program for exercise . . . , *ibid.*, pp. 60–61.
On a tour of Italy . . . , *ibid.*, p. 79.
"You do me cruel wrong . . . ," *ibid.*, p. 86.
49 ". . . a grand and graceful form . . . ," *ibid.*, p. 57.
During a tour of the Lake District . . . , *ibid.*, p. 90.
In Scotland he was entertained lavishly . . . , *ibid.*, p. 93.
At Carlsbad while taking a hike . . . , *ibid.*, p. 101.
50 He felt that American scholars . . . , *ibid.*, p. 108.
From Harvard came the offer . . . , *ibid.*, p. 133.
"George Bancroft literally and figuratively . . . ," Nye, p. 32.
51 Although Bancroft was unaware of it . . . , *ibid.*, p. 43.
"It is a fixed principle . . . ," *ibid.*, p. 37.
Now he found a very kindly man . . . , *ibid.*, p. 40.
51–52 They toasted the President . . . , *ibid.*, p. 45.
52 Then came the news that the Harvard Overseers . . . , *ibid.*, p. 48.
Once more he visited Goethe . . . , *ibid.*, p. 50.
53 "When I think of the time I ran about . . . ," *ibid.*, p. 54.
Bancroft pleased Byron . . . , *ibid.*, pp. 56–57.
Ticknor proposes lecture series, *Letters*, I, 322–323.
54 As Ticknor said . . . , *ibid.*, I, 324.
54–55 After one term he wrote bitterly . . . , Nye, pp. 61–62.
55 "He is weary of the imperfect system . . . ," Cogswell, *Life*, p. 134.
The times were not propitious . . . , Earnest, p. 24.
55–57 The Round Hill School, Nye, pp. 66–73, and Cogswell, *Life*, pp. 141–180.

57 It was Sam Ward . . . , Cogswell, *Life*, p. 204.
In his school at Raleigh . . . , *ibid.*, p. 191.
From the University of South Carolina . . . , *ibid.*, p. 193.
Another offer came from Jefferson College . . . , *ibid.*, pp. 204, 215.
After consulting Ticknor . . . , *ibid.*, pp. 221–222.
58 "I shall love my country . . . ," *ibid.*, pp. 210–211.
To C. S. Daveis, Ticknor wrote . . . , *Letters*, I, 399–401.
He was immediately invited to dine at Holland House . . . , *ibid.*, I, 408–409.
59 With a letter from Baron Humboldt . . . , *ibid.*, II, 16ff.
On a tour of the Lake District . . . , *ibid.*, II, 167.
60 In America, he replied . . . , *ibid.*, II, 50–51.
To Richard Henry Dana, Sr., Ticknor wrote . . . , *ibid.*, II, 75.
61 The fact was, he wrote to Miss Edgeworth . . . , *ibid.*, II, 174.
"The town, too, is a good town . . . ," *ibid.*, II, 188.
62 Shirley Brooks, writing in the London *Morning Chronicle* . . . , *ibid.*, II, 254.
At the age of sixty-five Ticknor made one more trip . . . , *ibid.*, II, 321ff.
64 He went on to say, "The popular voice . . . ," Nye, p. 87.
65 "The people is sovereign . . . ," *ibid.*, p. 109.
But Mrs. Bancroft's discovery . . . , *ibid.*, p. 160.
Bancroft writes Johnson's first message to Congress, *ibid.*, p. 230.
67 The former expatriate hailed Lincoln . . . , *ibid.*, pp. 231–234.
68 During the Franco-Prussian War . . . , *ibid.*, pp. 264–272.
69 In 1876 the revised edition . . . , *ibid.*, p. 287.

THE CHIP ON THE SHOULDER

71 "*The Red Rover* . . . ," James Fenimore Cooper, *Gleanings in Europe*, ed. Robert E. Spiller (New York, 1930), II, xiii.
72 Even before the Cooper family sailed . . . , James F. Cooper, *Correspondence of James Fenimore Cooper* (New Haven, 1922), I, 55.
"I suppose . . . ," *Gleanings*, I, 215.
By the time he had been in Europe . . . , Robert E. Spiller, *Fenimore Cooper, Critic of His Times* (New York, 1931), p. 192.
He felt that the government . . . , *Gleanings*, I, 9–11.
72–73 "To know when to pay . . . ," *ibid.*, I, 78.
73 But the cathedral . . . , *ibid.*, I, 76.
"The European who comes to America . . . ," *ibid.*, I, 57.
"I love to study a place . . . ," *ibid.*, I, 89.
Noting the contrast . . . , *ibid.*, I, 93.
73–74 "In America, I have always understood . . . ," *ibid.*, I, 122.
74 Cooper on American cooking, *ibid.*, I, 126.
75 To him there was something ponderous . . . , *ibid.*, I, 225–231.
Americans disliked the obsequiousness . . . , James Fenimore Cooper, *Notions of the Americans Picked up by a Travelling Bachelor* (Philadelphia, 1828), p. 67.
76 "I confess, I was a little startled . . . ," *ibid.*, p. 95.
"Twenty-two years before, an ardent boy . . . ," *Gleanings*, II, 9–10.
He had returned to astonish his friends . . . , *ibid.*, II, 44–45.

77 "I wish with all my heart . . . ," *ibid.*, II, 285.
"the intellectual spirits . . . ," *ibid.*, II, 36.
"The English do not like the Americans," *ibid.*, II, xxii–xxiii.
Several times Cooper felt . . . , *ibid.*, II, 28.
77–78 "I could have helped him . . . ," *ibid.*, II, 31.
78 "I then rapped *à ' la peer* . . . ," *ibid.*, II, 57.
"I would strenuously urge . . . ," *ibid.*, II, 77–78.
79 "Power, in America . . . ," *ibid.*, II, 298.
"Really, now, I do not see . . . ," *ibid.*, II, 290.
Cooper quoted with approval . . . , *ibid.*, I, 238.
Like other American visitors . . . , *ibid.*, II, 90.
French servants were treated . . . , *ibid.*, II, 253–256.
Despite his belief . . . , *ibid.*, II, 70, 181.
80 "I never witnessed an exhibition . . . ," *ibid.*, II, 161–162.
If Coleridge was scholastic . . . , *ibid.*, II, 234.
His final comment was . . . , *ibid.*, II, 394.
Very much a family man . . . , James Fenimore Cooper, "Leaves from His
Diary," *Putnam's Magazine*, I, No. 2 (Feb., 1868), 167–172.
80–81 Cooper's daughter Susan . . . , *Correspondence*, I, 71.
81 "Mr. Cooper has almost affronted the Lords . . . ," *ibid.*, I, 164.
in groupe . . . , Cooper's French was not always as good as he claimed it was.
"In a country like ours . . . ," *Correspondence*, I, 169.
82 "Your aunt Pomeroy is afraid . . . ," *ibid.*, I, 232.
"I have heard of the corruptions . . . ," *ibid.*, I, 238.
He admitted the charge . . . , *Notions*, pp. 195–197.
83 His answer on this occasion . . . , Spiller, p. 164.
At the suggestion of an Englishman . . . , *ibid.*, p. 179.
"I get up at eight . . . ," William Dunlap, *Diary of William Dunlap, 1766–
1839* (New York, 1831), III, 608.
84 Somewhat illogically . . . , *ibid.*, III, 645–646.
They felt it unjust . . . , Carleton Mabee, *American Leonardo, The Life of
Samuel F. B. Morse* (New York, 1943), p. 141.
Cooper himself said . . . , *Gleanings*, II, 316.
In his pugnacious *Letter* . . . , James Fenimore Cooper, *Letter to his Countrymen* (New York, 1834), pp. 11–12.
He said that he was attacked . . . , *Gleanings*, II, 316.
90–91 The Littlepage novels, Robert H. Zoellner, "Fenimore Cooper: Alienated
American," *American Quarterly*, XIII, No. 1 (Spring, 1961), 55. (A good
discussion of Cooper's "profound psychic split," especially as reflected in
these novels.)
91 "No tyranny of one . . . ," Quoted, Spiller, p. 249.
92 "In this particular . . . ," *Notions*, p. 67.

THE ARTISTS

94 "the premises of the artistic life . . . ," Van Wyck Brooks, *The Wine of the
Puritans* (London, 1908), pp. 120–121.
"They were obliged to reconcile . . . ," Suzanne La Follette, *Art in America*
(New York, 1929), pp. 65–66.

95 Europe "taunted us . . . ," Horatio Greenough, *The Travels, Observations, and Experience of a Yankee Stonecutter* (New York, 1852; reprinted Gainesville, Fla., 1958), p. 117.

"He always seemed like an eagle . . . ," Nathalia Wright, *Horatio Greenough, The First American Sculptor* (Philadelphia, 1963), p. 55.

"Allston starved spiritually . . . ," Henry James, *William Wetmore Story and His Friends* (London, 1903), I, 297–298.

96 "the damnest stupid wretches . . . ," Jared B. Flagg, *The Life and Letters of Washington Allston* (New York, 1892), p. 48.

"Titian, Tintoretto . . . ," *ibid.*, p. 55.

"To no other man . . . ," *ibid.*, p. 64.

96–97 The morning after his wedding . . . , *ibid.*, p. 83.

97 Morse said. . . . , *ibid.*, p. 87.

"Next to my own . . . ," *ibid.*, p. 118.

Prices for paintings, Edgar Richardson, *Washington Allston* (Chicago, 1948), p. 106.

". . . would probably have succeeded West," Flagg, p. 136.

"Another thought recurs . . . ," *ibid.*, p. 140.

97–98 ". . . in bringing it to America . . . ," *ibid.*, p. 346.

98 Paintings too large for buildings, Edgar Richardson, *A Short History of Painting in America* (New York, 1963), p. 99.

"But I fear it is a forlorn hope . . . ," Flagg, p. 233.

". . . with respect to the portrait . . . ," *ibid.*, p. 237.

99 Allston made a sketch . . . , *ibid.*, p. 350.

However, there is some evidence . . . , *ibid.*, pp. 282–283.

. . . wonderful dinners in Paris . . . , *ibid.*, p. 243.

Richardson on change in Allston's style . . . , Richardson, *Allston*, pp. 153, 161.

99–100 "I suppose you have heard of our Exhibition . . . ," Flagg, p. 214.

100 Mrs. Jameson on Allston's work, Richardson, *Allston*, p. 3.

"As his art grew quieter . . . ," Richardson, *History*, pp. 109–110.

100–101 Allston makes fundamental discoveries, Richardson, *Allston*, p. 60.

101 Allston learns from Titian, etc., *ibid.*, p. 87.

Coleridge's estimate, *ibid.*, p. 2.

Morse's complaints, Mabee, pp. 159, 208, 247.

"dissipated infidels," *ibid.*, p. 37.

Morse's bigotry, *ibid.*, pp. 129–132.

Morse on theaters, *ibid.*, p. 126.

102 "Samuel F. B. Morse, like Vanderlyn . . . ," Richardson, *History*, pp. 113–114.

Makes $9,000, Mabee, p. 72.

Peale's *Court of Death*, Richardson, *History*, pp. 112–113.

103 "The generation that nurtured . . . ," *ibid.*, p. 123.

"Artists have arisen in numbers . . . ," Greenough, *Travels*, p. 119.

104 Commissions to sculptors, Albert TenEyck Gardner, *Yankee Stonecutters, The First American School of Sculptors, 1800–1850* (New York, 1945), p. 8.

Powers told a visitor . . . , H. W. Bellows, "Seven Sittings with Powers, the Sculptor," *Appletons' Journal*, I, No. 15 (July 10, 1869), 471.

105 Greenough's teachers, Adeline Adams, "Horatio Greenough," *D.A.B.*, VIII, 586–588, and Horatio Greenough, *Letters of Horatio Greenough to his Brother, Henry Greenough*, ed. Frances Bott Greenough (Boston, 1887), pp. 42–43.
Cogswell's influence, Wright, p. 28.
106 Greenough in America, *ibid.*, pp. 51–52.
Return to Italy, *ibid.*, pp. 56–60.
"The carnival will be in its glory . . . ," *Letters*, p. 46.
"this beautiful but unhappy country . . . ," *ibid.*, p. 65.
Studies with Morse, Cole, etc., Wright, p. 80.
Asks Allston for painting, *ibid.*, p. 64.
107 "a pioneer . . . ," *ibid.*, p. 79.
"have looked so much abroad . . . ," *ibid.*, pp. 92–93.
"Fenimore Cooper saved me . . . ," Gardner, p. 40.
"The cherubs failed here . . . ," Quoted, Gardner, pp. 39–40.
Allston, hearing that Congress . . . , Gardner, p. 40.
108 "Still so many obstacles to study . . . ," Cooper, *Correspondence*, I, 308.
"I beg you will pity me . . . ," Wright, p. 109.
"no more of foreign lands . . . ," *ibid.*, p. 113.
"She is my only comfort . . . ," *ibid.*, p. 199.
In three years . . . , *ibid.*, p. 204.
Helps Powers, *ibid.*, p. 210.
109 "As respects your statue . . . ," Quoted, Gardner, p. 40.
Morse and Emerson praise statue . . . , Wright, p. 147.
Bad light in rotunda, *ibid.*, p. 146.
110 "By beauty I mean . . . ," Quoted, Gardner, p. 42.
"There are threads of relation . . . ," *ibid.*, p. 42.
110–111 "I understand, therefore, by embellishment . . . ," Horatio Greenough, *Form and Function*, ed. Harold A. Small (Berkeley and Los Angeles, 1947), pp. 74–75.
"There is no conceivable function . . . ," *ibid.*, pp. 85–86.
111 Honored in Florence and Boston, Wright, pp. 221, 226.
111–112 Praises democratic institutions, *ibid.*, p. 227.
112 "I thank God . . . ," *ibid.*, p. 266.
"I have not yet given up all thoughts . . . ," *Letters*, p. 237.
"the highest artistic authority . . . ," Wright, p. 274.
Powers made six copies . . . , *ibid.*, p. 29.
In Cincinnati a committee . . . , *D.A.B.*, V, 159–160.
113 When Hawthorne met Powers . . . , Nathaniel Hawthorne, *Passages from the French and Italian Note-Books* (Cambridge, Mass., 1883), pp. 309, 432.
"Make me as I am, Mr. Powers . . . ," Gardner, p. 30.
Senator Preston of South Carolina . . . , Bellows, *Appletons' Journal*, I, No. 13 (June 26, 1869), 404.
113–114 Although Powers later claimed . . . , Gardner, p. 31.
114 Powers arrived in the heyday . . . , Wright, p. 213.
When customers did not pay . . . , Bellows, *Appletons' Journal*, I, No. 19 (Aug. 7, 1869), 596.
114–15 "Thirty years away from home . . . ," *ibid.*, II, No. 22 (Aug. 28, 1869), 55.

115 To Sophia Hawthorne Eve looked "primal . . . ," Mrs. Nathaniel Hawthorne, *Notes in England and Italy* (New York, 1869), p. 366.

Nevertheless Hawthorne found Powers . . . , *French and Italian Note-Books,* p. 335.

115–16 "He told us that the skin . . . ," *Notes in England and Italy,* pp. 364–365.

116 "It is a rather bold thing . . . ," *French and Italian Note-Books,* p. 304.

One of them particularly impressed . . . , *ibid.,* pp. 362–363.

116–117 "He said that it would make him . . . ," *ibid.,* p. 432.

117 A later visitor . . . , Samuel Osgood, "American Artists in Italy," *Harper's New Monthly Magazine,* XLI, No. CCXLIII (Aug., 1870), 420.

To another visitor of the same period . . . , Bellows, *Appletons' Journal,* I, No. 15 (July 10, 1869), 471.

As for bringing up children . . . , *ibid.*

"In the busy studies . . . ," Gardner, p. 22.

He tended to agree with Mrs. Anna B. Jameson . . . , *French and Italian Note-Books,* p. 198.

118 Like other American sculptors . . . , Gardner, p. 22.

At twenty-three he married . . . , James, *William Wetmore Story,* I, 39–40.

His mother's comment was . . . , *ibid.,* I, 27.

119 To Lowell he wrote . . . , *ibid.,* I, 100–101.

"How shall I ever again endure . . . ," *ibid.,* I, 102.

"And now I am in Venice . . . ," *ibid.,* I, 190.

"Such a summer as we have had . . . ," *ibid.,* I, 249.

120 A year later he wrote . . . , *ibid.,* I, 266.

"As to what you say about Boston . . . ," *ibid.,* I, 313.

A friend described their apartment . . . , Mary E. Phillips, *Reminiscences of William Wetmore Story* (New York, 1897), p. 98.

121 "Mr. Story is the most variously accomplished . . . ," Quoted, Gardner, p. 34.

"What I have left undone . . . ," Andrew F. Rolle, "A Friendship across the Atlantic: Charles Sumner and William Wetmore Story," *American Quarterly,* XI, No. 1 (Spring, 1959), 48.

122 "I do love Italy . . . ," *ibid.,* p. 49.

"What a difference between this place . . . ," *ibid.,* p. 50.

"A walk in the streets of Rome . . . ," *ibid.*

Some authorities argue . . . , *ibid.,* p. 53.

The Roman artists . . . , *ibid.,* p. 51.

122–123 They had been sent there at the expense . . . , Gardner, p. 35.

On the other hand a modern critic . . . , *ibid.,* p. 35.

123 Story's poem "Cleopatra," *ibid.,* pp. 36–37.

124 "The Maenads carry the day . . . ," William Wetmore Story, *Conversations in a Studio* (Cambridge, Mass., 1890), II, 465–466.

"All the talk here is about dollars . . . ," James, II, 181.

But in Boston Story was feted . . . , Rolle, p. 54.

125 "Fancy the musty old professors . . . ," James, II, 175.

A few days later Story wrote . . . , *ibid.,* II, 185.

126. Visit to America in 1877, Gardner, p. 34.

The tower was to be crowned . . . , Phillips, p. 197.

Mrs. Story reported to their daughter . . . , Rolle, p. 56.

Lowell dedicated *Fireside Travels* . . . , *ibid.*

In later years Story's commissions . . . , Phillips, p. 240.

"We went to Mr. Story's studio . . . ," Quoted, Rolle, p. 52.

127 "In London, in Boston . . . ," James, II, 226.

ESCAPE FROM BOSTON

128 Studies Roman history . . . , *Memoirs of Margaret Fuller Ossoli*, ed. R. W. Emerson, J. F. Clarke, and W. H. Channing (Boston, 1852), I, 27ff.

She took up the study of French . . . , *ibid.*, I, 52–53.

After three months she was reading . . . , *ibid.*, I, 114.

128–129 She began to plan a biography . . . , *ibid.*, I, 129.

129 *"Very early I knew . . . ," ibid.*, I, 133.

Five days a week she gave lessons . . . , *ibid.*, I, 150.

Margaret had longed . . . , *ibid.*, I, 153.

The Farrars were sailing . . . , Faith Chipperfield, *In Quest of Love: The Life and Death of Margaret Fuller* (New York, 1957), p. 116.

Illness and father's statement . . . , *Memoirs*, I, 154–155.

130 "The new-year opens upon me . . . ," *ibid.*, I, 158.

"I was a great deal with Miss Martineau . . . ," *ibid.*, I, 159.

"If I am not to go with you . . . ," *ibid.*

"Circumstances have decided . . . ," *ibid.*, I, 161.

Groton, despite its beauty . . . , *ibid.*, I, 170.

131 Emerson disapproves of her belief in omens, *ibid.*, I, 219, and Chipperfield, p. 132.

Alcott, who had dared to introduce . . . , Chipperfield, p. 138.

The project started off well . . . , *ibid.*, p. 158.

One lady insisted . . . , *Memoirs*, I, 331–332.

132 "Utopia is impossible to build up . . . ," Chipperfield, p. 199.

132–133 As a preparation for this . . . , Margaret Fuller, *Summer on the Lakes* in *The Writings of Margaret Fuller*, selected and edited by Mason Wade (New York, 1941), p. 25.

133 "In older countries . . . ," *ibid.*, p. 22.

"the general dullness that broods over this land . . . ," *ibid.*, p. 28n.

"The villas and castles . . . ," *ibid.*, p. 32.

133–134 "Everywhere the fatal spirit . . . ," *ibid.*, p. 45.

134 Henry James, Sr., on Margaret, Chipperfield, pp. 206–207.

"No married woman can represent . . . ," Margaret Fuller, *Woman in the Nineteenth Century*, in Wade, p. 216.

135 "We would have every barrier thrown down," *ibid.*, p. 124.

She declared her "faith . . . ," *ibid.*, p. 127.

"I have been received here . . . ," Wade, "Prefatory Note," p. 107.

Marcus and Rebecca Spring, Arthur W. Brown, *Margaret Fuller* (New York, 1964), p. 90.

Borrows from Sam Ward, *ibid.*

136 ". . . we felt ourselves in a slower . . . ," Margaret Fuller Ossoli, *At Home and Abroad, or Things and Thoughts in America and Europe* (Boston, 1856), p. 121.

"The homes of England!," *ibid.*, p. 124.

137 Within a few paragraphs . . . , *ibid.*, pp. 131–133.

"Since Adam, there has been none . . . ," *ibid.*, p. 137.

"To the horrors and sorrows . . . ," *ibid.*, p. 150.
Like Hawthorne she commented . . . , *ibid.*, p. 159.
"Such a church is ruined . . . ," *ibid.*, p. 165.

138 On Carlyle . . . , *ibid.*, pp. 183–184.
"Mazzini, one of those noble refugees . . . ," *ibid.*, p. 182.

140 Margaret on George Sand, *Memoirs*, II, 193–194.
"She needs no defense . . . ," *ibid.*, II, 197.
But then the puritan asserted itself . . . , *ibid.*, II, 199.

141 The three had a pleasant conversation . . . , *ibid.*, II, 202.
These men were "the true kings . . . ," *At Home and Abroad*, p. 195.
"Ah! if physicians only understood . . . ," *ibid.*, p. 203.
"Your spirit is linked . . . ," Leopold Wellisz, *The Friendship of Margaret
Fuller Ossoli and Adam Mickiewicz* (New York, 1947), p. 13.

141–142 "Learn to appreciate yourself . . . ," *ibid.*, p. 18.

142 "I tried to make you understand . . . ," *ibid.*, pp. 23–24.
"You still live spiritually . . . ," Quoted, Chipperfield, p. 256.
Between Leghorn and Naples . . . , *Memoirs*, II, 208.
"I could not realize that I had actually touched . . . ," *At Home and Abroad*,
p. 217.
Yet there was an ambivalence . . . , *ibid.*, p. 219.
She visited the Grotto of Pausilippo . . . , *ibid.*, p. 218.

142–143 "What is the vulgarity . . . ," *ibid.*, p. 221.

143 "Art is not important . . . ," *Memoirs*, II, 209.
On their walks together . . . , *ibid.*, II, 282, and Wellisz, p. 20.

144 On the Greek Slave, *At Home and Abroad*, pp. 231–232, 372.
Greenough interested her for another reason . . . , *ibid.*, p. 246.
There were, she found, three classes . . . , *ibid.*, pp. 250–252.
She wondered if the idealistic young people . . . , *ibid.*, p. 256.

145 "Italy has been glorious to me . . . ," *Memoirs*, II, 224–225.
Mrs. Story as an afterthought . . . , Emelyn Story, "Account of Mrs. Ossoli's
Marriage," MSS, Boston Public Library. (The date seems to have been in-
serted later.)
"There is some evidence . . . ," Madeline B. Stern, *The Life of Margaret
Fuller* (New York, 1942), p. 430n.
"It is a time such as I always dreamed of . . . ," *Memoirs*, II, 235.
"The true aristocracy of a nation . . . ," *At Home and Abroad*, p. 306.
"The rich English traveller . . . ," *ibid.*, p. 361.

145–146 Mickiewicz came from France . . . , *Memoirs*, II, 233, and Wellisz, p. 28.

146 Asked to declare war . . . , *ibid.*, II, 238.
Despite her belief in a republican form . . . , *ibid.*, II, 243.
In May she went to Rieti . . . , Chipperfield, pp. 271, 274.
The situation would have been idyllic . . . , *Memoirs*, I, 244, 280–281.
Her reasons were threefold . . . , *ibid.*, I, 299.
"Of other circumstances . . . ," *ibid.*, II, 245.

147 When the siege began . . . , *ibid.*, II, 263.

148 "O Rome, my country . . . ," *ibid.*, II, 266.
As she told Channing . . . , *ibid.*, II, 267.
"But I could not let him go . . . ," *ibid.*, II, 301.
"I do not know whether . . . ," *ibid.*, II, 275.

"It is only since I have had . . . ," *ibid.*, II, 305.

"It made green her days . . . ," Emelyn Story MSS.

Margaret herself spoke of an interval of peace . . . , *Memoirs*, II, 306.

149 "Do not you die . . . ," *ibid.*, II, 306–307.

"If my mother is content . . . ," *ibid.*, II, 313.

149–150 "The journey home seems so long . . . ," *At Home and Abroad*, p. 437.

150 "Should anything hinder our meeting . . . ," *ibid.*, p. 440.

Already in debt to Sam Ward . . . , Chipperfield, p. 294.

150–151 The shipwreck, *Memoirs*, II, 341–349, and Stern, pp. 488–491.

THE AMBIVALENT PURITAN

153 They paid £160 a year . . . , Nathaniel Hawthorne, *The English Notebooks*, ed. Randall Stewart (New York, 1941), p. 21.

It seemed to him . . . , Nathaniel Hawthorne, *Our Old Home and English Note-Books* (Cambridge, Mass., 1891), pp. 25–26.

For the others he arranged a passage . . . , *ibid.*, p. 26.

153–54 On one occasion he found evidence . . . , *English Notebooks*, p. 112.

154 "There is a most dreadful state of things . . . ," *ibid.*, p. 267.

"Had he busied himself . . . ," Nathaniel Hawthorne, *Letters of Hawthorne to William D. Ticknor, 1851–1864* (Newark, 1910), II, 39.

He believed that philanthropy . . . , *English Notebooks*, p. 267.

"Not knowing whether I should . . . ," *Letters*, I, 93–94.

On the streets "with dreadful faces . . . ," *English Notebooks*, p. 17.

In a charity school . . . , *ibid.*, p. 13.

In December there were barefoot women . . . , *ibid.*, pp. 39–40.

The Scotch seemed to get drunk . . . , *ibid.*, p. 329.

155 After a civic banquet . . . , *ibid.*, p. 103.

"The women of England . . . ," *ibid.*, pp. 27–28.

". . . my experience is that an English lady . . . ," *ibid.*, p. 88.

155–156 Before he had been in England . . . , *Letters*, I, 43.

156 He could not read American newspapers . . . , *ibid.*, I, 54–55.

These things did not necessarily suffer . . . , *English Notebooks*, p. 77.

156–157 "There is a satisfaction . . . ," *ibid.*, p. 278.

157 "I doubt whether English cookery . . . ," Nathaniel Hawthorne, *Passages from the French and Italian Note-Books* (Cambridge, Mass., 1883), p. 17.

"It was all very good, and we respected ourselves . . . ," *ibid.*, pp. 30–31.

Even before he went abroad . . . , *Letters*, I, 5.

"I was about half seas over . . . ," *ibid.*, II, 14.

157–158 Despite the fact that another of his after-dinner speeches . . . , *English Notebooks*, p. 323.

158 "I need a residence of two or three years . . . ," *ibid.*, pp. 99–100.

During his first year in Liverpool . . . , *ibid.*, p. 98.

"Massachusetts must be a very uncomfortable place . . . ," *Letters*, I, 98.

"My mind has been considerably enlivened . . . ," *English Notebooks*, p. 230.

In October he told Ticknor . . . , *Letters*, I, 111.

"I HATE England . . . ," *ibid.*, I, 114.

"There are some English . . . ," *English Notebooks*, p. 270.

Only about a year later . . . , *Letters*, II, 37.

And in April of 1857 . . . , *ibid.*, II, 51.

159 "After all these bloody wars . . . ," *Our Old Home,* p. 33.
"I have been quite impressed . . . ," *Letters,* I, 42–43.
160 "But there seems to be no stormier prospect . . . ," *ibid.,* II, 29.
England was, he felt . . . , *Our Old Home,* p. 286.
He saw children carrying home gin . . . , *ibid.,* p. 327.
161 "Is, or is not, the system wrong . . . ," *ibid.,* p. 362.
"I wonder how many people live and die . . . ," *English Notebooks,* p. 278.
"We saw some ugly small manufacturing towns . . . ," Sophia Peabody
Hawthorne, *Notes in England and Italy* (New York, 1869), p. 7.
Nathaniel's tastes, he found . . . , *English Notebooks,* p. 269.
"I sometimes doubt whether this European residence . . . ," *Letters,* I, 114.
He came home one day with a black eye . . . , *ibid.,* II, 12.
162 "It is a strange, vagabond life . . . ," Quoted, Randall Stewart, *Nathaniel
Hawthorne, A Biography* (New Haven, 1948), p. 157.
They played battledore . . . , *ibid.,* p. 158.
At Lichfield he mused . . . , *English Notebooks,* p. 149.
And after seeing Salisbury . . . , *ibid.,* p. 359.
163 This was the spot which he "had dreamed about . . . ," *Our Old Home,* p.
287.
"Thomas à Kempis might here . . . ," Sophia Hawthorne, p. 16.
"Certainly beauty seems to haunt . . . ," *ibid.,* p. 19.
Often in visiting villages . . . , *Our Old Home,* p. 78.
". . . it thrills you with strange emotion . . . ," *ibid.,* p. 78, and *English Note-
books,* p. 124.
163–164 "Life is there fossilized . . . ," *Our Old Home,* p. 79.
"The present is burthened too much . . . ," *English Notebooks,* p. 294.
But a Venus was . . . , *ibid.,* p. 293.
From the Gallery he walked . . . , *ibid.*
In particular he liked the Old Dutch masters . . . , *ibid.,* p. 556.
164–165 But he became "weary . . . ," *ibid.,* p. 561.
165 Instead he hunted up Sophia . . . , *ibid.,* p. 553.
In his notebook Hawthorne remarked . . . , *ibid.,* p. 326.
"Good heavens! What an object . . . ," *ibid.,* p. 319.
165–166 "I did not know what the devil to say . . . ," *ibid.,* p. 299.
166 He found Tupper's vanity amusing . . . , *ibid.,* p. 300.
Milnes reminded him of Longfellow . . . , *ibid.,* p. 87.
167 "An Englishman," he noted . . . , *ibid.,* p. 383.
"He is a beautiful man . . . ," *ibid.,* p. 255.
"Melville, as he always does . . . ," *ibid.,* pp. 432–433.
168 He said he already felt much better . . . , *ibid.,* pp. 436–437.
He told Ticknor that in Italy . . . , *Letters,* II, 42.
If it were not for the children . . . , *ibid.,* II, 46.
168–169 Miss Shepard, a girl of twenty-one . . . , Stewart, p. 191.
169 To her fiancé, Clay Badger . . . , *ibid.,* p. 184.
Always concerned with the moral implications . . . , *ibid.,* p. 185.
But what chiefly impressed Hawthorne . . . , *ibid.*
"I am in Rome . . . ," *ibid.,* p. 187.
"How I like to write down . . . ," Sophia Hawthorne, p. 198.

170 "Rome struck me very disagreeably . . . ," *Letters*, II, 72.
   A year later he estimated . . . , *ibid.*, p. 76.
   In 1858 he had viewed the Carnival . . . , *ibid.*
   As Miss Lander was a Salem girl . . . , Stewart, p. 192.
   Nathaniel was somewhat put off . . . , *ibid.*
   "I liked her at once . . . ," Sophia Hawthorne, p. 265.
172 After visiting the studio of the American, E. S. Bartholomew . . . , *French and Italian Note-Books*, p. 171.
   Mrs. Anna B. Jameson . . . , *ibid.*, p. 199, and Stewart, p. 197.
   "I am partly sensible . . . ," *French and Italian Note-Books*, p. 159.
   In May, after four months in Rome . . . , *ibid.*, p. 272.
   For his part he would have all the Venuses . . . , *ibid.*, p. 502.
   "Classic statues escape you . . . ," *ibid.*, p. 399.
173 "Titian must have been a very good-for-nothing . . . ," *ibid.*, pp. 292, 331.
   He could not understand . . . , Nathaniel Hawthorne, *The Marble Faun.*
   Later when Browning talked . . . , Sophia Hawthorne, pp. 401–402.
   After the family had descended . . . , Stewart, pp. 202–203.
   "I hardly think there can be a place . . . ," *French and Italian Note-Books*, p. 277.
173–174 "His long absence . . . ," *ibid.*, p. 273.
174 In France he had attended a service . . . , *ibid.*, p. 179.
   Protestantism, he felt . . . , *ibid.*, p. 184.
175 "Saint Peter's offers itself . . . ," Julian Hawthorne, *Nathaniel Hawthorne and His Wife* (Boston, 1893), II, 178–179.
   Characteristically he added . . . , *ibid.*, p. 292.
   "In Italy," she wrote . . . , Sophia Hawthorne, p. 549.
176 It is generally recognized that Hilda . . . , Stanley T. Williams, "Nathaniel Hawthorne," *Literary History of the United States* (New York, 1948), I, 437.
   "I doubt not she could have slain a man . . . ," *English Notebooks*, p. 321.
177 "And now we sat down . . . ," Sophia Hawthorne, pp. 213–214.
   ". . . if I could take root . . . ," *French and Italian Note-Books*, p. 457.
177–178 Of one dinner . . . , Sophia Hawthorne, p. 529.
178 As they drew near Rome . . . , *French and Italian Note-Books*, p. 478.
   Mrs. Hawthorne wrote to her sister . . . , Stewart, p. 205.
   General Pierce . . . , *French and Italian Note-Books*, p. 503.
   They left three trunks . . . , *Letters*, II, 86.
179 "I shall really be glad to get home . . . ," *ibid.*, p. 90.
   An important reason . . . , *ibid.*, II, 94.
   "All the advantages of residing . . . ," *ibid.*, II, 96.
   In April he wrote . . . , *ibid.*, II, 103.
180 Here gathered Agassiz . . . , Stewart, p. 218.
   But the furor helped the sale . . . , *ibid.*, pp. 230–233.

THE CORK-LINED ROOM

182 "America of today . . . ," Ezra Pound, *Patria Mia* (Chicago, 1950), p. 47.
   "America was never kind . . . ," Mildred Howells, *Life and Letters of William Dean Howells* (New York, 1928), II, 395–396.
   "When I think . . . ," Van Wyck Brooks, *The Pilgrimage of Henry James* (New York, 1925), p. 28.

183 "I was again and again in the aftertime . . . ," Henry James, *The Middle Years* (New York, 1917), pp. 6–8.

184 "In fact it might be better . . . ," Robert LeClair, *Young Henry James, 1843–1870* (New York, 1955), pp. 54–55.

"The rupture with my grandfather's tradition . . . ," Henry James, *A Small Boy and Others* (New York, 1913), p. 190.

185 "Punch was England . . . ," Henry James, "George du Maurier," *Partial Portraits* (New York, 1888), pp. 327, 328, Quoted, Le Clair, p. 130.

To Coppet, James attributes . . . , Le Clair, p. 126.

During the family's residence in Berkeley Square . . . , *A Small Boy*, pp. 304, 308.

"American disorder is sweet . . . ," Le Clair, p. 221.

What Henry James, Sr., regarded . . . , Le Clair, pp. 229–230.

186 "It had been revealed to me . . . ," *A Small Boy*, pp. 87–88.

"I am a good patriot . . . ," Le Clair, p. 292.

After a few months . . . , *ibid.*, pp. 299ff.

"Life meanwhile I had a good deal of . . . ," Henry James, *Notes of a Son and Brother* (New York, 1914), p. 33.

186–187 "I fancied their saying . . . ," *ibid.*, pp. 31–32.

187 "You shall suffer . . . ," *ibid.*, p. 32.

"I think that if we are to live in America . . . ," Le Clair, p. 311.

"As it is we go home . . . ," *ibid.*, p. 324.

A year after his return . . . , *ibid.*, p. 353.

188 "Newport with its opera glass . . . ," *Son and Brother*, p. 304.

188–189 James's account of his injury . . . , *ibid.*, pp. 297–298. (For evidence of the psychosomatic nature of Henry's ailment, see Leon Edel, *Henry James* (New York, 1953), I, 173–183.

189 Edith Wharton says . . . , Edith Wharton, *A Backward Glance* (New York, 1934), p. 365.

"Scarce at all to be stated . . . ," *Son and Brother*, pp. 296–297.

189–190 Visit to army camp, *ibid.*, pp. 313–317.

190 It was as if the sense of Europe . . . , *ibid.*, p. 331.

Although the audience . . . , Le Clair, p. 360.

". . . there was the American spirit . . . ," *Son and Brother*, p. 321.

191 Norton publishes James's articles, Edel, I, 222.

James T. Fields of the *Atlantic* . . . , Le Clair, p. 376.

In his pilgrimages to the shrine . . . , Henry James, "Charles Eliot Norton . . . ," *The American Essays of Henry James*, ed. Leon Edel (New York, 1956), p. 121.

192 As Van Wyck Brooks noted . . . , *The Pilgrimage of Henry James*, p. 40.

Maxwell Geismar argues . . . , Maxwell Geismar, *Henry James and the Jacobites* (Boston, 1963), p. 35.

192–193 "It remained true, none the less . . . ," Henry James, *The Letters of Henry James*, ed. Percy Lubbock (New York, 1920), I, xxv.

193 "Within the somewhat narrow limits . . . ," Quoted, Richard Nicholas Foley, *Criticism in American Periodicals of the Works of Henry James from 1866 to 1916* (Washington, 1944), p. 5.

194 James on the Pre-Raphaelites, Henry James, *Parisian Sketches, Letters to the New York Tribune, 1875–1876*, ed. Leon Edel and Else Dusoir Lind (New York, 1957), pp. 131–132.

Even as late as 1898 . . . , *Letters*, I, 308.

"Plenty of gentle emotions from the scenery . . . ," *ibid.*, I, 26.

195 Blackmur on James . . . , R. P. Blackmur, "Introduction," *Washington Square, The Europeans* (The Laurel Henry James, 1959), p. 9.

196 "What is the meaning . . . ," *Letters*, I, 34.

Six months later . . . , *ibid.*, I, 36.

"Yet his own country seemed . . . ," *ibid.*, I, 38.

198 "Fancy Longfellow . . . ," *ibid.*, I, 46.

"I don't like their wares . . . ," *ibid.*, I, 49.

"Of pure Parisianism . . . ," *ibid.*, I, 48.

199 Meeting with Tennyson, *ibid.*, I, 53.

"So my interest in London . . . ," *ibid.*, I, 55.

199–200 "It is on manners . . . ," *ibid.*, I, 72.

200 In Paris he regarded the Variétés . . . , *Parisian Sketches*, p. 52.

For James a masked ball . . . , *ibid.*, p. 92.

201 "Her meagre knowledge . . . ," Leon Edel, "Introduction," *The Portrait of a Lady* (New York, 1956), p. xv.

202 Leon Edel speaks of the fairy-tale quality . . . , *ibid.*, p. ix.

"A new kind of heroine . . . ," *ibid.*, p. xi.

204 And of English country-house society . . . , *Letters*, I, 64.

"Each paid . . . $250," Edel, *Introduction*, p. viii.

"No other American writer . . . ," Foley, p. 143.

205 "the art of fiction . . . ," Quoted, Albert Mordell, *Discovery of a Genius* (New York, 1961), p. 121.

210 "The truth is that he belonged . . . ," *A Backward Glance*, pp. 175–176.

211 "New York is appalling . . . ," *Letters*, II, 23 (to W. E. Norris, 12/15/04).

"That altogether unspeakable city . . . ," *ibid.*, II, 25 (to Edmund Gosse, 2/16/05).

"It was after all in the great hall . . . ," Henry James, *The American Scene*, ed. with introduction by W. H. Auden (New York, 1946), p. 60.

212 "They were a huge, continuous . . . ," *ibid.*, p. 92.

"Doesn't it take the fact . . . ," *ibid.*, p. 96.

On the other hand "the comparatively windowless . . . ," *ibid.*, p. 77.

Throughout his journey . . . , *Letters*, II, 20 (to Edmund Gosse, 10/27/04).

"In the heart of the golden orange groves . . . ," *ibid.*, II, 32.

"I found my native land . . . ," *ibid.*, II, 48.

213 "As for the nonsense . . . ," *A Backward Glance*, pp. 175–176.

"Indeed I know that . . . ," Quoted, Van Wyck Brooks, *The Pilgrimage*, p. 156.

"If I were to live my life over . . . ," Hamlin Garland, *Roadside Meetings* (New York, 1931), p. 461.

Howells on James, Mildred Howells, ed., *Life and Letters of William Dean Howells* (Garden City, N.Y., 1928), II, 395–396.

214 "I see it now; I haven't done so . . . ," Quoted, F. W. Dupee, *Henry James* (New York, 1951), p. 234.

217 Meeting with Mr. Dooley, *A Backward Glance*, p. 178.

The Golden Bowl went through . . . , Van Wyck Brooks, *Scenes and Portraits* (New York, 1954), p. 112.

His friend, H. G. Wells . . . , H. G. Wells, *Boon* (London, 1915), p. 107.

"James has a very short list . . . ," Quoted, Herschel Bickell, "Aspects of the Novel," *The Virginia Quarterly Review*, XXI, No. 1 (Winter, 1949), 96.

André Gide, while recognizing . . . , André Gide, "Henry James," *The Question of Henry James: A Collection of Critical Essays*, ed. F. W. Dupee (New York, 1945), pp. 252–253.

218 "The celestial cheapness . . . ," Henry James, *William Wetmore Story*, I, 11.

"The deluge of people . . . ," Quoted, Edel, III, 378–379.

THE FLAMBOYANT AMERICAN

220 "Henry James is an effeminate old donkey . . . ," Thomas F. O'Donnell and Hoyt C. Franchere, *Harold Frederic* (New York, 1961), p. 155.

In addition he poured out . . . , *ibid.*, p. 12.

220–221 Comments on *Theron Ware, ibid.*, p. 148.

221 Grace Williams and Kate Lyon, *ibid.*, pp. 65–68.

Club memberships . . . , *ibid.*, pp. 12–13, 61.

222 Frank Harris remembered . . . , Frank Harris, "Harold Frederic Ad Memoriam," *Saturday Review of Politics, Literature, Science, and Art*, LXXXVI (Oct. 22, 1898), 527.

Collects statistics . . . , O'Donnell and Franchere, p. 61.

"He was of course, American . . . ," "Some Recollections of Harold Frederic," "By an Old Friend," *Saturday Review, loc. cit.*

Writes on cholera epidemic, O'Donnell and Franchere, p. 12.

Travels, *ibid.*, p. 63.

223 ". . . a drab tale of farm life . . . ," Vernon Louis Parrington, *Main Currents in American Thought* (New York, 1927 and 1930), III, 288.

Walter Taylor . . . , *Literary History of the United States* (New York, 1948), II, 992.

"The whole thing is between . . . ," Quoted, O'Donnell and Franchere, p. 77.

224 "In *Seth's Brother's Wife* . . . ," *ibid.*, p. 96.

228 "Concerned with the relationship of America to Europe . . . ," John Henry Raleigh, "Introduction" to Rinehart ed. of *Theron Ware* (New York, 1959), p. xv.

230 "Frederic represented the strength and weakness . . . ," Arthur Hobson Quinn, *American Fiction* (New York, 1939), p. 452.

Rejects social Darwinism . . . , O'Donnell and Franchere, p. 93.

236 The Americans are pictured . . . , Harold Frederic, "The War of 1812," *The English Illustrated Magazine*, XIV (March, 1896), 573–582.

A MOTOR FLIGHT FROM SOCIAL CHANGE

237 "No one quite knew . . . ," Percy Lubbock, *Portrait of Edith Wharton* (New York, 1947), p. 71.

"The only way to approach her . . . ," *ibid.*, p. 9.

In this last she boasted . . . , *A Backward Glance*, pp. 50–57.

"Happy misfortune . . . ," *ibid.*, p. 44.

"One of the most depressing impressions . . . ," *ibid.*, p. 54.

238 "Beauty, passion, and danger . . . ," Edith Wharton, "A Little Girl's New York," *Harper's Magazine*, CLXXVI (March, 1938), 358.

Madeira was a more important topic . . . , *A Backward Glance*, p. 58.

She always believed . . . , *ibid.*, p. 105.

She contrasted New Yorkers . . . , *ibid.*, pp. 61–62.

239 Edward Wharton . . . , Lubbock, pp. 62–63.

"He was indeed a person to whom she went . . . ," *ibid.*, p. 38.

As she put it . . . , *A Backward Glance*, p. 156.

In later life she speculated . . . , *ibid.*, p. 121.

240 "He alone not only encouraged me . . . ," *ibid.*, p. 116.

In fact she claimed . . . , Caresse Crosby, *The Passionate Years* (New York, 1953), p. 106.

In Paris his apartment . . . , *ibid.*, p. 109.

After Edith Wharton's divorce . . . , Robert Sencourt, "Edith Wharton," *The Cornhill Magazine*, CLVII, No. 942 (June, 1938), 723.

At his bedside . . . , Crosby, p. 107.

On his walls hung modern paintings . . . , *ibid.*, p. 216.

Edmund Wilson asserts . . . , Edmund Wilson, "Justice to Edith Wharton," *The New Republic*, XCV (June 29, 1938), 209.

241 "She came for talk . . . ," Lubbock, p. 49.

"While we were moving . . . ," *A Backward Glance*, p. 187.

Henry James spoke of the constant succession . . . , Lubbock, p. 82.

As Gaillard Lapsley said . . . , *ibid.*, p. 182.

Even in her reading . . . , *ibid.*, p. 101.

242 "Henry James would be summoned . . . ," *ibid.*, pp. 1, 5.

The appointments of her table . . . , Sencourt, p. 721.

There was a lack of spontaneous gaiety, Lubbock, pp. 163–164.

Distinguished transients . . . , *A Backward Glance*, p. 277 *et passim.*

Her friend, Robert Sencourt . . . , Sencourt, p. 722.

242–243 "She never became, she had no call to become . . . ," Lubbock, p. 50.

243 In her autobiography she stated . . . , *A Backward Glance*, p. 144.

Thus in Boston "her glittering plumage . . . ," Lubbock, p. 37.

A particular bête noire . . . , Edith Wharton, "The Great American Novel," *Yale Review*, XVI, No. 4 (July, 1927), 646–656.

244 "The woods of this wonderful Bois de Vincennes . . . , Edith Wharton, *A Motor-Flight Through France* (New York, 1908), p. 174.

In her essay for the *Yale Review*, "The Great American Novel," p. 647.

245 She found in them the same traits . . . , Blake Nevius, *Edith Wharton, A Study of Her Fiction* (Berkeley and Los Angeles, 1953), p. 74.

Writing of the institution of the salon . . . , *A Backward Glance*, p. 263.

On reading *The Age of Innocence* . . . , *ibid.*, p. 369.

It pleased her when . . . , *ibid.*, p. 175.

"She *must* be tethered in native pastures . . . ," James, *Letters*, I, 396.

. . . about money, "From top to bottom of *The House of Mirth* . . . the entire fabric revolves around money . . . ," Louis Auchincloss, "Edith Wharton and Her New York . . . ," *Partisan Review*, XVIII, No. 4 (July–August, 1951), 413.

Edith Wharton argued that Europe . . . , "The Great American Novel," p. 651.

246 Source of *Ethan Frome, A Backward Glance*, p. 296.

246–247 "In those days," she remembered . . . , *ibid.*, pp. 293–294.

248 In his study of Edith Wharton . . . , Nevius, p. 113.
Perhaps as she wrote of George Eliot . . . , *ibid.*, p. 111.
249 As Lapsley says, "The fact is . . . ," Quoted, Lubbock, pp. 149–150.
She was fond of quoting . . . , Nevius, p. 23.
"En effet, c'est seulement . . . ," Quoted, *ibid.*
Her friend Gaillard Lapsley said . . . , Quoted, Lubbock, p. 149.

AFTER THEY'VE SEEN PAREE

251 "As Malcolm Cowley says . . . ," Malcolm Cowley, *Exile's Return* (New York, 1934), p. 79.
"Indeed to young writers like ourselves . . . ," *ibid.*, p. 102.
Sylvia Beach mentions . . . , Sylvia Beach, *Shakespeare and Company* (New York, 1959), pp. 23–24.
"Everyday someone . . . ," *ibid.*
252 America, she said . . . , Gertrude Stein, "An American in France," in *Discovery of Europe*, ed. Philip Rahv (Cambridge, Mass., 1947), p. 571.
She added that France . . . , *ibid.*, p. 577.
This was echoed by Robert McAlmon . . . , Robert E. Knoll, *Robert McAlmon, Expatriate Publisher and Writer*, University of Nebraska Studies, new series, No. 18 (August, 1957), p. 12.
Speaking of the 1920's . . . , Harold Stearns, *A Street I Knew* (New York, 1935), p. 300.
Hemingway reported . . . , Ernest Hemingway, *A Moveable Feast* (New York, 1964), p. 20.
253 "To an extent almost incomprehensible . . . ," Harold Stearns, "The Intellectural Life," *Civilization in the United States* (New York, 1922), pp. 141, 147.
254 "Examine him at leisure . . . ," H. L. Mencken, "Politics," *ibid.*, p. 23.
"As a citizen, a workman . . . ," John Macy, "Journalism," *ibid.*, p. 36.
"What can we say . . . ," J. E. Spingarn, "Scholarship and Criticism," *ibid.*, p. 98.
"In no civilized country . . . ," George Jean Nathan, "The Theatre," *ibid.*, p. 249.
"What immediately strikes one . . . ," Van Wyck Brooks, "The Literary Life," *ibid.*, p. 179.
254–255 William Carlos Williams argues . . . , William Carlos Williams, *In the American Grain* (New York, 1925), p. 68.
"They seldom read American books . . . ," Van Wyck Brooks. *The Days of the Phoenix* (New York, 1957), p. 163.
"The royalism and the classicism . . . ," *ibid.*, p. 112.
It took him twenty years . . . , *ibid.*, pp. 3–4.
"The most hopeful thing . . . ," *Civilization in the United States*, p. 149.
256 When the editor of the *Outlook* . . . , Richard Aldington, *Life for Life's Sake* (New York, 1941), p. 219.
William Carlos Williams complained . . . , *The Autobiography of William Carlos Williams* (New York, 1951), p. 141.
At one time 500 copies . . . , Cowley, p. 132.
In Berlin typesetting and printing . . . , Harold Loeb, *The Way It Was* (New York, 1959), pp. 150–151.

257 Contact Publishing Company . . . , Knoll, pp. 33–35.
William Carlos Williams . . . , *Autobiography*, p. 181.
Some idea of the importance . . . , *ibid.*, p. 40.
With the help of a few small checks . . . , Cowley, p. 80.
258 It was a state of affairs . . . , *ibid.*, pp. 81–82.
In addition to himself, Malcolm Cowley lists . . . , *ibid.*, p. 38.
259 Even what he had seen of American . . . , Charles A. Fenton, *The Apprenticeship of Ernest Hemingway* (New York, 1956), pp. 112–113.
Filled with memories of conversations . . . , *ibid.*, p. 131.
"There was never a day so gay . . . ," Ford Maddox Ford, *It Was the Nightingale* (Philadelphia and London, 1933), p. 17.
"He didn't give a damn . . . ," Fenton, p. 138.
His debt to her . . . , *ibid.*, pp. 153–154.
At Sylvia Beach's . . . , Ernest Hemingway, *A Moveable Feast*, p. 134.
However prohibition and the puritanism of Toronto . . . , Fenton, p. 149.
260 Scott and Ernest met . . . , Arthur Mizener, *The Far Side of Paradise* (Cambridge, Mass., 1951), p. 183.
As Malcolm Cowley says . . . , Cowley, p. 273.
"Harry and I were actually escapists . . . ," Caresse Crosby, *The Passionate Years* (New York, 1953), p. 102.
When she met Harry in 1919 . . . , *ibid.*, p. 83.
"Bodily he survived . . . ," Cowley, pp. 250–251.
"I became a rebel . . . ," Caresse Crosby, p. 101.
261 The Crosbys also had private incomes . . . , *ibid.*, p. 128.
" 'Yes' and never 'no' . . . ," *ibid.*, p. 128.
From *The Picture of Dorian Gray* . . . , Cowley, p. 257.
"That crazy night . . . ," Caresse Crosby, pp. 132–133.
Again after he and Caresse . . . , Cowley, pp. 260–261.
262 They were to fly an airplane . . . , *ibid.*, p. 271.
They bought it for $2000 . . . , Caresse Crosby, pp. 204–205.
"We had decided . . . ," *ibid.*, p. 128.
A year later they started the Black Sun Press . . . , *ibid.*, pp. 265–266.
On a trip to Egypt . . . , *ibid.*, pp. 196–197.
After reading Lawrence's *The Plumed Serpent* . . . , *ibid.*, p. 218.
262–263 "Pure poetry is a lyrical absolute . . . ," Quoted, Cowley, pp. 276–277.
263 They put him up overnight . . . , Caresse Crosby, pp. 237ff.
Harry Crosby hired a lawyer . . . , Cowley, p. 233.
A few days later Harry borrowed . . . , Cowley, pp. 282–284.
264 In an article for the *Saturday Evening Post* . . . , Quoted, Mizener, p. 161.
Most Americans, he believed . . . , *A Street I Knew*, pp. 302, 338.
Hemingway stated . . . , Hemingway, *A Moveable Feast*, pp. 168–169.
"The Paris of the expatriate artist . . . ," Williams, *Autobiography*, p. 190.
265 Robert McAlmon tells of being poured off a train . . . , Robert McAlmon, *Being Geniuses Together* (London, 1938), p. 143.
People talked about the intolerance . . . , *A Street I Knew*, p. 299.
"It was a useless, silly life . . . ," *ibid.*, p. 277.
At the Cape d'Antibes . . . , Mizener, p. 185.
265–266 On another occasion . . . , *ibid.*, p. 199.
There was the ugly incident . . . , *ibid.*, pp. 187–188.

267 According to Arthur Mizener . . . , Mizener, pp. 184–185.

Theodore Chandler's version, *Fitzgerald Newsletter*, No. 7 (Fall, 1959), 1–2.

"Mr. Fitzgerald, your story lacks data . . . ," Andrew Trumbull, *Scott Fitzgerald* (New York, 1962), pp. 153–154.

In any case Mrs. Wharton . . . , *ibid.*, p. 154.

268 William Carlos Williams praised the French . . . , *Autobiography*, p. 196.

"no goods on the left bank . . . ," Grace Hegger Lewis, *With Love from Gracie* (New York, 1955), p. 291.

As Maxwell Geismar shows . . . , Maxwell Geismar, *Writers in Crisis* (Cambridge, Mass., 1942).

. . . Malcolm Cowley argued . . . , Cowley, pp. 94–95.

270 Cleveland's reading . . . , George F. Parker, "Grover Cleveland in Buffalo," *Saturday Evening Post*, August 28, 1920, p. 89.

Coolidge's reading . . . , William Allen White, *A Puritan in Babylon* (New York, 1940), p. 234.

Arthur Schlesinger lists . . . , Arthur Schlesinger, Jr., *The Age of Jackson* (Boston, 1945), pp. 369–370.

271 In 1913 Howells deplored . . . , William Dean Howells, "The Editor's Easy Chair," *Harper's Magazine* (March, 1913), 635.

271–272 "the real germ of the Middle Western literary movement . . . ," Ford, p. 27.

272–273 "Soon it became evident . . . ," Cowley, pp. 208–210.

273–274 Theodore Roosevelt greeted Mrs. Wharton . . . , *A Backward Glance*, p. 311.

274 Harold Stearns argued . . . , Harold Stearns, *Rediscovery of America* (New York, 1934), p. 338.

"Hemingway was no more Latin . . . ," Quoted, *ibid.*, p. 301.

She asserted that Cummings . . . , Gertrude Stein, *The Autobiography of Alice B. Toklas* (New York, 1933), pp. 268, 270.

Harold Loeb, the editor of *Broom* . . . , Loeb, pp. 8, 90.

"that pressing need for a kind of revitalizing . . . ," Conrad Aiken, *Ushant* (New York, 1962), pp. 279–280.

Malcolm Cowley argues . . . , Cowley, p. 95.

274–275 "We cannot escape a dim feeling . . . ," *Rediscovery of America*, p. 409.

275 "An irony of history . . . ," *ibid.*, pp. 135–136.

INDEX